MURAKAMI HARUKI AND OUR YEARS OF PILGRIMAGE

This book is a timely and expansive volume on Murakami Haruki, arguably Japan's most high-profile contemporary writer.

With contributions from prominent Murakami scholars, this book approaches the works of Murakami Haruki through interdisciplinary perspectives, discussing their significance and value through the lenses of history; geography; politics; gender and sexuality; translation; and literary influence and circulation. Together the chapters provide a multifaceted assessment on Murakami's literary oeuvre in the last four decades, vouching for its continuous importance in understanding the world and Japan in contemporary times. The book also features exclusive material that includes the cultural critic Katō Norihiro's final work on Murakami – his chapter here is one of the few works ever translated into English – to interviews with Murakami and discussions from his translators and editors, shedding light not only on Murakami's works as literature but as products of cross-cultural exchanges.

Murakami Haruki and Our Years of Pilgrimage will prove a valuable resource for students and scholars of Japanese studies, comparative and world literature, cultural studies, and beyond.

Gitte Marianne Hansen is Senior Lecturer in Japanese Studies at Newcastle University, UK. An AHRC Leadership Fellow, she is PI for the project 'Gendering Murakami Haruki: Characters, Transmedial Productions and Contemporary Japan' and the author of *Femininity, Self-harm and Eating Disorders in Japan: Navigating Contradiction in Narrative and Visual Culture* (2016).

Michael Tsang is due to take up lectureship in Japanese Studies at Birkbeck, University of London. He is a Leverhulme postdoctoral fellow at Newcastle University, UK. His research interests lie in world/postcolonial literatures and media with an East Asian focus. He has published in *Japan Forum*, *Inter-Asia Cultural Studies*, *Wasafiri*, and others, and is the founding editor of *Hong Kong Studies*.

MURAKAMI HARUKI AND OUR YEARS OF PILGRIMAGE

Edited by Gitte Marianne Hansen and Michael Tsang

Routledge
Taylor & Francis Group

LONDON AND NEW YORK

First published 2022
by Routledge
2 Park Square, Milton Park, Abingdon, Oxon OX14 4RN

and by Routledge
605 Third Avenue, New York, NY 10158

Routledge is an imprint of the Taylor & Francis Group, an informa business

British Library Cataloguing-in-Publication Data
A catalogue record for this book is available from the British Library

Library of Congress Cataloging-in-Publication Data
Names: Hansen, Gitte Marianne, editor. | Tsang, Michael (Editor), editor.
Title: Murakami Haruki and Our years of pilgrimage / edited by Gitte
Marianne Hansen and Michael Tsang.
Description: Milton Park, Abingdon, Oxon ; New York, NY : Routledge, 2022.
| Includes bibliographical references and indexes. | Identifiers: LCCN 2021008551 | ISBN 9780367181406
(hardback) | ISBN
9780367181413 (paperback) | ISBN 9780429059711 (ebook) | ISBN
9780429596209 (adobe pdf) | ISBN 9780429594915 (epub) | ISBN
9780429593628 (mobi)
Subjects: LCSH: Murakami, Haruki, 1949---Criticism and interpretation. |
Murakami, Haruki, 1949---Appreciation.
Classification: LCC PL856.U673 Z816 2022 | DDC 895.63/5--dc23
LC record available at https://lccn.loc.gov/2021008551

ISBN: 978-0-367-18140-6 (hbk)
ISBN: 978-0-367-18141-3 (pbk)
ISBN: 978-0-429-05971-1 (ebk)

Typeset in Garamond
by SPi Technologies India Pvt Ltd (Straive)

CONTENTS

LIST OF FIGURES AND TABLES

PREFACE

Gitte Marianne Hansen

While only a very short story within Murakami's extensive body of work, 'Midori iro no kemono' (1991; trans. 'The Little Green Monster' [1993]) is probably the single most important piece that inspired me to develop a research project on Murakami Haruki, part of which is now realised with this volume. With its housewife–narrator, this work stands out from the many stories told by the lonesome, male protagonist we know so well. It follows a formulaic storyline – a protagonist encounters a monster, a violent conflict ensues, and the protagonist conquers the monster – yet it is no typical story. The monster is cute and harmless, with pink arms and legs; and the protagonist is not heroic since her conquering acts cause the monsters' eyes to dissolve into emptiness, filling the room with the darkness of night, not light and joy. *Who* or *what* is this green monster, I wondered as I read, and *why* does the housewife have to make its eyes dissolve into emptiness? Each answer I found to my questions only set off a new query that brought me deeper into the Murakami world.

It was 2004 when I first read that story. I was a postgraduate exchange student at Waseda University and signed up for a class on contemporary Japanese literature taught by Katō Norihiro. I had read Murakami before (though to be honest not always with great enthusiasm), but it was not until hearing Katō-sensei's thought-provoking ideas every week that I was captured. Captured – not in the sense of being hooked because I had come to love Murakami's stories; it was more as if I found myself wanting to explore ways of reading his often strange tales, of making sense of them all. Since then time has passed. It is now more than 40 years ago that Murakami wrote his first novel, and more than 15 since I first met Katō-sensei from whom I had the privilege of learning for several years while working as his teaching and research assistant.

Whether we like Murakami's works or not, his entry onto the global literary scene has left its mark, asking us to explore his stories in diverse ways, not only in the field of literature but also in fields such as sociocultural history, translation, and gender.

I therefore tasked myself to read Murakami's entire body of fiction (not a small job as it turned out) to see how a research project on his works could take shape. Financially supported by the Arts and Humanities Research Council (AHRC), in 2018 I was finally able to realise my research ambition that first sprouted while I was at Waseda all those years earlier. Leveraging my background in gender and character construction, I now had my own ideas about who the green monster is and why the housewife–protagonist must make its eyes dissolve into emptiness. But there was still so much more in the Murakami world to be explored, and I wanted to create a project engaging ideas from the broad spectrum of Murakami scholarship I had seen emerge throughout the years.

To set off, my first task was to find scholars with whom to collaborate, engage and discuss. I was fortunate to gain the most excellent Research Associate for the project – Michael Tsang, who is the co-editor of this volume. In April 2018, we organised the event series 'Eyes on Murakami' and convened a diverse and inspiring group of international scholars, translators, artists, and filmmakers from all over the world to the North East of England. It was immensely exciting and enriching to bring together this strong international community to explore the past four decades of Murakami and to collectively question and share our distinctive sets of eyes and expertise. Although *Murakami Haruki and Our Years of Pilgrimage* only includes a fraction of the exciting scholarship that was presented at the '40 Years with Murakami' conference in Newcastle, I hope this volume will enable future discussion on Murakami and how his works are viewed around the world and within various disciplinary fields.

1

YES, MURAKAMI HARUKI IS A CHALLENGE

Gitte Marianne Hansen and Michael Tsang

A little more than four decades ago in 1978, a young Murakami Haruki sat down in his bar kitchen in Tokyo with the determination to write a novel. Having just watched a game of baseball at the Jingu Stadium, we have been told years later, it simply hit him that day that he could. The world was different then, and so was Japanese literature: very few could have imagined how deeply this young man's writings would come to influence Japanese literature and its place in the world. As we now know, Murakami's novels and short stories – and indeed also the story of his own journey to and from that very kitchen – have become global culture. His works have been translated into more than 50 languages, and his stories and characters are increasingly becoming transmedial, inspiring cultural producers from around the world such as filmmakers, artists, computer game programmers, travelogue writers, performing art producers, and dance choreographers. The Murakamian imaginary world with its peculiarly 'normal' – who therefore are not so normal – characters has thus travelled not only beyond that Tokyo bar kitchen, but also beyond both the Japanese language and the literary institution as medium of storytelling. But where does that leave us as critical readers?

After the publication of his kitchen-table novels – as he has come to call his first works – Murakami's stories were met with significant critique from many of the established literary circles in Japan which, throughout much of the 1980s and 1990s, saw his style as a threat to the rich tradition of *jun-bungaku* (pure literature). Miyoshi Masao, for example, called Murakami's (along with Yoshimoto Banana's and other new writers') works 'disposables' (1991: 33–37). Conversely, Murakami distanced himself from established literary circles, scholarship and prize committees in Japan, and later pointed out that the short story 'Tongariyaki no seisui' (1983; trans. 'The Rise and Fall of Sharpie Cakes' [2006]) was written as a response to his harsh experience with the Japanese literary tradition.[1] With this story, in which aggressive crows dig out each other's eyes over the quality and taste of a traditional type of cake, Murakami seems to have felt that established literary criticism was more focused on bringing each other down than up. Like the protagonist, who at first is keen to have his cakes approved by the crows but eventually decides to judge their value for himself, Murakami decided to be the judge of his own writings.

While generally disconnecting himself from literary criticism in Japan, from early on Murakami has been more willing to engage with literary critics and academics outside Japan, most notably through periods of writing fellowships at three US universities (Princeton, Tufts, and Harvard). Despite these and despite the fame from his breakthrough novel *Noruwei no mori* (1987; trans. *Norwegian Wood* [1989/2000]), he did not immediately gain attention in academic scholarship in the West. In fact, North American graduate students in the early 1990s found it difficult to find opportunities to discuss Murakami academically. In their *taidan* (dialogue) included in this volume, Murakami's translators Jay Rubin and Ted Goossen recall their panel at the 1992 Association for Asian Studies (AAS) annual conference and observe how back then Murakami was often dismissed as an 'entertaining' author popular with a young audience. Even 20 years later, a similar reluctance to include the writer in serious academic study in Europe was registered with co-editor of this volume Gitte Marianne Hansen during her doctorate at the University of Cambridge. This experience inspired her to call for academic attention to Murakami at a panel she organised at the 2011 Asian Studies Conference Japan. Although there was a high turnout, participants, who were largely affiliated with Western universities, lamented being judged for studying Murakami. In the same year, as the other co-editor Michael Tsang discovered during his master's studies in Hong Kong, Murakami was also not studied in literature departments, but at best sporadically touched upon in Japanese Studies departments in East Asia. Thus, although Murakami from early on had a massive following outside the academy, especially in East Asia, for a long time we could see a pattern where scholars – especially young scholars – with an interest in Murakami have felt that their work and academic thoughts were dismissed as unserious within the field of literature.

It has taken years to reach the point we are at today; in addition to the novelist himself producing an oeuvre of provocative works, it also took the accumulative endeavour of general and academic readers who tirelessly wrote, talked, or simply thought about Murakami. From the beginning of his career, only a handful of critics, most notably Katō Norihiro, recognised the new writing style and its importance for the future of Japanese literature. Later, as David Karashima shows in his book *Who we're reading when we're reading Murakami* (2020), Murakami's entry into the Anglo–American market in the late 1980s was not coincidental, but carefully planned by skilled translators and editors who knew what American readers and publishers would want, to the extent that some rather invasive omissions took place in the English translations of *Sekai no owari to hādoboirudo wandārando* (1985; trans. *Hard-Boiled Wonderland and the End of the World* [1991]) and *Nejimakidori kuronikuru* (1994–1995; trans. *The Wind-Up Bird Chronicle* [1997]). At that point, in English-speaking academia, scholars such as Matthew C. Strecher, Jay Rubin, and Rebecca Suter laid important groundwork for Murakami studies across the 1990s and 2000s. Both critical and marketing expertise have thus played a part in Murakami being awarded some of the world's most prestigious literary and cultural accolades, including the Franz Kafka Prize in 2006, the Jerusalem Prize for the Freedom of the Individual in Society in 2009, and *Time* magazine's 100 most influential people in 2015 under the category 'Icon'.

The fact stands that no matter how much Murakami may have tried to stay out of the spotlight, he has undoubtedly achieved celebrity status. There are several terms that describe the position he occupies in global culture, from the 'Murakami phenomenon' (Seats 2006: 25–41; Zielinska–Elliott 2015) to the 'Murakami effect' (Snyder 2016). While he undeniably is one of those artists who has managed to influence the established literary canon, the man who once sat writing in his Tokyo bar kitchen is now also subject to a type of fandom typically associated with popular culture. For instance, despite requests from the organisers to queue up in an orderly manner, fans scrambled and elbowed their way to the fore for a time-limited signing session at the 2014 Edinburgh International Book Festival. Later, on the same UK book tour, many readers lined up outside a London bookshop for as much as 18 hours to get a signed copy of *Colorless Tsukuru Tazaki and His Years of Pilgrimage* (2014) the English translation of *Shikisai o motanai Tazaki Tsukuru to, kare no junrei no toshi* (2013). Moreover, as we have pointed out in our discussion of Murakami and transmediality (Hansen and Tsang 2020), international success has now cyclically fuelled the writer's popularity in Japan, with overseas Murakami products being sold *back* to a Japanese audience: think, for example, of the German illustrator Kat Menschik's artistic drawings in *Schlaf* (2009) and *Die Bäckerüberfälle* (2012), illustrated German translations to 'Nemuri' (1989; trans. 'Sleep' [1992]) and the two bakery attack stories ('Pan'ya shūgeki' (1981; no trans. Attack on the Bakery); 'Pan'ya saishūgeki' (1985; trans. 'The Second Bakery Attack' [1992])), respectively. The rare picture book format prompted the Japanese publisher Shinchōsha to bring the stories back to the Japanese market, with Menschik's drawings untouched but the texts newly updated by Murakami (hence also stylised differently with the *hiragana*-only title *Nemuri* (2010) and the synonymous title *Pan'ya o osou* (2013).

Academic institutions have also gradually begun to recognise the significance of Murakami. As the first in the world, in 2012 Tamkang University in Taiwan established its Murakami Haruki Research Centre, which since then has held annual conferences on the writer. Furthermore, as we are finalising this edited volume, Murakami's alma mater, Waseda University, has announced its plans to establish the International House of Literature – otherwise to be known as 'The Haruki Murakami Library'. Murakami has stated that he intends to donate early manuscripts and notes to the new library as it opens later in 2021. Looking ahead, it remains to be seen how such institutional recognition will influence the future of Murakami studies and its place within the global academy.

However, the extensive international and critical acclaim has now ironically caused another problem for literary criticism. Katō identified this double bind in *Murakami Haruki wa, muzukashii* (2015; no trans. Murakami Haruki is, a Challenge): On the one hand, in tandem with Murakami's celebrated status as a global writer, the pejorative criticism against him in Japan died down, replaced by interest in his secret to success. For Katō, the space that allowed critics to argue about their interpretations of Murakami texts and about his literary accomplishment has been lost, and in recent years, long-term critics have found it difficult to criticise Murakami freely. On the other, Katō experienced situations where fellow novelists and literary critics from East Asia, such as the Chinese novelist Yan Lianke, were unfazed by Murakami's fame and uninterested in his works. Neither side of this double bind was productive for Katō, and until the end of his life he tirelessly championed and supported research that deliberates the literary value of Murakami's works; hence, 'Murakami Haruki is a challenge'.

It is with the trajectory sketched above that we named this volume *Murakami Haruki and Our Years of Pilgrimage*. An obvious reference to *Shikisai o motanai Tazaki Tsukuru to, kare no junrei no toshi* (cf. *Colorless Tsukuru Tazaki and His Years of Pilgrimage*), this title understands 'pilgrimage' not in the religious sense – by no means are we suggesting that Murakami is some sort of 'holy figure' in Japanese literature, but simply in the sense of a long, usually taxing journey in search of new meanings to one's belief, thought, and philosophy. As Tsukuru tries to make sense of what happened in his youth, so too have we – all readers, students, and researchers with an interest in Murakami – spent 'years' trying to think through his works. Hence, not only do we wish to second that, yes, it is a challenge to read Murakami Haruki critically, we also aim to rise to that very challenge and create a space of critique that Katō searched for – a space that allows everyone to muse on 'our' thoughts about Murakami liberally and enables those ideas to inspire our work going forward, just like Tsukuru's friend Haida says in the novel (2014: 44):

> I want to think deeply about things. Contemplate ideas in a pure, free sort of way.

Murakami as research project

As one of the few existing edited volumes in English devoted to Murakami, this collection of academic analyses and essays wishes to pay tribute to Katō's conviction that, while there is no doubt Murakami has helped transform Japanese literature in disturbing the division between 'pop' and 'pure' literature, it is no easy task to understand Murakami Haruki the novelist, essayist, translator, and cultural icon. It is simply impossible to reduce to any simplistic evaluation a writer who has been publishing for more than four decades, and who has generated such remarkable trans-national and transmedial reception but remains interestingly awkward with the literary establishment of his own country and elsewhere. This was indeed one of the main aims for the Arts and Humanities Research Council (AHRC)-funded project on Murakami Haruki that Hansen led at the School of Modern Languages, Newcastle University in 2018 – from which this volume took shape. The project sought to connect scholars from diverse fields to share their 'eyes' – thoughts, ideas, and expertise – through the event series 'Eyes on Murakami' co-organised by Tsang, which included an art exhibition and catalogue, a translation workshop and symposium, a film screening, and the academic conference '40 Years with Murakami Haruki'.[2] Over four days, we created a space for a highly diverse group of people – academic scholars, artists, professional and aspiring translators, filmmakers, and public readers – from all over the world to assemble in Newcastle and debate interpretations of Murakami's work. Some keynote speeches have already been published in a special issue of *Japan Forum* which we edited (Volume 32, No. 3 [2020]).

This present volume builds on that journal issue and includes several chapters that were first presented at the conference, as well as others that have been developed specifically for us. Either way, they showcase a multifarious range of research angles being undertaken on Murakami. We have ensured as much as possible a democratic and gender-balanced sample of backgrounds by including articles from established scholars to early career researchers, and indeed even editors and translators, based in Asia, Europe, North America, and Oceania. Some chapters take on interesting formats such as interviews, dialogues, essays, and adaptation from speeches, while others ground their approach in various academic disciplinary traditions from cultural studies, translation studies, and literary theory, to history, geography, and gender studies. Collaboratively, the contributions chronicle the 40-plus years that Murakami has been active, from the start of his career and the beginning of his global fame, to how he remains relevant in the present world. We hope the volume will be a testimony to how Murakami inspires and provokes such cross-generational, dia-chronic, transnational, multi-media, and of course, inter-disciplinary, responses.

This richness is also reflected in the cover image we have chosen for the volume. First displayed in the exhibition 'Beyond Words: Transmediating Murakami Haruki' at Long Gallery and Atrium, Fine Art Building, Newcastle University, between 6–9 March 2018 as part of the 'Eyes on Murakami' event series, Christopher Jones' *Slipping Through the Membrane #1* encapsulates the many prospects that may take place when one encounters a Murakami novel.[3] In this work, we see the juxtaposition of Japanese and English versions of the very first page of *Nejimakidori kuronikuru/ The Wind-Up Bird Chronicle*, superimposed by a ladder that leads to what can be understood as Murakami's iconic metaphysical motif of the well. Because we can only glimpse the words 'Bird' and 'Breasts' in the chapter title at the bottom of the well, we must figure out the depth hidden beyond these apparent signifiers for ourselves.

What this artwork shows is that there can in fact be infinite discussion on Murakami. To sustain a space for critique, *Murakami Haruki and Our Years of Pilgrimage* includes chapters that explore different aspects of both his identity as an author and his work. Before we proceed, however, we wish to comment on the conventions for this volume. Because people read Murakami in different languages, formats, and editions, the way he and his works are referred to or referenced also differs. One clichéd confusion is the way Japanese names often are reordered in Western European languages – hence Murakami Haruki becomes Haruki Murakami. In this volume, however, we seek to undo such persistent assumptions by consistently rendering purely East Asian names with their surnames first, that is, Murakami Haruki, unless in an already published title.[4] More problematic is the way contributors refer to his works: should one use Japanese or English titles? Given that noticeable omissions and edits have been done not only to the English translation but also translations in other languages, readers who read in Japanese may know a given work differently from those reading in translation. Far from positing that Japanese versions are the 'originals', we recognise that whether one reads a Murakami story in Japanese or in any other language, each work should be seen as its own original, with its own possibility for interpretations. Moreover, certain linguistic features are more prominent in the Japanese version, such as the use of the Japanese male first-person pronoun *boku* for many of his narrators. Acknowledging how these differences shape each of our unique ideas about Murakami's work means that it would be limiting to confine all mentions of his work to either the Japanese title or the translated title (bearing in mind that not all works have been translated). Instead, our editorial policy is to maintain consistency within a chapter, but allow variations *across* chapters. If a contributor works from the English versions of Murakami's work, titles will be in English throughout unless it is a work that has not been translated. If a chapter discusses issues related to the Japanese language or works from the Japanese versions, it will consistently use the Japanese title in modified Hepburn Romanisation and provide its own English translations of the work (because, as noted, the published English versions may contain omissions and edits). Either way, the other title (i.e. English titles for chapters that use Japanese ones, and vice versa) will be included the first time a work is mentioned in a chapter. We have also included a complete index of Murakami works cited in the volume with titles in both Japanese and English.

Indeed, this complication about story titles is symptomatic of a bigger challenge to gauge the critical potential of Murakami, who continues to transform with new texts and transmedial products. Underpinned by an astounding prolificacy with all his fictional and non-fictional works as well as interviews, essays, and speeches, his iconic authorship unites academics, translators, editors, and public readers. In this way, his works offer numerous possibilities for critical inquiry into a spectrum of social, political, cultural, linguistic, and literary topics. To capture these complex relationships, the chapters of this volume is organised into four parts:

Part I: Temporal and spatial dimensions

The volume opens with a section that considers how Murakami's fiction intersects with the axes of time and space. Each of the four chapters in this part demonstrates that thematic readings of Murakami can be grounded within broader temporal and/or spatial dimensions. We begin with **Katō Norihiro**, who periodises Murakami's oeuvre through the lens of humour and questions if Murakami has run into a certain predicament since *1Q84* (2009–2010; trans. *1Q84* [2011]) as his works became more and more 'committed' to the narrative and society as a whole. Dealing with a different notion of time, **Matthew C. Strecher** then examines what history means in Murakami's fiction, especially in the way he creates metaphysical narrative spaces with archetypal characters. Following on from that, **Barbara E. Thornbury** turns to geography and examines how the urban space of Tokyo, including named places and unnamed venues, is portrayed as a symbol fraught with sociocultural displacement, disconnection, and disorientation. Looking at a different, more enclosed space, the section ends with **Nihei Chikako**'s reading of the kitchen in the short story 'Zō no shōmetsu' (1985; trans. 'The Elephant Vanishes' [1993]) as illustrative of a broader transformation to the kitchen in Japan following the Second World War, and as a symbol that channels Murakami's critique of advanced capitalist society.

Part II: Narrative and genders

Not only is there little academic research that details Murakami's treatment of gender relations, that treatment is also often only criticised for reducing female characters to mere sexual objects, which Murakami briefly touched upon in his conversation with the writer Kawakami Mieko published in 2017. Hence, the second part comprises four chapters that elucidate and question the way gender is represented in Murakami narratives more broadly. In the opening chapter, **Gitte Marianne Hansen** paints broad strokes on Murakami's first-person narrator types and female character construction, laying the groundwork for several of the ensuing chapters. **Michael Tsang** then employs theories of discourse and of the male gaze to devise a model of narrativised gaze structure in *After Dark* (2007; *Afutādāku* [2004]), and shedding light on Murakami's gender representation in the novel. Using psychoanalysis, **Astrid Lac** brings to the table a different argument to Tsang's on the issue of gender, asserting that Murakami exemplifies the quintessential Lacanian idea that there can be no universal generalisation of Woman. In the final chapter of the section, **Anna Zielinska–Elliott** extends the inquiry on gender to examine the representation of gay characters in Murakami's work.

Part III: Literary dialogues

Part of the critique Murakami faced in the early days of his career was that his texts read more like English than Japanese, due to their more straightforward syntax and diction as well as numerous references to European and American literatures and cultures. Despite the fact that Murakami has only ever written in Japanese, this critique is strongly tied to his own claim of first writing the opening of *Kaze no uta o kike* (1979; trans. *Hear the Wind Sing* [1987/2015]) in English and later translating it back to Japanese, in order to find a voice and language that could be free of the restrictions he felt imposed by the Japanese literary tradition. Thus, from the outset of his career, questions of literary translation, inspiration, and cultural influence have been central, and the third part therefore contains chapters that unearth profound dialogues between him and other writers or genres of writing. First, **Giorgio Amitrano** studies how Murakami talks about literary inspiration, often in metaphors, both in his fictional and non-fictional works, and draws on other Japanese and non-Japanese authors for comparison. This is followed by two chapters acknowledging intertextual connections between Murakami and other authors. **Annette Thorsen Vilslev** recuperates a much-neglected influence of Japanese writers on Murakami's novels as she compares his coming-of-age novels with not only European and American Bildung classics but also with the works of the Meiji–Taishō writer Natsume Sōseki. Written during the Trump administration, **Patricia Welch** highlights three main ways Murakami's *1Q84* dialogues with George Orwell's dystopian classic *Nineteen Eighty-Four*, and makes a compelling case arguing for the importance of reading both authors in the current era. Finally, **Akashi Motoko** regards Murakami not only as a novelist but also as a literary translator; examining the manifestations of Murakami's trademark literary style in his translations, she makes an effective argument on Murakami's subjectivity as a translator–novelist.

Part IV: Personal stories from the industry

Murakami's global fame means that each reader has their own story of discovering, reading, and thinking about his work. Although it is a less common academic practice within literary studies to include personal accounts and reflections, we conclude this volume with three essays/interviews that not only offer insight into how he came to be appreciated and translated beyond Japan but also echo many of the perspectives, approaches, and thematics discussed in the other sections. As the first English editor of Murakami's work, **Elmer Luke** opens Part IV by sharing fascinating stories behind how he first came to read Murakami and help bring his work into an English readership in the late 1980s. Long-time English translators of Murakami, **Jay Rubin** and **Ted Goossen**, continue on from that by using the format of *taidan* often found in Japanese literary magazines, to share their own Murakami journey and discuss issues on Murakami's reception, gender representation, and more. These passionate recollections embody the organic relationship that Murakami has with his translators, editors, and critics in the context of his global popularity; just as Luke, Rubin, and Goossen have been impressed with his works, so too have they played a part in bringing him to the world inspiring more people. The volume ends with an interview by **Rebecca Suter** with none other than **Murakami Haruki** himself; readers will find the conversation adding interesting touches to the diverse understandings offered in this book.

At the closing discussion of the '40 Years with Murakami Haruki' conference in Newcastle, Katō said something to this effect: 'I came here and found out that the Murakami I thought I knew – I don't know at all'. With *Murakami Haruki and Our Years of Pilgrimage*, we aim to precisely showcase some of the numerous interpretations that we can adopt in Murakami studies. What is certain is that this will not be the last time scholars from multiple disciplines converge to discuss Murakami – the pilgrimage continues, and as Murakami himself says in Rebecca Suter's interview, time will do the work. By opening the floor, this volume hopes to become a key enabler of such future discussions.

Notes

1 Heard when Murakami was interviewed on stage at the small literary festival, 'Verdens literatur på Møn' (World literature on Møn island) in Denmark, 28–29 August 2010.
2 For full details on the event series including publications and the publicity generated, please visit https://research.ncl.ac.uk/murakami/.
3 For the full catalogue of the art exhibition, please visit https://research.ncl.ac.uk/murakami/publications.
4 There is increasing objection to the use of Western name order for Japanese names (e.g. Satō 2017).

References

Hansen, G. M. and Tsang, M. 2020. Politics in/of transmediality in Murakami Haruki's bakery attack stories. *Japan Forum* 32 (3): 404–431.

Karashima, D. 2020. *Who we're reading when we're reading Murakami*. New York: Soft Skull Press.

Katō N. 2015. *Murakami Haruki wa, muzukashii*. Tokyo: Iwanami Shoten.

Kawakami M. and Murakami H. 2017. *Mimizuku wa tasogare ni tabidatsu*. Tokyo: Shinchōsha.

Miyoshi M. 1991. Women's short stories in Japan. *Mānoa* 3 (2): 33–39.

Murakami H. 2014. *Colorless Tsukuru Tazaki and His Years of Pilgrimage*. Translated by Philip Gabriel. London: Harvill Secker.

Satō H. 2017. Reversing Japanese names for Western use? [online] *The Japan Times*, 22 January. Available from: https://www.japantimes.co.jp/opinion/2017/01/22/commentary/japan-commentary/reversing-japanese-names-western-use/ [Accessed 17 January 2021].

Seats, M. 2006. *Murakami Haruki: The simulacrum in contemporary Japanese culture*. New York, NY; Plymouth, UK: Lexington Books.

Snyder, S. 2016. Insistence and resistance: Murakami and Mizumura in translation. *New England Review* 37 (4): 133–142.

Zielinska–Elliott, A. 2015. Murakami international: The translation of a literary phenomenon. *Japanese Language and Literature* 49 (1): 93–107.

PART I

Temporal and spatial dimensions

2

FROM *HARA-HARA* TO *DOKI-DOKI*

Murakami Haruki's use of humour and his predicament since *1Q84*

Katō Norihiro, translated by Michael Tsang, with a tribute by the editors

For a long time now, I have been continuously and exhaustively discussing the works of Murakami Haruki. Having engaged with his works all these years, however, I have recently come to the opinion that Murakami has been met lately with a curious predicament. In this chapter I would like to discuss this problem and elaborate on some of my thoughts as they stand. Here are the reasons I believe Murakami has been trapped in a certain predicament since 2010.

My first concern is *1Q84*, published in 2009–2010 (trans. *1Q84* [2011]). Though undetectable when reading the English translation alone, the novel was in fact originally published in Japan in 2009 as a finished work in two volumes, BOOK 1 and BOOK 2, the latter of which ends with the suggested suicide of one of the protagonists, Aomame. Much to our surprise, Murakami then released BOOK 3 the following year, and here, the ending is clearly unresolved. This led to speculations in Japan at the time that there might be a BOOK 4, and such speculations were supported by two lines of reasoning.

First, the story is left unfinished at the end of BOOK 3. Not only is the mystery of Aomame's pregnancy left unexplained, but it is also suggested that when the protagonists manage to escape from the world of 1Q84, they do not return to the world of reality, but instead have entered into another parallel world. The evidence for this lies in the flipped position of the tiger on the Esso billboard. Second, as in BOOK 1 and BOOK 2, the Japanese version of BOOK 3 also ends with the suggestive phrase, 'BOOK 3 *owari*' [The End of BOOK 3]. Given that the three books so far are subtitled, respectively, April to June, July to September, and October to December, many believed that there could be a sequel (either a BOOK 4 or a BOOK 0, covering possibly January to March).

In addition, I have proposed in one of my books a third reasoning that I developed after reading BOOK 3: Aomame has killed someone (see Katō 2015). When the protagonist of a novel has killed somebody, and then escapes with her newfound lover into a new world where she is about to give birth, how can there be no further development to such a plot?

Yet, we all know that the saga ended with neither a BOOK 4 nor a BOOK 0 being published. The question then remains unsolved: What sort of problems did Murakami run into at the end of BOOK 3? Did he manage to solve them, and how? At the same time, another notable phenomenon occurred: BOOK 1 and BOOK 2 took the book market in Japan by storm, to the extent that various commentaries and reading guides were published to 'interpret' or 'decipher' the story for readers, but when BOOK 3 was released the following year, a similar hype did not recur.

Following the three volumes of *1Q84*, in 2013 Murakami published the novel *Shikisai o motanai Tazaki Tsukuru to, kare no junrei no toshi* (trans. *Colorless Tsukuru Tazaki and His Years of Pilgrimage* [2014]). This is a story where the protagonist Tsukuru, who guards himself strongly against other people and cannot love somebody a hundred per cent from the bottom of his heart, attempts to resolve his issues and break his psychological barrier from within. Born and raised in Nagoya, Tsukuru was ostracised by a group of friends and later relocated to Tokyo. On one level, this bears an interesting overlap with Murakami's own experience – a Japanese novelist who once left Japan (viz. Nagoya) for life overseas (viz. Tokyo) and felt isolated by his relationship with Japanese literature and the media.

However, with this work I feel that Murakami is going in circles. In the end, the protagonist goes to Finland, confesses his problems to an old female friend named Eri, and then discusses with her what he should do about his current lover in Tokyo. The advice he receives from Eri is: 'You know, Tsukuru, you need to make her your own' (*nee, Tsukuru, kimi wa kanojo o te ni ireru beki da yo*' (Murakami 2013: 322)). This is essentially an advice that asks Tsukuru to 'be strong' or 'toughen up'. However, the problem that one cannot commit to another person a hundred per cent is one that is commonly faced by many people nowadays. The key issue here, in my mind, is not to overcome such so-called vulnerability, but to first face it head on.

As a side note, the published English translation by Philip Gabriel renders this line into: 'You know, Tsukuru, you need to hang on to her' (Murakami 2014a: 259). Perhaps the translator also felt that 'making her your own' (*te ni ireru beki da yo*) sounded a little too strong and amended the line using his professional judgement as a translator without consulting Murakami. However, the English phrase 'to hang on to someone' is an advice that presumes the person to be 'weak' and reliant, while the Japanese '*te ni ireru beki*' is a piece of advice to a vulnerable person to toughen up.[1] Thus, as far as this particular phrase is concerned, the English translation misses the momentum of the advice; those who read the novel in English may not fully comprehend my following concern.

This shift from 'vulnerability/weakness' to 'toughness/resilience' has a symbolic meaning if we consider Murakami's work so far. Until now, whenever a similar dilemma has arisen, Murakami has always chosen to commit to the 'weaker' side. This default solidarity or commitment was first spotted in one of his earlier works, *Sekai no owari to hādoboirudo wandārando* (1985; trans. *Hard-Boiled Wonderland and the End of the World* [1991]), and was the reason the *boku* protagonist in 'The End of the World' part decided to remain in the Town. When his Shadow expresses that they should escape this fake, fabricated world – a reasonable and modern opinion – *boku* decides to commit himself to the vulnerabilities in this fake world, and gives up his chance to escape to the real world. Had this spirit of committing to the weak remained unchanged for Murakami after all these years, then, in my imagination, Eri's advice to Tsukuru might have been something like this:

> You know, Tsukuru, only you can solve your own problems, and you should not get your girlfriend involved in them. But, once you decide to endure everything on your own, your girlfriend may want to help you out. If that happens, you should accept her help with a grateful heart. That would become your commitment to the relationship.

This commitment should then be portrayed to the effect that Tsukuru would return to Japan and allow himself to be placed in this weaker position requiring help – a position available only thanks to the intervention of his girlfriend Sara. As it stands in the actual novel, however, Eri's advice to toughen up may be construed as an abandonment or betrayal of the commitment to the weak, which breeds a feeling of banality to the novel. I have argued elsewhere (see Katō 2016, esp. 262) that this creates a sense of emptiness in the novel's ending, which explains why Murakami had to throw in a convenient reminiscence – like an external shot in the arm or artificial boost of confidence – for Tsukuru to believe in the innocent hope that he and his friends used to have when they were young (Murakami 2013: 370).

After this novel, Murakami published in 2014 the short story collection *Onna no inai otokotachi* (trans. *Men Without Women* [2017]). Again, compared to his highly accomplished story collections in the past, such as *Pan'ya Saishūgeki* (1986; no trans. The Second Bakery Attack), or *Kami no kodomotachi wa mina odoru* (2000; trans. *after the quake* [2002]), this collection is uneven in its strengths and weaknesses, and offers little breakthrough in Murakami's writing. While there are good stories in the collection like 'Kino' (trans. 'Kino'), others are less stellar. For example, in the story 'Dokuritsu kikan' (trans. 'An Independent Organ') there are certain remarks that feel as if they were added in an offhand and careless way, such as when the protagonist's 'handsome secretary' is introduced with the random but hackneyed aside '(who was, of course, gay) [*mochiron gei data*]' (Murakami 2014b: 129), playing to stereotypes of handsomeness in Japan;[2] or when the protagonist, wounded by love, becomes interested in 'Nazi concentration camps' (ibid.: 141). Readers are tempted to raise this following question, one that even precedes a debate on literary value: Instead of being a passing mention, should these elements not require thorough preparation, careful arrangement, and plot necessity to justify their existence in the story? (See Katō 2014 for more of my opinion on the collection.)

The same could be said of Murakami's latest novel, *Kishidanchō goroshi* (2017; trans. *Killing Commendatore* [2018]), in which the treatment of the Nanjing Massacre and Auschwitz seems ornamental and unpolished to me, as if some 'serious' topics were imposed onto the text artificially, making the story unnecessarily 'heavy' (see Katō 2017b). One could even sense a tiny danger where, as the characters' inner commitment – which used to feature in Murakami's earlier works – weakens, the external, political themes and motifs have become more central in the latest works.

In fact, until recently, I was of the opinion that this would merely be a temporary phenomenon unworthy of attention. After all, everyone has had a bad hair day, every writer a bottleneck in their writing. However, I have since changed my position, and now I cannot help but think that Murakami is indeed facing a major difficulty in his writing.

The inspiration for such thoughts came from an interview with the Studio Ghibli animator Takahata Isao, who is widely known as the collaborative partner of Miyazaki Hayao. According to Takahata, anime nowadays are different from those in the past, having shifted from the '*hara-hara*' type to the '*doki-doki*' type. In the *doki-doki* type of fantasy, viewers stand 'in the same position as the protagonist', and because they 'cannot understand how the world is framed and operates', they can 'only follow the protagonist and keep having a feeling of *doki-doki* or, a heart-pounding excitement' (Takahata and Binard 2017: 247–248). However, this was not the case in the past. Viewers used to be able to stand at a metaphysical level and survey things 'objectively from the outside' or at a distance. And when 'an enemy approached the protagonist', they could 'say things to the protagonists like "Hey watch out!" or "You mustn't go there!"' As such, rather than *doki-doki*, viewers used to feel a palm-sweating sensation of *hara-hara* as they were kept on the edge for the main characters.

Why is this feeling of *hara-hara* important? Takahata then goes on to make this very important point: laughter emerges from distance. Conversely, when a work moves from *hara-hara* to *doki-doki* and immerses the reader into the point of view of the story, laughter disappears, or, humour vanishes. Takahata even makes the same criticism on his own collaborative partner, Miyazaki Hayao: 'while we could still laugh until *Tenkū no shiro Rapyuta* [1986, trans. *Castle in the Sky*] [...] works after that no longer brought us laughter apart from the occasional chuckle. [...] They have completely become the *doki-doki* type that dragged the viewer in' (ibid.: 248). Such critique may be very persuasive to those familiar with Miyazaki's animation. In short, since the release of *Mononoke hime* (trans. *Princess Mononoke*) in 1997, Miyazaki's animated works have shown a higher degree of *doki-doki* and a tendency to drag the audience into more serious stories; as a result, laughter, or humour, has been effaced.

Now, could we not say almost the same for Murakami's works?

Takahata's critique reminds me of a comment made by Murakami's translator Alfred Birnbaum, whom I invited to give a guest lecture at my university in 2009. When I asked him what, in his observation over the years, the biggest change in Murakami's work had been, he answered immediately that it was 'the disappearance of humour'. He thought it a pity that, ever since *Nejimakidori kuronikuru* (trans. *The Wind-Up Bird Chronicle* [1997]) was published in 1994–1995, Murakami's works have turned more serious at the expense of humour.

However, if we think through the issue again, we realise that this change in Murakami's literary style is not a particularly new argument. Roughly speaking, the shift from *hara-hara* to *doki-doki* is the other side of the same coin: Murakami's transformation as a novelist from 'detachment' to 'commitment', which many scholars have observed so far. In other words, the distance created in the *hara-hara* style between the reader and the subject is analogous to 'detachment', and the involvement that drags readers into the story in the *doki-doki* style can be seen as a serious 'commitment' towards the subject. The only difference here is that laughter, or humour, disappears as a result. Takahata's comment reminded me of this important negative aspect, which I believe many of us, myself included, have forgotten. (See Katō 2006 for the merits of the detachment approach.)

Following this train of thought, we can now offer a hypothesis for understanding why Murakami attempted to do something new in BOOK 1 and BOOK 2 of *1Q84*, namely, to introduce a world completely framed as entertainment.[3] My hypothesis is that, in order to secure and protect this space for detachment and humour in the story world of *1Q84*, Murakami introduced a world of entertainment – which takes reference from a popular Japanese TV drama – as a structural frame for the novel. One of the protagonists, Aomame, works as a professional assassinator. This idea comes from a TV programme with a similar plot called the *Hissatsu* series (trans. *Sure Death Killers*), which was in turn based on a famous samurai novel series in Japan. According to Wikipedia, the series has an archetypal plot that 'portrays the lives and actions of those who are paid to avenge at the behest of helpless people who are unable to do this by themselves. Most of the protagonists have decent jobs on the surface', and the murders 'are more a vengeance on behalf of the weak rather than a simple assassination' ('Hissatsu sirīzu' n.d.).

In *Sekai no owari to hādoboirudo wandārando*, Murakami also portrays a dichotomy between a sentimental, lyrical, heart-and-soul world on the one hand, and a dry hard-boiled world on the other. The former is a world of enthusiasm and dedication devoid of humour, while the latter is a world that reeks of apathetic, deadpan humour. The novel's narrative moves forward by oscillating between these two contrasting worlds. However, in *1Q84*, the same motif is portrayed not as a parallel world, but as a trajectory from the first half of the novel to the second half.

A precedence – or rather, prototype – of this two-part trajectory can be found in the short story 'Kaeru-kun, Tōkyō o sukuu' (2000; trans. 'Super-Frog saves Tokyo' [2002]) in the collection *Kami no kodomotachi wa mina odoru*. The first half of this story depicts matter-of-factly the supernatural Frog's battle of justice against evil, but such a dichotomous worldview collapses in the second half, which takes a turn down the path of mirthless gloom (rather than passion and ardour in *Sekai on owari*). After the protagonist Katagiri loses consciousness on the street, he wakes up to find Frog's body rotting away, maggots and worms crawling out from the corpse towards him. In a world of chaos, Katagiri no longer knows what is right and wrong. By the same token, among the three volumes of *1Q84*, the first half also reveals a dichotomous worldview of justice and evil under the framework of 'hard-boiled' entertainment, but the remaining half portrays a world where such dichotomy has collapsed and depicts the protagonists in a more serious light. The turning point for this occurs roughly at the midpoint of the three-volume version, that is, in Chapter 13 of BOOK 2 where

Aomame kills the leader of a religious cult called Sakigake on a stormy September night.[4] As a result, in BOOK 3, even Ushikawa, the private investigator who until then was a bit eccentric and comical, is promoted to protagonist status, playing a serious role in the story.

In other words, as suggested by the song lyrics quoted in the novel's epigraph – 'It's a Barnum and Bailey world, / Just as phony as it can be, / But it wouldn't be make-believe / If you believed in me' – the novel sports a trajectory from a 'phony' world of entertainment and dichotomy in the first half to a non-make-believe – i.e. 'serious'[5] – world in the second (see Katō 2017a for more).

With this in mind, my hypothesis for answering my earlier questions would go like this: Murakami feels a sense of crisis realising that 'humour' is gradually disappearing from his recent works as they become ever more 'serious'. To remedy this, he attempts to introduce elements of a popular novel/TV entertainment series into the structure of *1Q84*. However, I would argue that while this attempt is successful up to the end of BOOK 2, it then runs into a major problem as he stacks up the story with BOOK 3.

In a world of entertainment, where everything is 'as phony as it can be', it is acceptable for the protagonist to be a serial killer or the 'bad' person. Even before she kills the cult leader, Aomame has already killed a male domestic abuser who murdered her best friend. However, she then comes to know Sakigake's leader, and her worldview changes through an extended dialogue with him. With her love for Tengo at stake, this 'Barnum and Bailey world' turns serious and becomes the 'non-make-believe world'. With this, the Dowager, who until then can be seen as the embodiment of justice, begins to fade away, and the cult leader, who so far has been perceived as an embodiment of evil, becomes an enigmatic and compelling figure that rises above both justice and evil. After this, the novel continues into the second half with the element of entertainment expelled and, like 'Kaeru-kun, Tōkyō o sukuu', a 'non-make-believe' world of chaos is brought in.

As a result, however, Aomame is also faced with a new problem. As I said at the beginning of this chapter, this novel was first published in two volumes as BOOK 1 and BOOK 2 in Japan. This two-volume version ends with the cornered Aomame about to commit suicide in order to help Tengo, the person she loves. Someone who became a professional assassinator so as to seek 'justice' in the 'Barnum and Bailey' world of entertainment, gets a reset in the actual world of reality and dies in the name of 'love'. Though a bit simplistic, the structure of the novel is nicely settled with this ending. However, in BOOK 3 it is explained that in fact Aomame is not dead. This gives rise to the problem I presented earlier: 'when a protagonist has killed somebody, and then escapes with her lover into a new world where she will give birth, is it even conceivable that there is no further development to such a plot?' What has also emerged here is a different and rather difficult question: As the story transits from the world of phony entertainment into a 'real world', how does someone, who used to believe that she was committing murder in the name of 'justice', resurrect herself in the name of love and survive in a new world where that previous notion of justice has collapsed?

This was probably not a theme Murakami had planned for the novel at first, but rather, a new question that arose as he was writing the novel. Perhaps he was not well prepared to respond to this curious problem: should he write about what happens next, or should he stop at this point? I believe that this hesitation explains the unfinished ending of BOOK 3.

I will conclude this chapter by way of offering some partial findings. The key questions with which I am concerned in this chapter are: What is humour for a novel? And what does humour mean for Murakami's work?

My answer is that humour is something like the essence of Murakami's writing. In the beginning, what differentiated him from other Japanese novelists was a sensibility of 'detachment' from the world, a cognition of 'distance/separation' between the world and the land in which he was born and raised – and humour took root in that distance. This humour was also what caught the eyes of Alfred Birnbaum, who was the first to translate Murakami, and who set the young Murakami apart from other Japanese novelists.

Yet, most ironically, as Murakami's work began to carry a stronger sense of *doki-doki* and commitment since *Nejimakidori kuronikuru*, what had once been the essence of his works – i.e. the sensibility of detachment from the world – was lost. The space for *hara-hara*, from which humour emerged, was also disappearing. Perhaps this is just the tip of the iceberg reflecting a much bigger predicament in Japanese literature: the humour in Natsume Sōseki's early writing in the Meiji period also disappeared towards his later works in the Taishō era. I propose, as my parting thought, that this predicament is what confronts Murakami in his works nowadays, but it illustrates a major problem behind.

Postscript 1 (written in October 2018)

After my keynote speech at Newcastle University, Murakami Haruki published three short stories in the July 2018 issue of *Bungakukai* under the overall title 'Mittsu no mijikai hanashi' (Three Short Pieces). The three stories are: 'Ishi no makura ni' (trans. 'On a Stone Pillow'), 'Kurīmu' (trans. 'Cream') and 'Chārī Pākā Pureizu Bosanova' (trans. 'Charlie Parker Plays Bossa Nova'). However, none of the stories could persuade me to take back the judgement I made here on Murakami's post-2010 work. If anything, they only further confirm my assessment.

Postscript 2

This chapter is an edited and expanded version from my keynote speech given on 8 March 2018 at the '40 Years with Murakami Haruki' academic conference held at Newcastle University, UK. I thank the sponsors and organisers of the event, the Arts and Humanities Research Council, and Senior Lecturer Dr Gitte Marianne Hansen for their invitation and hospitality. I also thank Dr Michael Tsang for his comments on and translation of this speech.

Notes

1 Translator's note: Translating '*te ni ireru beki da yo*' into 'you need to make her your own' is my decision under full consultation with the chapter author Katō. Also, in the Japanese original, Katō understands Gabriel's 'hang on to her' as '*te hanashitewa ikenai yo*', which literally means 'you should not let go of her', using a negative construction (*ikenai*) that is absent in Gabriel's phrase. This may have played a part in Katō's understanding of the phrase 'hang on to her' and the presumption behind it. Given the novel's context, however, '*te hanashitewa ikenai*' is, despite the negative construction, more accurate than some other more literal translations of 'hang on to her' into Japanese, such as '*sugari tsuku*' or '*shigami tsuku*', since both carry a nuance of 'relying on somebody' that does not fit Tsukuru's relationship with his lover Sara. The complexity of this translation problem may be of further interest to scholars in translation studies.

2 Translator's note: For an in-depth analysis of Murakami's gay characters, see Zielinska–Elliott's chapter in this volume.

3 Translator's note: Readers may find it useful to go through Katō's article (2020) in *Japan Forum*, titled 'The problem of *tatemashi* in Murakami Haruki: Comparing *The Wind-Up Bird Chronicle* and *1Q84*', where he approaches the same problem in *1Q84* in a different way.

4 Translator's note: In Katō's keynote speech at the Newcastle conference, there was a slide showing how Chapter 13 of BOOK 2 is preceded by 36 chapters (24 in BOOK 1 and 12 in BOOK 2) and followed by 42 chapters (the remaining 11 in BOOK 2 and 31 in BOOK 3), hence 'roughly the mid-point'.

5 Translator's note: Again, a third-hand translation occurs here. Murakami translates the line 'it wouldn't be make-believe', which contains a negative construction, into '*subete ga honmono ni naru*', which turns the negative into a positive construction that roughly means 'everything becomes real'. Influenced by Murakami's use of '*honmono*', Katō therefore keeps using the words 'real' and 'serious'. I use 'non-make-believe' here to highlight where Katō's understanding of 'real' comes from.

References

Hissatsu sirīzu [online]. n.d. *Wikipedia*. Available from: https://ja.wikipedia.org/wiki/必殺シリーズ [Accessed 31 July 2019].

Katō N. 2006 [2000]. 'Masaka' to 'yare-yare'. In: Katō N. *Murakami Haruki ronshū Vol. I.* Tokyo: Wakakusa Shobō, 103–146.

———— 2014. 'Igokochi no yoi basho' kara no hōchiku – Murakami Haruki *Onna no inai otokotachi*. *Nihon Keizai Shinbun*, 28 April. Available from: https://www.nikkei.com/article/DGXDZO70464510W4A420C1MZB001/ [Accessed 26 July 2019].

———— 2015. *Murakami Haruki wa, muzukashii.* Tokyo: Iwanami Shinsho.

———— 2016. Shōsetsu ga jidai ni oinukareru toki – mitabi, Murakami Haruki *Shikisai o motanai Tazaki Tsukuru to, kare no junrei no toshi* ni tsuite. In: Katō N. *Sekai o wakaranai mono ni sodateru koto; bungaku, shisō ronshū.* Tokyo: Iwanami Shoten, 245–262.

———— 2017a. *1Q84* ni okeru chitsujo no hōkai, soshite saikōchiku – so no hensokuteki na shippitsu, kankō to 'kansei' made no sakuhin kōzō no dōtai o megutte. In: Numano M., ed. *Murakami Haruki ni okeru chitsujo.* Taiwan: Tamkang University Press, 1–53.

———— 2017b. Saisei e: hatei to tenkai no yochō. *Nihon Keizai Shinbun*, March 18. Available from: https://www.nikkei.com/article/DGKKZO14204100X10C17A3MY6000/ [Accessed 26 July 2019].

———— 2020. The problem of *tatemashi* in Murakami Haruki's work: Comparing *The Wind-up Bird Chronicle* and *1Q84*. *Japan Forum*, 32 (3), 318–337.

Murakami H. 1985. *Sekai no owari to hādoboirudo wandārando*. Tokyo: Shinchōsha.

———— 1994–1995. *Nejimakidori kuronikuru, dai 1, 2, 3 bu*. Tokyo: Shinchōsha.

———— 2000. *Kami no kodomotachi wa mina odoru*. Tokyo: Shinchōsha.

———— 2009–2010. *1Q84 BOOK 1, 2, 3*. Tokyo: Shinchōsha.

———— 2013. *Shikisai o motanai Tazaki Tsukuru to, kare no junrei no toshi*. Tokyo: Bungei Shunjū.

———— 2014a. *Colorless Tsukuru Tazaki and His Years of Pilgrimage*. London: Vintage.

———— 2014b. *Onna no inai otokotachi*. Tokyo: Bungei Shunjū.

———— 2017. *Kishidanchō goroshi dai 1, 2 bu*. Tokyo: Shinchōsha.

Takahata I. and Binard, A. 2017. Nagare ni 'notte iku' bokura no ima to mukashi. *In:* A. Binard, ed. *Shiranakatta, bokura no sensō*. Tokyo: Shōgakkan, 239–252.

A TRIBUTE TO KATŌ NORIHIRO FROM THE EDITORS, GITTE MARIANNE HANSEN AND MICHAEL TSANG

Born in Yamagata Prefecture during the immediate postwar period, Katō Norihiro (1948–2019) was a distinguished critic and intellectual. He held positions at Meiji Gakuin University and Waseda University, and was Emeritus Professor at the latter. For English readers he may be best known for the essay 'Goodbye Godzilla, Hello Kitty' (2006) published in The American Interest, *but his work is not often translated and tends to be under-appreciated outside Japan. In fact, he left behind an impressive and prolific list of publications, including several important books on postwar Japan such as* Nihon fūkeiron *(1990, no. trans. On the Japanese cultural milieu),* Haisengo ron *(1997; no trans. Theorising the defeat in the Second World War), and* Tekisuto kara tōku hanarete *(2004; no trans. Distancing far away from the text). A prominent critic of Murakami Haruki, he has also written and edited many books on the novelist, including* Murakami Haruki wa, muzukashii *(2015; no trans. Murakami Haruki is, a challenge),* Murakami Haruki o eigo de yomu, but writing about them in Japanese *(2011; no trans. Reading Murakami Haruki in English, but writing about them in Japanese), and* Murakami Haruki ierōpēji sakuhinbetsu (1979–1996) *(1996; no trans. The Murakami Haruki yellow pages by titles) among others. As early as the 1980s, he was a pioneer in appreciating and deliberating the significance of Murakami's oeuvre at a time when the Japanese literary establishment (*bundan*) had not yet warmed to the new type of writing that Murakami brought to the Japanese literary scene. One cannot overstate Katō-sensei's avant-garde contribution to Murakamian criticism, and we were extremely honoured to have him share his latest research at the '40 Years with Murakami Haruki' academic conference at Newcastle University in 2018, which forms the basis for his chapter here in this volume.*

His critical work aside, Katō-sensei was also a great educator. Gitte first met him at Waseda University in 2005 as an exchange student, and later had the privilege to work for him as his teaching and research assistant for several years, knowing him on a personal level. Ever since the first class in his contemporary Japanese literature course, he captured Gitte's fascination with the way he tied readings of Murakami to the history, politics, and life in contemporary Japan, and with his ability to argue meaning through careful analysis. Every week, the popular 1.5-hour zemi *(seminar) would turn into a 3-hour marathon with no student leaving early. He valued speaking to students and young scholars more than to established professors and intellectuals, for 'this is where new ideas can grow' as he once put it. No doubt thanks to his immense support throughout the years, Gitte won an Arts and Humanities Research Council Leadership Fellowship for a research project on Murakami. Michael, too, was very fortunate to have benefitted from his invaluable support and guidance, and to be able to translate some of his writings on Murakami into English, including the article 'The problem of* tatemashi *in Murakami Haruki's work: Comparing* The Wind-Up Bird Chronicle *and* 1Q84' (2020) in *Japan Forum. He was a rare mentor who gave us great insight not only on Japan, on literature, but also on life in general.*

Despite his immense recognition in Japan, Katō-sensei was a truly humble man who produced work because he was driven to do so. While some have said he was Japan's last public intellectual, he himself showed instead that literature is relevant to all people and not limited to the literary elite. With this in mind, we are grateful for his trust and full permission to translate and edit his keynote speech at the '40 Years with Murakami Haruki' conference for this volume. We hope this chapter, as one of his first academic works translated into English, will provide a glimpse to his perceptive assessment of Murakami's work. Although this chapter appears posthumously, we are confident that his legacy will inspire other students and academics of Japanese studies, as he continues to be a great influence to both of us.

3

HISTORY AND METAPHYSICAL NARRATIVE SPACE

Matthew C. Strecher

Introduction

This chapter opens with two fundamental dilemmas that should attend any serious discussion of the historical dimensions of Murakami Haruki's fictional work. The first concerns the narrative spaces in which historical discourses are enacted in Murakami's fiction, which are, most of the time, of a metaphysical nature. That is to say, the protagonist carries out his or her most important explorations of past events not in the everyday, material world of consciousness, but in an 'other world' of memory, of dreams, and of death. It is a narrative space in which time, as it functions in everyday life, does not exist, where 'past' and 'future' join with an eternal and unifying 'present' to form what St Augustine terms '*aeternitas*' – eternity, God's time – in *Confessions*, as he admonishes those who object that God's creations are bound by temporality: 'Try as they may to savour the taste of eternity [*aeternitas*], their thoughts still twist and turn upon the ebb and flow of things in past and future time' (1983: 261). So, how can we imagine a history – a representation of the past – that has been formulated in a narrative space wherein 'the past' does not exist?

The second challenge is that Murakami's 'histories', while concerned with major events in the recent Japanese past, are less concerned with those events themselves than they are with the roles played by individuals caught up in them. Moreover, Murakami's version of history is indelibly bound up in the abstract language of the metaphysical space, a language that is, in my view, more bound to image than to word. It is a narrative space of *archē*, of origins, of archetypal concepts that must be translated into the language of consciousness, into words that cannot represent them adequately. These archetypes, which are of a qualitative nature – power, greed, control, violence, conflict, and so on – are thus projected outward, in the context of historical events, to the material world in abstract, yet highly concentrated forms – a kind of 'code' that, through the surrounding narrative, expresses the essence of the archetype. 'Power' and 'control' emerge as a magical sheep in *Hitsuji o meguru bōken* (1990b [1982]; trans. *A Wild Sheep Chase* [1989]); 'love' takes the form of a pinball machine in *1973 nen no pinbōru* (1990a [1980]; trans. *Pinball, 1973* [1985/2015]); 'violence' and 'chaos' appear as a Scotch whisky icon called Jonī Wōkā (referencing precisely the whisky brand Johnnie Walker) in *Umibe no Kafuka* (2002; trans. *Kafka on the Shore* [2005]).[1] These projected images do not, in themselves, form a history, but they evoke one; they are living archetypes that awaken and enliven the individual memories of those characters who encounter them, and who are then prompted to confront and reconstruct their own pasts. What is more important still, however, is that those archetypes act in a similar way upon the reader.

In the present chapter we will examine a variety of texts, each of which offers a glimpse of how Murakami conceives of and writes history. As we shall see, in early works such as *Hitsuji o meguru bōken* and *Sekai no owari to hādoboirudo wandārando* (1990d [1985]; trans. *Hard-Boiled Wonderland and the End of the World* [1991]), his conception of 'history' is abstract to the extent that we cannot always be certain precisely what historic events are portrayed. In later works – *Nejimakidori kuronikuru* (1994–1995; trans. *The Wind-Up Bird Chronicle* [1997]), *Umibe no Kafuka*, and *Kishidanchō goroshi* (2017; trans. *Killing Commendatore* [2018]) – the narrative is more explicit in its references to the Second World War. What *all* of his texts have in common, however, is that they may be read as what might be termed 'archetypal' history, namely, that in which the perspective of the viewer – the Murakami protagonist, the reader – is situated in the metaphysical realm itself, observing specific events in the material world from the more generalising position of the 'other world'.

Reading and writing 'history' through the metaphysical lens of archetypal images, as we shall see, is a two-edged sword; on the one hand, the metaphysical narrative space here employed has the potential to stimulate the recovery of memories, both individual and collective, and ultimately history *is* memory, just as memory is narrative, mediated and represented through language. The imagistic language of the metaphysical narrative space remains a nearly untranslatable mystery; yet it *must* be translated, for the only means of constructing meaningful historical discourse is to decipher this language into recognisable forms. This is the principal challenge to all Murakami protagonists, and invariably it proves difficult, though not necessarily impossible, particularly in more recent texts. History, in these instances, is a matter of interpretation, construction, and often pure invention.

The key, then, to understanding the historical underpinnings of Murakami's fictional works is to recognise first that historical discourse – and the memories that feed it – is, for this author, always grounded in the metaphysical world. As such, its symbolic manifestations in 'this world' tend to resemble a Rorschach test, bound as they are to symbolic representations that are endlessly open to speculation and interpretation, much like any other symbol or text.

This chapter does not pretend to offer definitive readings for these symbols, but will instead focus on the mechanisms by which they come into being, how they represent various archetypes, and what they mean for the Murakami reader. For, as we shall see, Murakami's historical discourse does much more than narrate the historical past; its more important function is to link individual readers to their own renderings of a meta-historical past. This is, admittedly, true of any text to a certain extent; reception theory, for instance, suggests that every text remains a mere potentiality until the reader 'concretises' it, to borrow Wolfgang Iser's (1980) term, drawing upon the reader's experience to give specific meaning to its contents. Nonetheless, this is to approach the act of reading from the theoretical side, to suggest a method of reading; here we deal with an author who, arguably, constructs his texts specifically to be read in this manner. In contrast to a writer who places meanings into the text with the understanding that some readers will discover them, while others will not, Murakami provides a more generic, metaphysically grounded history that seeks the reader's active participation. These texts not only permit, but demand a symbolic reading of 'the Sheep', or of 'Jonī Wōkā', as representative of over-arching events from our collective past, that is, 'the Second World War', 'the Japanese student movement', 'the Holocaust', 'the Nanjing Massacre'. Through this process, a third narrative 'space' develops in the reader's mind, one that facilitates reconstruction of a more personal narrative version of the historical event under scrutiny, and invokes individual readers' memories of other, similar events, grounded in the same archetypes. Invocation of 'the Nanjing Massacre' for some will awaken thoughts of 19th-century pogroms in Russia, for others the killing fields of Cambodia, or the slaughter of the Tutsi in Rwanda. This is the power of history constructed via the metaphysical narrative space, but it is not without its risks, some of which will be discussed at the end of this chapter.

The status of 'history' in Murakami fiction

In moving forward, we are now aware of two immediate needs. The first is to provide greater insight into the nature of the narrative space we are describing here as 'metaphysical', its characteristics, usage, and its difference from the 'physical' narrative space. The second is to define, as far as possible, what 'history' means in the Murakami fictional landscape, how it functions for the narrative, and how it affects the reader.

We may consider the 'metaphysical narrative space' to be that in which the Murakami protagonist's most important action takes place. It is where he discovers his memories of the past, the dead, and the missing. As I have written previously (Strecher 2014), the qualities of this metaphysical space – dream-like, forbidding yet familiar, dimly-lit and mysterious, and above all, free from the constraints of physical time and space – connect it with other, perhaps more familiar forms of metaphysical space: Plato's 'realm of forms' (*kósmos noetós*), Plotinus's 'world soul' (*anima mundi*), or more recently, Carl Jung's 'collective unconscious', and Joseph Campbell's 'zone of magnified power'.[2] However we choose to characterise it, this 'space' (for want of a better term) forms a repository for all origins of human existence, and for all human memory from the beginning of time.

For both Plato and Jung, the metaphysical realm is home to *archē* (origins) or, in Jung's more modern nomenclature, archetypes, fundamental concepts that contain the pure essence of an idea (good, evil, love), event (birth, initiation, maturation, death), person (mother, teacher, god, demon), or motif (creation, extinction, apocalypse). These fundamental forms, which cannot be broken down beyond their core concepts, inform what we encounter in the physical world (for Plato, the material world; for Jung, consciousness). In this regard, the metaphysical realm should be seen as a mode of consciousness that may be accessed only through the mind, providing a general basis for all human thought, imagination, visions, and dreams.

Among scholars of Murakami's fiction, this realm is commonly known as *achiragawa* ('over there'), distinguishing it from *kochiragawa* ('over here'), which indicates the physical, usually conscious world of daily life (see Nakayama 2006; Atogami 2014; Strecher 2014). This metaphysical 'space' is so central to the Murakami literary landscape that its importance can hardly be overstated; it is where virtually *all* of the important action in the novels takes place. It is marked, particularly from *1973 nen no pinbōru*, by its sense of quiet gloom, its lack of regulated, physical time (clocks and watches are generally absent or non-functional there), and the pervasive idea that visitors gradually lose their sense of individual identity – their ego – the longer they remain there. *Achiragawa*, thus, represents an atavistic unity that absorbs everything into itself, erases all differences in time (past, present, future), identity (you versus me versus them), and even space (here and there).

For our purposes, this metaphysical realm and its contents are important because this is where Murakami characters invariably go to find answers to their most troubling questions. It is where the narrator of *1973 nen no pinbōru* goes to find his dead girlfriend, Naoko, and where the same narrator goes at the end of *Hitsuji o meguru bōken* to meet with his equally dead best friend, 'Rat'. It is the forbidding forest into which Tamura Kafuka ventures to say his farewells to 'Miss Saeki' – yes, she is dead, too – near the end of *Umibe no Kafuka*. But it is also where Okada Tōru goes to find and rescue his wife Kumiko (who is still alive), as well as to bludgeon her brother into a coma in *Nejimakidori kuronikuru*, and the place from which Aomame Masami rescues Kawana Tengo near the end of *1Q84* (2009–2010; trans. *1Q84* [2011]). In these later texts the metaphysical narrative space is not individual, but belongs to all and is, in theory, accessible to all. Okada Tōru discovers this when he has a sexy dream about another character in *Nejimakidori kuronikuru*, only to find out later that it happened for her as well.

What this tells us is that the metaphysical realm is both a means of connecting people and things across and beyond physical time and space – connecting the living with the dead, the past with the present, the conscious with the unconscious – and also a way of grounding and rendering comprehensible our experiences in the physical world. What we perceive through our five senses is rendered meaningful and comprehensible only through its connection with the contents of the metaphysical space, through the collective experience of all humanity, through all times. We understand the present only through the collective memories of experiences from the past. This sort of 'grounding' is given its clearest elucidation in the theories of Jung, who argues that the archetypes that inhabit the metaphysical realm – what he called the 'collective unconscious' – exist in order to help us make sense of the events, people, and situations we encounter in the physical world. But the idea is much older, dating back to Plato's theory of forms, in which the things of the material world are merely shadows of what exists, and has always existed, in the *kósmos noetós*.

When Murakami's characters enter the metaphysical realm – *achiragawa* – then, what they really find are the original forms (the *archē*) of what they meet in the material world. These original forms, or archetypes, are what help them to discover answers to the questions they pose about life. But because the metaphysical realm *is* freed from the constraints of physical time, conventional notions of 'history' as we understand it, presenting the stories of individual human beings at specific moments in human history, cannot function in quite the same way when seen *from* that realm.

We are now able to recognise the importance of this realm for the reconstruction of the historical past within the Murakami fictional landscape. The 'past' *as memory*, whatever its ontological status in philosophical discourse, is a very real thing in Murakami's works. It is a reality that exists, whose principal characters continue to exist, unchanging, in perpetuity, in the metaphysical realm. Murakami's protagonists use that realm for two significant purposes: first, to collect the 'testimony' of those who have already died or become otherwise incapable of sharing their stories; and second, to connect themselves with what I call the 'archetypal narratives' of history – the grounding concepts of human interaction and conflict that give meaning and continuity to events taking place in the physical world. The Murakami protagonist enters that realm, meets these characters – these memories, now part of the collective (archetypal) history – and collects their stories, their testimony, in order to unlock the mysteries of his own past. It is similar to psychoanalysis, except that he actually gains direct access to the parts of the mind normally hidden from us.

This brings us to the second of our dilemmas, namely, what history means to the Murakami text and to the reader. While it is true that all Murakami protagonists, to varying extents, search for answers to questions about their own lives, pasts, and identities, it is equally true that the author's narrative landscape is built upon a structure that superimposes the present atop the past. However contemporary the setting of a work may be, invariably there is a deeper historical past running parallel to it, like a subterranean river feeding pools of water that, here and there, emerge to the surface, providing useful landmarks for the protagonist.

History here is not merely a timeline, marked by 'big-picture' major events and world–historical figures; but neither is it, in the more recent, new historicist sense, a wide-angled 'snapshot' of a sociocultural milieu. For Murakami, history is something in between these two disciplinary approaches: a series of major events, but one whose real importance lies with the faceless, ordinary people who experienced them. His favourite underpinning historical narrative is the Second World War, which he sometimes *appears* to approach in a disarmingly vague and naïve way. On closer scrutiny, however, we recognise this to be a result of the author synecdochally invoking 'the War' while focusing almost exclusively on individuals caught up in it. The 1939 Nomonhan Incident discussed in *Nejimakidori kuronikuru* is, for Murakami, really about a single infantryman named Honda who served there. The Nanjing Massacre noted in *Kishidanchō goroshi* is actually the story of career soldiers bullying a young recruit. The B-29 air raids of 1944–1945, hinted at in *Umibe no Kafuka*, are merely a path to the story of a boy who, after an extended sojourn in the metaphysical realm in 1944, grows up into a mentally challenged man who can talk to cats. This is 'big-picture' history in which the entire point is, ironically, focused on individuals and their uniquely personal experiences. The big picture soon fades into the background, not to disappear, but to form a backdrop to the individual narrative.

Writing history in this way, while ignoring much of the sort of information normally found in histories – the what, where, when, who, why, and how – is by no means a meaningless exercise, nor is it altogether divorced from the ultimate purpose of writing history: to apply a coherent narrative to a confusing series of events or, in Hayden White's (1978) turn of phrase, 'to make a plausible story out of a congeries of "facts" which, in their unprocessed form, made no sense at all' (White 1978: 83). Defending his theory of history as constructed narrative, White argues that what historians really do is to recast the facts of history into narratives that are recognisable to us principally through their archetypal structure:

> The historical narrative thus mediates between the events reported in it on the one side and pregeneric plot structures conventionally used in our culture to endow unfamiliar events and situations with meanings, on the other.
>
> (White 1978: 88)

Put another way, the task of the historian is to collect data, and to organise – or 'emplot', to use White's term – those data into familiar narrative structures that make sense to us. And this emplotment, I would argue, is exactly what Murakami does with his reconstructions of history, though in a rather unconventional way. For, as we shall soon see, his reconstructions are emplotted not within recognisable narrative archetypes per se, but through highly abstract symbols which are themselves refined projections of the archetypal concepts noted above.

Why does Murakami write history?

Before demonstrating this through textual analysis, let us pose one last key question: why is Murakami interested in history, and specifically, the history of Japanese aggression in East Asia during the first half of the twentieth century? The answer to this will shed useful light on the peculiar methods Murakami uses to invoke histories for his readers.

To begin with, Murakami is and always has been concerned with the plight of the individual against a dominating state apparatus. He has always championed the lone wolf who stands against the collective rules of society, the single 'egg', to borrow a metaphor from his 2009 Jerusalem speech, that smashes itself against the 'wall' of the System – the powers-that-be – rather than give up its individual autonomy (Murakami 2009). And while this struggle between the individual and the state is perhaps an inevitable constant, it is also true, as Murakami told Ian Buruma in 1996, that war 'stretches the tension between individuals and the state to the very limit' (Buruma 1996: 62). That 'tension' refers not merely to controlling the behaviour of individuals in their daily life; rather, as we see prominently in works such as

Nejimakidori kuronikuru, *Umibe no Kafuka*, and *Kishidanchō goroshi*, it amounts to coercing individuals to commit acts of violence they would otherwise never commit.

On the other hand, this fixation is not merely a result of the author's liberalism. Early in 2019, Murakami revealed a more personal motivation: as a child, by his own account when he was no more than a primary school student, Murakami learned from his father that the latter, who served in the Imperial Army during the Second World War, had been involved in the brutal execution of Chinese prisoners of war. While Murakami is uncertain of his father's role in the incident, it clearly left an emotional scar on both father and son.

> Whether [my father] was merely an observer from the sidelines or was more deeply involved, I have no idea. I have no way of ascertaining whether my childhood memory is clouded, or my father used vague language. Either way [...] the event left a deep wound on the soul of my father, who was both a soldier and a Buddhist priest.
>
> (Murakami 2019: 253)

It clearly left an emotional scar on young Murakami Haruki as well, who feels a certain responsibility to preserve this memory.

> Put another way, some part of this thing that weighed so heavily on my father's heart for so long – today we would call it trauma – was passed along to his son, to me. Thus are human hearts joined, and history is like this as well. Its essence lies in the act, or maybe the ritual, of 'succession'. However unpleasant the contents, however much we might like to turn away, we must accept a part of it into ourselves. If not, then where is the meaning in history?
>
> (Murakami 2019: 253–254)

It was, one could surmise, this story of young recruits forced to commit murder that fostered in Murakami the child, and later in Murakami the novelist, the desire to write about individuals struggling to free themselves from the overpowering force of the state.

Murakami also alludes to revisionism in Japan with regard to its wartime past as one of his motivations. Speaking recently at the Théâtre National de la Colline in Paris, he noted:

> I try to write about war as much as I can in my novels. Even in Japan, historical revisionism has been a problem. Attempting to keep only history that we find convenient is a problem many countries face, but we must be against it.
>
> (qtd in Hikita 2019)

And while Murakami adds that '[t]he deliberate telling of false history has spread because of the Internet' (Hikita 2019), he is probably well aware that historical revisionism in Japan with regard to the Second World War goes back a good deal further.

Indeed, efforts to revise or eliminate narratives dealing with atrocities perpetrated by the Japanese military in Asia – particularly events like the Nanjing Massacre – from primary and secondary education in Japan became the centre of a virulent debate that began in the 1980s and continues in various forms to this day.[3]

Murakami as historian

But Japanese revisionism probably is not what interests Murakami most about the Second World War. Weighing the two principal motivations for writing about history noted above (his father's confession versus revisionist history), it seems obvious, even judging from his fictional texts alone, that his deeper concern lies with the role and fate of people caught up in events so vast that the individual is often forgotten. Methodologically speaking, Murakami lies somewhere between what historian Paul Ricoeur terms the 'positivist tradition' of political histories, and the social history of the 'new historians' (1984: 102). The former stress 'the primacy of the individual and of the pointlike event' (1984: 102), or, to put it another way, 'world–historic' persons and the events they bring about. 'Political history, including military, diplomatic, and ecclesiastical history, is where individuals – heads of state, generals, ministers, diplomats, prelates – are supposed to make history. It is also the realm where events go off like explosions' (Ricoeur 1984: 102). In opposition to this, 'the new historians [present history as] the "total social fact" [...] in every one of its human dimensions – economic, social, political, cultural, religious, etc.' (1984: 102).

It is not this 'total social fact', but the new historian's focus on *non*-world–historic figures, 'the bourgeois, artisans, peasants, and workers [as] the collective heroes of history' (Ricoeur 1984: 103), that seems to resonate with Murakami who, as a novelist, must concern himself with individuals functioning within a manageable narrative framework, but at the same time privileges the anonymous figures in those narratives. And in creating this structure in which the anonymous individual is placed side by side against the vast events of history – battles, uprisings, massacres, assassinations – Murakami reconstructs his egg-and-wall, or individual-versus-state, model again and again.

That model is not always recognisable as 'history', for the vast events and major figures he positions against his individuals are not always easily pinned down. This is particularly true in his early works, and so we shall now turn to the two prime examples of this noted above: *Hitsuji o meguru bōken*, and *Sekai no owari to hādoboirudo wandārando*.

History as archetype

Hitsuji o meguru bōken centres upon the narrator's quest to locate a semi-mythical, all-empowering Sheep, and at the same time, to find his best friend, known as 'Rat'. Interwoven through this quest narrative are historical titbits concerning the settling of Hokkaido, the raising of sheep for wool and mutton to supply the Japanese Imperial Army during the Russo–Japanese War of 1904–1905, the Japanese military–industrial complex of the Second World War, the rehabilitation of prewar and wartime national-ist politicians following Japan's defeat in 1945, and the student uprisings of 1967–1970 in Japan. Ultimately, though, this novel is about the Sheep, and about the mysterious right-wing figure the Sheep possesses and manipulates, Sensei, or, in the English translation, 'the Boss'.

If this text forms an allegory of some particular historical event or refers to specific historical figures, however, they remain, to the end, unnamed, a matter for interpreta-tion. Much of this interpretation must centre on Sensei and 'the Sheep', neither of whom actually appears in the story. Yet, they resonate for some readers in a peculiarly specific way. For instance, Katō Norihiro writes:

> The right-wing figure known as 'Sensei' reminded me of the real-world figure Kodama Yoshio, of his shady dealings in prewar Asia, and how he drove the postwar Japanese political scene. […] The appearance of 'the Sheep' is super-imposed on the February 26 Incident,[4] and in the youth who resists military conscription, depicted through 'the Sheepman'.
>
> (2015: 129)

For Katō, then, this novel allegorically depicts quite specific historical figures and events. Other critics have fixed on the mood of the novel, approaching it in terms of more recent historical events. Journalist and critic Kawamoto Saburō (1986), for instance, found himself 'shedding unexpected tears' at the point where the narrator reunites with Rat, but learns that his friend is already dead. This, for Kawamoto, hearkens back to the realities of the 1960s student uprisings, and the general sense of despair that attended their collapse. 'From the end of the 1960s through the beginning of the 1970s', writes Kawamoto, 'many of our friends really did disap-pear like Rat […] and like Murakami's protagonist, I wanted to go out looking for them' (Kawamoto 1986: 45). In a related vein, critic Yokoo Kazuhiro (1991) asso-ciates Rat's death at his mountain villa in Hokkaido with the 1972 Asama Sansō [mountain villa] Incident, in which a group of radical students made a final stand against the police, several of them losing their lives in the ensuing battle (Yokoo 1991: 16–18).

These readings, each of which focuses on a different aspect of *Hitsuji o meguru bōken*, as well as a different moment in history, reflect the flexible nature of Murakami's expression of the historical past at this point in his career. But how, we might wonder, would someone not of Murakami's generation or cultural/experiential background read this text? Given that the Sheep, in the process of occupying its 'host', appears to remove the host's individual identity and substitute its own, we might give the text a more contemporary spin, reading the Sheep as a symbol of Japan's vaunted 'managed society' (*kanri shakai*), as a concept dating from the 1960s that denoted excessive management of individual lives by government, corporate and media bureaucracies,[5] and as a prominent subject of public discussion at the time Murakami was writing the novel. In such a reading, 'the Sheep' becomes the perpetual shadow of overbearing state control over the individual.

Similar assertions can be made about *Sekai no owari to hādoboirudo wandārando*, whose opposition of the individual (again, the narrator) to the state – a faceless entity known as 'the System' – is even more obviously a reference to Japan's 'managed society'. In this novel, the narrator has been the unwitting subject of government-sponsored experiments in which his core consciousness has been modified, leaving him trapped in a crudely constructed, digitised replica of his inner mind. The utterly defenceless position in which the narrator finds himself is accentuated by the chilling words of his supervisor at the System: 'We are the State. There's nothing we can't do' (Murakami 1990d: IV, 217). As seen in Rat's suicide in *Hitsuji o meguru bōken*, these words prove to be quite true; there is nothing the hard-boiled protagonist can do to stop the awesome power of the System, other than to remove himself from it, so he remains *within* his inner mind, the one place the State can no longer touch him.

The futuristic *Sekai no owari to hādoboirudo wandārando* is more science fiction than history, yet the work is also very nearly a 'contemporary history', in the sense that it explores actual and observable struggles to control information at that time (and even more so today), and the ruthless nature of the 'management' side of this managed society. The novel is, moreover, only slightly apocalyptic, for much of what it describes is happening in the present, albeit in a slightly less cyberpunk form. Identity theft, cryptocurrencies, and international election tampering are only the latest irruptions of the realities described in Murakami's 'hard-boiled wonderland' but these predictions, while prophetic, were still largely fantastical when the novel was published in 1985, and thus probably more apt to be entertaining than alarming for many readers.

War on a personal scale

Despite frequent veiled, abstract references to the historical past, it seems likely that prior to the publication of *Nejimakidori kuronikuru* most readers of Murakami fiction did not perceive this author as a 'writer of history' per se. To that point, Murakami's interest in 'the past' – in memory – appeared more focused on understanding how his own generation of former student radicals had reached a point of political and social impotence, exchanging their *gebabō* (long sticks for attacking riot police) for the uniform blue suits of corporate Japan.

Nejimakidori kuronikuru, initially, looked like it might go in the same direction, for the main text is about a man seeking his missing wife – men seeking their missing women being a staple in the Murakami diet.[6] And like *Hitsuji o meguru bōken* – and indeed, *Sekai no owari to hādoboirudo wandārando*, in which some splendid 'documentary evidence' is located about unicorns – this novel contains a strong element of the historical past. The principal difference between this work and its predecessors is that its grounding historical events – the 1939 Nomonhan Incident and the Japanese retreat from Manchuria in 1945 – are both specific and predominantly factual.

Yet, it must be said that anyone who wishes to know something about the actual Nomonhan Incident, fought out by the Japanese and the Soviets at the border between Manchuria and Mongolia in the spring and summer of 1939, will learn little about that conflict from *Nejimakidori kuronikuru*. We do not learn, for instance, that roughly 60,000 casualties were suffered on each side, or that the Soviet forces were led by General Georgy Zhukov, who used the engagement as a testing ground for tactics he would later unleash on the German Wehrmacht in his push on Berlin six years later.[7] And some of this detail could have been useful; it might have helped readers to know that the fighting began in mid-May and lasted until late August, if only to place, chronologically, the ill-fated 'Yamamoto mission' across the Khalkha River, which Murakami sets in April of that year, some weeks before the start of the battle (cf. Murakami 1994–1995: I, Ch. 12–13). It might, for instance, give us better reason to suspect, based on the chronology, that this mission was not merely incidental to the battle, but one of its causes.

Like *Hitsuji o meguru bōken*, with its Sensei and Sheep, or *Sekai no owari to hādoboirudo wandārando* with its 'System' and 'Factory', *Nejimakidori kuronikuru* ascribes the true power of major events in history to iconic figures, and condenses all the evils of war and violence and fanaticism into a handful of characters. In this instance, those characters are 'Boris the Skinner', 'Yamamoto', and in the novel's concurrent era, 'Wataya Noboru'. It is, in fact, classic Murakami narrative craft to boil the coming conflict between the Soviets and the Japanese down to a battle between 'Boris' and 'Yamamoto', a conflict that, like Boris, the Soviets will eventually win. The suffering undergone by Yamamoto – staked to the ground and skinned alive – allegorically represents the suffering undergone by all Japanese troops in this meaningless and costly conflict, his screams echoing the cries of countless troops who were cut down charging Soviet tanks and flamethrowers with pistols and swords.

Yamamoto and Boris the Skinner are, in this sense, also icons for opposing ideologies, each a representative of the system that created him. In Yamamoto we see a man who is willing to undergo one of the most painful deaths imaginable without betraying his secrets (a sickening twist on the traditional act of *seppuku*), almost purely for the sake of his individual honour. Boris, by contrast, is a man who knows how to play the survival game in the Soviet system of the day: today's friend might be tomorrow's enemy, and no one was truly safe in Stalin's hierarchy.[8] Accordingly, Boris eventually winds up in a gulag himself, but bides his time until he can regain his position, all the while manipulating other prisoners in the gulag, including Japanese prisoners of war. Boris, unlike Yamamoto, is not a patriot but a self-interested powermonger, in a land that rewards those ruthless enough to take what they want.

And it is between these two ideologues – the patriot and the powermonger – that the forgotten nobodies of history must negotiate the labyrinth of life and death. The hapless narrator of Yamamoto and Boris's conflict, Lt Mamiya, is one such nobody. He is like the other Japanese prisoners of war, like the common infantrymen, like the prison guards, like the girls who service the gulag – just another nameless, faceless drone. But for his letters to Okada Tōru, he would have remained so. Thanks to his testimony, however, we learn much about Lt Mamiya, revealing a complex individual who embodies the difficulty of maintaining individual integrity in the face of conflict. We learn that he is a man of honour, that he has both pride and a conscience, and yet, owing to his careful work as Boris's personal secretary in the gulag, we also know that numberless other faceless drones lost their lives, while Boris grew wealthy. We discover that Lt Mamiya served Boris diligently and well, yet his motive in doing so was to find an opportunity to kill him, for 'I could not allow this man Boris to exist in this world' (Murakami 1995: III, 410). In the end, to his dismay, he fails to achieve his goal; Boris allows him two pistol shots, at point-blank range, and both times Lt Mamiya misses his mark. Boris's explanation for his failure is simply that '[y]ou lack the qualifications to kill me' (Murakami 1995: III, 415–416). One obvious implication of this statement is that the 'nobodies' of history can never overcome the powerful. History shows us again and again that the generals and prelates and bishops (as Ricoeur names them) make the rules, and the nameless, faceless common people die for them, anonymous and forgotten. Or, to borrow Murakami's metaphor, they are the eggs; their destiny is to build the wall, and then smash themselves against it in futile gestures of self-destruction.

Murakami achieves two things in *Nejimakidori kuronikuru* that are noteworthy: he restores a face and a name to one of the drones of history, and he offers an alternate narrative in which the *egg* knocks down the *wall*. The restoration of a name and a narrative to Lt Mamiya is clearly a gesture towards recovering the countless lost narratives of history, and represents, in its limited way, the stories of the individuals who built the pyramids of Egypt, or the Great Wall of China; the infantrymen slaughtered at Austerlitz for Napoleon's glory; the lost voices of African–American slaves who built a nation yet were denied a share in its promised liberty. In Lt Mamiya, Murakami demonstrates his interest in restoring a voice to those whose voices have been brutally silenced by the 'powers-that-be' of history.

As to the 'egg smashing the wall', obviously this is not the final result of Lt Mamiya's struggle against Boris. Rather, his quest comes to fruition some 40 years later, when another nobody called Okada Tōru squares off against the contemporary incarnation of 'Boris the Skinner', his brother-in-law and shady politician, Wataya Noboru. Journeying into the metaphysical realm, baseball bat in hand, Tōru, like Lt Mamiya, takes aim at Wataya Noboru's head. In this instance he does not miss, and Lt Mamiya is avenged. We see here the power of the metaphysical realm; in the material world, Wataya Noboru, like Boris, is untouchable, but 'over there', where all things are equalised, he is as vulnerable as the rest of us and, just for once, against all the odds of history, the egg succeeds in bringing down the wall.

However, this is not how it usually happens in history. Boris's statement that Lt Mamiya 'lacks the qualifications' to kill him speaks to the near invulnerability of those in positions of power. Through Lt Mamiya we may recall the German military high command, meeting with Adolf Hitler daily, any of whom might have unholstered his sidearm and ended the Fuhrer's life. We may recall Claus von Stauffenberg, who actually attempted to kill Hitler, yet failed.[9]

Readers who pursue the analogy this far might note further, in Lt Mamiya's diligent logistical work for Boris, parallels with Adolf Eichmann, the logistical brains behind the Nazi's 'final solution'.[10] Eichmann's 'gift' lay in the efficiency with which he organised the transportation (by cattle cars), murder, and disposal of the Jews. We hear echoes of this in Lt Mamiya's description of the gulag after Boris has taken it over:

> The camp transformed into a world in which total efficiency was all-important, and the strong devoured the weak. [...] When there weren't enough workers, new prisoners would be brought in by train like cattle.
>
> (Murakami 1995: III, 409)

There is a kind of counterfactual history at work here, then. Suppose Lt Mamiya had not missed? How would the history of this gulag – the lives of its inmates – have changed as a result? By analogy, suppose Stauffenberg had succeeded? How would the history of the Third Reich – and the countless lives it cost – have changed? Stauffenberg paid for his failure with torture and death; Lt Mamiya pays for his failure by returning to Japan a cursed man, never to know love or joy. Such is the result of failure. By re-enacting that fateful scene between Lt Mamiya and Boris through Okada Tōru and Wataya Noboru, Murakami shows us the successful scenario. We cannot know how many innocent lives are saved as a result.

There are risks in presenting history this way, through abstraction and analogy. Is Lt Mamiya to be likened to Stauffenberg, or to Eichmann? Based on his own account, we have little choice but to conclude that he was both. And if he was another Eichmann, however unwillingly, can he be absolved as a decent and principled man making the best of an impossible situation? If so, then by extension, are we also to absolve Eichmann for so efficiently engineering the murder of millions?

But absolution is not finally the point of these texts. In fact, Murakami's approach to history in these works suggests that he has no real interest in any 'world–historic' person. What he shows instead is the critical importance of the analogy, exposing the archetypal narrative that links someone like Eichmann with someone like Lt Mamiya. In so doing, he demonstrates that, based solely on the objective study of events, Lt Mamiya's experience shares certain key similarities to those of Eichmann, yet the two are nothing alike. The real point of Murakami's historical discourse, in my view, is to show that an all-powerful state is capable of turning *anyone* into a monster. This recognition cannot absolve the individual of wrongdoing, but it can demonstrate the culpability of the state as it subsumes the will of the individual. Such revelations can only come through the individual narrative, for viewing history solely from 'the facts' of the macrocosmic perspective, we may sometimes miss extenuating circumstances, the human dimension of an apparent monster. This is not about Eichmann, who was a true monster, but Lt Mamiya, who is not. Seen purely from 'the facts', Lt Mamiya is a collaborator, a traitor, even a facilitator of death – indeed, this is how his own men view him – but with the benefit of his own testimony we are able to balance this narrative with another view of Lt Mamiya as a man of conscience, and we are able to understand him, perhaps even to pity him. This is the true purpose of Murakami's superimposition of the grand view of history – the macrocosmic – onto the highly specific and individual, microcosmic one.

Another kind of war

Whereas any references to Adolf Eichmann are purely circumstantial in *Nejimakidori kuronikuru*, they are explicit in *Umibe no Kafuka*. Here, too, Murakami presents two characters, the eponymous Tamura Kafuka, and an elderly gentleman (and, truly, a gentle man) named Mr Nakata, who commit acts that, without the benefit of mitigating circumstances, would mark them as monsters. Yet once again, as he superimposes the spectre of the Second World War upon the events of a novel set in the contemporary era, Murakami guides readers toward a more informed response.

The actions of these two characters are driven by yet another iconic figure, that of Jonī Wōkā, the gentleman whose image appears on millions of Scotch whisky bottles worldwide. Like the Sheep and Sensei before him, Jonī Wōkā is a material manifestation of a particular archetype, in this case 'violent conflict'. Like an ancient god of war (Ares, Odin), Jonī Wōkā feeds – quite literally – on death and chaos, as we see in a grotesque scene in which he vivisects cats and eats their internal organs before the horrified eyes of Mr Nakata, who speaks the language of cats, and knows these animals as friends. Jonī Wōkā's ostensible purpose in doing this is to steal the souls of the cats to construct a flute, which he will play to attract other souls in order to construct an even larger flute, for larger souls, and so on (Murakami 2002: I, 242).

Nevertheless, even accepting as true this obvious allegorical reference to the act of conquest, of accumulating more (echoes of Hitler's *Lebensraum*, and of Japan's 'Greater East Asia Co-Prosperity Sphere' come to mind), Jonī Wōkā's real purpose is to awaken the killer spirit that lurks within the mild-mannered Mr Nakata, to make a 'soldier' of him, with the express purpose of killing Jonī Wōkā himself.[11] As Jonī Wōkā explains to Mr Nakata:

> When war starts, people are drafted as soldiers. [...] No one considers whether you like killing people or not. It's what you have to do. Or else you're the one who gets killed. [...] That's the gist of human history.
>
> (Murakami 2002: I, 246)

And Jonī Wōkā's plan succeeds: Mr Nakata feels 'something beginning to stir in his head [...] a severe confusion that was significantly changing the composition of his flesh' (Murakami 2002: I, 250–252), snatches up a kitchen knife, and hacks Jonī Wōkā to death.

But Mr Nakata is really only acting in place of another: according to prophecy, the 15-year-old Tamura Kafuka was destined to murder Jonī Wōkā – his own father – and then find and copulate with his long-lost mother and sister. Kafuka runs away from home, forcing Jonī Wōkā to recruit another killer, but in a general sense, the prophecy in the novel is fulfilled: it is Kafuka who awakens from a mysterious trance, hundreds of miles away, covered in fresh blood (Murakami 2002: I, 116–119), while

Mr Nakata finds himself in a vacant lot without a mark on him (Murakami 2002: I, 282). Kafuka further encounters Miss Saeki, a woman who *could be* his mother (and he more or less decides that she is), and he copulates with her (Murakami 2002: II, 91–92; II, 124–125). So between them, Mr Nakata and Tamura Kafuka have, potentially at least, committed murder and incest. What spares them the reader's censure, presumably, is the obvious reluctance of both characters, the clear sense that both are merely pawns – foot soldiers – in a much larger, cosmic chess game being played out eternally by the elemental earth spirits taking the form of 'Jonī Wōkā' (representing war, pain, death) and 'Kāneru Sandāsu' (referencing Colonel Sanders, representing peace, pleasure, fertility).

And yet, though the reader may absolve Kafuka and Mr Nakata, the two men cannot so easily absolve themselves. For Mr Nakata's part, while he routinely hides behind his oft-repeated statement that 'I am not very bright' (*atama ga warui*) (Murakami 2002: I, 79, *passim*), he does recognise his vulnerability to exploitation as a weapon by others. 'For instance, Nakata can make things fall from the sky', he tells a confidante. 'But I don't know what I'll make fall next. What could I do if it were ten thousand knives, or a big bomb, or poison gas?' (Murakami 2002: II, 140). Kafuka is similarly vulnerable to exploitation, confiding to a new friend called Sakura that 'Sometimes [...] I totally lose my temper, like I've blown a fuse. Like someone has hit a switch in my head, and my body moves before I can think. At times like that I am me, but I'm also not me' (Murakami 2002: I, 147). More than once, Kafuka confesses, he has done violence to others during these fits. He has no memory of having done so, but feels responsible all the same.

This would seem to be the point of Kafuka's interest in Adolf Eichmann, the story of whose trial he reads avidly while hiding from the police in a mountain forest in Shikoku. Unlike Eichmann, Kafuka feels a sense of responsibility for his actions, even those that take place only in his mind, for as he learns from a note scribbled in the book on Eichmann, '[i]t's all a matter of imagination. Our responsibility starts from our imagination. Yeats wrote this. In dreams begin the responsibilities' (Murakami 2002: I, 227). Unlike Eichmann, who evidently could not imagine the consequences of his careful logistical planning, Kafuka feels a sense of responsibility for his father's death, for the possibility that Miss Saeki really is his mother, and even for forcing himself sexually, while dreaming, on Sakura, who *could be* (but probably is not) his sister (Murakami 2002: II, 250–252).

What these events tell us, in terms of the historical past that delicately underpins the novel's present, is that, although undeniably guilty of 'crimes against humanity', neither Kafuka nor Mr Nakata is a monster, for both act out of impulses whose origins lie outside themselves. Moreover, both attempt to take responsibility for their actions. Mr Nakata, after attempting unsuccessfully to report his murder of Jonī Wōkā to the police, goes on a perilous journey to ensure that Jonī Wōkā cannot return to this world, a journey that costs him his life. Kafuka, on his side, makes an equally perilous journey to the land of the dead to discover the soul of Miss Saeki (who perishes after their tryst), and comes to terms with her. He then returns to Tokyo, prepared to explain himself to the police. This is in sharp contrast to Eichmann, who, as the novel states, 'felt no sense of guilt. Sitting in the defendant's chair behind bulletproof glass in Tel Aviv, Eichmann looked puzzled about why he was on trial. [...] He was just a technician who had found the most effective solution to the problem he had been given' (Murakami 2002: I, 227). Again, we are reminded of Lt Mamiya's highly successful efforts to raise efficiency in Boris's gulag.

This is not 'history' in the traditional sense. It is, rather, what Ricoeur expresses as 'the understanding of another person in everyday life' (1984: 118). Herein, though, lie the beginnings of a microcosmic history that impacted (and continues to impact) a macrocosmic history. This is a way of approaching, if not understanding, the Holocaust through a single lens, concentrated on individuals who were never even connected to it. Murakami is not writing a history of the Holocaust – how could he? – but is rather exploring the manner in which we, the readers of history, look upon those who make history. In his abstract way, Murakami draws our attention to the 'great events' of the historical past without seeming to do so, while demonstrating that, up close, things are not always so cut and dried.

History as artefact: *Kishidanchō goroshi*

This technique of intimating major events through the microcosmic lens of individual experience, often through completely unrelated, even fictitious events, has been a key feature of Murakami's fiction from the start. The author's most recent work, however, the 2017 novel *Kishidanchō goroshi*, suggests a turn toward more direct representations of those events, expressed in a new form of 'text'. *Kishidanchō goroshi* centres on the protagonist – a portrait painter known to us only as *watashi* – and his attempts to decipher a painting hidden by a dying artist named Amada Tomohiko. That painting, as we shall see, contains an abstract representation of two major events in the Second World War: the 1937 'Nanjing Massacre' and the 1938 Nazi takeover of Austria known as the Anschluss.[12]

These two 'big-picture' historical events figure importantly in the life of Amada Tomohiko on a personal level. In the case of Nanjing, Tomohiko's younger brother, Tsuguhiko, a classical pianist, was forced to participate in the beheading of Chinese prisoners during the massacre, not just once, but repeatedly until he had mastered the technique and become proficient with a sword. Not only was he forced by his commanding officer to carry out this unpleasant task, but he was ridiculed and beaten for his lack of aptitude. Shortly after his return to Japan, he committed suicide (Murakami 2017: II, 81–82; II, 94–97; II, 99–100).

With regard to the Anschluss, the connection is more direct, for Tomohiko was studying art in Vienna when the Nazis entered Austria. There he joined a group of fellow university students, including his lover, in a plot to assassinate the Nazi commandant of the city – the 'Commendatore', in effect. The plot was discovered through an informant, and the entire group was captured by the Gestapo (Murakami 2017: I, 421–423). While the Austrian conspirators were executed or deported to concentration camps, Tomohiko, after being held prisoner for two months, was deported back to Japan, where he was ordered to remain silent about the incident (Murakami 2017: II, 79–80). And while he kept his promise not to speak of the events in Vienna to anyone, he eventually painted *Kishidanchō goroshi*. It is *watashi*'s suspicion that this painting represents Tomohiko's memory of those events, a tangible 'text' of a narrative he could not otherwise share with anyone (Murakami 2017: I, 423).

These two events, and their artistic representation, are layered atop events befalling *watashi*, past and present, giving a new dimension to traumas that are linked archetypally through the metaphysical realm. *Watashi* suffers angst from memories of his sister's death during childhood, and more recently, the loss of his wife, who has announced her intention to divorce him. Thus, a layering of past and present trauma in *watashi*'s life, as well as a quest for recovery, overlays the hidden narrative of Amada Tomohiko in this complex tale.

As with Lt Mamiya in *Nejimakidori kuronikuru*, recovery is no longer possible for Tomohiko, who lies nearly comatose at a geriatric centre in Izu. Tomohiko's generation missed its chance to recover from the collective trauma of the war, for the war was not only lost, but literally 'unspeakable'. Dower (2000) points out that, even before the Allied Occupation forces landed in Japan at the beginning of September 1945, efforts were being made amongst public officials and military leaders to obscure their actions during the conflict. Indeed, even the emperor's surrender speech, recorded and broadcast to his people on 15 August 1945, represented an effort 'not merely to call a halt to a lost war, but to do so without disavowing Japan's war aims or acknowledging the nation's atrocities' (Dower 2000: 35). Both during and after the Allied Occupation (1945–1952), one imagines that 'talking through' the painful experiences of the war was a difficult process, to say the least, much as discussion of the war in Vietnam was difficult for many Americans, former soldiers and civilians alike, in the late 1970s. This complexity – this repression of feelings – is represented symbolically in Tomohiko, whose inability to 'talk out' his traumatic memories of a lost love and a lost brother began when he was forbidden by his own government to speak of it and later became habitual. Thus, Tomohiko, not unlike Murakami's own father, lived his whole life with tremendously powerful, emotionally damaging memories that had to remain locked tightly within himself. It is a most unhealthy situation, one with no real prospect for relief. For Tomohiko – and by extension, his generation – recovery is no longer possible.

By contrast, the middle-aged *watashi* continues his struggle to come to grips with his sister's childhood death and the end of his marriage. Taking refuge in Tomohiko's home, he is befriended by a mysterious neighbour called Menshiki, and by Menshiki's unacknowledged 13-year-old daughter, Marie.[13] The latter is important to *watashi*, both for the fact that she is nearly the same age as his sister when she died, and because she has the ability to 'read' the hidden meanings of paintings with the same keen eye as *watashi* himself. Her sudden disappearance in the latter stages of the narrative will afford *watashi* an opportunity to make a magical journey to rescue her, and in the process, to 'replay' both his own trauma of losing his sister, and Tomohiko's loss of his lover and his brother. In short, it will represent a rewriting of an archetypal tale of loss, this time with better results.

Let us return now to the painting. Entitled *Kishidanchō goroshi* (Killing Commendatore), the work depicts the scene from Mozart's *Don Giovanni* in which Giovanni murders the captain of the guard, *il Commendatore*, in pursuit of the latter's daughter, Donna Anna. The composition of the painting is worth noting here. At its centre stand Don Giovanni and *il Commendatore*, the former piercing the latter with his sword. Elsewhere in the painting, observing the scene, are Donna Anna and a male servant, possibly Leporello, Don Giovanni's body servant. Finally, peeping out of a square hole in the ground is another unnamed figure, a man with a long face who is known throughout the novel, appropriately, as 'Kaonaga', or 'longface' (Murakami 2017: I, 97–103).

But this is no ordinary painting. Not long after *watashi* discovers it, carefully hidden in the attic of Tomohiko's home, the eponymous character of *Kishidanchō*, the older man being stabbed to death, emerges from the painting and visits the protagonist. This figure, like the others in the painting dressed in Japanese Asuka Period (sixth century) clothing, speaks to *watashi* in a peculiar mixture of modern and faux-classical Japanese language, addressing him as *shokun* ('you', plural).

In addition to his clothing and manner of speech, our attention is drawn to *Kishidanchō*'s size – roughly that of a large doll – leading experienced Murakami readers, no doubt, to associate him with the 'Little People' of *1Q84*, earth spirits whose task is to mediate events between the physical and metaphysical realms in that novel; or with the 'TV people' from the story of that title, who climb out of the narrator's television one day and advise him that his wife will leave him (Murakami 1990e). Yet, setting aside his diminutive size, the real meaning and interest in *Kishidanchō* lies closer to characters like Jonī Wōkā and Kāneru Sandāzu in *Umibe no Kafuka*, as a metaphysical guide. Claiming to be neither ghost nor spirit nor deity, *Kishidanchō* declares himself to be an *idéa*, pronouncing the word 'ee-day-ah' to distinguish it from the more familiar English loan word 'idea' ('eye-dee-ah') commonly used in modern Japanese. In so doing, *Kishidanchō* marks himself as an archetypal figure. He explains to *watashi*, 'I am, in short, an *idéa*; at times, depending on who is looking, my appearance changes' (Murakami 2017: II, 317). While highly interesting as the latest in a long line of metaphysical Murakami characters, particularly in his construction as an apparent archetype, here it will suffice to note that *Kishidanchō* serves as a guide for the protagonist, advising him as to how he may draw out the final secrets of Tomohiko's painting by re-enacting its contents.[14]

The painting from which *Kishidanchō* emerges is a concrete representation of its creator's memories of the Second World War. Although on its surface it depicts a scene from Mozart's opera, its deeper connection to the Anschluss becomes clear with the revelation of Amada Tomohiko's participation in the assassination plot of the Nazi commandant of Vienna. With very little imagination, we recognise in the figure of Don Giovanni the painter himself, and in that of *il Commendatore*, the Nazi commandant.

Thus we encounter in Tomohiko's painting an event from the historical past, in a highly abstract, indeed, virtually unrecognisable form. There is no logical link between Don Giovanni's villainous murder of *il Commendatore* and the failed attempt to assassinate a Nazi official. Instead we find the means by which Amada Tomohiko sought to express a story he was forbidden to tell: that of a man trying to win the woman he loves by killing a symbol of power and authority. 'That painting', *watashi* surmises, 'may have been an imaginative depiction of the assassination that *should have occurred* (but had not actually occurred) in Vienna in 1938' (Murakami 2017: I, 423; emphasis in original). Instead, like Lt Mamiya, he failed to complete his mission and was deported, while the lover was captured and presumably executed. This reading of the painting is more or less confirmed late in the novel by *Kishidanchō*, who states that '[w]hat Tomohiko could not achieve in reality he changed in form through his painting. […] It is not what actually happened, but *what should have happened*' (Murakami 2017: II, 314–315; emphasis in original). This reminds us once again of Okada Tōru accomplishing what Lt Mamiya *should have accomplished* in *Nejimakidori kuronikuru*.

Yet again we see how events of the historical past – events with vast ramifications for a great many people – have been reduced to the representation of an essence, here to a fictitious murder. In *Kishidanchō goroshi*, in place of the Sheep, Sensei, or Jonī Wōkā, Murakami presents us a tangible, visual 'text' – a painting – and moreover, one virtually unintelligible without extensive deciphering. This leads *watashi* to engage in reconstructive historical discourse; while the painting may appear indecipherable, *watashi* demonstrates that there is a path to understanding its meaning. His method is simple, and quite like that of any other historian: he turns first to 'documentary' evidence, transmitted to him through Tomohiko's son, as well as the unusually well-informed Menshiki; finally, he approaches Tomohiko himself, though the latter is in no position to offer him direct testimony. The point is that the protagonist investigates, does the necessary digging, and learns what he needs to know in order to decipher the painting, which contains all of Tomohiko's 'testimony', reduced to a well disguised, abstract, yet tangible form.

Once again, this expression of past violence – and of failure – is re-enacted in the contemporary setting. *Watashi*'s interest in the painting 'Killing Commendatore' begins as a largely academic exercise, stemming from his personal curiosity, but when Marie disappears, solving the mystery of the painting by re-enacting it becomes the key – for reasons never quite explained in the novel – to rescuing her. Once more we see two 'events' that are connected only in the most general sense: the separation of Tomohiko and his lover in Vienna, and the separation of *watashi* and Marie. Tomohiko's painting, depicting 'what *should have happened*', becomes the model for *watashi*, who repeats what he has seen in the painting, this time determined to do what Tomohiko could not: save the girl.

This is accomplished, as noted above, by re-enacting the scene in the painting. Visiting Tomohiko's sickroom, prompted by *Kishidanchō*, *watashi* stabs him to death in front of Tomohiko (Murakami 2017: II, 321–323), whereupon a square hole opens in the floor of the room, causing Kaonaga to poke his face out (Murakami 2017: II, 326). Grasping him firmly before he can escape back into the hole, *watashi* forces Kaonaga to guide him into the hole, which leads to the metaphysical realm (Murakami 2017: II, 328–331), here taking a form reminiscent of the Underworld of

Greek mythology. Thus, 'interpreting' the image on the canvas is achieved by 'entering' the canvas, which has come to life right in front of *watashi* and Tomohiko.

What this scene shows us, then, is a particularly abstract means of gathering direct testimony from Tomohiko about what he experienced in 1938 Vienna. Silenced, first by his government and later by dementia, Tomohiko is incapable of expressing this testimony in words. In order to uncover the truth about Tomohiko's painting – the 'testimony' he has left behind – *watashi* can only re-enact the scene and watch Tomohiko's reaction, which awakens Kaonaga. We might surmise here that Kaonaga is a doppelgänger for Tomohiko himself, witnessing the killing that *should have* been accomplished by 'Don Giovanni', the man he himself *should have* been. If this is so, then Kaonaga represents the soul of Tomohiko, freed from the body that holds him prisoner to pass his task on to a successor – to *watashi*.

But awakening Tomohiko's soul does more than simply open a passage to the Underworld; rather, it has the more important function of linking Tomohiko's well-concealed past, on the archetypal level, with events from *watashi*'s own life. It is a process that resonates with Ricoeur's contention, noted earlier, that 'history is a form of knowledge only through the relation it establishes between the lived experience of people of other times and today's historian' (Ricoeur 1984: 99). The protagonist of *Kishidanchō goroshi* becomes the historian of today, establishing a relation between himself and the lived experience of Amada Tomohiko and his peers, but his goal is a recuperative one: to re-enact a scene from the past, and by doing so, rewrite the history of the present, with a more acceptable result. Whereas Tomohiko could neither save his lover nor his brother (echoed in *watashi*'s inability to save his sister), this time, through a re-enactment of past events and a magical journey to the metaphysical realm, which grounds all events in the material world, Marie *will* be saved.

The historical archetype

This brings us full circle to the discussion at the beginning of this chapter concerning the function of the metaphysical realm. What do the aforementioned Sheep, Sensei, Jonī Wōkā, and Amada Tomohiko's painting all have in common? Simply stated, all are material representations of archetypes that begin in the metaphysical realm, and this is precisely what is so disconcerting about how Murakami approaches 'history'. We are accustomed, after all, to historical discourse that is verifiable, coherent, and above all, specific. Genghis Khan and Adolf Hitler were both warlords, but they were different men, living in different eras, involved in separate, specific conquests. Yet, they share a connection with the archetypal concepts of 'violence', 'war', 'empire', and 'genocide'. This is not to suggest that Murakami equates Genghis Khan's rampage to the gates of Vienna with Hitler's conquest of western Europe – as noted earlier, his interest does not lie with world–historical figures; but I do suggest that, from an archetypal perspective, Murakami has constructed a model by which events of the distant past, the recent past, and the present, are linked to our collective memory, a strategy that enables readers to respond to the archetypal concepts that each event awakens. For some readers, 'Jonī Wōkā' will call up images of the Second World War; for others, he will be Vietnam, or Iraq, or the Crimea. Nomonhan – the 'forgotten war' of the Japanese Kwantung Army – may summon for American readers images of Korea, America's 'forgotten war', or of the so-called 'secret wars' fought by the US in Cambodia and Laos, El Salvador and Nicaragua. At issue are not the specifics of these conflicts, but the fact that, in all wars, people are required, by an impersonal, abstract state, to kill strangers, or be killed themselves. We do not learn much in *Nejimakidori kuronikuru* about Japan's war in Manchuria; we see, instead, up close and personal, how the stupid brutality, suffering, and loss of armed conflict affects the individual. We see, through individual cases, how war transforms civilised people to uncivilised beasts. And most important of all, to repeat Murakami's 1996 statement to Ian Buruma, we see how war exacerbates the 'tension between individuals and the state' (Buruma 1996: 62).

The document versus testimony

From the tension between 'individual' and 'state' noted above we might extrapolate an interesting and useful analogy with the status of historical sources. Not surprisingly in a discourse devoted to the uncovering of 'facts', historical documentary evidence is traditionally given more weight than individual testimony based on direct experience. This is unsurprising because documentary evidence is, presumably, based upon multiple accounts that corroborate one another.

Then again this analogy can be pushed further: if documentary evidence is the result of multiple accounts, then it becomes a concordance of varying points of view, more suitable to establishing the wider, 'macrocosmic' perspective of the 'big-picture' histories noted above. This is the foundation, indeed, on which most historical writing is based. Individual testimony may or may not be employed in such histories to lend credence or specificity, but such testimonies, grounded in the individual and his or her perception of events, is of uncertain value. Indeed, testimony that does not agree with 'the facts' at large is unlikely to be heard at all.

Ricoeur (1984), however, warns against over-valuing documentary evidence, reminding us:

> Documents themselves are not just given. Official archives are institutions that reflect an implicit choice in favor of history conceived of as an anthology of events and as the chronicle of a state. Since this choice was not stated, the historical fact could appear to be governed by the document and historians could appear to receive their problems from these things as given.
>
> (1984: 108)

Two problems are implicit in this statement: first, that the 'archives' (documents) themselves are used in service of the state to construct narratives that serve political ends; and second, that those archives gain the ontological status of 'truth' simply through being sanctioned by the very state that benefits from them. In other words, mere declaration that the archives are 'true' effectively lends them credence that may not be sufficiently problematised by historical discourse.

Perhaps this is why, in contradiction to the norms of the historian's trade, 'official' documentary evidence, while present in Murakami's fictional texts, frequently takes second place to the direct testimony of individuals. Murakami's protagonists would generally prefer to hear what the 'eggs' have to say, as opposed to the narrative sanctioned by the 'wall'. This is not to say that documentary evidence plays no part in his protagonists' efforts to reveal the past. Indeed, few readers are likely to have missed the sovereign position held by the symbolic and actual repository of all human knowledge – the library – in Murakami fiction.

Yet, the library, and the documentary evidence it contains, becomes for the author an ironic, and frequently facetious image. We note, for instance, that spurious 'documentary' evidence litters Murakami's work, beginning with the narratives of 'Derek Hartfield' in *Kaze no uta o kike* (1990c [1979]; trans. *Hear the Wind Sing* [1987/2015]). So convincing are Murakami's accounts of Hartfield – complete with titles of and quotations from his written works – that more than one reader surely went hunting through library catalogues in search of this fictitious entity, until Murakami finally sprang the joke, writing such an absurd end for Hartfield (who leaps off the Empire State Building in 1933 with an umbrella in one hand and a portrait of Hitler in the other) that we realise we have been played. Similar narratives attend the 'history' of pinball machines (*1973 nen no pinbōru*), of magic sheep and the settling of Hokkaido in the 19th century (*Hitsuji o meguru bōken*), and the discovery of fossilised unicorns in Russia (*Sekai no owari to hādoboirudo wandārando*), all grounded in 'documentary' evidence located in libraries in these various works. Indeed, by the time Murakami was ready to allude to the very real Nomonhan Incident in *Nejimakidori kuronikuru*, readers had probably lost their capacity to take him seriously.

While Murakami's protagonists do unquestionably spend a good deal of their time digging up textual support in their local libraries, the knowledge they gain is always supplemented – and frequently superseded – by the individual testimony of witnesses. The protagonist of *1973 nen no pinbōru*, while benefitting from a general knowledge of how pinball machines came into existence, really learns what he wants to know through conversations with a professor of Spanish with an encyclopaedic knowledge of the subject, and an even more stimulating conversation with the pinball machine itself. The narrator of *Hitsuji o meguru bōken*, after reading about the history of sheep ranching in Hokkaido, gets more in-depth information from an actual shepherd in the town of Jūnitakichō, and finally learns about the Sheep itself from his (dead) friend Rat. Fossilised unicorns remain a book-bound object of speculation for *watashi* in his 'Hard-Boiled Wonderland', but the protagonist of the 'End of the World' chapters in *Sekai no owari to hādoboirudo wandārando* comes to know these mythical beasts intimately by directly interacting with them. And whatever Okada Tōru of *Nejimakidori kuronikuru* learns about Japan's war in Manchuria from his library book, this has nothing of the impact and immediacy of the storytelling, verbal and epistolary, by 'Mr Honda' and 'Lieutenant Mamiya', both veterans of that campaign. In *Umibe no Kafuka*, Tamura Kafuka's reading on Adolf Eichmann's role in the Holocaust is informative, but what brings the realities of war home to him, individually, is his conversation with two Japanese Imperial Army deserters in the metaphysical forest on his way to meet Miss Saeki.

The opposition of document and experience is even more pronounced in *Kishidanchō goroshi*. For instance, some of the most disturbing images that form our documentary evidence of the Nanjing Massacre are photographs of Chinese civilians being buried alive by Japanese troops. Yet, the true sense of utter terror that must have accompanied this unspeakable fate comes through, for the extremely claustrophobic *watashi*, when he himself journeys into the Underworld and is forced to crawl through a tomb-like cave that presses in on him from every side. It is only through a superhuman effort, and the comforting voice of his dead sister encouraging him, that he emerges from the other side of this terrible ordeal, symbolically 'born again' as a new man.[15]

The privileging of testimony and experience over documentary evidence is important to this discussion, for it helps us recognise more clearly just what sort of a 'history' Murakami is after. It is not the 'social history' described by Ricoeur; in his daily life Murakami's protagonist sometimes appears to be an 'everyman' type figure – he is one of us – but he also possesses extraordinary qualities, and the histories he investigates, the events they reveal, are far from everyday. At the same time, this is not Ricoeur's 'political history' either, for those extraordinary events are told not in terms of the generals, prime ministers, and other 'world historical figures', but from the perspective of the nobodies of history, those who bear the brunt of every struggle, but enjoy none of the spoils. In these narratives, the 'world–historical figures' – Sensei, the Sheep, Wataya Noboru – are 'the state', and just as abstract, while Murakami – in true wall-and-egg fashion, reconstructs – really, he invents – the stories of 'individuals'. But his inventions, his reconstructions, frequently seem more real and powerful than the 'facts' of history.

That said, there is no denying the wholly subjective nature of all individual testimony. Ultimately, all testimony is grounded in experience, which is in turn grounded in perception, and in reconstruction according to the schemata that guide those perceptions (cf. Abercrombie 1960, Hall 2003, Danziger 2008). Two persons may witness the same event, yet reconstruct it differently in their minds according to their individual experiences, assumptions, biases, and so on. Since these reconstructions are grounded in and expressed through the unreliable tool of language, the likelihood of reconstructing the 'same' experience is virtually nil.

There is also no denying that all documentary evidence is grounded in individual testimony, in experience that has been sifted, distilled, reified into an intelligible narrative – again, what White (1978) calls 'emplotting'. That emplotment is done with a purpose, is nearly always political, and even when it is not, the emplotment of history represents an effort to bring order to chaos. But experience is not orderly. It is not tidy. It seldom has a recognisable beginning, middle, or end. Experience is messy, emotional, and intensely personal. It is felt as well as seen and heard. Documentary history can tell us what happened, but it cannot convey the complexity of emotions that might have accompanied being there. For this, we require testimony and, in Murakami's narrative worlds, we require experience too.

Conclusion

It may be argued convincingly that history is concerned with facts, while the emotional side of those facts is the purview of literature. I am inclined to agree. What takes Murakami's approach to history a step further, as I have sought to show, is that he combines these two discursive methods, and at the same time adds a third, metaphysical dimension to the narrative. That is, between the macrocosmic and microcosmic dimensions of historical events in the material (physical) world, he interposes the grounding, archetypal narratives of *achiragawa*, that mode of consciousness in which 'Nanjing' may be grounded as 'genocide', as 'bullying', or simply as 'terror'. And as these narratives join together as part of the collective narrative we all share, as part of the human experience, they evoke and awaken other real-world narratives in the reader that give them meaning and specificity for each individual reader. Juxtapositioning the name 'Nanjing' with the year '1937' prepares the reader to invoke 'genocide' as an archetypal core. By positioning a delicate, sensitive concert pianist at the centre of that narrative, however, Murakami disrupts those expectations, evoking an additional archetypal core that sheds light on a related, yet different problem: the helplessness of the individual (the 'egg') against the demands of the state (the 'wall').

The key to understanding the historical content in Murakami's fiction, then, is to grasp that (1) the specific historical events that underpin each text are intertextually relatable to countless other events that share similar characteristics; (2) the grand narratives of history – the major events, the world–historic figures – become virtually interchangeable with one another, for all are grounded in the same archetypes (power, greed, violence, genocide, conflict, terror, chaos, and so on); and (3) it is, finally, through the individual gaze of the disempowered – the 'egg' – that we may gain our best understanding of these events as experiences, by linking them with our own lives. From a macrocosmic perspective, the events are merely an endless repetition of human corruption, the callous use and waste of human lives. From a microcosmic point of view, on the other hand, they become intelligible through their relatability to the reader's own experience.

This is an effective and interesting approach to history, but it is not without its hazards. In radically reducing world–historic events and figures to absurd caricatures, or to a single painting, there is real danger of rendering impotent some of the truly significant events in human history. One is uncomfortable to see the murder of six million Jews, of 300,000 Chinese civilians, reduced to an archetype, particularly when that archetype diverts attention from a multitude of victims onto a single soldier, bullied into committing a barbarous act. It is troubling because our history is made in the material world, where each individual life is distinct from all others, and important in its own right. In the process of valorising 'the egg', there is an evident contradiction in focusing on the hyper-generalising archetype of 'bullying', or even of 'genocide'. In displacing the meaning of 'Nanjing' to a single soldier and his anguish, Murakami, perhaps unwittingly, risks deconstructing the 'Nanjing Massacre' into an apparently trivial signifier. From a narratological perspective he could easily have written the description of Tsuguhiko's killing of Chinese prisoners as an isolated attack on a nameless village, and still gained the sense of sympathy he sought for the character. Why, we might legitimately ask, did he choose to invoke something as emotionally and historically traumatic as Nanjing in the winter of 1937? He risks, if nothing else, being labelled an apologist for the Japanese Imperial Army.

It is not the first time he has run such a risk, and perhaps this, too, is part of his 'wall-and-egg' problem. When confronting the Aum Incident of 1995, Murakami took the audacious step of interviewing members of the cult who had participated in the most notorious act of domestic terrorism in modern Japanese history; and he appears to have been conscious of the danger of being seen as their defender. 'I feel profound anger toward the members of the Aum Shinrikyō who carried out the sarin gas subway attack (this includes both those who actually carried out the attack, and those involved in other ways)' (Murakami 1998: 17), he writes in the preface to *Yakusoku sareta basho de: Underground 2*.[16] The statement reads like a disclaimer, meant to defuse the impression people may have of him that, in trying to understand the actions of Aum Shinrikyō, he approves of them. We may surmise, then, that as he provides mitigating circumstances for Tsuguhiko's murder of Chinese prisoners, Murakami seeks not to excuse this act, but merely to understand it, and to recognise that at least some of those who took part were caught up in a struggle with an all-powerful state that they could not hope to win. Whether his Chinese readers will see things this way is another question altogether.

Perhaps *Kishidanchō goroshi* will need a disclaimer as well.

Notes

1 All translations from Japanese works in this chapter are the author's own, unless otherwise noted.

2 Plato's Realm of Forms is given thorough treatment in his *Republic*; Plotinus discusses the World Soul in the third book of *The Enneads*; Jung's discussions of the collective unconscious run throughout his published works, but a helpful description may be found in Jung (1972, esp. 237–280). Campbell's 'Zone of magnified power' is discussed in Campbell (1949).

3 See Brook (2002) and Lu (2004) for historical documentation of the Massacre. For a compelling discussion on the death toll, estimated at between 100,000 and 300,000, see Chang (2011 [1997]: esp. Ch. 4). For discussion of Japanese government efforts to cover up or diminish the scope of the event, see Chang (2011 [1997]: Ch. 10) and Bukh (2007). For more on the textbook controversy, see Bukh (2007), Sakaki (2012), and Takenaka (2014).

4 For brief introductions to the failed *coup d'etat* known as the February 26 Incident, see Gordon (2003: 198–199) and Tipton (2008: 122–126).

5 For a brief and useful discussion of Japan's *kanri shakai*, see Lummis and Kogawa (1992: 43–46).

6 See esp. Hansen (2017).

7 For more on the Nomonhan Incident, see Goldman (2012).

8 For a brief introduction to the Stalinist era known as 'the Terror' in the USSR, see Laver (2002: esp. 109–112).
9 There were at least 40 known plots to assassinate Hitler between 1932 and his death in 1945. For more see Fest (1996); cf. Manvell and Fraenkel (2018).
10 Short for the 'final solution to the Jewish question' (*Endlösung der Judenfrage*), the 'final solution' refers to plans drawn up by the Nazi leadership at the 1942 Wannsee Conference to exterminate Europe's 11 million Jews. Adolf Eichmann was in charge of logistics. For details on Eichmann's career, and his later capture and trial, see Arendt (1963).
11 Self-sacrifice of a god or spirit is not unheard of in the mythologies of the world: Odin did it for knowledge, Jesus did it to expunge sin. It is a particularly useful motif when exhorting soldiers to expend their lives on the battlefield.
12 The Nanjing Massacre took place between 13 December and the early part of February following the fall of Nanjing to Japanese Imperial forces. The Anschluss occurred on 12 March 1938 and led to the deportation and murder of countless Austrian Jews.
13 Pronounced as *ma-ri-eh*. The English translation of the novel uses the spelling 'Mariye'.
14 For more on the function of this archetypal character, see Strecher (2020). Interestingly, in conversation with Kawakami Mieko, Murakami affected to be unfamiliar with Plato's concept of forms, on which the character *Kishidanchō* appears to be based. It was a rather disingenuous denial for a man who studied classical Greek drama at university, and Kawakami, to her credit, expresses both surprise and doubt about Murakami's claim. See Kawakami and Murakami (2017: 158–159).
15 For the mythological implications of this rebirth, see Strecher (2020).
16 In 1997, Murakami published *Andāguraundo* [Underground], a collection of interviews with victims and families of victims of the 'sarin incident' on 20 March 1995. One year later in 1998, he released *Yakusoku sareta basho de: Underground 2* [*At the place that was promised: Underground 2*], for which he interviewed members of the cult itself. The two works were published together in English translation as a single volume in 2000.

References

Abercrombie, M. 1960. *The anatomy of judgment.* New York: Basic Books.
Arendt, H. 1963. *Eichmann in Jerusalem: A report on the banality of evil.* New York: Viking Press.
Atogami S. 2014. Murakami Haruki 'Kagami' no achiragawa to kochiragawa: 1980 nendai kara *1Q84* made [Over here and over there in Murakami Haruki's 'Mirror': From the 1980s to *1Q84*]. *Shōwa bungaku kenkyū* 68: 28–40.
Augustine. 1983. *Confessions.* Translated by R. S. Pine–Coffin. New York: Penguin Books.
Brook, T., ed. 2002. *Documents on the rape of Nanking.* Ann Arbor: University of Michigan Press.
Buruma, I. 1996. Turning Japanese. *The New Yorker,* 23 and 30 December, 60–71.
Bukh, A. 2007. Japan's history textbooks debate: National identity in narratives of victimhood and victimization. *Asian Survey* 47 (5): 683–704.
Campbell, J. 1949. *The hero with a thousand faces.* Princeton, NJ: Princeton University Press.
Chang, I. 2011 [1997]. *The rape of Nanking: The forgotten holocaust of World War II.* New York: Basic Books.
Danziger, K. 2008. *Marking the mind: A history of memory.* Cambridge, UK: Cambridge University Press.
Dower, J. 2000. *Embracing defeat: Japan in the wake of World War II.* New York: W.W. Norton & Company, The New Press.

Fest, J. 1996. *Plotting Hitler's death: German resistance to Hitler, 1933–1945*. Translated by B. Little. London: Orion Group.

Goldman, S. 2012. *Nomonhan 1939: The Red Army's victory that shaped World War II*. Annapolis, MD: Naval Institute Press.

Gordon, A. 2003. *A modern history of Japan: From Tokugawa times to the present*. Oxford and New York: Oxford University Press.

Hall, S., ed. 2003. *Representation*. London: Sage Publications.

Hansen, G. 2017. Not just asleep, dead or muted: Images of women in Murakami Haruki. *The Japan Society Proceedings* 154: 122–137.

Hikita S. 2019. Murakami to fans: Believe in the possibility of a better world [online]. *The Asahi Shinbun*, 25 February. Available from: http://www.asahi.com/ajw/articles/AJ201902250041.html [Accessed 11 March 2019].

Iser, W. 1980. *The act of reading: A theory of aesthetic response*. Baltimore and London: The Johns Hopkins University Press.

Jung, C. G. 1972. *The collected works of C. G. Jung*. Vol. 8. Princeton, NJ: Princeton University Press.

Katō N. 2015. *Murakami Haruki wa, muzukashii* [Murakami Haruki is, a challenge]. Tokyo: Iwanami Shinsho.

Kawakami M. and Murakami H. 2017. *Mimizuku wa tasogare ni tobitatsu* [The horned owl takes flight into the twilight]. Tokyo: Shinchōsha.

Kawamoto S. 1986. Murakami Haruki o meguru kaidoku [A wild Murakami Haruki chase]. *In:* Murakami R., ed. *Shīku & faindo Murakami Haruki* [Murakami Haruki hide & seek]. Tokyo: Seidōsha.

Laver, J. 2002. *The modernisation of Russia 1856–1985*. Oxford, Melbourne, Aukland: Heinemann Educational Publishers.

Lu S. 2004. *They were in Nanjing: The Nanjing Massacre witnessed by American and British Nationals*. Hong Kong: Hong Kong University Press.

Lummis, D. and Kogawa T. 1992. Kanri shakai – The managed society. *AMPO Japan–Asia Quarterly Review* 23 (4): 43–46.

Manvell, R. and Fraenkel, H. 2018 [1969]. *The Canaris conspiracy: The secret resistance to Hitler in the German army*. New York: Skyhorse Publishing.

Murakami H. 1990a. *1973 nen no pinbōru. Murakami Haruki zensakuhin 1979–1989* [Complete works of Murakami Haruki 1979–1989], vol. 1. Tokyo: Kōdansha.

——— 1990b. *Hitsuji o meguru bōken. Murakami Haruki zensakuhin 1979–1989*, vol. 2. Tokyo: Kōdansha.

——— 1990c. *Kaze no uta o kike. Murakami Haruki zensakuhin 1979–1989*, vol. 1. Tokyo: Kōdansha.

——— 1990d. *Sekai no owari to hādo boirudo wandārando. Murakami Haruki zensakuhin 1979–1989*, vol. 4. Tokyo: Kōdansha.

——— 1990e. *TV pīpuru*. Tokyo: Bungei Shunjū.

——— 1994. *Nejimakidori kuronikuru*. Vols. 1 and 2. Tokyo: Shinchōsha.

——— 1995. *Nejimakidori kuronikuru*. Vol. 3. Tokyo: Shinchōsha.

——— 1998. *Yakusoku sareta basho de: Underground 2*. Tokyo: Bungei Shunjū.

——— 2002. *Umibe no Kafuka*. Tokyo: Shinchōsha.

——— 2009. *The Novelist in Wartime* [online]. [Speech also titled 'On the Side of the Wall and Egg', presented on 15 February 2009, on the occasion of Murakami being awarded the Jerusalem Prize]. Available from: https://www.salon.com/2009/02/20/haruki_murakami/ [Accessed 11 March 2019].

——— 2009–2010. *1Q84*. Tokyo: Shinchōsha.

——— 2017. *Kishidanchō goroshi*. Tokyo: Shinchōsha.

———— 2019. Neko o suteru—chichioya ni tsuite kataru toki ni boku no kataru koto [Throwing out the cat—what I talk about when I talk about my father]. *Bungei Shunjū* 97 (6): 240–267.

Nakayama S. 2006. Murakami Haruki *Kami no kodomotachi wa mina odoru* ron: Achiragawa to kochiragawa no hazama ni ichi suru seinen [Study of Murakami Haruki's *All the Gods' Children Dance*: A youth in the narrow space between over there and over here]. *Kindai bungaku shiron* 44: 87–97.

Ricoeur, P. 1984. *Time and narrative*. Vol. 1. Translated by K. McLaughlin and D. Pellauer. Chicago and London: University of Chicago Press.

Sakaki A. 2012. Japanese–South Korean textbook talks: The necessity of political leadership. *Pacific Affairs* 85 (2): 263–285.

Strecher, M. 2014. *The forbidden worlds of Haruki Murakami*. Minneapolis: University of Minnesota Press.

———— 2020. Out of the (B)earth canal: The mythic journey in Murakami Haruki [online]. *Japan Forum* 32 (3): 338–360. Available from: https://doi.org/10.1080/09555803.2019.1 691628 [Accessed 20 September 2020].

Takenaka A. 2014. Reactionary nationalism and museum controversies: The case of 'Peace Osaka.' *The Public Historian* 36 (2): 75–98.

Tipton, E. 2008. *Modern Japan: A social and political history*. 2nd ed. London and New York: Routledge.

White, H. 1978. *The tropics of discourse: Essays in cultural criticism*. Baltimore and London: The Johns Hopkins University Press.

Yokoo, K. 1991. *Murakami Haruki to Dosutoēfusukī* [Murakami Haruki and Dostoevsky]. Tokyo: Kindai Bungeisha.

4

MURAKAMI HARUKI'S TOKYO

Spatial transformation and sociocultural displacement, disconnection, and disorientation

Barbara E. Thornbury

'Much has been made', as Richard Powers has observed, of Murakami Haruki's 'status as a leading practitioner of transnational fiction for a globalizing world' (2014: 193). Powers had in mind critics such as Miura Reiichi, who view Murakami as a writer whose work, in a sense, bypasses Japan and its culture in its quest to freely circulate across borders (see, for example, Miura 2014). In this chapter, I mostly sidestep the Japanese-or-global-writer debate (generated in large measure by the many references in Murakami's short stories and novels to American jazz and pop culture and even by what has been called his 'English-sounding' writing style) to draw increased attention to ways that his fiction defines, describes, and engages with Tokyo urban space. Almost from the very beginning of his career, Murakami has expressed in his writing a palpable sense of disquiet in reaction to the tearing down and building up that have been vastly changing the Japanese landscape in general, but especially the Tokyo cityscape. My purpose is not to resituate Murakami in Japan in a narrow sense, but to make the case that his fiction collectively forms a powerful response to and critique of Tokyo's ongoing 20th- and 21st-century spatial transformation and accompanying sociocultural displacement, disconnection, and disorientation – and, precisely by doing so, attracts and resonates with 'global' audiences for whom the urban experience is key.

For Murakami, as Matthew Strecher has written in *The forbidden worlds of Haruki Murakami*, Tokyo is 'an urban emblem of the contemporary' (2014: 196). Murakami's engagement with the capital city begins with his first novel *Here the Wind Sing* (2015; *Kaze no uta o kike* [1979]), in which the narrator recounts a beer-fuelled visit he made to his seaside hometown one August while on summer break from the university he attended in Tokyo. In section 39, labelled as a sequel to the main story, the now 29-year-old narrator says that he 'got married, and we live in Tokyo', adding that he and his wife 'are big Sam Peckinpah fans'. On the way home from taking in the director's latest film, they go to Hibiya Park, where they 'drink two beers each and feed popcorn to the pigeons' (Murakami 2015a [1979]: 98). The passage suggests that this young couple are cosmopolitan urbanites for whom Tokyo, with all that it offers those with wide-ranging cultural appetites, is the place where they feel most at home as they seriously embark on their adult life.

To look back at the four decades that have passed since the publication of that first novel is to see that images of Tokyo's enormous scale and complexity, wealth, and 24/7 cosmopolitan dynamism – contained in repeated references to areas such as Shibuya, Shinjuku, Aoyama, and Akasaka, along with numerous other sites on the city map – are integral to the body of Murakami's work. At the same time, Murakami also depicts a less readily visible, more anonymous Tokyo that is equally fundamental to his cityscape settings. The Tokyo spaces to which I am referring here are distinct from the 'other world' or metaphysical realm about which Matthew Strecher has written in his work on Murakami.[1] In the first of the two sections below, I focus on aspects of Murakami's fiction that manifest his growing sense of disquiet in response to the remarkable spatial transformation that has been taking place in Tokyo. In the section that follows, I then look at several examples of Murakami's less visible, more anonymous Tokyo – a closed-off alleyway, an empty building lot, the stairway of a luxury condo building, the city's sewer system, and an elevated highway – that are instrumental to his critique of sociocultural displacement, disconnection, and disorientation.

Tokyo's spatial transformation

Machimura Takashi described the 1980s – exactly when Murakami was emerging onto the scene as a new writer of note – as a watershed decade when Tokyo 'was at a turning point in its urban development' (1992: 127). The spatial transformation that had begun during the economic bubble years of the 1980s continued even after the bubble burst in the early 1990s, a time when urban renewal became a government priority. Policies aimed at economic reform that were introduced during this period, as Tsukamoto Yoshiharu and Fujimura Ryūji have noted, 'led to an unprecedented explosion in the number of construction projects which quickly – and radically – changed Japan's cityscapes unlike anything seen before' (2008: 33). This was true nowhere more than in Tokyo. Proof abounds in buildings and developments across the city, including skyline-altering structures such as the Mori Tower, the centrepiece of the expansive Roppongi Hills residential–hotel–retail–office complex that opened in 2003, and the Skytree communications tower, which was completed in 2012 – becoming the planet's second-tallest structure after Dubai's Burj Khalifa.

The process continues. In sum, as Robin Le Blanc has succinctly written, '[o]nce characterized by its massive sprawl of relatively low buildings and modest, snugly packed single-family homes, residential Tokyo is reconcentrating in more urbanized districts dominated by high-rise condominium developments'. Le Blanc cites a host of factors for 'Tokyo's physical remaking into a denser, high-rise city'. They range from 'the city's historically high "scrap and build" rate, improvements in building technologies, [and] changed regulation of urban real estate development projects' to 'increased pressures on household incomes, restructuring of capital in urban real estate development finance, and lifestyle preferences of the increasing numbers of double-income couples' (2016: 315–316).

Murakami's baseline impression of Tokyo was formed in 1967, when he arrived there from his boyhood home in Kobe as a Waseda University freshman. Ever since, except for several extended sojourns abroad, Murakami has been a resident of Tokyo and a firsthand observer of the city in flux. Although Tokyo was still a mostly low-rise city in the late 60s, advances in engineering techniques and innovations in earth-quake-resistant construction materials were just then making possible the capital's first skyscrapers, beginning with the 36-storey Kasumigaseki Building, which opened in 1968. With the completion in 1974 of the 52-storey Shinjuku Sumitomo Building, the area on the west side of Shinjuku Station – famous for its pre- and postwar black markets and as the setting of massive 1960s-era student demonstrations – would come to embody Tokyo's transformation to a high-rise city.

It is already in his second novel, *Pinball, 1973* (2015b; *1973 nen no pinbōru* [1980]) that Murakami begins historicising Tokyo's transformation and expressing a sense of disquiet in response to it. In a passage that describes the Tokyo suburb where the family of a woman named Naoko – one of the narrator's university classmates – had moved in 1961, he writes that, back then,

> Japan was changing – the Tokyo Olympics were held around this time [1964] – and an inexorable wave of urban development was moving toward them. Their homes had overlooked a rich sea of mulberry trees, but now bulldozers were crushing the trees and turning the land black, and a monotonous townscape was taking shape around the train station.
>
> The new residents were by and large mid-level office workers, the ubiquitous salarymen. They leapt out of bed at five o'clock in the morning, splashed water on their faces, and crammed themselves into commuter trains, returning half dead late at night.
>
> (Murakami 2015b: 117)

The narrator recalls visiting the place in 1973, when his university years, Naoko herself, and so much of the world he had come to know, already existed only in memory: 'I stepped down from the sorry old suburban local train […] and inhaled the smell of fresh grass. It was a fragrance from picnics long past; even the May breeze seemed to be reaching me from some distant time' (ibid.: 109).

The changing suburb is like the one Murakami takes to task in his story 'The Elephant Vanishes' (1993; 'Zō no shōmetsu' [1985]) for the surge of high-rise development occurring there (see Nihei in this volume for an analysis of this story). Despite being only 31 years old and having a career-track job that accords him financial stability and a degree of social status, the narrator feels a sense of unease toward the world around him. He learns about the missing elephant in the morning newspaper, which he carefully reads every day from beginning to end as if he might find in those printed pages answers to his metaphysical questions. One day, the headline in the newspaper's local-news section proclaimed 'Elephant Missing in Tokyo Suburb' (Murakami 1993: 308). It was, as the narrator drily notes, 'an old, well-established residential suburb', one that 'boasted a relatively affluent citizenry, and its financial footing was sound' (ibid.: 311) – not the sort of place where elephants go missing.

The tearing down and building up that was transforming geographically real Tokyo was also transforming Murakami's fictional Tokyo. The small, private zoo where the elephant had lived 'sold its land to a developer, who was planning to put up a high-rise condo building, and the town had already issued him a permit' (ibid.: 310). All the animals were relocated to other zoos – except for the elephant, 'a feeble old thing that looked as if it might die of a heart attack at any moment' (ibid.). It was agreed, in the end, that the town would pay a keeper to continue caring for the elephant on land given by the developer. For the narrator, the strangely magical relationship between the zoo's old elephant and its elderly keeper that he himself had frequently witnessed harboured some sort of compelling secret, one that could potentially be lost forever in the wave of late 20th-century development. 'I was getting sick of high-rise condos', as the narrator says, 'but I liked the idea of my town's owning an elephant' (ibid.: 312).

As Tokyo's surface has been reshaped by structures that reach ever higher, subway-line construction has similarly reconfigured the ground beneath people's feet. Today, there are over a dozen subway lines running through the centre of the city, several which now connect to aboveground rail lines in an uninterrupted surface and tunnel network that encompasses a large segment of the Tokyo metropolitan area and its neighbouring prefectures. Published in the same year as 'The Elephant Vanishes', *Hard-Boiled Wonderland and the End of the World* (1991; *Sekai no owari to hādoboirudo wandārando* [1985]) dramatises the fantastically scary consequences – encounters with monstrous creatures – of possibly going too far in developing the city's below-ground infrastructure. The character referred to as Professor sums up the situation: 'Those INKlings got control of the subway tracks. Maybe not durin' the daytime, but at night they're all over the stations like they own the place. Tokyo subway system construction dramatically expanded the sphere of INKling activity. Just made more passages for them' (Murakami 1991: 288). Subway construction did not create the INKlings (or *Yamikuro*, to use Murakami's original term), but it did give them ways to connect their own maze of tunnels with the passageways extending from the human realm.

Murakami eloquently gives literary expression to Tokyo's spatial transformation in *South of the Border, West of the Sun* (1998; *Kokkyō no minami, taiyō no nishi* [1992]) in words said to Hajime by his father-in-law as they gaze out of the window of the older man's construction company headquarters, on the seventh floor of an office building located in the city-central Yotsuya district. The father-in-law begins by gesturing toward the empty lots down below:

> Look out at Tokyo here. [...] There used to be old houses and buildings on those lots, but they've been torn down. The price of land has shot up so much old buildings aren't profitable anymore. You can't charge high rent, and it's

hard to find tenants. That's why they need newer, bigger buildings. And private homes in the city – well, people can't afford their property taxes or inheritance taxes. So they sell out and move to the suburbs. And professional real estate developers buy up the old houses, put 'em to the wrecking ball, and construct brand-new, more functional buildings.

(Murakami 1998: 127–128)

A prime example of that tear-down-the-old and replace-it-with-the-new process was the very edifice in which the two men were then standing – one of the properties in the father-in-law's own portfolio. The empty lots will disappear, he goes on to say.

In a couple of years you won't recognize Tokyo. There's no shortage of capital. The Japanese economy's booming, stocks are up. And banks are bursting at the seams with cash. If you have land as collateral, the banks'll lend you as much as you possibly could want. That's why all these buildings are going up one after another.

(ibid.)

Articulating the dangerous no-limits outlook that had taken hold in Japan during the bubble era, this is a remarkably prescient piece of writing by Murakami. Exactly at the time that *South of the Border, West of the Sun* was published, Japan's economy was about to see a precipitous decline in stock market and property valuations that would be followed by a long, bleak period of recession.

A new, darker view of Tokyo's spatial transformation can be found in *The Wind-Up Bird Chronicle* (1997; *Nejimakidori kuronikuru* [1994–1995]). The scene in which Toru Okada follows the man with the guitar case from the Shinjuku Station area contains a finely wrought description of a nostalgically familiar Tokyo of wooden houses and narrow streets that was being erased from memory. With Toru tailing him,

the man entered a hushed area of deserted streets lined with two-story wood-frame houses. The road was narrow and twisted, and the run-down houses were jammed up against each other. The lack of people here was almost weird. More than half the houses were vacant. Boards were nailed across the front doors of the vacant houses, and notices of planned construction were posted outside.

(Murakami 1997: 333)

Japan was in recession, and, for a time, lack of funding slowed or, quite often, halted building projects. In the part of the city being described, the one-time residents had already left. The only sign of life was the cats that famously roam through the neighbourhoods of Tokyo – and Murakami's fiction.

The essay 'A Walk to Kobe' (2013; 'Kōbe made aruku' [1997]), published just a few years after *The Wind-Up Bird Chronicle*, serves as a kind of *fin de siècle* summing up of Murakami's views on the spatial transformation that had already taken place

– and that would go on, and even accelerate, in the century to come. Here, Murakami speaks with palpable sadness about the changes visible in the place where he was raised – a sadness that can be said to extend to all he was witnessing in Tokyo where he now lives. In Kobe, he grew up with a clear view out to the sea.

> But now the sea isn't there any more. They cut down the mountains, hauled all the dirt off to the sea with trucks and conveyor belts and filled it in. […] Neat little residential communities have sprung up where the mountains used to be, and similarly neat little residential communities have popped up on the land-fill. All this happened after I moved to Tokyo, during the era of high growth in Japan, when the country was in the throes of a nationwide construction boom.
> (Murakami 2013: n. p.)

The changes that he saw happening in Kobe, where his childhood memories were formed, hit him hard when he returned there for a visit as an adult. Indeed, a decade and a half earlier, in *A Wild Sheep Chase* (1989; *Hitsuji o meguru bōken* [1982]), Murakami had already given voice to these sentiments about a visibly different Kobe. On a visit to J's new bar on the third floor of a four-storey building, the narrator looks 'out onto the line of hills and the area where the ocean used to be', noting that 'the oceanfront had been filled in a few years back, and the whole mile there was packed with gravestone rows of tall buildings'. As J himself ruefully remarks: 'they bulldoze the hills to put up houses, haul the dirt to the sea for landfill, then go and build there too. And they think it's all fine and proper' (Murakami 1989: 103).

Kobe had been reshaped, to be sure, but imagine, Murakami might be saying, how shocking Tokyo's transformation must feel to a person who had been born and grew up in the capital city, where the changes were many times more pronounced. Murakami's fiction, beginning with *Pinball, 1973*, vigorously expounds on these changes. Murakami's less visible, more anonymous Tokyo – exemplified by the spaces discussed in the following section – enable his critique of the sociocultural displacement, disconnection, and disorientation wrought by the city's spatial transformation.

Spaces of sociocultural displacement, disconnection, and disorientation

A closed-off alleyway

Thirty-year-old Toru, the protagonist of *The Wind-Up Bird Chronicle*, is a man adrift. In short order, he has left a fairly decent office job for no particular reason: 'If I was going to quit, now was the time to do it. If I stayed with the firm any longer, I'd be there for the rest of my life' (Murakami 1997: 9). At the same time, his wife, Kumiko, and their cat disappear. The closed-off alleyway behind the house where the couple and their cat are living in Setagaya Ward is a space of disconnection from the surrounding neighbourhood (and the world at large) that morphs into a pathway of discovery, if not recovery, for Toru. It leads him to his encounter with enigmatic teenager May Kasahara and to the spooky abandoned house and its well.

Murakami uses the word *roji*, which Jay Rubin translates into English as 'alley'. A term that resonates strongly in Tokyo cultural history, *roji* are iconic elements of *shitamachi* ('low city'/'downtown') nostalgia that call up images of flowerpot-lined, narrow lanes that run through densely-built neighbourhoods of wood-frame one- and two-storey homes and businesses (see Thornbury and Schulz 2018: xii–xiii). Only wide enough for pedestrians, bicycles, and the occasional motorbike, the idealised *roji* is a communal space that brings neighbours into contact with one another. As Jordan Sand notes, philosopher Yoshimoto Takaaki 'eulogiz[ed] the Tokyo alley [*roji*] as a locus of organic community' (2013: 46). Tokyo's *roji* are the subject of guidebooks (see, for example, Okamoto 2014) and even scholarly studies, such as Imai (2018).

Opening onto larger thoroughfares, *roji* by definition are not closed off and forgotten, as the alleyway in *The Wind-Up Bird Chronicle* is. In fact, the first time Murakami uses the word *roji* in the novel's Japanese version, he mulls over whether that is the right term – writing '"roji" to wa itte mo, sore wa honraiteki na imi de no roji de wa nai' (Murakami 2003: 23).[2] The reason for his doubts regarding the appropriateness of the term *roji* in this context is not just that the alleyway Toru enters is closed off, but that the people whose property abuts it are closed off from each other. Readers well acquainted with Tokyo know that *roji* are elements of the cityscape and, at the same time, signifiers of neighbourly interrelationships. But Murakami ends up staying with the term, with all its connotations, repeating the word some 30 times in the novel.

The *roji* in *The Wind-Up Bird Chronicle* is one that has been denatured by Tokyo's spatial transformation. The closed-off alleyway, as Toru recalls, 'used to have both an entrance and an exit and actually served the purpose of providing a shortcut between two streets'. Following years of postwar development and redevelopment, 'rows of new houses came to fill the empty lots on either side of the road, squeezing [the alleyway] down until it was little more than a narrow path'. As Tokyo's population grew, residents became increasingly concerned about their privacy and security. Step-by-step, property owners blocked off public access to the *roji*: 'As a result, the alley remained like some kind of abandoned canal, unused, serving as little more than a buffer zone between two rows of houses. Spiders spread their sticky webs in the overgrowth' (Murakami 1997: 12). In sum, community contact diminished and community bonds dissolved as a society that prized shared communal space was replaced by one with a preference for well-demarcated, individually owned and occupied plots of land.

Murakami amplifies the point in *The Wind-Up Bird Chronicle* in the same scene described above in which Toru follows the man with the guitar case from the vicinity of Shinjuku Station. Just before entering the house where he has the violent confrontation with the man, Toru says to himself: 'I couldn't just go on hanging around forever in this deserted alley' (ibid.: 334). 'Deserted alley' is the translation of 'hitodōri no nai roji' (Murakami 2003: 515) – literally, a *roji* without pedestrian traffic. The words communicate a sense of displacement – that something is amiss in society – when Tokyo's *roji* have become deserted or, as is the case of the alleyway that Toru enters behind his house, have become closed off because of Tokyo's spatial transformation.

An empty building lot

An empty building lot in *Kafka on the Shore* is the setting for things gone awry in a changing Tokyo. It is the hunting ground of the evil Johnnie Walker and the site where the life course of Satoru Nakata, the older man who cannot read but has the strangely marvellous ability to talk with cats, undergoes an enormous shift. Up until that point, Nakata led a relatively placid life, earning a little extra money in addition to his government welfare payments by helping his fellow residents of Nakano Ward track down their lost pet cats. One day he is informed by Mimi, a bright and articulate Siamese cat, that Goma – one of the missing felines Nakata is trying to find – was reported seen in the empty lot. She informs him that the warehouse that previously stood there was torn down to make way for a 'high-class' condominium building, but '[a] citizens' movement opposed the development, there was a legal battle, and the construction's been put on hold. The sort of thing that happens all the time these days' (Murakami 2005: 80).

Through this passage, Murakami underscores that he was not alone in feeling a sense of disquiet in response to the tearing down and building up that was taking place across the metropolis. For those inclined to activism, that unease has translated into occasional attempts to interrupt the ongoing construction of tall buildings that block access to sunlight and render the city less human-scale. Local residents who protest the encroachment of high-rise condos into their neighbourhoods, Robin Le Blanc has observed, also see such structures as 'an aesthetic disruption' that 'bring in crowds of new residents who do not contribute to community life' (2016: 317). When building lots are left undeveloped even temporarily, as Murakami writes in the same episode, nature quickly takes over: flowers bloom and creatures (like Tokyo's many stray and feral cats) congregate – undeterred, like Nakata, by fences and signs meant to keep trespassers out. In comparing the size of the building lot to that of a small playground, Murakami is perhaps suggesting that a better use for the space, now that the old warehouse is gone, may indeed be an area for children to run freely. Even if the construction of massive buildings does not entail the displacement of local residents from their own homes, the process still leaves them with a feeling of disorientation and even of being disconnected from a potentially more satisfying life in their own neighbourhoods.

The stairway of a luxury condo building

Citizens' attempts to resist the pace of change notwithstanding, the most emblematic images of Tokyo's spatial transformation are the sleek, glass and metal office and residential towers such as the one in the Shinagawa neighbourhood that is the setting for the story 'Where I'm Likely to Find It' (2006; 'Doko de are sore ga mitsukarisō na basho de' [2005]). Murakami turns a high-rise condo's emergency stairway into a welcoming alternative space for those residents of the units whose points of view – despite outward appearances to the contrary – might run counter to the ideology of 'our late-stage capitalist world' (2006b: 279). 'One of the reasons my husband bought this condo was that the stairs are wide and well lit', the wife of Mr Kurumizawa, the missing Merrill Lynch stockbroker, tells the investigator she wants to hire. 'Condo developers like to spend their money on places that attract attention – a library, a marble lobby. My husband, though, insisted that the stairs were the critical element – the backbone of a building, he liked to say' (ibid.: 280). The investigator soon discovers that 'it really was a memorable staircase. On the landing between the twenty-fifth and twenty-sixth floors', which Mr Kurumizawa would have traversed going to and from his apartment, 'next to a picture window, there was a sofa, a wall-length mirror, a standing ashtray, and a potted plant'. Although the picture window afforded a view of the world outside of the building, it was 'sealed and couldn't be opened' (ibid.) – as would be the case in most such climate-controlled buildings.

The extraordinary, amenity-laden stairway of the encapsulated, atomised domain of the building allows a self-selected cohort of residents to find (or, at least, seek) what they are looking for away from a world that has otherwise displaced them psychologically – leaving them with the disorienting sense that they do not belong in the environment they physically inhabit. The investigator – himself a mysterious figure who specialises 'in locating people who've disappeared' (ibid.: 279) but refuses to take payment for his work – inexplicably focuses his search for Mr Kurumizawa exclusively on the stairway. There he encounters several individuals, each of whom is in his or her own particular way among the displaced.

One of those individuals is a man in his 70s who uses the stairway as a place to partake in cigarettes, in part because his wife and son do not want the smell of smoke in the apartment where they live. 'I smoke only a couple of cigarettes a day', the man tells the investigator. He should quit, he says, but 'going to the store to buy cigarettes, coming down here for a smoke […] helps pass the time. Gets me up and moving and keeps me from thinking too much'. When the investigator wryly observes: 'You keep smoking for your health is what you're saying', the man responds '[e]xactly' (ibid.: 285). Another person the investigator meets is a little girl, perhaps just a first-grader, whose unfettered imagination and ability to see things that adults blithely ignore (such as the mirror on the landing that somehow does a better job at reflecting than other mirrors do) instinctively draw her to the stairway. Too young to be oppressed by an unrelenting work schedule or to be just worn down by life, the little girl expresses her feeling of displacement from the world around her by simply saying that '[t]he elevator's stinky' (ibid.: 286) – so she sometimes walks all the way up to her family's apartment on the 27th floor.

In the end, Mr Kurumizawa spontaneously turns up. His sense of displacement was seemingly so extreme that it caused him to somehow be catapulted – contrary to the laws of physics and common sense – from the condo building stairway to a bench in northeast Japan's Sendai train station. The glimmer of a rational explanation is given earlier in the story, when the man who used the stairway to smoke cigarettes mentioned to the investigator that he had apparently seen the missing Mr Kurumizawa sitting on the couch on the landing staring into space. When the investigator asked the smoker if it looked like Mr Kurumizawa was thinking about something, the man replied that he believed, 'contrary to Descartes, that we sometimes think in order *not* to be' (ibid.: 285, original italics) – meaning that the act of thinking itself is a kind of resistance to society's demands on the individual that takes the form of self-imposed displacement.

The city's sewer system

As Tokyo builds ever higher and digs ever deeper during its ongoing development, the relationship between the city and nature becomes increasingly fraught. 'A Shinagawa Monkey' (2006; 'Shinagawa saru' [2005]) dramatises this fraught relationship with its focus on a monkey living in the sewers beneath the streets of Shinagawa Ward that steals people's names. Mr Sakaki, section chief of the Shinagawa Public Works department (whose job includes oversight of the ward's sewers) had told his wife about the existence of the monkey. It did not take long before Mrs Sakaki – a counsellor trying to help a young woman named Mizuki recover her name – surmises that the monkey is the name-stealing culprit.

For all of its surreal elements, 'A Shinagawa Monkey' is rooted in the fact that monkeys – more precisely, macaques – can be found in the wild across a wide swath of mountainous area in Japan's northeast. Although they even live within the geographic borders of Tokyo – most famously in the wooded environs of Mount Takao (Takaosan) on the far western edge of the metropolis – the territory that Japan's monkeys naturally inhabit is not even remotely close to central, downtown Tokyo. This makes the creature in 'A Shinagawa Monkey' a figure of displacement – an extreme illustration of ways that people are transforming the natural world through development that encroaches further and further into the wild.

The aboveground transformation of Tokyo is necessarily accompanied by the development of an underground infrastructure that encompasses the city's massive sewer system. It is in that sewer system that the monkey finds refuge, angering Mr Sakaki's fellow Public Works employee Mr Sakurada, who views the animal as a kind of criminal with 'a hideout underneath Takanawa [a part of Shinagawa] that he used as a base for foraging operations all over Tokyo' (Murakami 2006a: 329). However, Sakurada does not have the last word. In Murakami's fiction, beings who normally do not have a voice can speak up in their own defence. 'There's no place for us to live in the city', the monkey retorts. 'There aren't many trees, few shady places in the daytime'. The stress is unrelenting: 'If we go aboveground, people gang up on us and try to catch us. Children throw things at us or shoot at us with BB guns. Huge dogs tear after us. [...] We never get any rest, so we have to hide underground' (ibid.).

Even though Mizuki recovers her name – and, in the process, gains, thanks to the monkey, valuable insight into her life and emotions – society requires that the 'criminal' must be punished. Giving in to the Sakakis' humanitarian solution to transport the animal to Mount Takao, Mr Sakurada harshly warns the monkey never to 'show your face round Shinagawa anymore', telling him that if he dares to come back, 'you aren't going to get out of here alive' (ibid.: 334). Having been forced to adapt to the human realm, the monkey is doubly displaced by being ejected from the city in which he had found a hiding place, if not a home.

An elevated highway

Starting in the run-up to the 1964 Olympics, elevated highways – built with the aim of enabling free-flowing mobility for a rapidly growing city – became a salient element of Tokyo's spatial transformation. 'In the long run', as André Sorensen has written, 'probably the greatest impact of the Olympics on Tokyo was the building of the inner-city elevated expressway system. The Metropolitan Expressway Corporation was established in June 1959, and the central network of five expressway routes […] [was] completed just in time for the opening of the games in 1964' (Sorensen 2002: 192). The network's impact on the city was tremendous: '[t]he expressway system so dominates the central area of Tokyo that it is impossible not to notice it. Some regret that it destroyed many of Tokyo's downtown canals, and forever changed Tokyo's relationship to its roots in water transport' (ibid.).

As the population of the city continued to increase over the next several decades, however, the dream of free-flowing passage along those elevated roads faded. 'Tokyo's already choked with cars', Hajime from *South of the Border, West of the Sun* observes in the scene in which his father-in-law, owner of a construction company, held forth expansively on the tear-down-and-rebuild fever gripping Tokyo. 'Any more skyscrapers, and the roads will turn into one huge parking lot' (Murakami 1998: 128). And, indeed, *1Q84* (2011; *1Q84* [2009–2010]) opens with Aomame sitting in a taxi stuck in gridlocked traffic on elevated Metropolitan Expressway Number 3 heading toward Shibuya. She is on her way to murder a man in revenge for the bone-shattering abuse his wife suffered at his hands.

Murakami maps Aomame's route with realistic precision. The taxi in which she is riding runs into stalled traffic outside of the Sangenjaya neighbourhood, not far from Shibuya: 'Only the side headed toward downtown Tokyo was tragically jammed. Inbound Expressway Number 3 would not normally back up at three in the afternoon, which was why Aomame had directed the driver to take it' (Murakami 2011: 8). The inscrutable taxi driver (who has no photographic registration card of the sort that is normally displayed) tells her that she can get on the Tokyu train line if she is willing to climb down a nearby emergency staircase – and she takes him up on the idea. Her final exit from the locked and fenced-in area situated between the inbound and outbound lanes of Route 246 that runs parallel to the expressway above is through an opening made by street people who use the space for nighttime shelter. In a word, Aomame is indirectly aided by anonymous folks who, having no stable abode of their own, inhabit the normally untraversed interstices of the city. 'The traffic on Route 246 was heavier than usual, probably because word had spread that an accident had stopped traffic on the parallel urban expressway. Aomame abandoned the idea of taking a cab and decided instead to take the Tokyu Shin-Tamagawa Line [which was later merged into the Den'entoshi line] from a nearby station' (ibid.: 41). Suddenly disconnected from 1984, she has entered the world of 1Q84.

The congested elevated highway is a potent metonym for Tokyo's transformation into a city overwhelmed by its own success. For Aomame and fellow protagonist Tengo, 1Q84 – or 'cat town', as he calls it – is a trap from which they must escape before it is too late. However, even the real world of 1984 sets its own traps – represented in the novel by the stalled traffic on elevated Metropolitan Expressway Number 3. When Aomame first tries to get out of 1Q84, not having imagined that she could actually be reunited with Tengo, she reasons that she should repeat the process of going down the emergency stairway from the elevated highway. She starts by getting into a taxi in Koenji (the location of the safe house where she was put up after assassinating Sakigake cult's 'Leader'), telling the driver to go to Yoga and then take Metropolitan Expressway Number 3 as far as the Ikejiri exit. The cab driver understandably balks and advises Aomame of a potential traffic jam. And, indeed: '[t]he inbound side of Metropolitan Expressway Number 3 was, as the driver had predicted, beautifully backed up. The slowdown started less than a hundred yards from the entrance, an almost perfect specimen of chaos, which was exactly what Aomame wanted' (ibid.: 712). All goes according to plan until she finds that 'in the world of 1Q84, the emergency stairway no longer existed' (ibid.: 715).

The congested elevated highway is the portal between 1Q84 and 1984 – but the key to her return to 1984, as Aomame (now with Tengo by her side) finally realises, is to climb back up the same emergency stairway that she climbed down at the beginning of the novel. Once the couple reach the roadbed of Metropolitan Expressway Number 3, they find that '[t]he traffic on the expressway was bumper to bumper, just as she had left it. The Shibuya-bound traffic was barely inching along' (ibid.: 1148). Whether or not she and Tengo are actually back in 1984 or have been transported into yet a different space/time – 'Aomame was struck by a sudden thought. Something was different, but she couldn't put her finger on it' (ibid.: 1150) – they have at least freed themselves from the unsettling, two-moon world of 1Q84. What remains consistent, however, is Tokyo's dystopic urban gridlock.

Conclusion

Tim Parks is not alone among those critics who have pointed to the many 'tropes, images, and cultural references from Western literature, classical music, and pop culture' as indicators that Murakami has 'pioneer[ed] a new global literature whose stories, whether real, surreal, or "magical", are not radically located in any place or culture precisely in order to appeal to a worldwide audience' (2016: 247). To the contrary, I would argue, Murakami's writing appeals to a worldwide audience to a great extent because of its notable geographic (and cultural) specificity – manifested especially in the ways it skillfully deploys the expressive power of the Tokyo cityscape.

Much of Murakami's fiction is set in the very centre of Tokyo. 'This was the middle of Tokyo' (Murakami 1997: 220), as Toru unequivocally declares in *The Wind-Up*

Bird Chronicle about the Setagaya Ward neighbourhood where he and Kumiko live. Later in the novel, the character makes virtually the same observation about the area into which he follows the man with the guitar case (Murakami 2003: 514). The points on the map of Tokyo that take shape within the framework of Murakami's narratives include Akasaka, Akasaka Mitsuke Station, Aoyama, Aoyama Boulevard, Aoyama-Itchome Station, Asagaya, Azabu, Chiyoda Ward, Denenchofu, Gaienmae Station, Ginza, the Ginza subway line, Harajuku, Harumi Pier, Hibiya Park, Hiroo, the Imperial Palace, Jiyugaoka, Kanda, Koenji, Kojimachi, the Marunouchi subway line, Meguro, Meiji Jingu Baseball Stadium, Minato Ward, Ochanomizu Station, the Odakyu train line, Okura Hotel, Omotesando, Sangenjaya, Sendagaya, Setagaya, Shibuya, Shinagawa, Shinagawa Station, Shinbashi, Shinjuku, Shinjuku Boulevard, Shinjuku Imperial Gardens, Shinjuku Station, Tama River, Tokyo Bay, Tokyo Station, the Tozai subway line, Ueno Zoo, Wako Building, the Yamanote Line, Yotsuya, Yoyogi, and Yoyogi Park. Despite its length, this list gives just some of the more prominent Tokyo locales in his short stories and novels.

The assumptions that Murakami makes about the knowledge possessed by readers of his work relate both to the cartographic location of these many references and to their cultural and historical resonances. These assumptions necessarily apply not only to those who read his work in Japanese but also to those who access it in translation. Regarding literature from Japan being translated into English as well as other languages, it is fair to say that translators, publishers, and their readers recognise, 'that global literacy in the twenty-first century requires a rapidly expanding cultural and geographical vocabulary and knowledge' (Thornbury, 2017: 133). Moreover, '[t]he linguistic demands on readers of fiction translated from Japanese – and expectations about the cross-cultural knowledge that they possess – are markedly intensifying' (ibid.). Globally literate readers outside of Japan who may already 'know' New York, London, and Paris in fiction – that is, who are already conversant with the geographic and symbolic components of those cityscapes – are getting to know Tokyo in the same way through the translated work of Murakami, along with that of other writers such as Higashino Keigo, Kirino Natsuo, Nakamura Fuminori, and Yoshida Shūichi. Flynn (2016), Hantke (2007), and Suzuki (2013) are examples of scholarly work that focuses on or includes reference to the role of Tokyo in Murakami's fiction. Examples of literary–geographic guides to Murakami's work, which feature the Tokyo locations, include Lawrence (2016) and Anderson (2011). Here readers can experience a guided tour of Murakami's Tokyo.

Expressions of disquiet in response to Tokyo's ongoing 20th- and 21st-century spatial transformation are a prominent feature of Murakami's work – leading his characters literally to wonder: Where am I? When trying to follow the man with the guitar case, Toru from *The Wind-Up Bird Chronicle* reflects to himself: 'The geography of this place was lost on me. I couldn't tell north from south. I guessed that I was in the triangular area between Yoyogi and Sendagaya and Harajuku, but I could not be sure' (Murakami 1997: 333). Murakami uses the actual geography of Tokyo to communicate Toru's disorientation as he enters a space beyond what is real to him. In addition to well-known locations such as Shibuya, Shinjuku, Aoyama, and Akasaka, Murakami evokes for readers a less readily visible, more anonymous Tokyo that is equally fundamental to his cityscape settings. Murakami's critique of sociocultural displacement, disconnection, and disorientation arising from Tokyo's ongoing spatial transformation finds expression in locations as varied as a once open, but now closed-off alleyway; an empty building lot that was once the site of a warehouse, but is now where flowers bloom and cats roam within fenced-off areas marked with no-trespassing signs; and a remarkably amenity-laden stairway set within the atomised world of a luxury condo building. As developers dig ever deeper and build ever higher, it may also find expression in the form of encounters with creatures that enter spaces (sewer systems, among them) we humans have claimed for ourselves and the massive traffic jams that we have inflicted on ourselves on elevated highways built with the intention of ensuring free-flowing mobility.

Familiarity with those less visible, more anonymous spaces – together with the city's better-known ones – contributes to a nuanced understanding of Tokyo urban space in Murakami's fiction for readers both in Japan and beyond its borders. Those ever-transforming spaces illustrate, to quote the character Frog in 'Super-Frog Saves Tokyo' (2002; 'Kaeru-kun, Tōkyō o sukuu [1999]), 'what a fragile condition the intensive collectivity known as "city" really is' (Murakami 2002: 117) – and, by extension, also illustrate the fragile condition of characters whose lives are inextricably linked with that intensive urban collectivity.

Notes

1 The 'other world' or metaphysical realm in Murakami's fiction is perhaps best summarised by the character Oshima in *Kafka on the Shore* (2005; *Umibe no Kafuka* [2002]): 'There's another world that parallels our own, and to a certain degree you're able to step into that other world and come back safely. As long as you're careful. But go past a certain point and you'll lose the path out. It's a labyrinth' (Murakami 2005: 352).
2 Murakami's struggle with the term is reflected in Jay Rubin's translation of the line: 'It was not an "alley" in the proper sense of the word, but then, there was probably no word for what it was' (Murakami 1997: 12).

References

Anderson, S. 2011. Murakami's Tokyo [online]. *The New York Times*. Available from: https://archive.nytimes.com/www.nytimes.com/interactive/2011/10/23/magazine/20Mag-Murakami-Tokyo.html?ref=magazine [Accessed 5 June 2019].
Flynn, D. 2016. The transcreation of Tokyo: The universality of Murakami's urban landscape. *In*: Strecher, M. C. and Thomas, P. L., eds. *Haruki Murakami: Challenging authors*. Rotterdam: Sense Publishers, 87–100.
Hantke, S. 2007. Postmodernism and genre fiction as deferred action: Haruki Murakami and the noir tradition. *Critique: Studies in Contemporary Fiction* 49 (1): 3–24.
Imai H. 2018. *Tokyo roji: The diversity and versatility of alleys in a city in transition*. New York: Routledge.
Lawrence, K. 2016. *The Murakami pilgrimage: A guide to the real-life places of Haruki Murakami's fiction*. Jackson: Sailingstone Press.

Le Blanc, R. M. 2016. What high-rise living means for Tokyo civic life: Changing residential architecture and the specter of rising privacy. *The Journal of Japanese Studies* 42 (2): 315–341.

Machimura T. 1992. The urban restructuring process in Tokyo in the 1980s: Transforming Tokyo into a world city. *International Journal of Urban and Regional Research* 16 (1): 114–128.

Miura R. 2014. *Murakami Haruki to posutomodan Japan: gurōbaru-ka no bunka to bungaku.* Tokyo: Sairyūsha.

Murakami H. 1989 [1982]. *A Wild Sheep Chase.* Translated by A. Birnbaum. New York: Vintage Books.

———— 1991 [1985]. *Hard-Boiled Wonderland and the End of the World.* Translated by A. Birnbaum. New York: Vintage Books.

———— 1993 [1985]. The Elephant Vanishes. Translated by J. Rubin. *In*: Murakami H. *The Elephant Vanishes: Stories by Haruki Murakami.* New York: Vintage Books, 307–327.

———— 1997 [1994–1995]. *The Wind-Up Bird Chronicle.* Translated by J. Rubin. New York: Vintage Books.

———— 1998 [1992]. *South of the Border, West of the Sun.* Translated by P. Gabriel. New York: Vintage Books.

———— 2002 [1999]. Super-Frog Saves Tokyo. Translated by J. Rubin. *In*: Murakami H. *After the Quake.* New York: Alfred A. Knopf, 111–140.

———— 2003 [1994–1995]. *Nejimakidori kuronikuru, vol. 1. Murakami Haruki zensakuhin 1990–2000*, vol. 4. Tokyo: Kōdansha.

———— 2005 [2002]. *Kafka on the Shore.* Translated by P. Gabriel. New York: Vintage Books.

———— 2006a [2005]. A Shinagawa Monkey. Translated by P. Gabriel. *In*: Murakami H. *Blind Willow, Sleeping Woman: Twenty-Four Stories.* New York: Alfred A. Knopf, 309–334.

———— 2006b [2005]. Where I'm Likely to Find It. Translated by P. Gabriel. *In*: Murakami H. *Blind Willow, Sleeping Woman: Twenty-Four Stories.* New York: Alfred A. Knopf, 273–290.

———— 2011 [2009–2010]. *1Q84.* Translated by J. Rubin and P. Gabriel. New York: Vintage Books.

———— 2013 [1997]. A Walk to Kobe [online]. Translated by P. Gabriel. *Granta* 124. Available from: https://granta.com/a-walk-to-kobe/ [Accessed 5 June 2019].

———— 2015a [1979]. *Hear the Wind Sing.* Translated by T. Goossen. *In*: Murakami H. *Wind/Pinball: Two Novels.* New York: Alfred A. Knopf, 1–101.

———— 2015b [1980]. *Pinball, 1973.* Translated by T. Goossen. *In*: Murakami H. *Wind/Pinball: Two Novels.* New York: Alfred A. Knopf, 103–234.

Okamoto S. 2014. *Tōkyō 'rojiura' bura aruki: rojiura no tatsujin ga 'tsū no tanoshimikata' o tettei gaido!* Tokyo: Kōdansha.

Parks, T. 2016. *Life and work: Writers, readers, and the conversations between them.* New Haven: Yale University Press.

Powers, R. 2014. The global distributed self-mirroring subterranean neurological soul-sharing picture show: On Haruki Murakami's fiction. *In*: Goossen, T. and Shibata, M., eds. *Monkey Business: New Writing from Japan* 4. Brooklyn: A Public Space Literary Projects, Inc., 187–195.

Sand, J. 2013. *Tokyo vernacular: Common spaces, local histories, found objects.* Berkeley: University of California Press.

Sorensen, A. 2002. *The making of urban Japan: Cities and planning from Edo to the twenty-first century.* New York: Routledge.

Strecher, M. C. 2014. *The forbidden worlds of Haruki Murakami.* Minneapolis: University of Minnesota Press.

Suzuki A. 2013. Mapping the subterranean of Haruki Murakami's literary world. *The IAFOR Journal of Literature and Librarianship* 2 (1): 17–41.

Thornbury, B. E. 2017. Cultural references in the novels of Fuminori Nakamura: A case study in current Japanese-to-English literary translation practices and challenges. *Asia Pacific Translation and Intercultural Studies* 4 (2): 132–146.

Thornbury, B. E. and Schulz, E. 2018. Introduction. *In*: Thornbury, B. E. and Schulz, E., eds. *Tokyo: Memory, imagination, and the city*. New York: Lexington Books, vii–xxii.

Tsukamoto Y. and Fujimura R. 2008. Typo-Morphology of Tokyo. Translated by E. Shiner. *Perspecta* 40: 32–41.

5

FOOD CULTURE, CONSUMERISM, AND MURAKAMI HARUKI

The kitchen in 'Zō no shōmetsu'[1]

Nihei Chikako

Food scenes and advanced consumerist capitalism

Murakami's novels are often replete with food scenes – scenes of both eating and cooking. Many of his protagonists and characters are good cooks who enjoy cooking for themselves and for their guests. The dishes are usually simple enough to be reproduced by anyone (for they are often made with ingredients immediately available), but elaborate enough to impress and give great pleasure to the guest. Whether as lovers or as friends, when a meal goes well, it often signals a positive relationship between two characters – consider for instance the protagonist in *Sekai no owari to hādoboirudo wandārando* (1985; trans. *Hard-Boiled Wonderland and the End of the World* [1991]), who cooks for the librarian girl with a huge appetite; Midori in *Noruwei no mori* (1987; trans. *Norwegian Wood* [1989/2000]), who invites her romantic interest, the protagonist Watanabe, to her house for lunch; and the protagonist in *Dansu dansu dansu* (1988; trans. *Dance Dance Dance* [1994]), who uses his cooking skills to become friends with the 13-year-old girl Yuki whom he is tasked to escort from Hokkaido back to Tokyo after being abandoned by her mother. Conversely, tasteless meals often reflect dysfunctional relationships, such as the breakfast the protagonist in *Hitsuji o meguru bōken* (1982; trans. *A Wild Sheep Chase* [1989]) has after his divorce; or Kumiko in *Nejimakidori kuronikuru* (1994–1995; trans. *The Wind-Up Bird Chronicle* [1997]) refusing to eat what her husband, the protagonist Okada Tōru, prepares; or the uneaten breakfast Yuki from *Dansu dansu dansu* has in Hokkaido before being abandoned by her mother.

These scenes with food and cooking tend to be well received by critics and are popular among Murakami's readers. For example, Uchida Tatsuru calls Murakami's food descriptions the most skilful among Japanese novelists (2014: 32), and Matsumoto Umi attributes the lesser popularity of *Afutādāku* (2004; trans. *After Dark* [2007]) to the absence of tempting food (2019: 202). Similar to how musical pieces mentioned in Murakami's novels are compiled as playlists and sold as CDs, dishes from his stories have also been turned into recipes and published as books (e.g. *Daidokoro de yomu*

Murakami Haruki no kai 2001), on personal blogs, and on recipe websites such as *Cookpad*.

At the same time, the portrayal of food in Murakami's work can be understood in terms of the author's critique of consumer capitalist society. Returning to Japan in 1989 from a three-year 'escape' to Italy and Greece, Murakami commented that Japan, having enjoyed rapid economic growth and transitioned into a consumer capitalist society that peaked in the 1970s and 1980s, reminded him of 'a gigantic suction machine, which gulps everything including the organic and the inorganic, the known and the unknown, the physical and the metaphysical' (Murakami 2006: 559–560).[2] This critique of a growing consumerist culture is embodied in the characterisation of Murakami's male protagonists (sometimes doubling as the first-person narrator, *boku*), who is often a freelance writer, part-time worker, or househusband – somebody who refuses to work in major corporations, or 'the System' as Murakami calls it in his famous speech 'Kabe to tamago' (Walls and Eggs) delivered at the acceptance of the 2009 Jerusalem Prize. In sharp contrast to the corporate worker – the male ideal within consumerist society – these occupations allow Murakami's protagonists to spend long hours at home in the kitchen cooking and eating, hence becoming good cooks. An iconic example is *Nejimakidori kuronikuru*, which features one of the most memorable opening scenes for a Murakami novel, in which Okada Tōru, having left his job at a legal firm, fusses over picking up a mysterious phone call while boiling a pot of spaghetti, a moment that will go on to set off the rest of the story.

Another notable example, however, is the contrast between the protagonist *boku* and his foil Gotanda in *Dansu dansu dansu*. Having reconnected with Gotanda after many years since their junior high days, *boku* experiences the 'utopia' of capitalist consumerism as Gotanda, now a film star, brings *boku* to dine at high-end restaurants and sleep with prostitutes, all paid by Gotanda's agent. As a successful actor, Gotanda sells commercialised products through his endorsements, advertisements, and commercials, and in turn becomes a commercial product himself selling his own image in a consumerist society. Losing sight of when he is acting and when he is not, he commits murder and ultimately suicide. *Boku*, on the other hand, is a freelance gourmet writer who reviews restaurants for popular magazines – a job that requires him to visit several restaurants a day and, since he leaves most of the food uneaten, create food waste. While enjoying the benefits of capitalism via both his own job and Gotanda's indulgence, *boku* is aware of his complicity and identifies 'waste' as 'the biggest virtue' in what he calls 'advanced capitalist society' (*kōdo shihonshugi shakai*; Murakami 1997: 40), later claiming that 'advanced capitalism finds value in any trash' (ibid.: 159). This awareness of complicity with the System is a common theme across Murakami's writings; in 'Kabe to tamago' he cautions that while '[w]e must not allow the System to exploit us', we are not innocent either because 'we made the System' (2009: 169).

What prevents *boku* – who cherishes his friendship with Gotanda so much that he says Gotanda 'was my only friend, he was part of me' (Murakami 1998: 282) – from becoming (self-)destructive is, I propose, his association with cooking, which ultimately shelters him from the invasive influence of consumerism in advanced capitalism. As mentioned, *boku* puts his cooking skills to good use for developing trust and friendship with Yuki, putting her in a better mood for accepting her mother's abandonment. Meanwhile, Gotanda praises *boku* as a genius for his cooking, to which *boku* replies '[w]hat's important is to make the most of what you have in your fridge' (Murakami 1997: 165). This is an important line, because it shows *boku* gaining satisfaction from enjoying cooking and feeding his guests without depending on wasteful consumption of ingredients and commercial goods.

The *boku*–Gotanda pair from *Dansu dansu dansu* is thus an example illustrating how character traits – the combination of a non-corporate worker and a good cook – and scenes of food consumption/production may be seen to reflect Murakami's own resistance to what Matthew Strecher calls 'the consumerist economic utopia of late twentieth-century Japan' (1999: 295). Indeed, critics have pointed out that this novel reflects one of Murakami's more critical views of capitalism: this is the first time he uses the term *kōdo shihonshugi shakai* (advanced capitalist society) in his novels (Fukatsu 2014: 60), a phrase which other scholars (e.g. Dil 2010: 35; Ellis 1995: 146) have argued corresponds to Fredric Jameson's term 'late capitalism' (1989) encompassing the period from the end of the Second World War to the 1970s. However, our discussion on food culture in Murakami and its relationship with advanced/late capitalism will not be complete if we do not also give due attention to the kitchen, that is, the *place* of food production. The kitchen is an important venue, not least because Murakami's career started there: while running the jazz bar Peter Cat in Tokyo, he wrote his first two novels outside business hours in the bar kitchen, leading him later to term those works 'kitchen-table novels' (Murakami 2007: i). More importantly, the kitchen in Japanese homes underwent a remarkable transformation after the Second World War that was in tandem with both the country's capitalist development generally and housing policy specifically. Among Murakami's works, the short story 'Zō no shōmetsu' (1985; trans. 'The Elephant Vanishes' [1993]) precisely elucidates this change in the role of kitchen for the postwar family. The main aim of the rest of the chapter is therefore to complement the discussion on practices of food consumption/production with an examination of the kitchen in this story as a symbol of critique of consumer capitalist society.

In this light, the brief treatment on *Dansu dansu dansu*'s *boku* also provides a useful counterpoint to our discussion below. As in *Dansu dansu dansu*, the protagonist (also a *boku*) in 'Zō no shōmetsu' is aware of his complicity with the System, which can in turn be seen to reflect Japanese society in what is now known as the bubble years (late 1980s to early 1990s) before the burst of Japan's economy. However, *boku* in this short story is significantly different in one aspect: he works for the public relations section of a major manufacturer and is in charge of the publicity of kitchen equipment. Rather than rejecting the corporate world, this *boku* has seemingly embraced the position of the ideal man in late capitalist consumerist society. Despite this embrace, however, I will show that *boku* in fact turns the space of the kitchen upside down and into a sign of the consumerist society itself; thus the story does not simply criticise

Japanese society through its plot about an elephant that has vanished, but uses the kitchen as a hinge that dovetails Murakami's own opinion about people's complicity with the System. To help us understand the story better, in the following section I will begin by providing some brief information about the transformation of the kitchen in postwar Japan and its association with the accelerating consumer capitalist system.

Japan's postwar kitchen transformation

In order to deal with the rapid population increase and housing shortages in cities, a policy was instituted in the 1950s to promote homogenised housing and develop residential suburbs all through Japan. The gender division of labour was regarded as the most productive and effective way to drive national economic and industrial development: the husband was supposed to devote himself to commercial work and the wife to support him as a full-time housewife. The urban nuclear family became the archetypal postwar family, replacing the traditional patriarchal system and emphasising a more democratic communication between family members. House design therefore placed emphasis on space for family gathering, and during this time the kitchen, a space for both cooking and eating, became the most meaningful room for the family (Ueno 1996: 10).

The Japanese kitchen underwent change, however, beginning from the late 1950s and coming into full force in the 1970s. The import of American TV dramas such as *Father Knows Best* (1954–1960) in Japan from the late 1950s came with a new experience of foreign lifestyle. In these series, the American middle-class suburban families were seen possessing the latest home appliances and in general consuming the latest technology, fashion, and leisure activities. Thus, the American lifestyle became a model for Japanese audience with mothers dreaming about preparing food in stylish-looking kitchens similar to those shown on TV (Miura 1996, 1999). Later, in the 1970s, when Japan achieved the second-highest Gross National Product (GNP) and the third-highest Gross Domestic Product (GDP) in the world, the so-called *shisutemu kitchin* (system kitchen), a type of built-in kitchen modelled on the German Frankfurt kitchen, was introduced in urban areas. Perfect for the many new high-rise apartment buildings being built at the time, the system kitchen was focused on compact design and function: a range of colours were available but there was a sense of homogenised unity in appearance, colour, and function, and the effective use of space for storage optimised working space (Sakai and Dewancker 2005: 759). As a result, the kitchen became a much smaller space compared to previously, leading to a reduction in the importance of home cooking and the growth of the food industry and food-service industry. Processed foods and ingredients became necessary for cooking in the smaller and less functional kitchen (Ōne 2010: 213). As Yamaguchi Masahiro (1996: 64) points out, in many households from around the 1970s, the home kitchen became a 'secondary food factory', in which processed foods from supermarkets were reheated or mixed with other ingredients and sometimes simply plated with some vegetables.

In addition to people's shift in attitude towards cooking, changes to the role of the kitchen were further buttressed by a change in women's role as consumers. In a capitalist system, the gender division of labour – men work outside, women stay inside – assigns no market value to the labour women do as housewives. That is, while men were seen as 'paid' workers producing value for Japan's economic success, women became 'unpaid' workers, a view that ultimately devalued and even demonised domestic labour as menial, unproductive, and unintellectual work – and hence should be done as effortlessly as possible (Ochiai 2002; Pollan 2009; Lupton 1996: 38). It is in this context that women's role as consumers became important for the sales of kitchens and food-related industries. Women started to rely on recipes introduced in the many new women's magazines or TV shows aimed at women, in which there were also tie-in commercials linked to industrialised ingredients and newly released kitchen appliances. The Japanese gendered ideology *ryōsaikenbo*, or 'Good Wife, Wise Mother', then came to mean the woman who actively mastered or absorbed new information on the latest food technology. In this way, Japan's kitchen transformation and development of food industries were closely linked to the nation's economic growth and the rise of consumerism, which necessitated the mediation of women as consumers. The kitchen now appealed to housewives as a room that embodied modern lifestyle rather than, or no longer, simply as a place to efficiently conduct cooking and feeding.

This transformation in meaning underlines, more broadly, Japan's shift from a society of stable production and distribution of goods to a postmodern, depthless, culturally saturated society in late capitalism, characterised by 'the circulation of a "surfeit of signs and images"' (Featherstone 2007: xiv). As Jean Baudrillard has argued, in a society of overproduction and oversupply, products become symbolic goods rather than necessities, and sign value (i.e. the symbolic prestige a commodity gives to its owner) becomes more important than use value (Baudrillard 1976). This indicates that consumption as we have seen in postwar Japanese capitalist society is not simply an economic behaviour but includes social, psychological, and symbolic aspects. The proliferation of signs and images of commodities means that there is a loss of stable meaning to these signs, since goods are now defined through an endless comparison with other goods, which encourages consumers to find 'better' products to purchase and to engage in 'an endless and fruitless quest for satisfaction' (Wilk 2006: 192). Certainly, the idea of consumers being part of consumerist society echoes Murakami's view on people's complicity with the System or advanced capitalism mentioned earlier. As I embark on my analysis of 'Zō no shōmetsu' below, it will become clear that *boku*'s attempt to negotiate his distance from the System hinges on the kitchen as well as the elephant in the story.

From *daidokoro* to *kitchin*: The vanishing of 'things you can't sell'

The protagonist of 'Zō no shōmetsu' at first appears to be the typical lonesome Murakami *boku*-narrator who has enough time on his hands to concern himself with an unusual situation – the vanishing of an elephant. The tale begins as he is reading the newspaper when he comes across the story about the vanished elephant. Suggesting insignificance, the information about the disappeared elephant is tugged away in the local news section, but as it turns out, the story holds much significance to *boku* who has followed the 'elephant problem' right from the start: the elephant became homeless when the town zoo went bankrupt and a real estate developer acquired the land to build high-rise apartment buildings. While most animals were moved to other zoos, no one was willing to take the old elephant that looked as if 'it might die of a heart attack at any moment' (Murakami 1989: 41). After a significant amount of dispute amongst the locals and the drafting of a carefully negotiated financial plan between the town and the real estate developer, it was decided that the town would take ownership of the elephant and make it 'the town's symbol', a decision supported by citizens because 'people liked the idea of saving the homeless elephant by adopting it' (ibid.: 44). A year after the elephant was relocated to a rear mountain where it was fed the remains of local school lunches, both the elephant and its keeper vanish without a trace.

Collecting newspaper clippings, *boku* seems extraordinarily interested in the elephant both before and after its disappearance; he attends various events and even makes it his habit to watch the animal from a covert spot. Up until this point in the story, the narrator is thus quite similar to Murakami's usual *boku* who is reluctant to work in major corporations and therefore has a significant amount of free time. However, more than halfway through 'Zō no shōmetsu' the image of the familiar Murakamian *boku* abruptly disappears when we are suddenly informed that this *boku* is indeed very much part of 'the System':

> I was working for the PR section of a major manufacturer of electrical appliances, and I was in charge of the publicity for the new series of kitchen equipment, which was scheduled to enter the market in time for the coming wedding season in the fall and the bonus period in winter. My job was to negotiate with some women's magazines for tie-in articles. It was not the kind of work that requires intelligence, but I had to check if the articles they wrote didn't 'smell' of advertising.
>
> (Murakami 1989: 54)

While *boku*'s unusual interest in the elephant problem sets him apart from other mere onlookers in the town and thereby reminds us of Murakami's familiar *boku*, his perceived embrace of the System as an employee of a major corporation is a rare find within Murakami's stories, and clearly merits more examination. Furthermore, because it is, of all things, 'the coordinated line of kitchen equipment' that he is in charge of promoting to consumers, *boku*'s job asks us to recall the transformation of the Japanese kitchen throughout the postwar period. Thus, it is in the contradiction of *boku*'s interest in the old elephant and his job as a promoter of modern kitchens where the meaning of this story lies.

At a campaign party where *boku* promotes the company's new Italian kitchen appliances to a magazine editor, he places emphasis on *tōitsusei* (unity) as the most important element of the contemporary kitchen:

'The most important point is unity', I explained. 'Any beautifully designed item dies if it doesn't have a good balance with its surroundings. Unity of colour, unity of design, unity of function: This is what today's kitchen needs the most. Research shows housewives spend the largest part of the day in their kitchen. The kitchen is their workplace, their study, their living room. For this reason, they try their best to make the kitchen a space comfortable to be in. The size is not important. Whether it's large or small, there is only one fundamental principle that matters, which is unity'.

(Murakami 1989: 55)

Both *boku*'s persuasion to a women's magazine editor and his description of the kitchen reflect women's growing contribution to the market as consumers and the increasing reliance on modern food technologies described in the previous section on Japan's housing and kitchen transformation since the Second World War. As was also discussed, this transformation led to a change in food preparation practice, and we can find a possible echo of this in *boku*, who admits to the editor 'with a professional smile' that he 'do[es] like to cook. Nothing special, but I cook for myself every day' (Murakami 1989: 55). Although the daily cooking habit reminds us of Murakami's other cooking characters, thereby suggesting that this corporate *boku* still has a homely anti-System side to him, this is the only mention of cooking in the story, and the brevity of this line combined with the 'professional smile' allows us to wonder if, unlike other Murakami characters, there is a somewhat offhanded, dismissive attitude towards home cooking in disguise that alludes to 1970s Japan when cooking no longer meant preparing meals from scratch, but simply reheating and plating processed food and industrialised ingredients.

Together with this sense of transformation into 'today's kitchen' comes a need to give the kitchen a different nomenclature, and the significance of this terminology may not dawn on the English reader immediately. When the magazine editor uses the old Japanese term for cooking space, '*daidokoro*', *boku* immediately corrects her with the word '*kitchin*' (Murakami 1989: 56), a loanword from the English 'kitchen' that established distance to the Japanese traditional kitchen. Indeed, in tandem with the Japanese government's housing policy in the 1950s, '*kitchin*' as a word was imported and gradually edged out '*daidokoro*' (Yamaguchi 1996: 89). With this new term, *boku* goes on to explain the difference when she pushes him to give his 'personal' opinion: 'A *daidokoro* probably *does* need a few things more than unity. But those elements are things you can't sell. And in this pragmatic society, the factors that can't sell don't mean much' (Murakami 1989: 56). Here, *boku* establishes an 'out with the *daidokoro*, in with the *kitchin*' mentality that tallies with Japan as a late capitalist society: out with things that one cannot sell, in with things that one can. Such mentality, arguably, changes even people's worldview. Later in the story, *boku* states that, 'people are looking for a kind of unity in the kitchen, which we call the world' (ibid.: 68). In this way the kitchen carries broader symbolic significance: since the kitchen's unity is comparable to the world's unity, the antithesis of the modern kitchen – 'things you can't sell' from the traditional *daidokoro* – is also a metaphor for things in the world that lie on the opposite side of market and sign values, and must therefore be excluded from society.

Contrasting *boku*'s corporate identity and consumerist mindset, on the other hand, is his peculiar interest in an old elephant that loses its home to capitalist real estate development. But it is only in this textual flow, I argue, that we can make sense of the elephant as the chief symbol of 'things you can't sell' in the story that, therefore, like the *daidokoro*, is doomed to be made to disappear in the new capitalist world of consumption. Indeed, the elephant's relocation bears resemblance to the design philosophy of the system kitchen: like how utensils need to be stored behind a variety of shelves designed to maintain the 'unity' of the system kitchen's appearance, the act of building high-rise apartments where the zoo once was is a way to increase 'unity' in the town's housing system per Japan's homogenised housing policy. Since it would have been impossible to kill the elephant because it would be too hard to cover up, the elephant therefore needs to be stored away behind a mountain. Considering also that the kitchen appliances *boku* sells are the products that are likely to be equipped in the system kitchens installed in new high-rise apartments building, *boku* by way of his job is not entirely innocent in helping to remove and persecute the elephant.

Now that we have established what *boku*'s job means in the story and how it plays a part in the elephant's vanishing, the symbolism of the elephant becomes clearer. The elephant's transition from boom to doom reveals how it is subject to the manipulation of meanings. Early on in the story the elephant dilemma lay partly in its maintenance cost but was temporarily solved by clever negotiations with the real estate developer, turning the elephant into 'the town's symbol' and feeding it scraps from left over school lunches – at this point food 'waste' can still be turned into something useful, i.e. nourishment. Public opinion was in support because of the symbolic advantage to the town's morality over monetary cost. However, once the elephant and the keeper have mysteriously 'vanished', the public is more concerned about the town's security rather than the elephant's safety, with a mother expressing in the newspaper her anxiety about letting her children out to play. A double bind is formed: the elephant is both the town's symbol and a latent threat. The fast transition from a welcomed symbol to a dangerous creature – not least manipulated by the media such as newspapers where *boku* gets his information – shows how the elephant was treated as a sign whose meaning is replaceable. The *daidokoro* undergoes a similar change as it gets replaced by new values in late capitalist society, represented by the 'unity' of the modern *kitchin*.

The common thread between the elephant and the *daidokoro* both representing something of the past is strengthened with *boku*'s ponderment on the word *shōmetsu* (vanishing). Although the newspaper articles used the word *dassō* (escape), *boku* believes that *shōmetsu* is the word that should be used because there is no trace left to prove the elephant's escape, a point that is again perhaps not immediately clear to the English reader. In his discussion of the story, Katō Norihiro (2011: 299) draws attention to Murakami's word choice of *shōmetsu* rather than another word *shissō* (*shi*

= loss, *sō* = trace), and points out that *shōmetsu* emphasises the inability to detect the process of disappearance, while *shissō* requires a trace of the object's movement and therefore suggests a sense of loss. Katō (ibid.: 297) further associates the vanished elephant with the counterculture movement that Murakami's generation experienced in the late 1960s, stressing that their experience of the fight against the System and power is now no longer meaningful to or understood by the generations born after them, although Murakami's generation continue to suffer from a sense of loss because the past movement took the form of *shissō*. Katō's argument reveals how *shōmetsu* indicates a cutoff with history: because the elephant vanished without a trace, *boku* says people later 'seem to have forgotten that the elephant used to be in the town' (Murakami 1989: 68). If the elephant in this story signifies the past, the elephant's vanishing means a world where people are deprived of the means to remember the past under capitalism's endless pursuit of newer products and technology.

The relevance of food-related metaphors continues as the absence of the past is also compared with a 'gut-less' state. *Boku*, reading the newspaper report on the elephant's vanishing for the first time, commented that the empty elephant house looked like 'a huge, dehydrated creature from which the gut [*zōbutsu*] had been removed' (Murakami 1989: 40). Yet, the empty elephant house is metaphorical of the town itself which has also lost its elephant. The metaphorical chain continues, and hence what is gutless is not only the empty elephant house, but the town society itself which has turned inorganic and lost its means (gut) to process/digest the past. Going back to *boku*'s 'out with the *daidokoro*' ideology, however, a similarity can be seen here between the edging out of the *daidokoro*, the vanishing of the elephant, and the gutless society – all of them 'things you can't sell' and to be replaced by a single event: the capitalist activity of building high-rise apartments. The 'huge, dehydrated creature' (Murakami 1989: 40) also reminds us of the 'gigantic suction machine' metaphor that Murakami used to describe the bottomless appetite of consumption he observed in Tokyo upon his return from Europe in 1989. What is important is that Murakami frequently uses images of devouring and metaphors related to eating to describe the tight grip the consumer capitalist system has on our lives, which in turn induce a fundamental change in food production with the advent of the *kitchin*.

Read this way, then, the comfort *boku* used to find in the elephant implies his hidden alienation in consumer society which, following the elephant's vanishment, puts *boku* into discomfort. For *boku*, who conforms to the corporate norm in order to make a living, the elephant seems undisturbed by the isolation in the consumer capitalist system that *boku* finds difficult to cope with. *Boku*'s hidden social isolation was thus temporarily alleviated by observing this socially vulnerable yet ideologically unaffected animal. With the disappearance of the elephant, however, *boku* has lost his means to keep his mental balance between what he had to do and what he longed for:

> I would try to do something, but then I would become incapable of distinguishing between the possible results of doing it and of not doing it. I often feel that things surrounding me have lost their proper balance. […] Since the

elephant incident, some balance in me probably has collapsed and that causes some external phenomena appear strange to my eyes. [...] I continue to sell refrigerators and toaster ovens and coffee-makers in the pragmatic world working based on pragmatic memory system. The more pragmatic I try to become, the more products I can sell [...] I become more welcomed by people.

(Murakami 1989: 68)

Boku's loss of ability to distinguish 'between the possible results of doing it and of not doing it' reflects precisely the mentality in consumerist capitalism: in a world without 'things you can't sell', any actions will be turned into the process of producing 'things you can sell'. This loss of mental balance pushes him to become a more 'pragmatic' worker than ever (pragmatism implying a dissociation from 'things you can't sell'). With the elephant's vanishment, *boku*'s only method of negotiating his distance with the System is gone and the transition from *daidokoro* to *kitchin* is complete; in order to survive in a capitalist world, his only path is to be an efficient and pragmatic worker, selling images of modern lifestyle more successfully.

To sum up, through a complex chain of metaphors between the *daidokoro*, the *kitchin*, the elephant, and the gut, 'Zō no shōmetsu' critiques the growing impact the consumer capitalist society has on people's daily lives and thoughts. The transformation that happened to the kitchen space in Japanese homes as a result of late capitalism is expressed plot-wise by *boku*'s job to eliminate the *daidokoro* for the *kitchin* and the system kitchen, and this is layered both with the elephant as a symbol of 'things you can't sell' that has to be put away in the mountain, and with the gut-less state of the empty elephant house qua society as a metaphor for severing links with the past.

Complicity and resistance in the System

This chapter opened with an overall discussion on food culture in Murakami's world and drew specific attention to the kitchen. Specifically, I showed how in the short story 'Zō no shōmetsu' the kitchen can be read as a critique of consumer culture and the capitalist system. In this story, the diptych of *boku*'s job to promote modern-style *kitchin* equipment and the town's decision to relocate the elephant to the mountains to make room for apartment construction – in short, to promote 'things you can sell' and hide 'things you can't sell' – illustrates a broader shift in Japan, and more widely in the world, into late capitalism. The vanishing of the elephant, then, is more than a mystical happening; it is a wider metaphor for things that society has sacrificed as it turns consumerist.

I would like to end with the final note that, while Murakami's fiction in this way is consistently critical of the System, it is also important to recognise that, like *boku* in both *Dansu dansu dansu* and 'Zō no shōmetsu', Murakami's successful career has undeniably both contributed to and benefitted from the consumer culture. His success is not only in terms of direct sales of his works (including translations of his works overseas and his own translation of foreign literatures), but has developed into an industry that generates a range of transmedial commercial and creative products,[3] from explanation guides on his work, music played in his fiction, and collections of recipes cooked by his characters. Considering Murakami's worldwide popularity, he is no longer the controversial author who wrote his kitchen-table novels in the early 1970s in opposition to the changing world around him; he *is* now a celebrity like Gotanda from *Dansu dansu dansu*. Just as he critiques people's complicity with the System, Murakami himself is aware of his own complicity with it, expressing in interviews the dilemma that he experienced when his *Noruwei no mori* sold millions and his fear that the popularity would turn his work into a commercial product (Murakami 1991; Kelts 2002).

This awareness provides a textual linkage back to his characters and their complicity as they acknowledge their unavoidable association with the benefits created through the System, like *boku* in 'Zō no shōmetsu'. Yet, Murakami has never stopped creating characters who attempt to resist the System by relating themselves with 'things you can't sell' such as home cooking, as a defence against the influential force of the consumer capitalist society. There is, then, a more nuanced meaning to these characters: they are not merely rebellious, but they try to appreciate what exists or is given in their life (a practice that does not conform to consumerism) before perhaps ultimately wanting more (a sign that they cannot escape consumption). A close look into the replete description of food scenes in Murakami's fiction thus provides a different perspective to understand his view on the System, a key theme that constructs his fiction.

Notes

1 I would like to thank Dr Gitte Marianne Hansen and Dr Michael Tsang for their invaluable help and advice on this chapter.
2 All translations from the Japanese are mine unless stated otherwise.
3 For more on transmediality and Murakami, see Hansen and Tsang (2020).

References

Baudrillard, J. 1976. *Symbolic exchange and death*. London: Sage.
Daidokoro de yomu Murakami Haruki no kai. 2001. *Murakami reshipi*. Tokyo: Asuka Shinsha.
Dil, J. 2010. Haruki Murakami and ideology of late-capitalist Japan: Learning how to *Dance Dance Dance*. Asiatic 4 (2): 34–48.
Ellis, T. 1995. Literature: Questioning modernism and postmodernism in Japanese literature. *In*: Y. Sugimoto and J. P. Arnason, eds. *Japanese encounters with postmodernity*. London: Kegan Paul International, 133–153.
Featherstone, M. 2007. *Consumer culture and postmodernism*. Los Angeles: Sage.
Fukatsu K. 2014. Murakami Haruki 'Warera no jidai no fōkuroa – Kōdoshihonshugi zenshi' ron. *Kyōritsu joshi daigaku bungei gakubu kiyō* 60: 59–72.
Jameson, F. 1989. *Postmodernism, or the cultural logic of late capitalism*. Durham: Duke UP.
Hansen, G. M. and Tsang, M. 2020. Politics of/in transmediality in Murakami Haruki's bakery attack stories. *Japan Forum* 32 (3): 404–431.
Katō N. 2011. *Murakami Haruki no tanpen o eigo de yomu 1979–2011*. Tokyo: Kōdansha.

Kelts, R. 2002. Writers on the borderline [online]. *The Japan Times*, 1 December. Available from: http://www.japantimes.co.jp/community/2002/12/01/general/writer-on-the-border-line/ [Accessed 2 October 2011].

Lupton, D. 1996. *Food, the body and the self.* London: Sage Publication.

Matsumoto U. 2019. Murakami Haruki *Afutādāku* ni okeru 'shoku': Eiga *Alfaviru* to Jōji Ōweru o hojosen toshite. *JunCture* 10: 202–212.

Miura A. 1996. Yokubō suru kazoku, yokubō sareta kazoku. *In*: C. Ueno, ed. *Iro to yoku.* Tokyo: Shōgakukan, 27–46.

——— 1999. *'Kazoku' to 'kōfuku' no sengoshi.* Tokyo: Daishindō.

Murakami H. 1989. *Panya saishūgeki.* Tokyo: Bunshū Bunko.

——— 1991. Intabyū: Monogatari no chikara ni tsuite—Jon Āvingu. *Bungakukai*, 45 (5), 131–146.

——— 1997. *Dansu dansu dansu, jō.* Tokyo: Kōdansha.

——— 1998. *Dansu dansu dansu, ge.* Tokyo: Kōdansha.

——— 2006. *Tōi taiko.* Tokyo: Kōdansha.

——— 2007. *Murakami Haruki zensakuhin 1979–1989.* Vol. 1. Tokyo: Kōdansha.

——— 2009. Boku wa naze Erusaremu ni itta no ka. *Bungei Shunjū* 87 (4): 156–169.

Ochiai E. 2002. *21 seiki kazoku e.* Tokyo: Yuhikaku.

Ōne K. 2010. Shoku no itonami no henka: Orutanatibu na shoku to komyunitī no saisei o motomete. *Tagen bunka* 10: 209–222.

Pollan, M. 2009. Out of the kitchen, onto the couch [online]. *The New York Times*, 29 July. Available from: http://www.nytimes.com/2009/08/02/magazine/02cooking-t.html?mcubz=1 [Accessed 8 August 2017].

Sakai R. and Dewancker, B. 2005. Shisutemu kitchin ni itaru made no daidokoro no hensen ni kansuru kenkyū. *Architectural Institute of Japan Report* 44: 757–760.

Strecher, M. C. 1999. Magical realism and the search for identity in the fiction of Murakami Haruki. *Journal of Japanese Studies* 25 (2): 263–298.

Uchida T. 2014. *Mōichido Murakami Haruki ni goyōjin.* Tokyo: Bungei Shunjū.

Ueno C. 1996. Sengo nihon no yokubō to shōhi. *In*: C. Ueno, ed. *Iro to yoku.* Tokyo: Shōgakukan, 5–25.

Wilk, R. 2006. *Home cooking in the global village: Caribbean food from buccaneers to ecotourists.* Oxford: Berg.

Yamaguchi M. 1996. Daidokoro sengoshi. *In*: C. Ueno, ed. *Iro to yoku.* Tokyo: Shōgakukan, 69–102.

PART II
Narrative and genders

6

MURAKAMI'S FIRST-PERSON NARRATORS AND FEMALE CHARACTER CONSTRUCTION

Gitte Marianne Hansen

The title of Murakami's short story collection *Onna no inai otokotachi* (2014a; trans. *Men Without Women* [2017]) is ironic, since only rarely are Murakami's male characters without women.[1] Although we can find numerous works with absent women – either because they are asleep, dead, have disappeared, or simply never existed – throughout the past 40 years we find just three works, all very short stories, without women.[2] It is therefore an important task to examine the construction of his female characters. I am currently in the process of undertaking a comprehensive study of Murakami's female character construction and it is yet premature to conclude much about women's overall position across his works. However, until now several scholars and critics have stated that Murakami's story worlds rely on the patriarchal structure of Japanese society (Ishihara 2007: 73) with women serving as sexual objects for male subjectivities; or as novelist Kawakami Mieko phrases it, they must 'shed blood' in sacrifice for male self-realisation (Kawakami and Murakami, 2017). The novel *Noruwei no mori* (1987; trans. *Norwegian Wood* [1989/2000]) where the male protagonist sleeps with numerous women while torn between the two main female characters Naoko and Midori, is unsurprisingly referred to in this manner (Ueno et al. 1992: 253–312).

While this setup between male and female might understandably lead us to conclude that Murakami's works portray problematic male–female relations, this criticism of his breakthrough novel has troubled me for some time now. The reason for this is tied to the novel's narrator type; that is, the tool that conveys the story, its characters, and events. *Noruwei no mori* is presented to us by Watanabe Tōru, a male first-person narrator who recalls his experiences as a university student 18 years earlier. The story and characters of *Noruwei no mori* are therefore a biased product of his memory and fantasy. From the start, this is the premise of the story and its characters, and this must therefore be considered in any analysis or criticism. When aiming to discover women's position in Murakami's world, a good place to start is therefore to take a closer look at their narrators.

As I have already shown elsewhere (Hansen 2010, 2017), Murakami's narrator types can be divided into five groups – three first-person singular narrated story types, the third-person narrator, and the first-person plural *watashitachi* or we-narrator (see Tsang in this volume for a discussion of the *watashitachi* narrated work, *After Dark* (2007; *Afutādāku* [2004])). In this chapter, I focus on Murakami's main narrator type, namely the singular first-person narrator, and discuss the significance of 'I' for female character construction. Rather than analysing a few selected works in detail, my aim here is to provide an overview, a survey type of examination across a large spectrum of his works. After an introduction to the complexities of Japanese first-person personal pronouns,[3] I divide Murakami's first-person narrators into three types: *boku*, male *watashi*, and female *watashi*. As the chapter will show, the few female narrated stories we find amongst his works provide an alternative glimpse into the expression of female agency, or rather, the challenges particular to the expression of that agency. While these narrator categories are useful to gain an overview of Murakami's first-person narrator types and can reveal how their position influences the construction of female characters, the voices and visions that convey a Murakami story are often not limited to the overall narrator whose words we might not even be wise to trust. Concepts of 'voice', 'focalisation', 'participation', and 'reliability' therefore play an important part in the techniques and narrative strategies for female character construction in Murakami's worlds, as will be discussed towards the end of the chapter.

First-person pronouns and narrator types

Unlike English and many other languages, Japanese has several expressions for the first-person pronoun 'I', such as *watashi, watakushi, boku, ore, atashi, uchi, washi*. Speakers and writers of Japanese therefore have a range of choices when uttering 'I'. This is practical; depending on variables such as the speaker's and listener's age, rank, relationship, and situation, users of Japanese can choose an appropriate first-person pronoun to refer to themselves. This ability to choose, however, has consequences since each 'I', to a greater or lesser extent, is coded with specific cultural meaning and expectation. A mismatch of the selected pronoun and the perception of the user's subject position will necessarily impact how that individual or character is received. The various 'I' pronouns are often also gendered. First-person pronouns such as *boku* and the rougher *ore* are, for example, associated with the male sex and gender, and when women or female characters use these to refer to themselves, it – intentionally or unintentionally – stirs confusion about sex and gender. The most broadly applicable word for 'I' in Japanese is *watashi*. Unlike *boku* and *ore*, in mainstream Japanese, *watashi* is not strongly associated with a specific gender, although men's usage is typically limited to formal or polite speech, whereas women tend to use *watashi* in both informal and formal situations (Miyazaki 2004: 271). Still, getting it right for the specific sociolinguistic situation and position of the speaker is very important for both women and men. Yet at the same time, the possibility of using various pronouns to refer to oneself can also be an expression of creativity. In literary works, which often give readers extended glimpses into a character's use of various pronouns at different times, this becomes an opportunity for analysis, allowing readers to understand characters' shifting identities and subjectivities. Thus, because the Japanese language offers speakers and writers a choice, 'I' always comes with a coded depth that obviously is a difficult element to translate into languages devoid of such plentiful options for referring to oneself.

Within Murakami's works, male characters primarily use *boku* but sometimes also *ore* or *watashi* (see Akashi in this volume for a discussion of *boku*), whereas female characters almost consistently use *watashi*, and we therefore frequently come across three or more different first-person pronouns in the same story. Because pronouns evoke certain personality traits in the uttering characters, this array of first-person pronouns can not only function to express self-reference for different characters (in the same situation), but also self-reference for the same character in different situations. In *Dansu dansu dansu* (1988; trans. *Dance Dance Dance* [1994]), for example, the protagonist who generally uses *boku* to refer to himself, quotes his own thoughts using *ore* (Murakami 1988: 199), and in *Kishidanchō goroshi* (2017; trans. *Killing Commendatore* [2018]) the protagonist, who primarily uses *watashi*, refers several times to himself as *boku* when conversing with others.[4] Early Murakami works often show significant consciousness regarding the choice of first-person pronoun, especially when the text involves multiple narrative layers. For example, in the short story 'Shika to kamisama to Sei-Seshiria' (1981; no trans. Deer and Gods and Saint Cecilia), the *boku*-narrator sets out to write a story – which he narrates using *watashi* – for the literary magazine *Waseda bungaku*. And in *Kaze no uta o kike* (1979; trans. *Hear the Wind Sing* [1987/2015]), the narrating *boku* conveys a story made up by his friend Nezumi (Rat/Mouse) – in which the narrator calls himself *ore*.

The various 'I's in a Murakami text can also function to indicate split or double personalities. An interesting work in this respect is *Sekai no owari to hādoboirudo wandārando* (1985a; trans. *Hard-Boiled Wonderland and the End of the World* [1991]), in which chapters are alternately told by *boku* and by *watashi*. As already pointed out by other scholars, the two first-person pronouns of this novel can be understood to express two sides of the same male protagonist – his outer world (*watashi*) and his inner world (*boku*) (Katō 2006 [1996]: 200–201), and their relationship is that of alter egos (Napier 1996: 212). However, while chapters consistently are divided into *boku* and *watashi*, there are a few situations where *boku* uses *watashi* to refer to himself, such as in Chapter 13 when speaking to the two strange men who break down the steel door to *boku*'s apartment: '"*boku* no doa" to *watashi* wa itta' ['my door', I said] (1985a: 191). On the one hand, such instances express the text's clear divisions of story levels and worlds controlled by the narrating self who then becomes an observer of himself; but on the other hand, they merge the inner and outer self to create one composite protagonist.

In addition to the *watashi* and *boku* selves, it is also important to note that within the *boku*-narrated chapters, the protagonist's own shadow (*kage*) also becomes a character when disconnected from *boku* upon their entry into the town with the tall wall (which can be understood as the protagonist's inner world). The shadow consistently uses the rougher male personal pronoun, *ore*, when referring to himself in dialogue with the narrator, *boku*.[5] Expressed through the richness of personal pronouns in Japanese, the main character of the story is therefore split into a double narration (with *watashi* and *boku*), but in fact contains not just two, but three selves; *watashi*, *boku*, and *ore* (the shadow). Without alternative options for 'I', translators of *Sekai no owari to hādoboirudo wandārando* had to think creatively about how to recreate the distinctness of the selves and their worlds. As a solution, in Alfred Birnbaum's translation, *watashi*'s 'hard-boiled wonderland' chapters are written in the typical past tense, whereas *boku*'s 'end of the world' chapters are written in the present tense. Although this allows English readers to sense some sort of difference between the two narrators and their worlds, the difference between *boku* and *ore* could not be completely addressed.

First-person stories have a significant place in the modern Japanese literary tradition, most prominently as the genre of I-novels (*shishōsetsu/ watakushi shōsetsu*), which are typically told through *watashi* or the more polite *watakushi* (they share the same *kanji* character). Murakami's first-person stories are most frequently told by *boku* and only occasionally by *watashi*, and with their use of multiple first-person pronouns and layers of subjectivities, they depart from previous traditions.[6] However, even though he is particularly known for his *boku*-narrators – Saitō Minako has even called him 'the king of *boku-shōsetsu-ka* [*boku*-novel writer]' (1994: 75) – it should be noted that *boku* is not unique to Murakami. From the postwar period onwards, male writers (and later, indeed some female too) have increasingly equipped their narrators with this male-gendered pronoun. A few key examples come to mind, such as Ōe Kenzaburō (1935–) and Yasuoka Shōtarō (1920–2013, especially his story 'Garasu no kutsu' ([1951]; trans. 'Glass Slipper' [2008])). Yet, as Jay Rubin has suggested, Murakami's development of the *boku* personality as known in his works is probably 'unique':

> [T]he personality with which Murakami invested his Boku was unique. First of all it resembled his own [Murakami's], with a generous fund of curiosity and a cool, detached, bemused acceptance of the inherent strangeness of life.
>
> (Rubin 2005: 37)

But as much as Murakami's male *boku* may be characteristic to a majority of his literary worlds, it is not the only first-person narrator type we find amongst his works, and for our purpose here we can categorise Murakami's first-person narrated works into two gender specific groups: *boku*- and male *watashi*-stories on the one hand; and female *watashi*-stories on the other. These male and female types of narrators – and their respective impact on female character construction – will be discussed in the following two sections.

His construction: *Boku* and male *watashi*-narrators

The most well-known male 'I' narrator we meet in Murakami's works is without doubt *boku*. Starting with his debut novel *Kaze no uta o kike* and its follow-up *1973 nen no pinbōru* (1980b; trans. *Pinball, 1973* [1985/2015]) *boku* is the narrator of a majority of Murakami's novels and short stories including *Noruwei no mori*. In fact, a headcount across all his works of fiction reveals that a total of 83 are told by a *boku*-narrator.[7] It is no wonder, then, that many readers feel most familiar with this narrator type, with some even suggesting that the fictitious *boku* – particularly in *Noruwei no mori* – is (Yeung 2011: 3), or feels like (Rubin 2005: 150), an autobiographical character. Relying on narratological ideas where the author and narrator are always considered separate beings (Rimmon–Kenan 2002: 84–88),[8] however, allows us to understand Murakami the author as different and not interchangeable with any narrator of his novels – even in the few works where the *boku*-narrator explicitly is named Murakami.[9]

Besides the well-known *boku*-narrator, in five works Murakami's male narrators also unwound their stories using *watashi*. We come across the first example of this already in 1982 with the short story 'Sausu Bei sutoratto – Dūbī Burazāzu "Sausu Bei sutoratto" no tame no BGM' (1986a [1982]; no trans. The BGM [background music] for South Bay Strut, Doobie Brothers' 'South Bay Strut'), in which *watashi* is a private detective in South Bay city, a rough part of southern California. Because Murakami's male narrators primarily convey their stories via *boku*, the use of the pronoun *watashi* immediately sets a different tone and expectation. In fact, since female characters generally use *watashi* within his works, the appearance of a *watashi*-narrator might add qualities of uncertainty or mystery regarding sex and gender. This is the case in 'Doko de are sore ga mitsukarisō na basho de' (2005b; trans. 'Where I'm Likely to Find it' [2005]), until we are told that *watashi* in fact shaves his beard, a piece of information that encourages us to understand the narrator as male (Murakami 2005b: 100).[10] Thus, while the *boku* pronoun by default informs us that a specific narrator is male, more information is needed about *watashi*-narrators in order to determine their gender. To illustrate this, we can think of Murakami's rather experimental stories in which the protagonist or narrator is a sea lion rather than a human being. Since it is uncommon for Murakami to use sea lions as protagonists (in fact, we can find only three), these stories are likely to make us feel unsettled and unfamiliar at first. However, the *boku*-narrated story 'Ashika matsuri' (1986b [1982]; no trans. Sea Lion Festival) differs from the *watashi*-narrated work 'Gekkan "Ashika bungei"' (1991d [1982]; no trans. Monthly Magazine *Sea Lion Literary Arts*) and the third-person narrated 'Ashika' (1991e [1981]; no trans. Sea Lion) in that here the gender of the narrating creature is at least immediately marked as male.

Murakami's *boku* is frequently a rather ordinary, lonesome man with little success and aspiration within the consumerist and corporate world (see Nihei in this volume for an exception). He often lives in a Tokyo-like setting, listens to music, cooks spaghetti, and in many cases ends up in search of something – a cat, a sheep, an old friend, but very often his wife or long-lost girlfriend – and along the way he encounters women who tend to take centre stage of his story – at least for a while. By contrast to this familiarity of *boku*, Murakami's five male *watashi*-narrators seem more experimental and do not have a similar strong personality that unifies them as a type. In fact, some male *watashi*-narrators seem to resemble the circumstance and personality of the iconic *boku*; in the full-length novel *Kishidanchō goroshi*, *watashi* is, for example, a lonesome man who begins his tale after his wife asks for a divorce, and in 'Sausu Bei sutoratto – Dūbī Burazāzu Sausu Bei sutoratto no tame no BGM', it is a woman who the *watashi* private detective seeks. But while on the one hand it may not be possible to argue for an iconic male *watashi* as an alternative or opposition to Murakami's iconic *boku* (with Murakami's work so far), making no distinction between *boku* and *watashi* at all would, on the other hand, limit our acknowledgement of the richness found in Murakami's first-person male narrators. Just like *watashi* says after looking himself in the mirror in 'Ichininshō tansū' (2020a; trans. 'First Person Singular' [2021]), 'I who is not actually I' ('jissai no watashi dewanai watashi'), we should generally remain aware that 'I' across Murakami's works is not simply 'I'.

However, for our purpose here, whether a story is narrated by *watashi* or *boku*, what unites these two types of narrators is their narrating position as males. This means that the female characters of both these story types are in the first instance products of his construction; we have access to them via his tale and experience of events. As the narrating subject, the male narrator creates their beings, and their construction is therefore dependent on a highly gendered system where the male constructs the female. The women in these first-person narrated stories are subjected to the male narrator's storytelling and are potentially positioned merely as objects for his advancement. This is not to say that they do not occupy important positions – indeed it is often women who move the story forward in their function as a classic 'plot device',[11] and without them, there would be no story to tell at all. Consider for example how the narrator of *Kishidanchō goroshi* only begins his tale because his wife divorces him; without the dead Naoko and the living Midori in *Noruwei no mori*, Watanabe would have no reason to tell his tale, similar to how the narrators of *Dansu dansu dansu* and *Nejimakidori kuronikuru* (1994–1995; trans. *The Wind-Up Bird Chronicle* [1997]) would struggle to move their stories along without the disappeared Kiki and the disappearing Kumiko (for a psychoanalytic study on how women drive Murakami's stories forward, see Lac in this volume). While most of the prominent female characters we meet in Murakami's male-narrated works in various ways are plot devices, even when women only play a small explicit role within the entire story, they often function as supporting characters that seem to hold much symbolism. The woman in the Nissan Skyline in *Sekai no owari to hādoboirudo wandārando*, of whom the male narrator only sees a glimpse, is an example of this. Despite her very brief physical existence in his world, again and again *boku*'s thoughts return to the two silver bracelets on her wrist, suggesting that they contain significant symbolic meaning.

The gender criticism of *Noruwei no mori* mentioned at the beginning of this chapter is based precisely on this observation – that the female characters exist merely as objects for the development of the male protagonist. We should not dispute this fact; Naoko, Midori, and Reiko all function each in their own way to mature *boku* as he becomes an adult man (see Vilslev in this volume for a reading of *Noruwei no mori* as a classic coming-of-age novel). Various types of objectification of women are indeed seen across Murakami's male-narrated works. In his most recent novel *Kishidanchō goroshi*, for example, *watashi* makes a list of the women he has slept with after his separation from his wife, a treatment of women as consumer products that we have seen in much of Murakami's works, starting already with his first novel *Kaze no uta o kike*, where *boku* lists his sexual conquests habitually. However, while we find many instances of such utterly explicit sexualisation of female characters, the male narrator also often expresses regret about himself, including his past relationships with, and treatment of women. We see this in *Noruwei no mori* when *boku* self-critically recalls how in those days:

> I was thinking about myself. I thought about the beautiful woman walking beside me. I thought about me and her together, and then I thought about myself again. (Murakami 1987: vol. I, 8)

Similarly filled with regret, upon learning that an ex-girlfriend has committed suicide, *boku* of 'Onna no inai otokotachi' (2014b; trans. 'Men Without Women' [2017]) reveals how he believes they should have met at aged 14 under the circumstance of sharing an eraser – a highly symbolic image that might imply his wish to erase the past (that brought her to commit suicide).

Such reflections and confessions by the male narrator are clearly important for how we understand him and generally come to feel sympathy towards him despite his shortcomings. Yet, whether the male narrator explicitly sexualises women as consumer products, or whether he confesses his own regret about such treatment, the textual position of the female characters he narrates does not change; they remain objects of his storytelling. Thus, on the narratological level we can conclude that because the I-narrators are all male in these works whether narrated by *boku* or *watashi*, the female characters are constructed through the male narrator's tale as edited products of his world – a fact of which the male narrator is often painfully aware. As *boku* confesses in *Nejimakidori kuronikuru* when he is about to tell the story of Akasaka Natsumegu,

> Akasaka Natsumegu spent several months telling me her life story. Her tale was long, without end and full of countless side-tracks. Here, I am therefore producing a kind of simple (though having said that, not so short) summary of those words, but to be honest, I am not confident as to whether I am conveying the essentials of the story.
>
> (Murakami 1994–1995: vol. 3, 231)

Boku's confession of editing, while really not comprehending the story of the woman he constructs, means that we cannot help but long for the full tale as told by Akasaka Natsumegu herself and, by extension, the tales of all the other female characters whom we only reach through Murakami's male narrators. This desire to read the women's stories as narrated by themselves is often intensified, because the male storytellers frequently show signs of not understanding much about the women they narrate. In *Noruwei no mori*, for instance, *boku* cannot grasp the point when Midori explains how she will forever love a man who would just offer her another type of cake after she has thrown the strawberry shortcake – which she herself requested but no longer wants – out the window (Murakami 1987: vol. I, 140–141). Since *boku*, as the narrating subject, never understands Midori's ideas about love, it is also unclear to us what strawberry shortcake has to do with love. Thus, while *boku*- and male *watashi*-narrated works always are *his* story and the women in them by default are his constructs – as readers and as critics, we might find ourselves longing for women's stories beyond the limits of the male narrator.

A (silent) voice of her own: Female *watashi*-narrators

While stories told by the male 'I' are the most typical narrative technique found within Murakami's works, we also find a small number of *watashi*-narrated short stories – four to be exact – in which the narrator is female, typically a lonesome house-wife. These works were published over a span of three years (1989–1991), shortly fol-lowing *boku*-narrated novels such as *Noruwei no mori* (1987) and *Dansu dansu dansu* (1988), but before *Nejimakidori kuronikuru* (1994–1995). The first, and probably the best-known female *watashi*-story is 'Nemuri' (2005d [1989]; trans. 'Sleep', [1992]), which Murakami edited and republished as an independent short illustrated novel in 2010.[12] This story, about a housewife who is awake for 17 days as she literally wakes up to her routine life as wife and mother, sets the tone and themes for the other three works: 'Kanō Kureta' (1990; no trans. Kanō Kureta), titled after its narrator, Kanō Kureta, who is cursed to meet abusive men; 'Midori iro no kemono' (1991a; trans. 'The Little Green Monster' [1993]) in which the housewife narrator battles a harm-less green monster who has an ancient message; and 'Kōri otoko' (1996 [1991]; trans. 'The Ice Man' [2003]), where *watashi* marries an 'iceman' out of love, but soon finds herself surrounded by ice in the South Pole with no flights out. Because the first-per-son narrator in this group of work is not male, but female, the setup is no longer that of the male storyteller constructing the female character; here, female characters have been given a voice to construct themselves and their own worlds. Let us take a brief look at how these four women make use of their subjectivity as their own narrating 'I'.

Rebecca Suter (2008: 141–162) understands 'Nemuri' as a parody of Western feminist literature.[13] But since 'sleep' and 'awakening' are also metaphors used in feminist literature from Japan (Hansen 2016: 102–103), the story can also be read as a Japanese feminist 'wakeup' story. Like most Japanese women who are not actively engaged in organised feminist movements, however, the *watashi* of 'Nemuri' is sub-missive and keeps her awakening and rebellion to herself late at night. She neither speaks of her complaints nor disturbs anyone, and as she repeatedly points out, her husband and son do not know that she is awake and remain unaware of the changes in her body and mind. As I have previously suggested, 'Nemuri' can be read as the story of a woman trying to navigate 'contradictive femininity' (Hansen 2016: 102–106); by giving up sleep the narrator manages to navigate all her contradictive positionings as wife, mother, and individual self. However, in contrast to how a typical femi-nist awakening tale might allow the protagonist to successfully break free, *watashi*'s narration ends in an awoken nightmare because 'doing it all' is ultimately impos-sible. *Watashi* realises that she is unable to escape from her entrapment, and the story concludes abruptly with *watashi* locked inside her small car as two male shadows rock it back and forth. She knows she needs to get out, but the men shake the car violently, attempting to flip it over, at which point she drops the key, and with nothing left to do, gives up, and cries. *Watashi*'s awakening is therefore silent and secretive, and this important circumstance of her awakening only becomes possible to convey textually because it is she, and not someone else, who narrates the story, which therefore can become her own.

Although we find less explicit feminist metaphors as we do in 'Nemuri', story ownership is most clearly emphasised in 'Kanō Kureta' through the identical story title and narrator name – this is clearly the story of Kanō Kureta by Kanō Kureta. But while this suggests a strong potential for female liberation, the *watashi* of 'Kanō Kureta', like the *watashi* of 'Nemuri', attempts but still fails to free herself. Following years of hiding from male violence in the mountains with her sister Maruta, she eventually decides to venture out into the world again with the aim of becoming a famous architect (at which she succeeds). However, even though she takes strict precautions and installs electronic locks on her door, and hires a gay bodyguard (whose sexual orientation presumably eliminates him as a male threat; see Zielinska–Elliott in this volume for male–male sexuality in Murakami's works), she cannot escape her violent destiny as a woman. Even more so than in 'Nemuri', this strange story ends abruptly when we learn that *watashi*'s efforts to liberate herself are ultimately impossible:

> He was a very big man with burning green eyes. He disabled all the alarms, ripped off the locks, beat up my guard, and kicked down my door. I stood in front of him, fearless, but the man didn't care one bit. He ripped off my clothes and dropped his trousers to his knees. Then, after he forced himself on me, he slit my throat with a knife. It was a very sharp knife. He split open my throat, as if cutting through warm butter. The knife was so sharp, I almost didn't realize that my throat had been slit open.
>
> (Murakami 1990: 115)

Despite that *watashi* is the narrator throughout the story, the violent description of her throat being slit open with a knife suggests her character's death, meaning that she in effect gives voice to her own murder – an unusual narrative closure that bittersweetly underscores how *watashi* owns her own story, even in death.

As with 'Kanō Kureta', violence is also an important topic in 'Midori iro no kemono'. Like the narrator of 'Nemuri', in this story, *watashi* is a housewife who is home alone after her husband has left for work as usual. With nothing left to do she is looking out of the window when a green monster crawls up from the ground and enters her house, uninvited. Since 'women behind windows' is a frequent feminist imagery used in Japan and elsewhere to illustrate that women are suppressed in the private inside (as housewives), unable to take part in the outside social world (Hansen 2016: 99–101), it is clear from the story opening that this *watashi* also longs to break out of her housewife position. Soon after the monster arrives, *watashi* realises that it can read her mind and that the two can communicate by 'thinking' (*omou*), and this story therefore depicts the female protagonist's inner struggle between her two selves – the *watashi*-self and the monster-self – and the violence with which the monster is suppressed therefore becomes acts of self-harm (Hansen 2016: 167–171). Similar to 'Kanō Kureta', in 'Midori iro no kemono' the violent acts are therefore directed at the female body, and because *watashi* tells us that the monster 'means no harm' and has come to 'express its love', we can imagine that its undelivered 'ancient message' is of a loving – if not feminist – nature. Regardless of the message's content, however, since we can only guess what the monster wanted to say, it is clear that the narrator uses her narrative subjectivity to self-censor and suppress her own inner voice, and this is an important difference between Murakami's first two female *watashi*-narrators and this third: although the narrator of 'Nemuri' remains silent towards her husband and her outside world, and the narrator of 'Kanō Kureta' is finally silenced by the hands of a very big man, both these narrators lay bare their thoughts and desire to escape through their narrated text. By sharp contrast, the narrator of 'Midori iro no kemono' uses violence to silence her own voice, and we do not even gain access to her thoughts and desires for a different life – only small hints and perhaps the story's placement amongst Murakami's other female narrated works gives us such clues.

In 'Kōri otoko', Murakami's final female narrated work, as the recently married *watashi* flies to the South Pole with her iceman husband, it seems clear that she is en route to a lonely housewife life similar to the narrators of 'Nemuri' and 'Midori iro no kemono'. But while those *watashi*-narrators could at least look out the window, in this story the windows are so full of snow and ice that *watashi* cannot even see outside, and her entrapment with no means of return is strongly emphasised at the end when she finds herself pregnant in the South Pole, with no flights out. Although it was *watashi*'s idea to travel, as soon as the newlyweds arrive at their destination, the husband who, after all, is an iceman, fits perfectly with the new life in the cold environment. Liked by everyone, he immediately comprehends the language spoken and interacts freely with the locals. In contrast to his smooth transition, the new life alienates *watashi* who only seems to become more and more isolated as she realises that her 'husband is not my husband' (Murakami 1996 [1991]: 117), and that she cannot make herself understood: 'the language I speak, not even a single word, was understandable to them' (Murakami 1996 [1991]: 117). Despite her effort to learn the language of the South Pole, we are informed that she cannot – a rather bizarre point given that in the Free Territory of the South Pole all languages are officially recognised (though English and Russian are the most commonly spoken). Following that, we should therefore not understand *watashi*'s language barrier to be related to her (Japanese) nationality or ethnicity, but instead to her person and situation. Despite her acquired subjectivity to occupy the powerful position of narrator, as with the other three female storytellers, this *watashi* also becomes silenced on the story level because she cannot communicate with her surroundings.

Paradoxically, then, although these four narrators are bestowed with the ability to tell their own stories of individual hardship, the text is their only witness. But while this lack of an audience on the story level can seem to counter the idea that they are enriched with subjectivity to tell their own stories, their ability to tell this silence is precisely the point. We can indeed think of many *boku*-stories where women confess their personal inner life and hardship to the *boku*-narrator (and often in much more detail), who is then responsible for telling their stories to us – in *Noruwei no mori*, for example, we find Midori, Naoko, and Reiko who all have stories to tell, while in *Nejimakidori kuronikuru* we have Kanō Kureta and Akasaka Natsumegu. But unlike the *watashi*-narrators in 'Nemuri', 'Kanō Kureta', 'Midori iro no kemono' and 'Kōri otoko', these female characters have already broken their silence by telling *boku*, who then becomes our informant. In these four stories, by contrast, we are at the point where silence is *being* broken.

In terms of female character construction, what is different about this group of works is that we get direct insight into the inner struggles as women when they begin to break their silence. Equipped with their own narrating voice, these female narrators have the opportunity to act as subjects in their own worlds and tell their own stories as they themselves experience them in silence – a silence to which we otherwise rarely have access: the silence of women who never find their way out of an unhappy marriage; the silence of raped and murdered women who cannot speak up; the silence of women harming the female self in private; and the silence of women who discover that marriage is not the happy life promised by social discourse. Thus, Murakami's four female narrators convey women's struggle to break silence, a topic that has concerned global feminists for a long time. As acknowledged by the 1960s and 1970s feminist slogan 'the personal is political',[14] what appears to be women's private problems are not personal, but instead political, caused by an oppressive system, and the first step to create awareness about this system is for women to break their silence and tell their personal stories including their suffering and hardship. However, as Murakami's works show, breaking the silence may in fact be the most difficult part of the process to break free. Female *watashi*-narrated works are thus important because in these stories female characters are not constructed by the male narrative in the male world, but by the female narrative in her specific female silenced world.

Despite that we find only very few examples of this type of works and most are relatively unknown, this group of stories are vital for understanding the position of female characters within the world of Murakami. Via reappearing characters or intertextual elements, several of the works function beyond their own textual boundaries, encouraging us to reconsider existing interpretations of major Murakami novels, including *Noruwei no mori*, which I have previously argued is intertextually linked to 'Midori iro no kemono' (Hansen 2016: 167–171), and *Nejimakidori kuronikuru*, which is tied to 'Kanō Kureta' through the reappearance of its narrator Kanō Kureta and her sister Maruta as characters constructed by the novel's *boku*-narrator. Bringing attention to this group of Murakami fiction can therefore encourage us to reread and rethink some of his other works.

Voice, focalisation, and participation: Who really tells her story?

While Murakami's first-person narrated works can be divided into *boku*-stories, male *watashi*-stories, and female *watashi*-stories as we have done so far, such categorisation only acknowledges the *overall* narrator as the grammatical subject who conveys the complete story of a specific work. The narrative structure within many of Murakami's works tends to be highly complex, however, and this information is often insufficient to examine how specific female characters are constructed. When reading a *boku*-story, for instance, we will often find that in addition to the technique of the over-all *boku*-narrator, several passages of the story are conveyed by a female character, who uses *watashi* to tell her story to *boku*, thus reminding us of a female *watashi*-story. Examples of this include Reiko's tale in *Noruwei no mori* and Kanō Kureta's in *Nejimakidori kuronikuru*. Such passages influence not only how we can understand *boku's* position as narrator, but also the construction of specific female characters. Therefore, while the categorisations can help us identify *who* the overall narrator is and who thereby is responsible for the telling of the full story, this knowledge does not tell us much about what *kind* of narrator we are dealing with, nor *whose* voice or vision it is that colours the story, as narrative theorist H. Porter Abbott points out (2008: 74). In 'Ichininshō tansū', for example, after the male *watashi*-narrator looks in the mirror and sees 'I who is not actually I', he narrates a conversation with a female character who – to his own disbelief – informs him that he did something revolting to a mutual friend three years ago (Murakami 2020a: 231–232). This discrepancy in knowledge about *watashi's* past doings, it could be said, challenges the narrator's control of his own story. It is therefore often important to ask whether it is the nar-rator who tells the *entire* story; whether narrated events and characters are seen with the eyes of the narrator only or through the eyes of other characters; and whether the narrator takes part in the actions in the full story world or stands outside the told story world. Answers to such questions can potentially shift the system of who constructs whom. Three concepts are helpful in this regard: voice, focalisation, and narrator participation.[15]

Among Murakami's *boku*-stories we frequently come across passages, chapters, or entire stories in which the story seems to be carried forward by a voice or voices other than *boku's*, and this influences the construction of his narrated characters. Specifically, in *Noruwei no mori*, information about the character Naoko is given in the follow-ing forms: Naoko's letters as presented within the text (sometimes as full chapters on their own), her speech as expressed in quotation marks (direct speech), her words as reported by *boku* without quotation marks (indirect speech), and descriptions of her as heard, read, seen, or remembered by *boku*. Although *boku* is the overall narrator of the full story, the letters and directly quoted speech appear to be Naoko's own words, and Naoko seems therefore not only constructed through *boku's* narrating voice, but also through her own. The voice of the character Reiko also plays a part in the con-struction of Naoko since she recalls Naoko to *boku* in both conversations and letters. It is therefore important to explore whose voices participate in the storytelling, and necessary to ask whether a female character is equipped with a voice of her own. Based on this we must then decide how much power we attribute to the overall narrator.

In several *boku*-narrated works, *boku's* role is in part (and sometimes in full) more that of a listener than an active character and protagonist. Characteristically to these works, we find ourselves reading page after page as *boku* passively listens to female (and male) characters report events seen and experienced with their own eyes and bodies – Reiko's tale in *Noruwei no mori* and Kanō Kureta's in *Nejimakidori kuronikuru* are obvious examples. As a result, *boku* becomes distant from his told story world; the story is not only about him per se but also about the women he introduces to the narrative. Frequently, we even get the impression that it is he, as much as we, who has to make sense of their strange tales. In such works, however, *boku* never really leaves the protagonist position: the women's stories are plot devices for him as he progresses on his own journey. We see this especially clearly in *Noruwei no mori*, where *boku* looks back and remembers his youth, but also in *Nejimakidori kuronikuru* and many other *boku-* and male *watashi*-stories. Once all the presented story worlds are pieced together in our reading experience, we are in no doubt that it is *boku* who is the main character and protagonist; it is his life experiences we follow, and the other characters and their stories are encounters along his way. Admittedly, rather than riding a forward-moving train, Murakami's works sometimes make us feel more like we are dragged into a labyrinth with circles and dead ends; but this does not change the perception of whose overall story it is that we are witnessing.

Unlike works such as *Noruwei no mori* and *Nejimakidori kuronikuru* where *boku* only temporarily vacates positions of voice, focaliser, and protagonist, we can also find works where *boku* is so removed from all story worlds that he can hardly be said to be the protagonist at all. The 2005 revised version of 'Rēdāhōzen' (2005c; trans. 'Lederhosen' [1993]) is an excellent example of this. The story begins with *boku* telling the reader that his wife's friend comes to visit while his wife is out. After watching TV, the friend begins to tell him a story about how her parents divorced over a pair of German lederhosen. Within her tale, we find another tale, a detailed story about events in Germany as experienced by her mother. The short story thus contains three story worlds as illustrated in Figure 6.1.

While *boku* is the overall narrator who is responsible for conveying to us the story about two women and a divorce involving a pair of lederhosen, the majority of the work is not about him and his experiences, but about the two female characters, the wife's friend, and her mother. Throughout the story we come to know much about these two, and only very little about *boku*, suggesting that they, and not he, are the story's main characters and protagonists. Apart from the few times *boku* makes comments and provides us with his own observations, the role of focaliser is placed primarily with the two women – it is through their eyes, rather than *boku*'s, that we see story world II and III, respectively. Thus, although grammatically a first-person-narrated work, *boku*'s status as narrator in much of the story becomes almost comparable to a typical third-person narrator who is positioned outside the told story world; he does not participate in the unfolding events and furthermore is neither the protagonist nor the story's main focaliser. By the end of the story, as we very briefly return to story world I when the positions of voice and focaliser are returned exclusively to *boku*, it seems that he – as much as we the reader – does not really understand the meaning of what he heard. This becomes evident when the wife's friend asks, 'you do understand that the important thing is the lederhosen, right?', and he never answers her, but instead simply comments to the reader, 'a substitute pair of lederhosen, which I don't

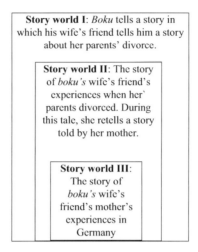

Story world I: *Boku* tells a story in which his wife's friend tells him a story about her parents' divorce.

Story world II: The story of *boku's* wife's friend's experiences when her parents divorced. During this tale, she retells a story told by her mother.

Story world III: The story of *boku's* wife's friend's mother's experiences in Germany

FIGURE 6.1 Story world layers in 'Rēdāhōzen'

even think the father ever got' (Murakami 2005c: 180). As the story concludes, *boku* seems unable to understand what he heard and as a result, he and the two women therefore remain (story)worlds apart.

'Rēdāhōzen' was first published in *Kaiten mokuba no detto hīto* in 1985 (1985e; no trans. Dead Heat on a Merry-Go-Round) before it was translated with significant changes and included in the collection *The Elephant Vanishes* in 1993; based on the translation, the short story was then republished and included in *Zō no shōmetsu* in 2005.[16] Remarkably, my discussion here of 'Rēdāhōzen' applies to the 2005 version only; the changes between the original 1985 version and the newer one have major implications for the position of protagonist, voice, and focaliser. Not only does *boku* generally provide more comments throughout the original version, he also begins his narration with a rather long introduction that reveals more about himself and why he tells this story (i.e. he has never told such a story before and wants to try just once). While *boku* is the listener to the women's tales about lederhosen and divorce in both versions, in the 1985 version he is more clearly a participating character in the story himself and cannot as easily be removed from the powerful positions of protagonist, voice, and focaliser. The ending also reflects this difference, since the 1985 version concludes with *boku* actually agreeing with the daughter – that the point of the story *is* the lederhosen (Murakami 1985c: 33). Unlike the later 2005 version, this suggests that *boku* understands why the lederhosen are significant; why the mother came to want a divorce after witnessing a pair being made in Germany; and why the daughter understood her. In this earlier version, it is only us who are left to wonder: Why would a Japanese mother and wife decide to divorce after seeing three German men chatting away in a language she does not comprehend as they produce a pair of lederhosen for her husband? And why would her daughter understand and approve of her decision to divorce only after hearing her story about the lederhosen?

We shall consider the significance of the lederhosen in 'Rēdāhōzen' on a different occasion; the important point here is that, like the voice(s), the focaliser(s) of a story impacts the construction of specific female characters – even in I-narrated works. In *boku*-stories, while the male 'I' is responsible for narrating the story, the vision and voice that bring the story's events and characters to him are not necessarily his, but can be hers or someone else's entirely. The different feelings we are left with from the two versions of 'Rēdāhōzen' can be explained by how involved *boku* is with his story. The less he occupies the roles of voice, focaliser, and protagonist, the less he participates in the tale. Thus, the extent to which the narrator participates in the narrated story and enters the story worlds of his narrated characters cannot always simply be answered by acknowledging whether the overall narrator tells the story in the first or third person; sometimes a first-person narrator can be absent as a character in the told story world (Abbott 2008: 75), as is the case in two of the three story worlds in 'Rēdāhōzen'.

While overall narrators are powerful agents who are responsible for conveying the full story, their level of power may depend on whether they, or someone else, occupy the positions of voice and focaliser, and the degree of their involvement in the story they tell. The relationship between these textual positions and the overall narrator is especially important to consider for any examination of female character construction, as it potentially influences our perception of 'her' – is she just an object of his construction, or a subject–participant in her own construction? Scholars of literature have approached this differently, with some identifying narrating power according to the narrator's participation in the story (Rimmon–Kenan 2002: 97–100). However, there are other questions to be considered, such as whether quotations within a narrative belong to the narrator or to the quoted character (Abbott 2008: 69–70). Depending on how we answer this question, Naoko's letters and her direct speech passages in *Noruwei no mori*, for example, can be viewed very differently: either as truly hers or as *boku*'s construction, and therefore no different from her indirect speech passages and the purely descriptive information about her as voiced by him.

In my view, although *boku* is not the protagonist, voice, or focaliser at all times in, for example, 'Rēdāhōzen' or *Noruwei no mori*, the accounts of events and characters we are presented in both these stories are given to us as experienced, heard, remembered, or imagined by him. As the narrating subject *boku* creates and edits the female characters' beings, their words, and their actions. The many letters *boku* receives from Naoko and Reiko in *Noruwei no mori* are conveyed to us by him – we have to trust him to deliver these unedited. Even in *Supūtoniku no koibito* (1999; trans. *Sputnik Sweetheart* [2001]) – a novel which can be said to present female characters' thinking and consciousness in a way we do not typically see in Murakami's *boku*-works and which therefore can seem to be 'presented by an all-knowing narrator who is omnipresent in the world of the story' (Yeung 2011: 7–8) – it is still *boku* who is the overall narrator. Therefore, despite the fact that the explicit level of power is seemingly different in different stories (and parts of stories) – and this certainly should form part of our analysis of specific female characters – the overall narrator inhabits the most powerful position of all. Just as *boku* is the link that joins us to the female characters we encounter in *boku*-stories, so is *watashi* our link in female *watashi*-stories. Murakami narrators are often aware, or become aware, of their own power, as we are reminded in *Supūtoniku no koibito* when *boku* says:

> Of course, this is Sumire's story; not mine. Nevertheless, the person called Sumire is told as seen through my eyes.
>
> (Murakami 1999: 80)

Acknowledging the overall narrator's powerful position means that the four short female *watashi*-stories we find among Murakami's works are vital to examine, since only through these stories can we gain access to female characters who are constructed, not by male or gender-ambiguous narrators, but by the female narrating characters themselves.

It's my story and I'll lie if I want to: Trust and reliability

As Abbott (2008: 68) and Rimmon–Kenan (2002: 97–100) point out, the reliability of narrators when telling their stories is an important issue for narrative studies. We have already established how Naoko's direct speech and letters as well as her indirect speech and the purely descriptive information given about her are all constructed by her narrator (*boku*), but whether we accept his quotations of her words and his descriptions of her person as adequate, depends on how much we feel we can trust him as narrator. While Murakami's I-narrators often appear brutally honest as they confess their own mediocrity, sense of loss and desire, their tales are usually also told under a number of circumstances that, logically at least, significantly decrease their level of reliability. Some of the most recurring conditions are: time lapse, forgetfulness, intoxication, sleep (or lack thereof), death, and encounter with the fantastic. Let us look at some examples.

Many of Murakami's works are stories that convey something about the protagonist's past. As others have pointed out, we see a temporal difference between the time of narration and the narrated events (Yeung 2011: 1). More often than not, we are informed of the rather precise amount of time that has passed since the occurrence of the narrated incidents. In *Dansu dansu dansu* (1988: vol. I, 6–7) *boku* states for instance: 'When was that? Four years ago. No, four and a half to be exact. At the time I was still only in my twenties'. The narrator may also provide historical details such as his own age then and now, or how much time has passed since a historical event – for example the death of John Lennon in 'Pan'ya shūgeki' (1991f [1981]; no trans. The Bakery Attack). Such easy-to-use information allows us to calculate the elapsed time rather precisely.[17] The longer the time span between the told event and its occurrence, the more the narrator's reliability decreases, since we – and often also the narrators themselves – begin to question whether they actually remember the details accurately. Although fiction generally includes an element of disbelief, in a story like *Noruwei no mori*, which is the result of *boku*'s experiences in the late 1960s as remembered by him in the late 1980s, we might be wise to wonder whether *boku*'s recollections from almost 20 years ago are accurate – especially since his motivation for telling the story in the first place is that he is beginning to forget Naoko, despite his promise to always remember (Murakami 1987: vol. I, 10, 17).

Forgetfulness is often conveniently a part of the Murakami first-person narrators' repertoire; while they remember the most bizarre minute details, they tend to forget major elements. Male narrators often cannot remember women's names; in *Hitsuji o meguru bōken* (1982; trans. *A Wild Sheep Chase* [1989]), for instance, *boku* cannot remember the name of the girl he and everyone else used to sleep with:

> I completely forgot her name.
> I could perhaps pull out the obituary clipping one more time and remind my-self once more, but the name doesn't matter now. I completely forgot her name. That's all there is to it.
>
> (Murakami 1982: 14)

When *boku* and his friends referred to her, they simply used to call her 'the girl who slept with everyone', which then becomes her defining characteristic as *boku* seals her fate by adding that 'that is her name'. In this way the narrator's lack of memory has a major impact on the construction of this female character. Through *boku*'s forget-fulness, she loses the possibility of a personal identity and agency; her new 'name' de-humanises her and reduces her to a sexual object for *boku* and his friends. While confessions of having forgotten something can come across as earnest, even poten-tially increasing a narrator's reliability, the forgetfulness we see in Murakami's narra-tors often appears to be highly selective, suggesting that it is a convenient excuse that allows them to avoid disclosing select information.

While Murakami's I-narrators may or may not intentionally forget elements of their story, it is certain that they repeatedly narrate events and encounters they expe-rienced under the influence of alcohol, and sometimes also other intoxicating sub-stances – as in the short story 'Naya o yaku' (1984 [1983]; trans. 'Barn Burning' [1993]), where *boku* and a male character who likes to burn barns smoke marijuana. These intoxicated narrators are particularly prominent in early works; if it were pos-sible to measure the alcohol content in *boku*'s blood as he drinks at J's bar throughout the Rat trilogy (i.e. *Kaze no uta o kike* [1979]; *1973 nen no pinbōru* [1980b]; *Hitsuji o meguru bōken* [1982]), we would surely find that an average person in his place would already have passed out. It is therefore relevant to question whether we can trust such a storyteller. Indeed, *boku* first meets his friend Nezumi when they wake up together in a car crash; how they got into the car, neither of them remembers (Murakami 1979: 18).

Furthermore, on several occasions *boku*'s acquaintances and girlfriends become unconscious from drinking, and the reliability of the narrator becomes not only an issue for us, but also for the female character whom his narrative constructs. In *Kaze no uta o kike*, *boku*'s relationship with the four-fingered girl (whose name this *boku* also cannot remember) begins after he finds her passed out on the bathroom floor of

J's bar. Waking up naked with *boku* in her apartment, she refuses to believe that he did not take advantage of her sexually while she was drunk. However, upon saying that she cannot believe his explanations, *boku* simply replies, 'you have no choice':

> 'Hey, can you prove you really didn't do anything?'
> 'Go ahead and check for yourself'.
> 'How could I do that?' It was as if she was seriously pissed off.
> 'I give you my word'.
> 'I can't trust you'.
> 'You have no choice but to trust me' [*shinjiru shikanai*].
> After I said this, an unpleasant feeling hit me [*iya na kimochi ni natta*].
>
> (Murakami 1979: 50–51)

Her accusations continue until more than halfway through the novel when she finally decides to trust *boku* for reasons he declines to hear, and to which we therefore also are denied access (1979: 113–114). However, despite being told that the four-fingered girl eventually trusts her own narrator, we may still be filled with doubt – why then was *boku* also naked when he woke up before her in her apartment (1979: 36)? And why did it take him ten seconds to think about how he 'could say it in a way that would persuade her' (1979: 39)? Is he lying, or was he perhaps also so drunk that he himself cannot remember? As with many of the intoxicated narrators, this doubt seems to linger without ever being affirmed.

Intoxicated I-narrators are not a monopoly of male storytellers; one of the female *watashi*-narrators also reports events that occur while inebriated. In 'Nemuri' (2005d [1989]) where *watashi* is awake for an astonishing 17 days, the narrator spends her awakened nights – and later her days too – drinking brandy while reading books and eating chocolate. In this short story, however, it is not only the intake of alcohol that undermines the narrator's reliability. Since insomnia and lack of sleep usually make a person lightheaded, *watashi*'s wakefulness is also a factor that potentially lowers our trust in her. Far from experiencing the world in a haze as we might expect, *watashi* claims that her time awake only makes everything 'clearer than usual' (1989: 133). Yet, although this information might lower her reliability as a narrator, it is clear that here reality is not concerned with objective scientific truth. Underscored by the fact that *watashi*'s time awake is much longer than the 11-day real world record of sleeplessness, this story is instead a record of the personal developments taking place within the narrator's mind. As she is keen to point out, her condition is not 'insomnia' [*fuminshō*], but 'awakening' [*kakusei*], suggesting further that her story can be read as a tale of self-discovery or feminist awakening.

Insofar as wakefulness is one sleep-related circumstance that may affect a narrator's reliability, so are the acts of putting to sleep, being asleep, and sleepiness. The short story 'Nemui' (1983 [1981]; no trans. Sleepy) is a humorous example of this.

Struggling to stay awake, *boku* is so sleepy that he drops the soup spoon with a loud sound while attending a wedding reception. Although his girlfriend pleads with him to stay awake for her sake, and he indeed makes much effort to do so by spelling difficult English words, he is constantly on the verge of falling asleep until the very end of the story when the reception ends and he suddenly has the energy to go swimming, suggesting of course that his sleepiness is not physical, but mental, connected somehow to the wedding situation – the ultimate commitment made between two individuals. Ironically, although the entire narrative of 'Nemui' is about the narrator's own sleepiness at a wedding reception, this sleepiness as a circumstance for creating the narrative in the first place is exactly what makes *boku* less trustworthy: we cannot be sure whether *boku*'s efforts to stay awake actually are successful or whether he at times in fact doses off (and for how long), for example, when he drops the spoon. Since the story is narrated in the past tense, it is also uncertain whether *boku*'s recollections are based on what actually happened while he was in a hazy state of sleepiness or constructed by him later.

However, in addition to being a threat to reliability, sleep in various forms is often a much more serious matter, which potentially influences the construction of characters and the entire story. As we have already seen in Murakami's debut novel in the initial encounter between *boku* and the drunken four-fingered girl, it often seems that Murakami's narrators conveniently put their witnesses to sleep. We see this for instance in 'Naya o yaku' with the girl who later goes missing, and in *Nejimakidori kuronikuru* with *boku*'s wife, Kumiko, before she disappears. From the perspective of reliability, the narrative effect of putting a character to sleep is that she, as a witness, is both silenced and blinded; the voice and focalisation of the narrated scene are placed solely with the narrator. We might be plenty suspicious, but because the text offers no other information, we are made to feel like the four-fingered girl to whom *boku* says 'you have no choice but to trust me' when she declares her disbelief. In other words, *boku*'s line may also be seen as a comment on the relationship between the narrator and the reader – when he tells the girl 'I give you my word', all we are given, too, are *his* words. Even *boku* himself seems to feel weary about this, evident from his comment: 'After I said this, an unpleasant feeling hit me'. But despite that we know of his unpleasant feeling from reading the story (while the girl does not), and our suspicions (*something* must have happened while she was asleep – why else would he need to 'say it in a way that would persuade her') therefore may be grounded further, we essentially know nothing more, and are thus placed in the same position as her.

Murakami's narrators do not only induce others to sleep, they frequently also narrate their own sleep, dreams, and disorientation from sleep after they wake up not knowing what time or day it is, as we see in *Sekai no owari to hādoboirudo wandārando* (Murakami 1985a: 98) and *Kishidanchō goroshi* (Murakami 2017: vol. II, 56). These departures from the conscious world are also significant obstacles to reliability that impact the construction of characters and story worlds. In *Noruwei no mori*, for example, *boku* is in doubt about whether he is asleep or awake when Naoko appears at his bedside, showing her naked body (Murakami 1987: vol. I, 204). This uncertainty means that we do not know whether the narrated image of Naoko's naked body results from Naoko's acts as a narrated subject who undresses herself – and thereby actively seems to participate in the story – or whether it results from her objectification in *boku*'s dream where he then is the undressing subject. In this example, sleep and the world of dreams make the narrator's tale unreliable even to himself.

Including countless I-narrated stories, throughout Murakami's works we find many dead or dying women, and so his narrators do not just put women to sleep; they also kill them. We learn about female characters' suicide and murders from numerous *boku*-narrators, including, for example, *Noruwei no mori*, *Dansu dansu dansu*, and 'Onna no inai otokotachi'. By narrating the death of these women, the narrator ultimately silences and removes the female characters from the story in a more powerful manner than when they are just put to sleep. As he disables them entirely from their own construction, we are left with only the narrator's perspective. This becomes problematic especially in stories where the narrator is highly involved with the cause of death. In *Kishidanchō goroshi*, the male *watashi*-narrator returns again and again to his fragmented memories of strangling a woman who apparently begged him to do so during some kind of sexual game, and it seems he gradually begins to realise the traumatic fact that he himself may have killed her, much in a similar way to how Tazaki Tsukuru fears that he may have killed and raped Shiro in *Shikisai o motanai Tazaki Tsukuru to, kare no junrei no toshi* (2013; trans. *Colorless Tsukuru Tazaki and His Years of Pilgrimage* [2014]). However, whereas Tazaki Tsukuru is not the narrator (the novel is written in the third person but with Tsukuru as the focaliser), *watashi* in *Kishidanchō goroshi* is indeed the overall narrator, and this means we are in effect given a confession of murder rather than simply a narration of death.

However, women are not only silenced to death by the male narrating hand. As we have seen in 'Kanō Kureta', the female *watashi*-narrator gives voice to her own murder. This immediately becomes a reliability issue, because how can we understand a narrator who narrates her own death? Is her narrative a lie – is her neck not slit after all – or is the narrator not *the* narrator? Even if we accept the fantastic premise that narrators can still narrate posthumously, the factors that contribute to *watashi*'s death nevertheless become an important consideration for determining her agency. While her character is murdered by a big man with a knife, textually she commits suicide by silencing herself as narrator and thereby maintains narrating subjectivity. But the dilemma travels beyond the short story itself. As previously observed, Murakami's novels often have direct links to previous short stories (Katō 2020), and because the narrator of 'Kanō Kureta' reappears as a character in *Nejimakidori kuronikuru*, we also have to wonder whether she is already dead when *boku* meets her in his search for the cat and Kumiko. With clues from the female *watashi*-narrator of the short story, we can perhaps better understand the mysterious Kanō Kureta in the *boku*-narrated novel who 'preserves an appearance from the early 1960s' (Murakami 1994–1995: vol. 1, 153). If we trust the narrator of the short story 'Kanō Kureta', then the character Kanō Kureta is indeed stuck in time as a ghostly being, suggesting that we read her character in the novel as yet another fantastic Murakami element.

Distinctive among Murakami's full-length novels, *Noruwei no mori* does not contain explicit fantastic elements. However, it is the sense that another world exists below the surface of the conscious reality – an underworld reached through sleep, dreams, and spirituality (Strecher 2020) – that contributes to the unreliability of the narrator. Sometimes fantastic elements are more subtly included in the story world of a specific work. For example, as already pointed out, the lack of sleep in 'Nemuri' is a fantastic element due to its impossible duration. Our suspicion towards the narrator of 'Nemuri' stems from this fact; if we apply knowledge from the factual real world, *watashi* is either lying, dreaming, or hallucinating. However, if we accuse narrators of lying each time we come across a fantastic element in Murakami's works, we would have to call most of them liars, which would go against the premise for fiction that, by definition, means that the story is *made up*.

As Humne reminds us (1984: 21), in order to accept the fantastic in the first place, we have to be willing to 'depart from consensus reality' as we know it, and admit things we usually would not to be true. In other words, acceptance of a new fantastic reality or world is contingent on the prerequisite that we first know how to question the reliability of our existing world. In addition to these spiritual other worlds and subtle fantastic elements, we have for example accepted that in specific Murakami works cats can in fact speak (as in *Umibe no Kafuka* [2002], trans. *Kafka on the Shore* [2005]) and green monsters can show up knocking on doors of ordinary housewives (as in 'Midori iro no kemono'). The premise for a narrative set in a fantastic world is that our knowledge from the real world is not necessarily applicable as a guide when we judge whether the narrator is telling the truth. Yet, while it is necessary to acknowledge this premise of the fantastic, it is also important to point out that in Murakami's works narrators are themselves frequently perplexed by their own encounter with the fantastic, suggesting that as much as a specific element may be fantastic to us readers, it is also fantastic and not part of consensus reality in the story world in which it occurs. In 'Nemuri', for example, *watashi* is at first perplexed by her own awoken state, and in *Dansu dansu dansu*, *boku* cannot comprehend what he experiences in the elevator and in the strange room with the human skeletons. It is of course because we can find such magical happenings in an otherwise realistic setting that many scholars place Murakami's worlds within 'magic realism' (Strecher 1999: 267).

Logically, time lapse, forgetfulness, intoxication, sleep, and death as well as encounter with the fantastic are some examples of circumstances that should make us question the reliability of Murakami's narrators. But whether or not we decide to trust *boku* as the narrator of, for example, *Noruwei no mori*, his narration about Naoko gives us insight into what Naoko said and how she looked as he experienced her, or – and this is just as important to acknowledge – how he wanted her to speak and look. This information is still important for our perception of her because the text often gives us nothing else. While narrator reliability is an important issue for our examination of female characters, my position is that regardless of whether narrators deliberately forget and regardless of whether they were drunk or asleep and so forth, the story is still theirs. A *boku*-story is *boku*'s story and just as he can edit it when he sees the need, he can also lie if he wants to. And that he does, as he admits in *Kaze no uta o kike*:

'Do you love me?'
'Of course.'
'Do you want to marry?'
'Right at this moment?'
'At some point … in the future.'
'Of course, I want to marry.'
'But until I asked you, not once have you said that.'
'I forgot to say.'
'… How many children do you want?'
'Three.'
'Boys? Girls?'
'Two girls and a boy.'
She took a swallow of coffee to wash down the rest of the bread, and looked me straight in the face.
'LIAR!' she said.
But she was wrong. I had lied only once.

(Murakami 1979: 165–166)

Conclusion: Acknowledging narrator limitation

This chapter has explored Murakami's first-person narrators and discussed their impact on the construction of his female characters. Among his works we find two types of male first-person narrators, *boku* and *watashi*, and the female first-person narrator, *watashi*. These three categories are to some degree fluid, since within a first-person narrator type, we can find examples of narrators who are involved with the story they tell to different extents. In *Supūtoniku no koibito*, *boku* is almost as powerful as an omniscient narrator who constructs even the women's thoughts and feelings, whereas in works such as 'Rēdāhōzen' and parts of *Noruwei no mori* and *Nejimakidori kuronikuru*, he partly vacates his positions of voice and focaliser and instead simply listens to women, who then seem to become *watashi*-narrators themselves. It matters whether the male narrator steps aside and lets a female character speak for herself, or whether he 'monitors' her 'as she becomes a character in the realization of his fantasy to possess her' (Yamada 2009: 8) as has been argued about *boku* in *Supūtoniku no koibito*. Potentially, it marks the difference between whether we can understand her to have been allowed to have a voice and vision of her own and thus to participate in her own construction, or whether she has not been equipped with these tools.

However, this matters only within the story world, not on the overall narratological level. Even when the overall narrator's role within the story world appear to be merely that of listeners, they are still the ones who reveal to us the story and its various story worlds, since we must assume that it is them who make voices and focalisers available to us through their retelling, quoting, or imagining. No matter how little *boku* or the male *watashi*-narrators participate in their narrated story world, ultimately this does not change much for the construction of female characters, since the position of *boku* and male *watashi* as overall narrators means that it is the male who constructs the female. It is from this fact that my initial scepticism towards feminist critiques of *Noruwei no mori* began: although the three female characters, Naoko, Midori, and Reiko, are central to the story and we seem to learn more about these three women than we do about *boku* himself, it is not theirs, but *his* story. *Boku* is the subject and the women he meets are the objects whom he desires and seeks – but generally fails – to understand. The point is that regardless of whether Naoko is quoted directly or simply described, whether or not *boku* occupies the position of protagonist, voice, and focaliser, he, as the overall narrator, still remains in control of the full narrative. Our access to the voices and focalisers participating in the construction of specific female characters is always filtered by him – that is the basic premise of the novel's composition as a first-person-narrated work.

Therefore, despite it being necessary to acknowledge that the explicit level of the narrator's power is possibly different in different stories (and parts of stories), it is the overall narrator who inhabits the most powerful position of all. They choose what to tell, what to silence, and what to make up; and Murakami's narrators are often aware of this power, as the young *boku* in *Umibe no Kafuka* realises when, to the astonishment of his new acquaintance Sakura (who could be his sister), he asks her permission to imagine her naked:

> She smiled as if amused. 'I don't get it. Why not just keep quiet about it and imagine whatever you like? You don't need my permission for every single thing. I won't know what you're imagining anyway'. But she was wrong. What I imagine is probably very important for this world.
>
> (Murakami 2002: vol. I, 229)

This awareness of power is why the four female *watashi*-stories are so important within Murakami's worlds: it is the only textual space where female characters are positioned so that they can fully construct themselves. The short story 'Kanō Kureta', where Kanō Kureta herself occupies not only positions of voice and focaliser but also acts as overall narrator, is different from Kanō Kureta's story in *Nejimakidori kuronikuru* where *boku* is the overall narrator despite the passive listening position he has assumed during her tale. This is because in *Nejimakidori kuronikuru* Kanō Kureta is a plot device that drives *boku*'s tale forward, while in 'Kanō Kureta' Kanō Kureta is herself the narrator in search of plot devices, which in this story are the numerous violent men she encounters. While in both stories Kanō Kureta is a voice for victims of men's violence against women, it is due to the difference in her narratological position that we can read her in the short story as a (paradoxically) empowered subject, whereas in the novel she becomes a mysterious object.

However, although the four *watashi*-stories clearly are important to examine because they offer a different type of female character construction than what we can observe in all other Murakami works, it is necessary to underscore that they do not tell a truth about Murakami's women that we cannot otherwise find. As this chapter has shown, although Murakami's narrators seem brutally honest, a number of reoccurring issues lower the overall narrators' (whether male or female) reliability asking us to always question whether we can trust them at all. These include time lapse, forgetfulness, intoxication, sleep (and lack thereof), death, and encounters with the fantastic. Yet, whether or not we decide to trust the narrator, their narratives give us clues about female character construction; in *Noruwei no mori*, *boku*'s descriptions may not give us an objective truth, but instead offer insight into what *he* experienced or what *he* imagined Naoko said and looked, and this is still what constructs her as a character. To criticise that female characters in works such as *Noruwei no mori* are mere objects for the male subjects is a refusal to read the story on its narratological terms, and thus becomes a criticism of the novel's narrator type. Said differently, such criticism is a wish for a completely different story and narrator.

I contend that we will come to see a different picture of Murakami's female characters if we begin our analysis by acknowledging the limitations of their narrators – Naoko, Midori, and Reiko, for example, can never tell their own stories, and this is not the premise with which they were constructed. While the silent female *watashi*-narrators may seem to have less subjectivity than many of Murakami's other outspoken female characters such as Midori in *Noruwei no mori*, it is in fact the other way round: through their position as narrators, they are empowered to construct themselves and to tell their own stories. However, their narratological privilege is limited by their position as women in each of their respective worlds. This is what Murakami shows so well in these four works.

Notes

1 Unless otherwise stated, all translations from the Japanese are the author's own and might not correspond to the official translation.

2 Stories without women – not even a single mention – include, 'Kaitsuburi' (1986c [1981]; trans. 'Dabchick' [2006]); 'Odamaki zake no yoru' (1991c [1982]; no trans. The Evening of Columbine Sake); Haineken bīru no akikan o fumu zō ni tsuite no tanbun (1991b [1985]; no trans. A Short Piece About an Elephant that Steps on an Empty Heineken Beer Can).

3 Some scholars (e.g. Kanaya 2002) argue that the Japanese language is 'pronoun-less'. It is irrelevant for this chapter to enter this disciplinary discussion, and I rely generally on linguist Ishiyama Osamu, who considers Japanese pronouns to come from two major sources, lexical nouns and spatial expressions such as demonstratives (2008: xv).

4 In these incidences, however, it is noteworthy that the narrator of *Kishidanchō goroshi* uses *boku* written in *hiragana* (e.g. see Murakami 2017: vol. 1, 121), and not in *kanji* as is usually the case in Murakami's works, suggesting perhaps that his character has several voice levels.

5 In the earlier work 'Machi to, sono futashika na kabe' (1980a; no trans. The Town and its Uncertain Wall), which is strongly related to *Sekai no owari to hādoboirudo wandārando*, the shadow character also uses *ore*.

6 Scholars of Japanese literature have debated Japanese I-novels (*shishōsetsu/watakushi shōsetsu*), especially that of the modern period, for a long time. Interested readers should consult works such as Fowler (1988), Karatani (1993), Hijiya–Kirschnereit (1996), and Suzuki (1996). In this chapter I do not explore Murakami's I-narrators in relation to the concept of the I-novel.

7 This number includes both stories in which *boku* is written in *kanji* and in *hiragana* – *Supūtoniku no koibito* (1999; trans. *Sputnik Sweetheart* [2001]) and 'Kurīmu' (2018; trans. 'Cream' [2019]) are, for example, narrated by a hiragana-written *boku* – as well as a few works were the narrator is difficult to determine including, for instance, the short story 'Hantingu naifu' (1985d [1984]; trans. 'Hunting Knife' [2006]) which begins with a plural first-person narrator, *ware-ware* (we) who then turns into *boku*.

8 The author, implied author, and the narrator are different and not interchangeable. We cannot rely on the narrator to act as a direct, or indirect, representative of the implied author, who is 'often far superior in intelligence and moral standards to the actual men and women who are the real author' (Rimmon–Kenan 2002: 84–88).

9 *Boku* is named Murakami in: 'Amayadori' (1985g [1983]; no trans. Shelter); 'Ima wa naki ōjo no tame no' (1985e [1984]; no trans. For the Sake of the Now Dead Princess); 'Ōto 1979' (1985f [1984]; trans. 'Nausea 1979' [2006]); 'Gūzen no tabibito' (2005a; trans. 'Chance Traveler' [2006]); 'Yakuruto Suwārozu shishū' (2020b [2019]; trans. 'The Yakult Swallows Poetry Collection' [2021]).

10 Assigning characters with gender is a complex process that I will not discuss here. See Hansen (2016: 9–12) for my discussion of how characters become gendered beings.

11 For more on 'plot device' see Pfeil (1990: 267).

12 The difference between the 1989 and the 2010 versions was expressed through a subtle title change, from 眠り to ねむり, both pronounced 'nemuri' but with the stem of the word ('nemu') altered from *kanji* to *hiragana* (Murakami 2010: 90–93).

13 Suter points to works such as Charlotte Perkins Gilman's 'The Yellow Wallpaper' from 1892 and in particular Kate Chopin's *The Awakening* from 1899.

14 'The personal is political' is from an essay by American Carol Hanish used by 1960s and 1970s feminists. Hanish, however, denounced authorship of the slogan, and the phrase has since been used by feminist thinkers and activists worldwide, including Japan.

15 See voice and focalisation as concepts in narrative discourse in Genette (1983 [1980]: 161–268). Focalisation was developed by literary theorist Gérard Genette as a means to identify the eyes or lens through which we see a narrative. The concept has since then been rethought by several literary theorists. We can think of the focaliser as the agent that sees, and the focalised as the object being seen (Rimmon–Kenan 2002: 73) but including the one who experiences the told in a broader sense; the focaliser may be identical to the narrator and the voice of the narrative, but can also be different.

16 See Hansen and Tsang (2020) for a discussion of 'backselling' Murakami's works to Japanese readers.

17 The often very precise historical facts provided in Murakami's works may, however, not always correspond to the series of events we know from history books, creating instead confusion about time and setting. The two bakery attack stories are an example of this (Hansen and Tsang 2020: 8).

References

Abbott, H. P. 2008. *The Cambridge introduction to narrative*. Cambridge: Cambridge University Press.

Chopin, K. 1899. *The Awakening*. New York: H. S. Stone & Co.

Fowler, E. 1988. *The rhetoric of confession: Shishōsetsu in early twentieth-century Japanese fiction*. Berkeley and Los Angeles: University of California Press.

Genette, G. 1983 [1980]. *Narrative discourse: An essay in method*. Ithaca and New York: Cornell University Press.

Gilman, C. P. 2009 [1892]. *The Yellow Wallpaper*. Cedar Lake: Feather Lake Press.

Hansen, G. M. 2010. Murakami Haruki's female narratives: Ignored works show awareness of women's issues. *Japan Studies Association Journal* 8: 229–238.

———— 2016. *Femininity, self-harm and eating disorders in Japan: Navigating contradiction in narrative and visual culture*. London and New York: Routledge.

———— 2017. Not just asleep, dead or muted: Images of women in Murakami Haruki. *The Japan Society Proceedings* 154: 122–137.

Hansen, G. M. and Tsang M. 2020. Politics in/of transmediality in Murakami Haruki's bakery attack stories. *Japan Forum* 32 (3): 404–431.

Hijiya–Kirschnereit, I. 1996. *Rituals of self-revelation: Shishōsetsu as literary genre and socio-cultural phenomenon*. Cambridge and London: Harvard University Press.

Humne, K. 1984. *Fantasy and mimesis: Responses to reality in Western literature*. New York: Methuen.

Ishihara C. 2007. *Nazo toki Murakami Haruki*. Tokyo: Kōbunsha Shinsho.

Ishiyama O. 2008. *Diachronic perspectives on personal pronouns in Japanese*. PhD dissertation, State University of New York at Buffalo.

Kanaya T. 2002. *Nihongo ni shugo wa iranai*. Tokyo: Kōdansha.

Karatani K. 1993. *Origin of modern Japanese literature*. Durham and London: Duke University Press.

Katō N. 2006 [1996]. *Murakami Haruki ierōpēji*. Tokyo: Gentōsha Bunko.

———— 2020. The problem of *tatemashi* in Murakami Haruki's work: Comparing *The Wind-Up Bird Chronicle* and *1Q84*. *Japan Forum* 32 (3): 318–337.

Kawakami M. and Murakami H. 2017. *Mimizuku wa kōkon ni tobitatsu*. Tokyo: Shinchōsha.

Miyazaki A. 2004. Japanese junior high school girls' and boys' first-person pronoun use and their social world. *In:* Okamoto S. and J. S. Shibamoto Smith, eds. *Japanese language, gender and ideology: Cultural models and real people*. New York: Oxford University Press, 256–274.

Murakami H. 1979. *Kaze no uta o kike*. Tokyo: Kōdansha.

———— 1980a. Machi to, sono futashika na kabe. *Bungakukai* 9: 46–99.

———— 1980b. *1973 nen no pinbōru*. Tokyo: Kōdansha.

———— 1981. Shika to kamisama to Sei-Seshiria. *Waseda bungaku* 6: 6–10.

———— 1982. *Hitsuji o meguru bōken*. Tokyo: Kōdansha.

———— 1983 [1981]. Nemui. *In: Kangarū biyori*. Tokyo: Heibonsha, 27–36.

———— 1984 [1983]. Naya o yaku. *In: Hotaru; naya o yaku; sono hoka no tanpen*. Tokyo: Shinchōsha, 49–80.

———— 1985a. *Sekai no owari to hādoboirudo wandārando*. Tokyo: Shinchōsha.

———— 1985b. Rēdāhōzen. *In: Kaitenmokuba no detto hīto*. Tokyo: Kōdansha, 15–33.

———— 1985c. *Kaitenmokuba no detto hīto*. Tokyo: Kōdansha.

———— 1985d [1984]. Hantingu naifu. *In: Kaitenmokuba no detto hīto*. Tokyo: Kōdansha, 165–196.

———— 1985e [1984]. Ima wa naki ōjo no tame no. *In: Kaitenmokuba no detto hīto*. Tokyo: Kōdansha, 79–100.

———— 1985f [1984]. Ōto 1979. *In: Kaitenmokuba no detto hīto.* Tokyo: Kōdansha, 101–121.

———— 1985g [1983]. Amayadori. *In: Kaitenmokuba no detto hīto.* Tokyo: Kōdansha, 123–144.

———— 1986a [1982]. Sausu Bei sutorattō – Dūbī Burazāzu 'sausubei sutoratto' no tame no BGM. *In: Kangarū hiyori.* Tokyo: Heibonsha, 177–184.

———— 1986b [1982]. Ashika matsuri. *In: Kangarū biyori.* Tokyo: Heibonsha, 59–66.

———— 1986c [1981]. Kaitsuburi. *In: Kangarū biyori.* Tokyo: Heibonsha, 165–175.

———— 1987. *Noruwei no mori.* Tokyo: Kōdansha.

———— 1989. *Dansu dansu dansu.* Tokyo: Kōdansha.

———— 1990. Kanō Kureta. *In: TV pīpuru.* Tokyo: Bungei Shunjū, 105–116.

———— 1991a. Midori iro no kemono. *Bungakukai 4* (Special edition): 30–34.

———— 1991b. Haineken bīru no akikan o fumu zō ni tsuite no tanbun. *In: Murakami Haruki zensakuhin 1979–1989*, vol. 8. Tokyo: Kōdansha, 63–66.

———— 1991c. Odamaki zake no yoru. *In: Murakami Haruki zensakuhin 1979–1989*, vol. 5. Tokyo: Kōdansha, 233–238.

———— 1991d. Gekkan 'Ashika bungei'. *In: Murakami Haruki zensakuhin 1979–1989*, vol. 5. Tokyo: Kōdansha, 217–223.

———— 1991e. Ashika. *In: Murakami Haruki zensakuhin 1979–1989*, vol. 5. Tokyo: Kōdansha, 213–216.

———— 1991f. Pan'ya shūgeki. *In: Murakami Haruki zensakuhin 1979–1989*, vol. 8. Tokyo: Kōdansha, 31–36.

———— 1994–1995. *Nejimakidori kuronikuru.* Tokyo: Shinchōsha.

———— 1996 [1991]. Kōri otoko. *In: Rekishinton no yūrei.* Tokyo: Bungei Shunjū, 95–119.

———— 1999. *Supūtoniku no koibito.* Tokyo: Kōdansha.

———— 2002. *Umibe no Kafuka.* Tokyo: Shinchōsha.

———— 2004. *Afutādāku.* Tokyo: Kōdansha.

———— 2005a. Gūzen no tabibito. *In: Tōkyō kitanshū.* Tokyo: Shinchōsha, 7–42.

———— 2005b. Doko de are sore ga mitsukarisō na basho de. *In: Tōkyō kitanshū.* Tokyo: Shinchōsha, 81–119.

———— 2005c. Rēdāhōzen. *In: Zō no shōmetsu.* Tokyo: Shinchōsha, 167–180.

———— 2005d [1989]. Nemuri. *In: Zō no shōmetsu.* Tokyo: Shinchōsha, 113–155.

———— 2010. *Nemuri.* Tokyo: Shinchōsha.

———— 2013. *Shikisai o motanai Tazaki Tsukuru to, kare no junrei no toshi.* Tokyo: Bungei Shunjū.

———— 2014a. *Onna no inai otokotachi.* Tokyo: Bungei Shunjū.

———— 2014b. Onna no inai otokotachi. *In: Onna no inai otokotachi.* Tokyo: Bungei Shunjū, 263–285.

———— 2017. *Kishidanchō goroshi.* Tokyo: Shinchōsha.

———— 2020a. Ichininshō tansū. *In: Ichininshō tansū.* Tokyo: Bungei Shunjū, 217–235.

———— 2020b. Yakuruto Suwārozu shishū. *In: Ichininshō tansū.* Tokyo: Bungei Shunjū, 123–149.

Napier, S. J. 1996. *The fantastic in modern Japanese literature: The subversion of modernity.* New York: Routledge.

Pfeil, F. 1990. *Another tale to tell: Politics and narrative in postmodern culture.* New York: Verso Books.

Rimmon–Kenan, S. 2002. *Narrative fiction: Contemporary poetics.* London and New York: Routledge.

Rubin, J. 2005. *Haruki Murakami and the music of words.* London: Vintage.

Saitō M. 1994. *Ninshin shōsetsu.* Tokyo: Chikuma Shobō.

Strecher, M. C. 1999. Magical realism and the search for identity in the fiction of Murakami Haruki. *The Journal of Japanese Studies* 25 (2): 263–298.

——— 2020. Out of the (B)earth canal: The mythic journey in Murakami Haruki. *Japan Forum* 32 (3): 338–360.

Suter, R. 2008. *The Japanization of modernity: Murakami Haruki between Japan and the United States*. Cambridge: Harvard University Press.

Suzuki T. 1996. *Narrating the self: Fictions of Japanese modernity*. Stanford: Stanford University Press.

Ueno C., Tomioka T., Ogura C. 1992. *Danryū bungakuron*. Tokyo: Chikuma Shobō.

Yamada M. 2009. Exposing the private origins of public stories: Narrative perspective and the appropriation of selfhood in Murakami Haruki's post-AUM metafiction. *Japanese Language and Literature* 43 (1): 1–26.

Yasuoka S. 1971 [1951]. *Garasu no kutsu*. Tokyo: Kōdansha.

Yeung, V. 2011. A narratological study of Murakami Haruki's *Norwegian Wood* and *Sputnik Sweetheart*. *Transnational Literature* 3 (2): 1–10.

7

VOYEURISTIC GAZE, NARRATOLOGICAL CONSTRUCTION, AND THE GENDER PROBLEM IN MURAKAMI HARUKI'S *AFTER DARK*

Michael Tsang

Introduction

This chapter aims to examine the mode of narration in Murakami Haruki's *After Dark*[1] (2008 [2007]; *Afutādāku* [2004]) and the power structure of gazing associated with the novel's narrative mode. One of my goals here is to devise an analytical framework that is not only applicable for analysing the gaze structure in this short Murakami novel, but one that may have a wider application to prose fiction that involves gazing in general.

In performing my analysis I will build my framework around Laura Mulvey's male gaze theory. Since male gaze is a theory that studies unequal gender and power relations, another aim of this chapter, naturally, is to provide a more concrete evaluation of gender relations in Murakami's work. Murakami has been generally criticised for his treatment of female characters – in most of his novels, female characters often act as plot device for the male first-person narrator so that the latter can undergo some sort of journey of self-discovery (see also Hansen in this volume). When the novelist Kawakami Mieko brings up the topic of gender treatment in her conversation with Murakami, touching on the criticism that 'female characters portrayed by male writers are mere fantasies' (2017: 35), he responds vaguely that every woman thinks differently (ibid.: 35–36), as if to imply that there is no ideal way to represent women in reality. However, Murakami's answer is confusing if we juxtapose it with his celebrated acceptance speech, 'Always on the Side of the Egg', at the 2009 Jerusalem Prize, where he compares the human individual as an egg and what he calls 'the System' as a wall. 'Each of us is, more or less, an egg,' says he, 'a unique, irreplaceable soul enclosed in a fragile shell', and the high wall that is the System sometimes 'kill[s] us and cause[s] us to kill others – coldly, efficiently, systematically' (Murakami 2009). He claims that the novelist's job is 'to bring the dignity of the individual soul to the surface and shine a light upon it' and 'clarify the uniqueness of each individual soul by writing stories' (ibid.). Hence, the issue with Murakami's gender treatment is not whether male writers can or cannot represent women faithfully, but whether Murakami's work – with their characterisations, settings, plotlines, narratological structures, themes, and so on – live up to his own celebrated aim of novel-writing – whether female characters, in particular, are treated *as* unique individual souls.

Nonetheless, while there may be a general opinion on the way female characters are represented (or mis-represented) in Murakami's novels, there are few academic works that provide close-reading analysis on the manner and extent of oppression of female characters in Murakami's work, particularly from a gender studies *and* literary studies perspective. This chapter seeks to remedy this research gap by deconstructing the gaze structure in *After Dark*, and, by doing so, hopes to attract more fine-grained analyses of gender relations in Murakami.

In choosing to focus on *After Dark*, this chapter also aims to recover the significance of this mid-length novel in Murakami's oeuvre. *After Dark* is not necessarily the most iconic, well-known, or well-discussed work by Murakami either in Japanese or international academia. Matsumoto Umi (2019: 202) has attempted to attribute this lower popularity partly to the absence of attractive food scenes that usually pepper Murakami's other novels, in which protagonists prepare home-made food like pasta or enjoy variations of coffee or alcohol; instead, *After Dark*'s only food-related episode is about an unappetising piece of toast in the chain family restaurant Denny's. While this may be a valid reason, *After Dark* does also depart from Murakami's oeuvre in that it lacks a first-person *boku* narrator typically found in many of his novels – especially the most popular ones. In fact, as I will explain in this chapter, *After Dark* has a uniquely complex narratological design that may have alienated readers from the Murakami with which they are familiar, but that at the same time merits analytical scrutiny. This narratological design, unfortunately, has often gone amiss when scholars do discuss *After Dark*, such as Ōtomo Rio's (2009) analysis of the notions of danger and home or Oda Masayasu's (2017) spatial analysis of Tokyo's nightscape. By analysing the novel's narrative structure, the chapter will suggest that the novel contains material that is equally rich and worthwhile for analysis as Murakami's more high-profile novels.

In the following, I will first discuss the narrative mode of *After Dark*, before moving on to a theory of male gaze in literature, and finally coming back to the novel by examining its structure of gaze. I argue that the novel's narrative structure has produced multiple and complex layers of gazing, to which certain female characters in particular are subject.

Narrator/character confusion in *After Dark*

In his review of the English translation of *After Dark*, David Dalgleish of *January Magazine* notes that, for the first 20 years of Murakami's career, his typical first-person protagonist is 'a young, somewhat disaffected man in his 20s or 30s with a particular worldview, a tone of voice, and a set of likes […] which changed very little from one book to the next' (2007). Against this typical protagonist Dalgleish notes that in *After*

Dark Murakami 'abandons the first-person voice entirely' and features the first female lead in his novel-length works, Mari Asai. Dalgleish views these changes positively and considers them evidence of Murakami's 'continuing growth as a writer', presenting us 'with a broader range of people from a more neutral perspective'.

However, the question of narrative voice is not as straightforward as it seems. Elsewhere in the same review, Dalgleish contradicts his own comment on the 'entire' abandonment of 'first-person voice' by writing that the novel is 'told in the present tense by an unnamed, unknown "we"[2] who [...] can observe humans and their problems, but is unable to intervene' (ibid.). But the use of a first-person plural pronoun can only prove that Murakami abandons his typical first-person *singular* male narrator, and cannot prove that Murakami abandons first-person narration 'entirely'. To complicate things further, in a long interview with a Japanese magazine, Murakami (2010b: 30) himself says that *Afutādāku* is written in 'third-person narration' (*sanninshō*), disregarding the 'we' narrator. While not every reader sees the novel as only a third-person novel (see for instance Hansen 2010: 231), the confusion here from Dalgleish and Murakami on first-person plural and third-person narration thus calls for a careful investigation in narratology.

In fact, the confusion arises partly from the novel's narrative structure. It has a double plot line alternating each other for the most part, a technique that Murakami has used numerous times in his oeuvre, from as early as *Hard-Boiled Wonderland and the End of the World* (1991; *Sekai no owari to hādoboirudo wandārando* [1985]) to as recently as *1Q84* (2011; *1Q84* [2009–2010]), but none of these adopts a pluralistic narrative mode. In the first plot line of *After Dark*, the nameless narrator 'we' is compared to a pure 'point of view' and a 'mid-air camera' swooping down on midnight Tokyo (Murakami 2008: 25) and starts the novel by focusing on 19-year-old Mari reading in a Denny's restaurant. She is interrupted by Takahashi, who claims they have double-dated with his friend and her elder sister, Eri Asai. Soon after, Takahashi leaves for band practice, and Mari is interrupted by a woman working in a love hotel who needs Mari's help. Meanwhile, in the other story arc, the camera jumps to Eri who is in a deep sleep in her bedroom, not having woken up visibly for the last two months. Later, she is transported to an unknown, empty place which is connected solely by her bedroom TV, and there, in the world within the TV screen, she wakes up. The camera then goes back to Mari, who offers help to a Chinese prostitute who has been robbed and abused, and has a long talk with the love hotel staff about her relationship with Eri. At the end of the night and as the sun begins to rise, Mari again meets Takahashi, who wants to keep in touch with her despite her upcoming study trip to Beijing. In the last scene, Mari returns home and sleeps beside her elder sister.

It must then be noted that *After Dark* adopts a mixed mode of narration, and understanding the mode of narration in this double plot structure is imperative to solving the narratological confusion mentioned above. When the story focuses on Mari (the first arc), the 'we' narrator seldom appears except at the very beginning when 'we' swoop down into Denny's, after which Mari's storyline unfolds on its own. An example of what is known in narratology as 'extradiegitic' narration – i.e. a narrator who stands outside ('extra') the story universe ('diegesis') – the effacement of the 'we' pronoun attempts to erase 'our' existence in this plotline, as if 'we' simply sit back and watch Mari, Takahashi, and other characters interact. Thus, while the 'we' narrator does exist, it is not involved with the action of the characters. In the other story arc involving Eri, however, 'we' enter her room and make comments as 'we' watch how she is transported to and wakes up in the world within the TV screen. Later, in a feat of magical realism, 'we' are even able to 'separate from the flesh, leave all substance behind, and allow ourselves to become a conceptual point of view devoid of mass' so that we can transport 'ourselves' into the TV screen (Murakami 2008: 108). Not only is the pronoun 'we' often used, but 'we' even take part actively in the plot line with movement and thoughts. Contrary to Mari's story arc, the 'we' narrator becomes prominent in Eri's arc and intrudes more into the flow of the plot. Needless to say, this is a type of 'intradiegetic' narration where the narrator can also be considered a character in the narrative (Rimmon–Kenan 1989: 94).

Indeed, diegesis and narration operate interconnectedly. In the long interview, when Murakami agrees with his interviewer that *Afutādāku* is written in the third person (*sanninshō*), the interviewer defines *sanninshō* as 'strangers wholly unrelated to the *kakite*' (Murakami 2010b: 30). While *kakite* can mean the writer or the author, I do not believe the interviewer is referring to Murakami here. The literal meaning of *kakite* – the hand (*te*) that writes (*kaki*) – suggests a split between the thoughts of the author, and the hand that actually does the writing. In this way, each sentence in a literary work is seen as being 'written' twice, the first time in the author's head, and the second time with the author's hand. A possible rendition of *kakite* into English, therefore, may be 'the implied author'. Furthermore, the interviewer's choice to use the term *kakite* is remarkable vis-à-vis another similar term, *katarite* – literally the hand (*te*) that speaks (*katari*), thus more accurately rendered as 'the narrator'. On one level, the distinction between these two terms has to do with medium: *kakite* suggests a written medium (e.g. novels), while *katarite* suggests an oral/aural medium (e.g. films). On the other hand, the two terms can both be understood as interim categories between the actual author (Murakami himself) and the text. A minute difference between the two is that an implied author is closer to the author and more conscious about the act of writing on a metanarrative level, while a narrator is closer to the story universe of the text (diegesis) and less conscious about the story being a 'written' piece of work. Since *After Dark* opens with the cinematic trope of a mid-air camera swooping down on Tokyo, the novel blurs the distinction between the written and the audiovisual. For this reason, we see no implied author or a Murakami-like figure being conscious about the act of writing; rather, from the very beginning *After Dark* is a novel *presented like a film*. Therefore, I argue that *kakite* in this context can be directly understood as a proxy agent who tells the story at the textual level on the author's behalf – for which the term 'narrator' is a close enough resemblance.

Following this, the interviewer's definition of the third person as 'strangers wholly unrelated to the *kakite* [= narrator]' in fact matches how literary scholars define third-person narration. For example, M. H. Abrams and Geoffrey Harpham define the third-person narrator in *A Glossary of Literary Terms* as 'someone outside the story proper who refers to all the characters in the story by name' or by third-person pronouns (2009: 272). In other words, the third person is used because it is conventionally assumed that the narrator (*kakite*) is extradiegetic, who stands '"above" or superior to the story he [sic] narrates' (Rimmon–Kenan 1989: 94). What is key here is that a narrator always exists, and third-person narration is contingent on the fact that the narrator does not participate in the action of the story. But what if the narrator *does* participate in the story? The narrator then becomes intradiegetic, and when this narrator refers to him/herself, first-person pronouns naturally have to be used.

Dalgleish's and Murakami's claim that the novel is written in the third person, then, is flawed, because they fail to consider the novel's double plot structure. The claim *seems* valid insofar as Mari's plotline gives the illusion of third-person narration due to the effacement of 'we'; effacement, but not disappearance. Because of its unique mix of extra- and intradiegesis, *After Dark* cannot be accurately argued as written in the third person; the precise formulation should be that it oscillates between intradiegetic first-person narration and extradiegetic first-person narration. The first-person narrator/*kakite* never disappears, for even in Mari's narrative arc, 'we' do appear in the very beginning as 'we' swoop down on Denny's. But more importantly, both the confusion about third-person narration demonstrated by Dalgleish and Murakami's interviewer – and the accompanying disregard for diegesis – reveals how they do not regard 'we' as both a narrator and a *character* (for at least one half of the story in Eri's plot line). By emphasising diegesis rather than narration, I argue to the contrary that 'we' should be considered carefully in both capacities: 'we' shift back and forth between being an extradiegetic narrator in Mari's arc and an intradiegetic narrator-cum-character in Eri's part.

The above discussion on narration, diegesis, and characterisation is fundamental to my ensuing synthesis of a theory of narrative voice that addresses the gaze structure in *After Dark*: as a narrator-cum-character, 'we' subjugate Eri under an unequal power structure by gazing at her sleep. Moreover, drawing on Laura Mulvey's male gaze theory and Lacanian psychoanalysis, I will show that the narrative structure in *After Dark* makes the reader an accomplice in this voyeuristic gaze on the female body, hence subjecting female characters to an oppressed powerless position.

Towards a theory of narrativised male gaze

Laura Mulvey's theory of the male gaze in her landmark essay 'Visual pleasure and narrative cinema' (1999 [1975]) is pertinent to a discussion on gazing in *After Dark*, not only because of the obvious focus on gazing, but more importantly, because male gaze – as seen from Mulvey's essay title – is first and foremost a theory on cinema. Hence, this theory, supposedly on film, becomes a useful tool when *After Dark* opens with an explicit comparison of the 'we' narrator to 'a mid-air camera' as 'we' enter Eri Asai's room for the first time to peek at her sleep (Murakami 2008: 25). With its eye-shaped lens strongly associated with the act of looking and gazing, what the mid-air camera sees is what 'we' (the narrator and the reader) see. In effect, then, the camera serves as a mediation between Tokyo's night scene and the readers, inviting readers to gaze at the characters and making the reading experience comparable to watching a film.

Employing Lacanian psychoanalysis, Mulvey first gives an account of Lacan's mirror stage, which she sees as the origin of the cinema audience's voyeuristic desire to gaze at the female. The mirror stage, for Lacan, concerns the development of a child's ego and the recognition of the ego–ideal. In the mirror stage, the child sees its own image through a symbolic mirror (such as its mother) but experiences an incongruence because its 'motor impotence and nursling dependence' (i.e. limited limb movements) affects its ability to govern and completely control this image (Lacan 1966: 95). The ego is then born in the child because it identifies with this ideal image that provides it with 'a sense of unification and wholeness' (Homer 2005: 25). Meanwhile, the image, mis-recognised as 'superior' to the way the child experiences its own body, is projected 'as an ego ideal [which] gives rise to the future generation of identification with others' (Mulvey 1999: 836). Mulvey sees the mirror stage as the origin of 'the long love affair/despair between image and self-image which has found [...] such joyous recognition in the cinema audience'; in other words, she attributes the audience's voyeuristic pleasure from gazing at the female on screen to the baby's primordial act of looking at its image in the symbolic mirror (ibid.). Using examples from mainstream Hollywood films, Mulvey demonstrates how women on screen are subject to the audience's 'controlling and curious gaze', and hence objectified for the audience's voyeuristic pleasure as a projection of fantasy (ibid.: 833–835). In the final part of the essay, she breaks down the male gaze into three different kinds of cinematic looks:

1) '[the look] of the camera as it records the pro-filmic event',
2) 'that of the audience as it watches the final product', and
3) 'that of the characters at each other within the screen illusion'. (ibid.: 843)

As Jackie Stacey clarifies, these three tiers in the gaze structure mediate between themselves in such a way that '[t]he spectator identifies with the powerful look of the male character on the screen, and his position in relation to it is produced by the camera(man)'s/director's look' (Stacey 21). Moreover, Mulvey maintains that in film conventions the camera must not appear on screen, (because if it does, the spectator may realise that they are watching but an illusionary world), so that only the male gaze among the film characters is shown, and the male characters act as surrogates of the spectator gazing at the female (ibid.: 843–844).

To apply Mulvey's theory to a study of fiction, the three-tier gaze structure in film needs to be mapped onto a story's discourse structure. As proposed by Mick Short (1996), there also exists a three-layer discourse structure in prose (Figure 7.1).

Short's model here expands on the linguist Roman Jakobson's classic dictum for communication, where an addresser sends a message to an addressee (1960). Moreover, the model has three layers: through a book of fiction, the novelist transmits some sort of message to the reader in the first layer; once the reading experience commences, a narrator tells the story (the message) to the narratee – which may or may not be the reader – at the second layer; and finally, the third layer unfolds with interactions *within* the story between the characters in the form of speech or action.

The different roles in the novel's discourse structure (namely the novelist, the reader, the narrator etc. in Figure 7.1), can now be mapped back to Mulvey's three-tier male gaze structure in film-watching, so that the novelist in the diagram is replaced by the director, the reader by the spectator.[3]

Since this is a model addressing the narrative structure of films, we can now combine Mulvey's three-layer structure of the male gaze with the narrative structure proposed by Mick Short to understand how the male gaze is entwined in a film's narrative framework (Figure 7.2).

While my theorisation is only halfway and Figure 7.2 is but an interim figure, two things are of note here. First, the middle layer, the narrator–narratee level, is missing. This is because Mulvey sees no need to acknowledge a narrator in film structure, and indeed, other film analysts such as David Bordwell would perhaps agree that there is no such need (see Cobley 2001: 153). However, for *After Dark* there is a need to recognise the narrator level because it is a novel for which a narrator always exists. Second, if we then accept that there is a narrative figure (*kakite*) who should be treated

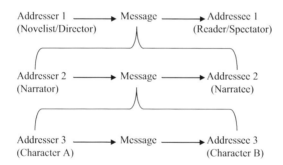

FIGURE 7.1   Discourse structure of a novel, combining two diagrams from Short 1996: 39, 257

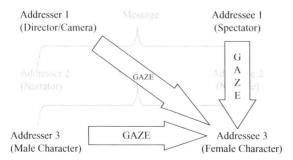

FIGURE 7.2   Types of male gaze in film

separately from the author, then we must also posit that the narrator likewise takes part in gazing at the female character. In her essay, Mulvey assumes that the camera and the director occupy the same position (see Figure 7.2) because she only uses the term 'camera', and subsequent scholars tend to equate the camera with the director.[4] Yet, for my purpose here I see it necessary to separate the camera from the director, since the camera in a film functions on a level of discourse different from the director's. In the actual process of filming, the director typically communicates with the actors before the camera rolls. Once the camera is rolling, the director stays silent. Yet, because the camera movements and expressions are subject to the director's control, it becomes the agent or proxy of the director's gaze through its various shots, angles, and perspectives. In the meantime, the actors do not only act for the director's sake: Since their acting will ultimately be watched by the cinematic audience, the eye-shaped tool that is the camera is also the audience's proxy for recording sounds and actions during the filming process. In effect, then, the camera represents neither the director's nor the audience's gaze fully, but is a combination of both, and hence should be treated as a new type of gaze. The communication between the director and the actors behind the camera is not entirely the same as the interaction between the actors and the camera during filming.

With this, I posit that the camera overlaps partly in its function to a narrator in fiction, because both act as a mouthpiece for the director or author, the mastermind behind the story. Just as Roland Barthes has warned us that the 'author of a narrative is in no way to be confused with the narrator of that narrative' (1982: 282), the camera should not be confused with the director. While I by no means suggest the camera and the narrator operate in identical ways, the mediatory nature of the narrator being positioned amid the author and the character is analogous to the camera standing in between the director and the actor. Hence, I propose to split the camera from the director in Mulvey's gaze tiers, and instead place the camera and the narrator on the same second level in the discourse structure, as seen in Figure 7.3 below. The implication of this is that the camera/narrator can also become involved in a kind of gazing that is neither reducible to the author/director's nor the reader/spectator's. The result is that there are four, not three, tiers of male gaze, with a gaze each coming from the author/director, the narrator/camera, the male character, and the spectator.

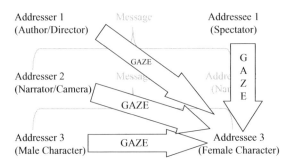

FIGURE 7.3 A model of narrativised gaze structure

This diagram highlights a model of narrativised gaze structure which I will deploy below in my analysis of *After Dark*. The model may have wider application to other novels, but not every literary work will contain all four levels, and collapses or expansions are possible. Indeed, as an example of such collapse, I will argue below that the filmic quality of the novel and the use of a first-person plural narrator enable various gazes to condense into one single form of gaze, directed at the female character Eri Asai.

Narration and gazing in *After Dark*

Although there are four possible gazes in a novel's discourse, *After Dark* integrates them together into one single form of gaze by playing on the special configuration of the first-person plural pronoun, 'we'. Uri Margolin explains the nature of the 'we' narrator in the formula 'we = I + other(s)', and goes on to split the formula into two different variations: 'we = I + he/she' and 'we = I + you' (Margolin 2001: 242–246). In the 'I + he/she' variation, the use of third-person pronouns denotes someone neither the narrator (who would have referred to him/herself with the first-person 'I') nor the narratee (who would have been referred to as the second-person 'you'), but most probably a character in the story – whom the narrator addresses in the third person. Many studies in narratology (e.g. Margolin 2001; Richardson 2006, 2009) have looked at texts that feature the 'I + he/she' formula. A typical example of this is the American writer William Faulkner's 'A Rose for Emily' (1930), in which the 'we' narrator represents the voice of the inhabitants in an unidentified town in southern US, who are also characters in the short story.

The implication of the 'I + you' variant is less often analysed. In this formula, the 'I' refers to the narrator, 'you' the addressee of the narration, and 'we' a united front where the narrator and narratee join hands and share the same vision. This narratee figure can be the reader (especially when the narrator uses phrases such as 'Dear Reader' that acknowledge the figure of the reader directly), or an imaginary person, such as another character in the story (for example, when the narrator writes a letter to another character). In *After Dark*, although there are no such phrases as 'Dear Reader', we can still deduce that the default narratee of the novel is the reader, because there is no evidence in the text that suggests the narrator is speaking to another character within the story. Hence, *After Dark* is one of the few novels that uses the 'we = I + you' formula, where 'I' is the unnamed narrator, and 'you' can be taken as the reader,[5] to whom the 'I' tells the story. The pronoun 'we' first appears in the second sentence of the novel: 'Through the eyes of a high-flying night bird, we take in the scene from midair' (Murakami 2008: 3). Yet, it appears so naturally without any preceding explanation of how 'we' even come into existence; and at such an early point of the novel, we as readers naturally assume that we are the one being addressed through the narration; we are part of 'we'. In effect, the pronoun 'we' serves to invite the readers into the story, to transport us into the story's setting of midnight Tokyo, so that both the reader and the narrator are on the same front and share the same point of view. Here is then the most crucial implication of this first-person plural pronoun 'we': what should have been distinctive categories of narrator, narratee, and reader are simplified and singularised into *one* single point of view represented by a sole signifier, 'we'. This pronoun neutralises the boundaries between the narrator and the reader, so that they operate as a collective whole. The reader is brought onto the same level with the narrator once they open the book and encounter the novel's second sentence.

This 'lumping together' and singularisation of the narrator and the reader is evident when the narrator dictates the reader's vision and responses. For instance, when Takahashi first enters Denny's, the narrative voice attempts to give several explanations of his messy hair: 'Perhaps he has had no chance to wash it in some days. Perhaps he has just crawled out of the underbrush somewhere. Or perhaps he just finds it more natural and comfortable to have messy hair' (Murakami 2008: 7). The narrator cleverly throws out these guesses as if it anticipates that readers will ask the question: 'why is his hair so untidy?' This can be read as an attempt to preempt the reader's potential wonder in order to maintain the unity between the narrator and the reader, a technique known as gap-filling in narratology.

As Wolfgang Iser theorises in the essay 'The Reading Process', 'individual sentences [in a literary work] not only work together to shade in what is to come; they also form an expectation' (1972: 282). A gap is the absence of information that a reader expects to know in order to comprehend the story – in this sense it is also a narratological tool to motivate the reader to continue reading. A gap is *prospective* if the reader is aware of a gap during reading, and *retrospective* if the reader is not aware of it until the end of the story (Rimmon–Kenan 1989: 129). In a sense, then, fiction is essentially an art of gap management in which the narrator controls what and how much information it feeds to the reader. In *After Dark*, however, the narrator shares all the information it knows and sees with the reader precisely with a view to eliminate the categorical distinction between narrator and narratee. In the textual example above, 'why is Takahashi's hair so untidy' is a prospective gap that the reader may become aware of. Yet, if the reader is aware of this gap, they will also realise that the narrator and the readers are two distinct voices, going against the nature of 'we' narration (one voice that encompasses multiple beings). Thus, the narrator must eliminate such gaps to continue to unify with the reader and maintain a singular point of view.

Apart from the technique of gap-filling, the novel also uses metaphor and explicitly compares the viewpoint of the 'we' narrator to 'a mid-air camera that can move freely' (Murakami 2008: 25). At this point, a chain of metonymic references is established for the first-person plural pronoun 'we'.

Now that we have worked out how one single 'pronoun' approximates and flattens – but note that it does not entirely remove – the distinctive boundaries between the mid-air camera, the narrator, and the narratee/reader, we have paved the groundwork

FIGURE 7.4 Metonymic chain of the first-person plural pronoun

for analysing the novel's male gaze. Through this metonymic chain, what the mid-air camera sees becomes what 'we' – the narrator and the reader – see, and by extension, whatever power and pleasure achieved in the act of gazing is also shared between the narrator and the reader.

On this, Lacanian psychoanalysis would dovetail the argument that through gazing, the fiction reader or film spectator gains pleasure and has his/her desire satisfied. Alexandre Kojève contends that 'desire is always revealed as *my* desire, and to reveal desire, one must use the word "I"' (1969: 37, italics original). Also, as Jerry A. Flieger maintains, reading is a transaction of pleasure between the writer and the reader, where the writer, using his/her techniques and art, must draw the reader into the story with 'a bribe of pleasure, enlisting the reader's cooperation in a pleasure-circuit which would otherwise remain incomplete' (Flieger 1983: 958–959). Due to the blurring effect of the 'we' pronoun in *After Dark*, desire becomes 'our' desire instead, and the pleasure of gazing is shared with the reader. It is through the pronoun 'we' that the pleasure of gazing and voyeurism is articulated, shared, managed, and satisfied between the narrator and reader – a bribe of voyeuristic pleasure to gaze at not only the beautiful female character Eri Asai, but also at everything in midnight Tokyo that the camera presents to us. In this sense the reader is no longer innocent; if, according to Mulvey's charge, the film spectator is guilty of gazing at the female character, then any reader of *After Dark*, too, regardless of their gender, is brought into the same powerful position of the spectator, and is guilty of gazing at Eri Asai, an idea I will unpack in the next section.

First, however, a word of caution: 'regardless of the reader's gender' is crucial here, for gazing denotes first and foremost not a gender or anatomical difference, but a power difference in which the privileged gazer peeks at the gazed object. Just like psychoanalysis which seeks to theorise as its primary aim the psychosexual development of humans and, only as a result, derives different theories for boys and girls, the power of voyeuristic pleasure in the case of *After Dark* is awarded to the *category* of reader/spectator, not their *gender*.[6] By extension, the object of the gaze is also not necessarily limited to Eri Asai alone, but to those living in the 'shadowy middle ground' between light and dark in Tokyo (Murakami 2008: 186). However, the prominence of 'we' and 'our' gazing at Eri Asai's deep slumber is the chief manifestation of the politics of gazing in the novel.

Gazing at Eri Asai

Eri Asai's unconscious sleep is the chief example of gazing in the novel because, as I have already established earlier, the 'we' narrator in this plot line is intradiegetic, meaning that 'we' are also a character in the story universe directly interacting with Eri. This means that, per Figure 7.3, 'we' gaze at Eri not only as a narrator and reader, but also as a character, combining three gazes into one and inflicting it upon her. In this regard Eri Asai is designed as a prey of an unequal power (gaze) structure.

Eri Asai is a girl destined for spectatorship. Takahashi points out succinctly: 'From the time [Eri Asai] was a little girl, her job was to play her assigned role and satisfy the people around her. She worked hard to be a perfect little Snow White' (Murakami 2008: 128–129). This explains her obsession with dieting and her busy schedule to model for girls' magazines (ibid.: 122–127). Beautiful and slender, she is set to look pretty for the gazing pleasure of other people. The metaphor of a fish tank is used to underscore her existence as a gazed-at object: when 'we' watch through the TV how Eri wakes up on the other side of the TV screen and tries to speak, she is compared to 'a person [who] had wandered into an empty fish tank at an aquarium and was trying to explain the predicament to a visitor through the thick glass' (ibid.: 150). The need to explain a predicament to a visitor is ironic because she is searching for a way out by appealing to the very people – the imaginary spectators behind the TV screen, i.e. 'we' including the narrator and the reader – who formulate her in a gaze.

Still, the tragedy of Eri Asai is not only that she is gazed at when she is awake; even when she is deeply asleep, she is still subjected to a gaze – 'our' gaze. Gazing is what 'we' do as a character in Eri's portion of the novel. This is most evident in the way 'we' consume Eri's image of a sleeping beauty. Ever since the beginning, 'we' are drawn to Eri Asai's sleeping figure and scrutinise her sleeping face and other features:

> At the moment, the camera is situated directly above the bed and is focused on her sleeping face. Our angle changes at intervals as regular as the blinking of an eye. Her small, well-shaped lips are tightened into a straight line. [...] [S]taring hard we can make out a slight – a very slight – movement at the base of her throat. [...] Her eyelids are closed like hard winter buds. [...] Her slender white neck preserves the dense tranquility of a handcrafted product. Her small chin traces a clean angle like a well-shaped headland.
> (Murakami 2008: 25–26)

With each change of the camera angle – reflected stylistically with each new sentence – 'we' turn 'our' attention to a new part on her body or face, dissecting and consuming her appearance in a series of camera images. Moreover, the laudatory adjectives and delicate metaphors used to describe her, such as 'hard winter buds' and 'well-shaped headland', also reflect a consumer behaviour to evaluate the images that 'we' have consumed.

As 'we' invest more of our interest in her, however, the nature of the narration gradually shifts from a description of outward appearances to a spectacle where 'we' as the spectator anticipate something to happen to her. In Chapter 10, when Eri has already been transported to the mysterious world within the TV screen, 'we' 'keep our eyes trained on the motionless image' of a sleeping Eri displayed on TV because 'we' sense by intuition that 'something alive [... is] lurk[ing] beneath the surface' of that calm sleep (Murakami 2008: 106–107). Right after this intuition, 'we' notice two microscopic movements of her mouth. These hints transform the nature of Eri's sleep from a girl's deep repose to a spectacle where 'we' expect something more than just a beautiful girl sleeping, or a peep show with Eri the performer asleep at centre-stage in a studio and 'us' the audience anticipating her performance – her awaking. Robert Con Davis points out that a voyeuristic gaze is 'a perverse activity' (1983: 987) and 'our' gaze becomes similarly perverse. At this point, Eri no longer simply sleeps; she sleeps *so that* she can later display signs of waking up for an audience like 'us'. When later in the novel she does wake up, she wakes up not because she wants to, but because we want her to and can sense the awake coming, a performance that responds to our anticipation and satisfies our voyeuristic desire. As if this does not already reduce her to a position powerless enough, the camera even cooperates with our desire to see more and shows a close-up of Eri's mouth 'as if sensing our will [to look closer at Eri]' (Murakami 2008: 107). In an earlier scene when Eri is just transported into the TV, this telepathy also occurs when the camera moves around the room that imprisons Eri 'as if responding to our thoughts' until the sleeping Eri appears on the TV screen (ibid.: 89). The purposeful camera movement simultaneously reveals two things: the camera's ability to sense what 'we' want to gaze at, and the helpless and objectified position to which Eri, unconscious and thus unable to reject being watched, is exposed.

To sum up, the gaze inflicted upon Eri Asai undoubtedly echoes the most important contribution of Mulvey's male gaze theory, namely, that female characters are gazed-at objects exposed under an unequal, multilayered power structure of gazing 'for the [...] enjoyment of men, the active controllers of the look' (1999: 840). While Mulvey focuses on film, the model of narrativised gaze structure derived in the last section allows us to delineate how the gaze is manifest in this novel: through the flattening effect of the first-person plural pronoun, the gaze of the intradiegetic 'we' narrator-cum-character divaricates into three levels of voyeuristic gaze imposed on Eri Asai – namely, the narrator's gaze, the narratee/reader's gaze, and the character's gaze – devouring the images of her deep sleep. The reader, in particular, is invited in this hierarchical mechanism to assume the powerful position of the gazer and visit voyeuristic violence onto the less powerful Eri.

Desire, the dual nature of voyeurism, and 'the System'

In the meantime, however, we must pay attention to the inherently dual nature of voyeurism. In psychoanalysis, this dual nature is highlighted by both Freud and Lacan, who insist that the looker's active voyeurism is turned upside down because the gazed-at object also holds the looker in a gaze. In a reading experience, for example, Robert Con Davis explains:

> we [readers] turn to and read a text as if, by giving attention to it, we look into it and master or possess it *as an object*. But while reading, in fact, we are focused upon and held by a Gaze that comes through the agency of the object text.
>
> (1983: 988, italics original)

The looker then also becomes an object, and eventually, a new gazer will emerge to take up the original powerful position of gazing, eventually making even the original looker 'an object for another watcher (ibid.: 986). In *After Dark*, while on the one hand 'we' actively gaze at Eri Asai, on the other hand 'we' are also captivated by the images 'we' see, hence held by the object – Eri herself. It is imperative to recognise that this is not a reciprocal gaze and we must not over-accord agency to Eri, for we simply cannot say that Eri gazes back at 'us' (she is asleep for most of the time), but we may say that the sleeping Eri arrests 'our' gaze upon her. Crucially, the power difference is not turned upside down even if 'we' cannot take 'our' eyes off her. Even when she becomes temporarily awake in the world of the TV screen, 'we' are still not visible to her, and her gaze is not directed at any specific person or being; all the while, 'our' gaze remains directly fixed on her. Instead of being a counter-argument that threatens my reading of Eri's gazed-at position, this dual nature should be read as a hint for the 'new gazer' described in Davis's quote. That 'we' both gaze at Eri but are also being gazed at by another gazer is revealed at the end of Chapter 10 when, after being in the same world as Eri within the TV, 'we' are suddenly pulled away from that world and forced to 'draw back [from Eri …] beyond our control' to return to Eri's room (Murakami 2008: 116). Being forced to leave Eri exposes the limited ability of 'we'. Although the camera sometimes responds to 'our' wish to focus on certain body parts of Eri, there exists a supreme force, an unidentified gazer whose faculty is far greater, who ultimately grants 'us' the ability to enter different places freely.

I propose to read this supreme force over the 'we' narrator as the System that Murakami refers to in his Jerusalem acceptance speech. As an existence that 'takes on a life of its own' so that it 'kill[s] us and cause[s] us to kill others' (Murakami 2009), the System's omnipotence mimics the supreme force in *After Dark* such that 'we' are able to transcend into a mid-air camera entering physical spaces like Eri's bedroom and metaphysical locales like the world in the TV. By extension, then, 'our' oppressive gaze is therefore also validated by the System. Through its narrativised gaze structure, the novel reveals how we the reader, in the process of reading and however unknowingly, are dragged into the System's complicity in inflicting violence on Eri Asai, robbing her of her agency.

But it is also with this that I argue *After Dark* is ultimately not so much about the lives of Mari or Takahashi or Eri as it is about 'us', the 'we' narrator. To this extent I agree with Ōtomo's warning that the novel should not be read 'as a text of social realism' (2009: 361), or rather, not *only* as a text of social realism. More importantly, judging from how Eri's sleep turns into a show for 'us' to anticipate her waking, I see the novel as a fulfilment of the voyeuristic pleasure of the 'we' narrator inasmuch as it is a book about the lives of the nightly outcasts. Evidence for this is provided at the novel's ending, when a certain sense of hope burgeons as dawn breaks and Mari returns home. She 'briefly presses her lips to Eri's' before sleeping in the same bed, and right before the novel ends, 'Eri's small mouth does move slightly […] an impression [that] comes to us with certainty' (Murakami 2008: 195, 201), thus partially fulfilling a prophecy made earlier in the novel that 'somebody'll kiss [Eri] and wake her up' (ibid.: 164). Speaking of this ending, Murakami explains in an interview that 'Eri and Mari are getting out of darkness in separate directions at the same time. […] And then dawn comes, and the story ends when the two of them are finally about to be *saved* in their own ways' (Murakami 2010a: 308–309; my emphasis). Yet, the critical part here is that the asleep Mari does not witness Eri's mouth movement, and if this tiny lip twitch should be read as a possibility of Eri's hopeful waking, a symbol of her being 'saved', it is only a sign of hope meant for the 'we' narrator – and us, the reader – to catch, becoming yet another item on the menu of 'our' gaze. Therefore, this story is not only written to narrate the stories of night people, but also written *for* us, the reader to hope – hope for a good ending for the characters, but also to carry a broader, more general sense of hope and optimism.

Here, then, is what is to me the biggest problem in Murakami's treatment of gender. *After Dark* shows that through the single device of a plural pronoun, the reader, regardless of gender, is bribed by the System to gain voyeuristic pleasure through gazing at powerless characters, only then to also earn a hope of life via Eri's tiny mouth movement, designed to be comprehended by no other character in the novel. Even though the reader is degendered, the quintessential Murakamian victim is both female and feminine (i.e. occupying the powerless gazed-at position), and always beyond redemption to the extent that not only can her awakening happen only in the metaphysical realm of the TV screen, but even a final hint of her salvation remains undetected by herself and becomes a spectacle for the reader, whose power is awarded by the purported target against which Murakami writes fiction: the System.

Conclusion

Murakami makes the following comment in his long interview in 2010:

> In *After Dark*, I wanted to take on the digital modern society in a digital way. […] Similar to coarse images taken simultaneously with a handy digital camera, only dialogues were written in the beginning, and on top of it descriptive passages were then added to make the form of a fiction.
>
> (2010b: 30)

Murakami here acknowledges how comparable reading this 'digital' novel is to watching through a digital camera. Permitted by the System and through the operation of the first-person plural narrator, we readers intrude into the lives of Mari, Eri, Takahashi, and other characters, leaving no trace behind but observing and consuming their stories without their knowing and consent. Particularly in our gaze at Eri Asai, power hierarchy is reinscribed through reducing her sleep to a spectacle or performance that anticipates her waking. The novel therefore aptly demonstrates how, to use Murakami's egg-and-wall metaphor, the wall 'cause[s] us [the eggs] to kill others' (Murakami 2009) – the System grants the reader privilege to inflict non-reciprocal gaze on a female character, and from this act the reader even gains hope. But in this transaction of pleasure lies a most damning fate that awaits the female character.

I opened this chapter by suggesting that the model of narrativised gaze structure devised here for the purpose of analysing *After Dark* may be applied to other novels involving gazing. In fact, many of Murakami's novels featuring a first-person male narrator and his adventures surrounding female characters can also be analysed in similar ways, albeit without the fascinating plural narrator 'we' which is a one-off appearance among Murakami's full-length novels. In *Sputnik Sweetheart* (2001, *Supūtoniku no koibito* [1999]), despite the abundant focalisation on female characters like Sumire and Myu, the story is still framed through the gaze of the comparatively effaced male narrator K. It is not until 2009 when Murakami's magnum opus trilogy *1Q84* was published that he truly wrote a third-person novel. How the gaze structures evolve in these works and across Murakami's oeuvre will be topics for future research.

Notes

1 Since I am quoting from the English translation, character names follow the English convention with given name first and surname last, because this is how it appears in the translation. However, all other Japanese names, such as Murakami Haruki, follow the Japanese 'surname first' convention in this edited volume. Apart from Murakami's works, all other translations from the Japanese are mine unless otherwise specified.

2 'We' is of course a literal translation of the Japanese first-person plural pronoun, *watashita-chi*, which is also what Murakami uses in the Japanese original. For this reason I will treat 'we' in *After Dark* and *watashitachi* in *Afutādāku* as bearing the same effect on the novel, meaning that what I argue about 'we' in the English also applies to *watashitachi* in the Japanese.

3 Film theorists will be correct to protest that the literary reader is not entirely interchangeable as the filmic spectator. For example, in his essay 'The viewer's activity' (1985), film analyst David Bordwell discusses the similarities and differences between the spectator and the reader. For my purpose in this chapter, however, the reader and the spectator can be interchanged because both occupy the same role in the addresser–addressee interaction as the recipient of the addresser's (novelist or director) message.

4 Jackie Stacey (1994: 21), for example, writes that the spectator's position in relation to the on-screen male character is 'produced by the camera(man)'s/director's look', the slash showing that she makes little distinction between the camera and the director.

5 Note that 'the reader' is a category referring to the collective of all imaginary readers of this novel, rather than any specific, named person who has read the book in any particular way.

6 In this sense, the feminist theory of female gazing is most productively understood as an activism that articulates the potential of a female point of view in film qua resistance to the patriarchal gaze.

References

Abrams, M. H. and Harpham, G. G. 2009. *A glossary of literary terms*. 9th Ed. Boston: Wadsworth.

Barthes, R. 1982. Introduction to the structural analysis of narratives. *In*: S. Sontag, ed. *A Barthes reader*. New York: Hill and Wang, 251–295.

Cobley, P. 2001. *Narrative*. London: Routledge.

Dalgleish, D. 2007. Murakami grows. Review of *After Dark*, by Murakami Haruki. *January Magazine*, July 2007. Available from: https://www.januarymagazine.com/fiction/afterdark.html [Accessed 3 May 2011].

Davis, R. C. 1983. Lacan, Poe, and narrative repression. *In*: R. C. Davis, ed. *Lacan and narration: The psychoanalytic difference in narrative theory*. Baltimore: The Johns Hopkins University Press, 983–1005.

Flieger, J. A. 1983. The purloined punchline: Joke as textual paradigm. *In*: R. C. Davis, ed. *Lacan and narration: The psychoanalytic difference in narrative theory*. Baltimore: The Johns Hopkins University Press, 941–967.

Hansen, G. 2010. Murakami Haruki's female narratives: Ignored works show awareness of women's issues. *Japan Studies Association Journal* 8: 229–238.

Homer, S. 2005. *Jacques Lacan*. Oxon: Routledge.

Iser, W. 1972. The reading process: A phenomenological approach. *New Literary History* 3 (2): 279–299.

Jakobson, R. 1960. *Style and language*. Edited by T. A. Sebeok. Cambridge, Mass.: MIT Press.

Kawakami M. and Murakami H. 2017. *Mimizuku wa tasogare ni tobitatsu*. Tokyo: Shinchōsha.

Kojève A. 1969. *Introduction to the reading of Hegel*. Translated by J. H. Nichols. Edited by A. Bloom. New York; London: Basic Books.

Lacan, J. 1966. The mirror stage as formative of the *I* function as revealed in psychoanalytic experience. *Écrits*. Paris: Seuil, 93–100.

Margolin, U. 2001. Collective perspective, individual perspective, and the speaker in between: On 'we' literary narratives. *In*: W. van Peer and S. Chatman, eds. *New perspectives on narrative perspective*. Albany: State University of New York Press, 241–254.

Matsumoto U. 2019. Murakami Haruki *Afutādāku* ni okeru 'shoku': Eiga *Arufaviru* to Jōji Ōweru o hojosen toshite. *JunCture* 10: 202–212.

Mulvey, L. 1999 [1975]. Visual pleasure and narrative cinema. *In*: L. Braudy and M. Cohen, eds. *Film theory and criticism: Introductory readings*. New York: Oxford University Press, 833–844.

Murakami H. 2008 [2007]. *After Dark*. Trans. Jay Rubin. London: Vintage.

——— 2009. Always on the side of the egg. Speech given at the award ceremony of the Jerusalem Prize for the Freedom of the Individual in Society, 24th Jerusalem International Book Fair, Israel. 15 Feb. Available from: https://www.haaretz.com/israel-news/culture/1.5076881 [Accessed 3 May 2011].

——— 2010a. Kyōfu o kugurinukenakereba hontō no seichō wa arimasen. Interview with *Bungakukai*, April 2005. *In*: H. Murakami, ed. *Yume o miru tame ni maiasa boku wa mezameru no desu. Murakami Haruki Intabyūshū 1997–2009* [*I wake up every day to see dreams. Interview Collection of Murakami Haruki 1997–2009*]. Tokyo: Bungei Shunjū, 287–324.

——— 2010b. Murakami Haruki rongu intabyū. *Kangaeru Hito*, August 2010: 13–101.

Oda M. 2017. A spatial analysis of Haruki Murakami's *After Dark* – The city at night as a place to encounter 'darkness'. *Regional Views* 30: 1–13.

Otomo R. 2009. Risk and home: *After Dark* by Murakami Haruki. *Japanese Studies* 29 (3): 353–366.

Richardson, B. 2006. *Unnatural voices: Extreme narration in modern and contemporary fiction.* Columbus: The Ohio State University Press.

———— 2009. Plural focalization, Singular voices: Wandering perspectives in 'we'-narration. *In*: P. Hühn, W. Schmid and J. Schönert, eds. *Point of view, perspective, and focalization: Modeling mediation in narrative.* Berlin & New York: Walter de Gruyter, 143–159.

Rimmon–Kenan, S. 1989. *Narrative fiction: Contemporary poetics.* London; New York: Routledge.

Short, M. 1996. *Exploring the language of poems, plays and prose.* London: Longman.

Stacey, J. 1994. From the male gaze to the female spectator. *In*: J. Stacey, ed. *Star-gazing: Hollywood cinema and female spectatorship.* London: Routledge, 19–48.

8

MAN WITHOUT ~~WOMAN~~

The sexual relationship in the postmodern era

Astrid Lac

The foremost magical element in Murakami Haruki's fiction seems to be the hero, a recurring figure who appears in the guise of various narrative characters throughout the prolific author's vast oeuvre. The debate over whether this hero is 'ordinary' or 'extraordinary' elides the kernel of his 'magic', assigning historical–political value while ignoring literary qua phantasmatic significance. Such a debate can do no more than alternately, contradictorily, celebrate 'his consciousness […] leftover from the *Zenkyōtō* [All-Campus Joint Struggle] [university student] protests of the late sixties […] unreconciled to the blandness of contemporary life' and deplore his 'exceedingly ordinary' personality unable to 'shoulder the burden of great ideas' (Hillenbrand 2007: 267). What finally invalidates this binary characterisation is a textual irony sustained between constative and performative acts: the hero is said to be so devoid of distinct features as to appear extraordinary; or, conversely, his extraordinary features are recounted in a language stripped of claims of ownership in the way of modification, emphasis, or negation. Either way, the effect is the same: dissonance in the order of fantasy. For what is fantasy if not the subject's – and the text's – endeavor to make up for the lack in language qua symbolic order? Diametrically opposite views continue to circulate: in his isolation, Murakami's hero simply mirrors, on the one hand, the 'alienated life style characteristic of cosmopolitan city people' (Murakami F. 2002: 127–128), 'superficial, yet comfortable' (Treat 2013: 94); and, on the other, 'usually self-employed, freelance, a part-timer or a house-husband', he manages 'careful distancing from and engagement with society, without full dependency or absolute resistance', thereby earning 'individuality' and reflecting 'Murakami's rejection of the system' (Nihei 2013: 71). It would be a betrayal of the text to vacillate between them without considering what renders them all valid.

I propose to read Murakami's iconic hero, shot through with contradiction and as such definitive of a single oeuvre, by way of the psychoanalytical concept of the subject at the intersection of sexual difference qua structural division and its sociocultural significance. The most familiar rendition of this hero, doubling as the first-person narrator, goes by the masculine first-person pronoun *boku* in the original Japanese which, distinct from the more gender-neutral and (as such) modern individualistic *watashi* or emphatically gendered *ore*, is already marked by a certain cool distance at the level of enunciation. Murakami reifies this quality to the extreme only to reveal its truth to be precisely its opposite, that is, the hero ever found on the precipice from which to descend into the quicksand of fantasy. This reversal defines nearly all of Murakami's heroes, first- or third-person, thus warranting the designation of the 'Murakamian' hero as a particular subject position and the reading of Murakami's fiction as a theoretical adventure on the question of the subject. Likewise, if there is anything 'postmodern' about the Murakamian hero – and Murakami's fiction centred on him – as much of scholarly debate has led us to believe (see Iwamoto 1993; Strecher 1998; Murakami F. 2002; Kawakami 2002; Seats 2006), it should be located not in what he does or does not do, but how he positions himself vis-à-vis the world, that is, of the Other, others, or women.

Desire in the colour of sexual difference

One of Murakami's more recent novels, *Colorless Tsukuru Tazaki and His Years of Pilgrimage* (2014; *Shikisai o motanai Tazaki Tsukuru to, kare no junrei no toshi* [2013]), presents a representative specimen of the Murakamian hero qua subject. It is fitting that Murakami defines the hero Tsukuru as 'colourless' (*shikisai o motanai*, literally, without possession of colour). What he lacks is not so much particular features – for the absence of features is also a feature – as desire, whose status is serendipitously marked by the active lexeme 'possess' (*motsu*). What is desire if not desire for difference? Carl Cassegård's observation regarding Murakami's 'protagonists' is relevant in this sense: '[for them] each second is as good as the next and nothing ever seems to change' (2007: 162). The pseudo-Zen composure that pervades the Murakamian hero's world owes itself to this dispassion, and the narrative language that simultaneously reflects and constitutes it. Colour then, denoting what can be added, lacking, or dispensable, signifies superfluous yet (or, as such) never sufficient *difference*. Yet, his life is far from colourless, indeed often teeming with extraordinary events that would astonish any ordinary individual who wears his desire on his sleeve.

A possibility of resolving this perceived contradiction between the absence of desire and life configured to demand full subjective engagement – which is what proper desire does – is found in Jacques Lacan's concept of aphanisis. Unlike Ernest Jones, who first seized upon the Greek term to mean the 'extinction' of 'sexual capacity and enjoyment' at the experiential level (1927: 461), Lacan sees it as a fundamental psychical structure, the 'fading of the subject' (1998a: 208). To paraphrase Lacan, I first have desire – and thus become constituted as a subject who can know and speak – when I know that my mother qua first Other has desire/lack; simultaneously, I become reduced or constituted as this originary reduction to what is represented by one signifier (i.e. mother's desire) for another (i.e. the phallus qua signifier of desire), thus also lacking in being. In short, for Lacan the subject is split or divided: 'when the subject appears somewhere as meaning, he is manifested elsewhere as "fading", as disappearance' (Lacan 1998a: 218). The Lacanian subject is constituted as lacking, that is, when the spectre of its own demise answers, and thus preserves itself against the lack in the Other – 'the superimposition of two lacks' (1998a: 214). The minimal lesson is that aphanisis is the condition of, rather than (or, as much as) a barrier to, 'sexual capacity and enjoyment'.

At first glance, Murakami's hero seems impoverished not only in terms of particular desires but also desire qua desire of the Other which is the premise of the subject function, and this may be the reason for his 'strange aphasia': 'There is no ready-made language with which he is completely at home' (Hirata 2005: 50). Yet, it would be wrong to conclude that there is no functioning Other here. Not only is the hero not psychotic, but he must, and can only, 'first [appear] in the Other' to be at all susceptible to fantasy, of which we see a perverse variety overtake him, leading him to new social bonds (Lacan 1998a: 218). Another of Lacan's concepts provides an opening for further interpretation here: the trouble with the Murakamian hero is that of *objet a*, or the object–cause of desire. *Objet a* denotes the fundamental antagonism or negativity inherent to desire ('*a*' as in the first letter of *autre*, French for 'other'), that is, desire split from within between object and cause, which cannot finally coincide, and thus ever elusive and ever insistent. Lacan thus declares: '[In] its fundamental use, fantasy is the means by which the subject maintains himself at the level of his vanishing desire, vanishing inasmuch as the very satisfaction of demand deprives him of his object' (2006: 532). In other words, desire qua cause appears in the place from which the object of demand has vanished. Desire qua object has no status but the subject's pursuit of one object after another, each of which can only appear in the frame of the demand and accordingly vanish, thereby confirming the reign of desire qua cause. Put in these terms, the Murakamian hero lacks desire qua object – it is worth noting that he never makes demands on anyone – to the extent that he is lingering at the threshold of desire qua cause – a hypothesis that can diffuse the contradiction of the colourless hero's excessively colourful fantasy.

In Murakami's fiction, the hero's daily routine works like a physical mantra continually obliterating the possibility of difference, while female characters are extremely mobile – fulfilling, we might venture, what is proper to their sex: difference. On the surface, they awaken him to desires, to recognise and correct what is amiss in reality. Underneath, however, what drives him in this new mode of activity is not any particular (object of) desire but the very possibility of desire (qua cause) – hence the radical coming face to face with fantasy, or the magical interstices of the world. He never arrives at desiring some *thing*, but until the end wanders passively at the bidding of desire qua difference. Along with Tsukuru of *Colorless Tsukuru Tazaki*, recall Toru Watanabe of *Norwegian Wood* (2000; *Noruwei no mori* [1987]), Toru Okada of *The Wind-Up Bird Chronicle* (1997; *Nejimakidori kuronikuru* [1994–1995]) and Tengo of *1Q84* (2011; *1Q84* [2009–2010]). Their pursuits are invariably responses to external urgencies introduced by women, responses arising from unresisting affirmation rather than (re)active volition or intention. For instance, in *Norwegian Wood*, Toru accepts without a second thought nearly all the demands made on him, demonstrating that his capacity is to affirm desire as such, qua cause, rather than satisfy individual desires for particular objects. Situating the Murakamian hero between object and cause of desire, we can also cast new light on the 'postmodernity' of Murakami's work. The dispassionate hero is precisely an instance of subjective endeavours negotiating the postmodern condition of desire, which tends towards attenuation and, to use Frederic Jameson's oft-quoted phrase, the consequent 'waning of affect'. What form then do these endeavours take?

The textual answer is as already stated: women, the markers of colour qua difference qua cause of desire. They thrust the colourless hero into a signifying/desiring circuit, often nearly to the point of death, enacting a new rite of castration.[1] Obviously, castration in this case occurs not under the paternal agency outlined in psychoanalysis – as the classic Freudian father with the superior phallic organ or the Lacanian Name-of-the-Father – but, instead, by women. Simultaneously, however, women do what they do for the Murakamian hero because he has some *thing*, hence their attraction to him. Put simply, he has the penis – a point that requires further elaboration. Leaving detailed discussion for the analysis below, here I will simply point out how Murakami's textual position presents an alternative to the conventional postmodern debate on terminology, which frequently concludes by privileging the 'phallus' for its symbolic valence over the 'penis's' biological facticity. By illuminating the penis precisely as an organ that comes into conflict with the phallus (e.g. when erection is the cause of abjection rather than the sign of potency), in conjunction with the questioning (deconstructing) of desire, Murakami's texts regress to the forgotten *époque* in the development of the individual when desire qua psychical regime premised on the phallus subjugated the penis. From the psychoanalytical perspective then, the fantasy of Murakami's fiction is properly infantile and as such traumatic. Let us now return to the question of colour and conclude this prologue on the Murakamian hero, desire, and sexual difference.

Colour is an exceptionally apt figure for desire because it signals the spectrum of affect, that is, as a figure of speech. More importantly, insofar as its (figurative) ontology is that of supplement rather than substance, colour becomes women, or femininity as the absolute Other of man who thinks he possesses the phallus, the ground of signification and desire. *Colorless Tsukuru Tazaki* illustrates this idea of sexual difference almost diagrammatically. Of Tsukuru's four 'colourful' friends, two are male and named after primary colours, red (*Aka*) and blue (*Ao*), and the other two female, whose colours are ambiguous, indeed shades of noncolour: white (*Shiro*) and black (*Kuro*). Particularly suggestive is Shiro who, unbeknown to Tsukuru, spread accusations that he had raped her. The resulting ostracism drove Tsukuru to an experience verging on Lacanian 'subjective destitution' whereby he was forced out of the intersubjective dialectic with a lasting consequence: 'Like Jonah in the belly of the whale, Tsukuru had fallen into the bowels of death, one untold day after another, lost in a dark, stagnant void' (Murakami 2014a: 4). White, a (non-)colour that renders other colours visible, is a genuine metaphor for the Lacanian cause of desire and, we might add, the Derridean difference ('*différance*') that is both a term for and the condition of differential relation. Thus, Shiro, in being the object of desire – qua site of truth of Tsukuru's present reality – in fact represents the ontology of the cause of desire.

By contrast, Sara, Tsukuru's girlfriend, is not marked by any colour, and she knows exactly what she desires (from him), namely, manhood built on full self-knowledge: 'to come face-to-face with the past, not as some naive, easily wounded boy, but as a grown-up, independent professional' (2014a: 115). The important point is that Sara's function (focalised on object qua purpose) is secondary to Shiro's (qua motivating cause) when it comes to Tsukuru's subjective mobility, and this contradiction between Shiro and Sara has metatextual significance bearing on Murakami's entire oeuvre. On the one hand, man lacking colour holds the possibility of sexual relationship even if it is destined to prove impossible, while woman lacking colour, precisely by presuming the existence of such a thing as a sexual relationship, bodes the end of that possibility.[2] On the other hand, man doubtful of desire (qua object) is put on the path of further subjectivisation by desiring woman (qua cause).

Given the fundamentally pathological structure of desire, the exceptional clarity of Sara's desire should be doubtful. Alternatively, Sara is possibly the most masculine of all Murakami's characters, if masculinity is understood as a subjective structure founded on the fantasy of the phallus, presence, and meaning; and, as Lacan says, '[m]eaning [*sens*] indicates the direction toward which it fails [*échoue*]' (1998b: 79). The 'Saras' qua phallic women of the Murakamian hero's world are no lovers in the end, as we will confirm shortly, a textual discernment demonstrative of a theoretical consistency. In contrast, Kuro, who loves (Tsukuru in the past) and who creates (she is a potter in the present), was named a (non-)colour and yet (as such) has come to see *beyond* colours, hence her final dispensing with colourful nicknames and request that Tsukuru call her Eri instead (Murakami 2014a: 300). The relation between Shiro and Kuro offers a nearly complete trajectory of the Lacanian subject, from its onset (with *objet a* qua cause of desire) to the traversal thereof (i.e., of colour qua fantasy).

If white is the colour most colourless, we find that Tsukuru and Shiro in fact share an affinity. In the context of Tsukuru's saga of becoming once again a subject – better, recognising afresh his subjecthood, '[t]he Tsukuru who makes things' (Murakami 2014a: 300) – Shiro is a kind of mirror image *à la* Lacan, that is, not identical but ideal, in her own process of subjectivisation, for Tsukuru to desire and identify with, so as to constitute himself as subject. This dovetails with the Lacanian definition of femininity: precisely by being *not-all* ('*pas-tout*' in French, because there is more to her than being situated, in the phallic order), woman can *also* be like man. This duality, or what Freud rather quickly calls female bisexuality, operates differently in the case of Sara, who actively pursues the phallic function on the sole premise of desire and signification. The postmodern male subject *à la* Murakami thus emerges as a symptom of two alternative femininities, one taking on *narrative* (Shiro's lies, for instance) as modern hysterical ambivalence *à la* Freud, and the other, as the postmodern phallic–feminist certitude. The ambiguous ending for which Murakami's fiction is famous can now be read as the point of non-arrival for the hero, reflective of the work of the postmodern subject as *subject-to-be* in an era when sexual difference, the fundamental structuring principle of the subject, is changing sexes, if never equally or reciprocally. This limit is no error but another iteration of sexual difference as such.

What *Colorless Tsukuru Tazaki* codifies into a metaphorical diagram of colours, the short story collection *Men Without Women* (2017; *Onna no inai otokotachi* [2014]) fully articulates in thorough narrative studies. Puzzling out the fundamental problematic of sexual difference through banal binaries – e.g. feminine deception and masculine disappointment – the sum of the stories illustrates a culture of the Lacanian dictum: there is no such thing as a sexual relationship (*il n'y a pas de rapport sexuel*). That is, even when the sexes seem to change places, sexual difference remains that which obstructs the relation of the sexes, *one with the Other*. Nevertheless, or for that reason, *Men Without Women* is shot through with the question of love, as if echoing Lacan's discussion of the nonexistent sexual relationship punctuated with questions of love: e.g., 'Isn't it on the basis of the confrontation with this impasse, with this impossibility by which a real is defined, that love is put to the test?' (1998b: 144). My purpose in the following discussion is to clarify what the absence – 'without' in Murakami's title – signifies, and how it might be configured in relation to the other absence – 'colourless'. It becomes possible thereby to illuminate sexual difference as the textual logic of *Men Without Women* – also the template, I argue, of Murakami's fiction on the whole.

Men without women, women without men

All six stories in the original Japanese edition of *Men Without Women* thematise emphatically feminine deception – from enigmatic charms to downright betrayal – and uniformly suggest that, for women, sexual maturity is inseparable from performative relation to the world. Murakami's textual configuration of performance in the context of the feminine sex, however, is not to be confused with the widely circulated de/constructivist notion of 'gender performance', which has become a critical norm since its popularisation by Judith Butler in the 1990s. While the theory of performativity sheds light on the making of a sex qua gender and thereby shows the way to sex's unmaking, Murakami's fiction demonstrates with what intransigence performance adheres to woman qua sexed being, to order her world often to fatal effect. Simultaneously, this feminine performance or deception is not without a psychosexual developmental history. The entire volume is configured around the momentous shift whereby the little girl becomes a woman and thus makes inevitable the failure – or as Lacan would say, the nonexistence – of the sexual relationship. This is not to say that Murakami blames the feminine sex. To the contrary, the volume holds true to what has been argued above, that women denote colour, of (the possibility of) desire, subjective function *par excellence*. Murakami seems to be saying: without women exercising their birthright of difference, actualising what is true to their sexuality, there is no hope for men. The Murakamian hero's default withdrawal into colourlessness marks this impasse as the starting point – a textual task. He then invariably *answers* feminine demands which are impossible to *meet*, and thereby arrives at a new subjective position that has a relation to that impossibility. It is thus that *Men Without Women* never ceases to intimate how the nonexistent relationship between the sexes might nevertheless lead to love – a shorthand for what might possibly lie beyond the phallic order that the sexes may access by way of each other.

Women lie

'Drive My car' ('Doraibu mai kā'), the first story in the collection, tells the story of a man whose wife dies without confessing to her extramarital affairs, leaving him to his own detective work. The main concern of his investigation turns out not to be sordid details (who, when, where, etc.) but the mystery of her desire. It begins with Kafuku, the cuckolded husband, commenting that 'female drivers' are either 'a little too aggressive or a little too timid' (Murakami 2017a: 3). This is not a gratuitously misogynistic remark. In view of Kafuku's profession as an actor and his marriage to an actress involved in a series of extramarital affairs, the phrase 'a little too' gains theatrical significance with an ontological dimension. On the one hand, the wife's ability to act – i.e. deceive her husband – up to the point of her death, is essentialised into feminine mystery. On the other hand, it turns out that Kafuku knew of the affairs all along, yet never revealed this knowledge to his wife: 'The most excruciating thing, though, had been maintaining a normal life knowing his partner's secret – the effort it required to keep her in the dark' (2017a: 17). Who is acting really? Neither the character nor the narrative development acknowledges this irony. Nevertheless, Kafuku is said to have a 'blind spot' both literally due to glaucoma (2017a: 11), and metaphorically: '*we men are all living with the same sort of blind spot*' (2017a: 35; emphasis in the original Japanese). Thus, his own deception seems largely exonerated as an effect of this handicap as opposed to the feminine enterprise. The consequence is not insignificant, however. Declared unfit to drive on account of his visual impairment, he abdicates the driver's seat to Misaki, an exceptionally reliable 24-year-old female driver, signalling the possibility of the sexes coming eye to eye. However, this hopeful end promises no simple solution for deception as the first articulation of sexual difference.

Indeed, the rest of *Men Without Women* goes a long way towards substantiating the ontological significance of this missed encounter between the sexes, or sexual encounter precisely as this missing. The first complication is that feminine deception operates in the absence of conscious intention, as described in 'An Independent Organ' ('Dokuritsu kikan'), the third story in the volume:

> Women are all born with a special, independent organ that allows them to lie. [...] [At] a certain point in their lives, all women tell lies, and they lie about important things. They lie about unimportant things, too, but they also don't hesitate to lie about the most important things. And when they do, most women's expressions and voices don't change at all, since it's not them lying, but this independent organ they're equipped with that's acting on its own.
>
> (Murakami 2017c: 111)

This fissure that opens (in) woman's speech finds a clear explanation in psychoanalysis. At one level, subjectivity as such is feminine. Freud characterises passivity qua femininity as the inherent principle of sexual development for *both* sexes: 'the castration complex always operates in the sense implied in its subject matter: it inhibits and limits masculinity and encourages femininity' (1961: 256). We have already seen that for Lacan the subject is by definition a split subject: it simultaneously is and is not (itself), or it *is* only as a place of absence, precipitated as an interruption in language and persisting as the desire of the Other. In sum, the feminine lie, precisely for its lack of sovereignty, points to the truth of the subject as such. No wonder Kafuku's obsession with his wife's deception as the truth of femininity has the ironic effect of drawing out the untruth that drives *all* speech acts: 'Once you really get into a role, it's hard to find the right moment to stop. No matter how it preys on your emotions, you have to go with the flow until the performance has taken its shape, the point where its true meaning becomes clear' (Murakami 2017a: 24). Taking for truth the paradox that 'true meaning' arises precisely from the 'performance' of a 'role', this little reflection by Kafuku bears out the fundamental condition and possibility of the subject, that is, 'I' never coincides with itself but can only appear in 'the field of the Other' (Lacan 1998a: 204). How then can woman be differentiated from the inherently lacking subject? What is the lack that is specific to the feminine sex, which allows untruth to be the truth of *her* speech in a way that it is not *his*?

Freud provides a systematic investigation of the way in which the two sexes come to desire, that is, the itinerary of earliest affects, object choice, identification, etc., with the focus on their incommensurate experiences of the castration complex and the Oedipus complex. The fundamental difference between the little boy and the little girl is the negative origin of the latter's desire: the little girl desires her father out of disappointment with her mother's love, which is doubly insufficient or inadequate on account of her desire/lack and castrated sex, leading possibly to a deep hatred which she might not conquer even in adulthood. The boy, in contrast, holds steadfastly to the original object of desire, if at the expense of profound anxiety and consequent compromises. The crux of the matter is the masculine and the feminine forms of, and relations to, the lack or split inherent to the subject. Put in Lacan's terms, the object of desire carries with it the nebulous history of the cause of desire like an inexpungible stain, that is, *objet a*, which simultaneously motivates and inhibits object relation. Lacan takes this objectal, desire-based difference in the direction of ontology to claim the nonexistence of Woman ('Woman'): Woman does not exist to the extent that, unlike man, not all (*pas tout*) of her is under the sway of the phallic function, and is thus not only split within the Symbolic, but marks the beyond of the Symbolic where enunciation (of meaning) is impossible (see Copjec 1994: 217–227).[3] It is in this spirit that Lacan posits the possibility of feminine *jouissance* not only undercutting the phallic foundation of desire, but even highlighting the *jouissance* of language, which he calls llanguage (*lalangue*) (Lacan 1998b: 138).

Note how Kafuku's desire is unambiguously professed: 'Kafuku adored his wife' (Murakami 2017a: 15). By contrast, the wife's infidelity with a series of men – without exception, her counterparts in movies – is itself generative of *questioning* without definite questions. The single positive act attributed to her is refusal: 'Judging from the way Takatsuki [the partner in her last affair] spoke, Kafuku's wife had been the one to call a halt to their affair. "It's best we not meet anymore", was probably how she had put it. [...] As far as Kafuku knew, that was the pattern of all her amours' (ibid.). Her 'amours', marked by nonchalant fusion of performance and truth, foreclose (ac) countability of desire, and simultaneously cast a melancholy qua knowledge of the lack over her figure in its entirety. Renata Salecl defines 'women's dilemma [as] concerning what kind of an object they are for men', which then 'might result in [their immersing] themselves in melancholic indifference' (2002: 94–95). In this sense, Kafuku once again approximates, if without coinciding with, femininity, as he professes his desire to know the desire of the Other: 'I wanted to understand. Why she slept with him, why he was the one she wanted' (Murakami 2017a: 23). This affinity, as we will see, is a chance at love, which nonetheless (or, by the very virtue of it) freshly affirms sexual difference.

Puberty: The second sexual efflorescence or the beginning of the end of sexual relationship

As is well known, Freud posits two *époques* of sexual efflorescence in the individual's life, namely, Oedipal and pubertal. Yet, structurally speaking, the significance of puberty is only nominal. The transformations that take place during this phase concern only the most normative milestones of sexual development – the primacy of the genital zones and the object choice in accordance, constitutive of the 'final, normal' organisation – the foundation of which is in fact already, decisively, laid down during the Oedipus complex (Freud 1953: 207). It is rather at a phenomenal level that puberty marks a crucial event for the sexes, occasioning a fresh manifestation of their nonequivalence. While the boy learns the 'highest degree of pleasure' in 'the discharge of the sexual products' (ibid.), the girl needs to be acquainted with a whole new sexual part, that is, the vagina. Freud notes: 'Puberty, which brings about so great an accession of libido in boys, is marked in girls by a fresh wave of *repression*, in which it is precisely clitoridal sexuality that is affected' (ibid.: 220; Freud's emphasis). As I have explained, the girl's sexual development was marked by negation at its origin – the pre-Oedipal castration complex in relation to the mother – and is now once again subjected to negation by this anatomical transition that is the jettisoning of the clitoris, precisely the infantile equivalent of the penis. A woman's greatest problem seems then to be that she never gets to desire *straightforwardly*, in the phallic manner. How then is this pubertal complication related to the feminine lie discussed above, which dominates the adult female subject? Murakami's fiction does more than answer this question, locating the cause of the impossibility of sexual relationship (*à la* Lacan) in puberty as Freud distinguishes it for the two sexes. Women, we learn, deal with the exorbitant sexual task largely in two ways, the narrative elucidation of which moreover provides commentary on contemporary sociocultural discourse on sexuality.

One of the more memorable examples is the trauma at the heart of *Norwegian Wood*, consisting of Kizuki's suicide and Naoko's subsequent mental illness and eventual suicide. Naoko and Kizuki, an inseparable couple since early childhood, have as their only other friend the narrator–protagonist Toru in high school. It requires only minimal insight to see through the strange exception: despite their seemingly complete union (or, for that very reason), they need an Other, the Third. Even with this intervention, the exceptional intimacy is charged with pathological foreboding. Put simply, 'trauma' in this instance does not refer to any of the deaths – for Naoko, Kizuki's and her own sister's; for Toru, Kizuki's and Naoko's. Its precise construction should be identified in Naoko's relationship with Toru in the narrative foreground. The crucial problem there is Naoko's sexuality. Why did she open up to Toru, only to retreat suddenly after their first intercourse? To Toru, who assumed Naoko's past physical intimacy with Kizuki and is shocked to discover that she is a virgin, Naoko explains: 'I was ready to sleep with him. [...] And of course he wanted to sleep with me. So we tried. We tried a lot. But it never worked. We couldn't do it. I didn't know why then, and I still don't know why. [...] I couldn't get wet. [...] I never opened to him. So it always hurt. I was just too dry, it hurt too much' (Murakami 2000: 111–112). What has baffled and distressed her is her own discovery that in fact she can enjoy sex perfectly well: 'I mean, I was plenty wet the time I slept with you, wasn't I? [...] I was wet from the minute you walked into my apartment' (ibid.: 112). The glitch in Naoko and Kizuki's union, we now discover, was this second rite of sexuality, whereby tender affection must yield to erotic love. Freud articulates the challenge as follows:

> The object–choice of the pubertal period is obliged to dispense with the objects of childhood and to start afresh as a 'sensual current'. Should these two currents [affectionate and sensual] fail to converge, the result is often that one of the ideals of sexual life, the focusing of all desires upon a single object, will be unattainable.
>
> (Freud 1953: 200)

Naoko never gets wet again, perishing at the threshold of feminine sexuality proper.

In *Men Without Women*, Murakami offers an alternative scenario of the pubertal malaise. 'Yesterday' ('Iesutadei'), the second story in the volume, has the same premise as *Norwegian Wood*, that is, the supposedly 'natural' transition from infantile affection to adult sexuality, but adds another factor (or reveals what was concealed there), namely, that this transition is largely conditioned by cultural discourse, whose coercive power could have the opposite effect, that is, of interference, and even psychical crisis. Two friends, Kitaru and Tanimura, reminiscent of Kizuki and Toru, respectively, discuss the former's romantic situation with Erika (Naoko's counterpart), his girlfriend since elementary school:

> 'I kiss her, of course, and hold her hand. I've touched her breasts, through her clothes. But it's like we're just fooling around, y'know, playing.'
> [...]
> 'Instead of waiting for signs or anything, shouldn't *you* be the one to make things happen, and take the next step?'
>
> (Murakami 2017b: 53–54)

Tanimura adds an internal comment, '[t]hat's what *people call* sexual desire' (my emphasis). Erika vents in her turn, also privately to Tanimura: '*As a general rule* [...]

when a guy and a girl go out for a long time and get to know each other really well, the guy has a physical interest in the girl, right? [...] But [Kitaru] doesn't. When we're alone, he doesn't want to go any further' (2017b: 62; my emphasis). This further textualisation sheds new light on Naoko's claim of guilt: it might be that Kizuki (also) failed to desire *properly* and thereby left her body frigid. Indeed, their sexual impasse ought to be situated in the larger context of Kizuki's subjectivity-cum-sexuality in the precise *époque* of puberty, as the text explores in regard to Nagasawa, another of Toru's friends. A flawless young man with an equally perfect girlfriend, Nagasawa nonetheless suffers from a seemingly pathological drive to have casual sex. For both Nagasawa and Kizuki, the problem seems to be the gap between the penis qua organ and the phallus qua symbolic value harbouring sociocultural injunction in the form of regulatory discourse. Indeed, is not the perennial cause of male anxiety that 'their organ might disappoint them when they need it most' (Salecl 2002: 93–94), or, we might add, prove unruly in the opposite way? The only escape is fantasy, read deception, at which these male characters are exceptionally inept. This should explain their general melancholy, which has the absence of desire as its cause. Most of Murakami's heroes share this quality. While Toru's oft-noted speech form – minimal and straightforward – is a positive manifestation of this ineptitude, Nagasawa articulates the truth of this lack with stinging insight: '[Toru] may be a nice guy, but deep down in his heart he's incapable of loving anybody. There's always some part of him somewhere that's wide awake and detached' (Murakami 2000: 210).

Tanimura, the narrator of 'Yesterday', is unable to see through the subtleties of the situation and offers only banal counsel. To Erika who wonders, '[s]ometimes it feels like [Kitaru] doesn't have any sexual desire for me', he answers, 'I'm sure he does. But it might be a little embarrassing for him to admit it' (Murakami 2017b: 63). Kitaru, on the other hand, playfully distorts the Beatles song 'Yesterday', turning it from a sentimental ballad about a young man's growth through love and heartbreak into a farce (Freudian joke?) about linear time: 'Yesterday/Is two days before tomorrow, / The day after two days ago' (Murakami 2017b: 41). Through this transfiguration, Kitaru voices and embraces the uncertainty regarding the traumatic cut that is the *époque* of genital sexuality. It is clear that the textual sympathy lies with Kitaru, as Tanimura, the guy who can be 'sometimes a little *too* normal', voices an uncharacteristic anger, at the anonymous world, in defence of Kitaru: 'You should do what you want and forget about what other people think' (Murakami 2017b: 68; emphasis in the English translation). By the same token, Erika's demand that Kitaru quickly make the transition to manhood betrays a certain ability to dissimulate reality, to narrativise and thereby assimilate it into the 'general rule' of 'sexual desire' – a refrain on the larger theme of feminine performance qua deception. Now we see more clearly the determinant of Naoko's fate in *Norwegian Wood*; she failed where Erika succeeds and consequently fell victim to *après coup* – the logic/time of trauma, the price of sexual enjoyment.

The title character of 'Scheherazade' ('Sheerazādo'), the fourth story in the volume, is a woman who is 'assigned' to deliver supplies and offer sexual companionship to Habara, a man in confinement for an unspecified reason. The narrative climax occurs when Scheherazade, so called by Habara for the reason that 'their lovemaking and her storytelling are so closely linked', divulges an intimate story from her girlhood (Murakami 2017d: 123). This particular story plays on the same theme of female puberty as in 'Yesterday' and *Norwegian Wood*, but from the opposite direction. Scheherazade's sexual awakening at the age of 17 was as powerful as the absence of her object of desire was complete: 'She buried her face in his shirt and greedily breathed in the sweaty fragrance. Now she could feel a languid sensation in the lower part of her body. Her nipples were stiffened as well. Could her period be on the way? [...] Was this sexual desire? [...] She had no idea' (Murakami 2017d: 137). Her extraordinary absorption in sensual pleasure, the ability to 'get off on' random objects in the absence of phantasmatic support, points to the narrow yet infinite region of *jouissance* posited in opposition to the dominance of adult genital sexuality. Without the discursive, narrative, compensation (for what, if not the lack of enjoyment?) attending this last, Scheherazade's enjoyment is both more and less than 'sexual'; certainly not 'romantic', it approaches 'mystical'. Lacan takes the mystic's *jouissance* as a rare example of feminine *jouissance* distinguished from its phallic counterpart: 'There's no doubt about it [that "she's coming"]. What is she getting off on? It is clear that the essential testimony of the mystics consists in saying that they experience it, but know nothing about it' (Lacan 1998b: 76). Scheherazade echoes Lacan: 'What I had contracted was not something *like* sickness but the real thing. As long as it lasted, I couldn't think straight' (Murakami 2017d: 142; emphasis in the original Japanese). Nevertheless, she 'forgot all about him once [she] graduated': 'What was it about him that made the seventeen-year-old me fall so hard? Try as I might, I couldn't remember' (ibid.).

A striking image encapsulates the nonexistent relationship between man of phallic *jouissance* and woman of its feminine (non)counterpart: 'Lampreys live like that, hidden among the weeds. Lying in wait. Then, when a trout passes overhead, they dart up and fasten onto it with their suckers. Inside their suckers are these tongue-like things with teeth, which rub back and forth against the trout's belly until a hole opens up and they can start eating the flesh, bit by bit' (ibid.: 119). This is one of Scheherazade's stories, once again part of her own life – 'a former life' when she was one such lamprey eel (ibid.: 118). These sea creatures are a perfect embodiment of the *pas-tout* ontology of ~~Woman~~, as their parasitic (not-whole) ex-sistence directly manifests the 'opening' towards the Other's nonexistence. Habara the male captive confesses, '[h]e imagined that he was one of [the lampreys], waiting for a trout to appear. But no trout passed by, no matter how long he waited' (ibid.: 145).

In the end, however, even Scheherazade is claimed by genital sexuality premised on phallic fantasy. She can now tell stories – read 'lies' in the larger textual context – to supplement sex lacking in enjoyment, 'not what you'd call passionate [but not] exactly businesslike' (Murakami 2017d: 122–123). We confirm the same narrative thesis as in earlier stories: girlhood, insofar as it is defined by pre-genital sexuality or not-yet-femininity, signifies the absence of story qua deception; and insofar as story qua fantasy compensates for the absent object – the phallus not found in the penis

– her newfound narrative talent marks her fate to be *without men*. Nevertheless, when the story traverses the fantasy, she is again the girl that she once was, enjoying: 'She was able to direct her incredible storytelling powers at herself. Like a master hypnotist hypnotizing himself by looking in a mirror' (ibid.: 138). Overwhelmed by her own storytelling, an instance of Lacanian *lalangue*, a 'symbolic without an Other' (Copjec 1994: 227), Scheherazade invites Habara to a new round of sex in which '[t]he two of them made love as never before' (Murakami 2017d: 139). This split in her *jouissance* is what Lacan explains as a kind of choice: 'Nothing can be said of woman. Woman has a relation with S(Ⱥ) [the Lacanian algebraic symbol for the signifier of the lack in the Other], and it is already in that respect that she is doubled, that she is not-whole, since she can also have a relation with Φ [the Lacanian symbol for the phallus]' (1998b: 81). In other words, while man only has a relation with *objet a*, woman doubles up by relating to the phallus (e.g. man as her object of desire), and also to the Other that does not exist, which has a signifier in her own domain of sexuality (e.g. God); indeterminacy-cum-overdetermination is written into femininity of Woman. Insofar as femininity is a structure and not a substance, significantly, '[o]ne can also situate oneself on the side of the not-whole. There are men who are just as good as women' (Lacan 1998b: 76). The question is whether the Murakamian hero is as good as that.

So women kill themselves

As the single story in the volume in which the protagonist doubles as the nameless narrator, and whose concern is the deepest melancholy of sexual difference, 'Men Without Women' ('Onna no inai otokotachi') constitutes a point of summation of Murakami's textuality centred on subjectivity that is inseparable from sexuality. In the middle of the night, the narrator-cum-sole character in the narrative present is woken by a phone call from the husband of an ex-girlfriend from long ago informing him that she has killed herself. No explanation comes forward as to why he is calling, how he knows about this ex-boyfriend, or the reason or means of suicide. In the vacuum left by this sudden news, he reflects on the peculiar history of his: 'This woman was the third woman I'd gone out with who'd killed herself' (Murakami 2017g: 214). As for this particular woman: 'Truthfully I like to think of M as a girl I met when she was fourteen. That didn't actually happen, but here, at least, I'd like to imagine it did' (ibid.: 215); '[w]hat I want to say is, M is the woman I should have fallen in love with when I was fourteen' (ibid.: 218). The age of 14 is significant here because, as I have argued, in Murakami's fiction puberty functions as a kind of vanishing point of femininity (it disappears as soon as it appears). For the girl, the demand to have tender, affectionate, infantile sexual desire meet genital sexual initiation thereby completing the final, normal, organisation of sexuality, entails surrendering to the phallic logic to the exclusion of her Other relation or, failing that, expiring. Put differently, 'femininity' often manifests itself in irony, either in the form of masquerade – to *be* the phallus – or '*hommosexualité*,' that is, to 'play the part of the man [*homme*]' and to therefore love one who is the same (*homo*) as herself. Either way it loses the specifically feminine kind of enjoyment (Lacan 1998b: 85).[4] In short, the story's protagonist would have liked to meet M before she had *necessarily* suffered the effects of adult female sexuality. To his regret, they failed to meet at that age:

> But it was only much later that I fell in love with her, and by then, sadly, she was fourteen no more. [...] A fourteen-year-old girl still resided within her, however. That girl was complete inside of her, not just fragments. [...] When she lay in my arms as we made love, she would turn old one minute, then become a young girl in the next.
>
> (Murakami 2017g: 218)

For their ill-fated relationship, the narrator blames other men rather than her 'femininity': 'But, of course, the time came when I lost her again. All the sailors around the world, after all, had her in their sights. I couldn't be expected to protect her all by myself. [...] There was always, in the background, the unambiguous shadow of a sailor' (ibid.: 218). Who are the sailors? We find an intertextual explanation in another of Murakami's novel, *1Q84*. For the hero Tengo, who 'wanted most of all [...] uninterrupted free time' and only to 'have sex on a regular basis' and therefore 'had nothing more to ask of a woman' (Murakami 2011: 252), the sailors are fools suffering an excess of machismo:

> It didn't work this way when he had sex with younger women. He would have to think from the beginning to end, making choices and judgments. [...] All the responsibilities fell on his shoulders. He felt like the captain of a small boat on a stormy sea, having to take the rudder, inspect the setting of the sails, keep in mind the barometric pressure and the wind direction, and modulate his own behavior so as to boost the crew's trust in him. The slightest mistake or accident could lead to tragedy. This felt less like sex than the discharging of a duty.
>
> (ibid.: 277)

Sailors are, in other words, men who have completely settled in their phallic fantasy and therefore have nothing more to do than encourage women on the path of 'feminine' (self-)deception toward masquerade or *hommosexualité*, thus actively perpetuating their shared fate to be without 'sexual relationship' (*rapport sexuel*).

The narrator of 'Men Without Women', self-identified as one of the men who 'oppose' the sailors (Murakami 2017g: 220), is wiser than Tengo in the way of love. He seems to know that women fall for sailors precisely because they do *not* desire men. Recall the story 'Drive My Car', in which Misaki makes this canny observation concerning Kafuku's unfaithful wife: 'Isn't it possible that your wife didn't fall for him at all? [...] And that's why she slept with him? [...] Women can be like that' (Murakami 2017a: 39–40). Infidelity is nothing but the truth – of the failure – of desire guaranteed by the phallus. As for these women's subjective journey, we have only an external view; and the little that the text reveals is nonetheless, or all the more, startling: 'Or else the women have nothing to do with sailors, and take their own lives' (Murakami 2017g: 223). In short, once a girl becomes a woman, she can either go with the sailors or perish. The psychoanalytical implications of these choices should be clear by now: either phallic fantasy (feminine falsehoods) to conceal the lack (redoubled as subjective and feminine), or death; either as the consequence of fantasy's failure, or, conversely, full identification with the failure, and thus traversal of fantasy.

How love can be possible

Having established the double-bind, the necessary bond, that is 'femininity' between the 'fresh repression' of sexuality during the girl's puberty and the deception inherent to adult female sexuality, which precisely obliterates femininity, we are now ready to speak of love. To draw on *1Q84* again, we find there a rare example of a couple in Murakami's fiction who succeed in their romantic relationship, an exceptional case proving the rule sketched above. Aomame and Tengo first fall in love at the age of ten only to be separated for the next 20 years. This love, cherished by both throughout their separation, sustains them through a series of life-threatening adventures and finally brings them together and out of the dangerous alternate world of 1Q84. It is easy to see how they can avoid the pitfall to which Kizuki and Naoko, as well as Kitaru and Erika, succumb. While their bond is formed during the pre-genital *époque*, they are serendipitously separated during the traumatic period in which they assumed their respective genital sexuality and thus spared the task of redefining their relationship under the pressure of the psychical reality of the body and cultural discourse of 'sexual desire'. True, it takes no less than 20 years and an alternate world with two moons in the sky for them to be reunited. Man and woman in love, Murakami seems to say, are nothing short of a miracle. This explanation is reasonable for the case at hand, but what about the broader problem of sexual difference that disturbs and drives Murakami's fiction in general? For not all men and women receive a cosmically ordained second chance. Besides, it is worth noting, *1Q84*'s neat denouement harbours purposeful hints of the *forced* fulfilment of the Oedipal wish: Tengo and Aomame's child is conceived before their sexual union – as if to insist that *there shall be no sexual relationship*. A happy ending is more, and simultaneously less, than what sexual difference can give.

Against this single 'ideal' case in *1Q84*, *Men Without Women* presents several possibilities for the (nonexistent) sexual relationship between man and woman. At the narrative level, 'Drive My Car' presents an optimistic outlook on the future of the sexes that seems to depend on two conditions. First, quite miraculously, Kafuku was born in the same year as Misaki's father (Murakami 2017a: 37) and Kafuku's daughter would have been Misaki's age if she had lived instead of dying soon after birth (2017a: 18). Thus the kind of femininity with which Kafuku can be at ease, the kind which knows how to drive without theatrical surplus, the kind which does not lure men into mimetic deception, is imagined for the daughter's generation. The wife's death signifies the end of her generation, of any hope for its capacity to discover or reconstitute what is *not* phallic. Misaki's portrayal of her harsh mother adds to this generational rupture within femininity (2017a: 22, 40).

'Samsa in Love' ('Koi suru Zamuza'), an addition made to the English edition of *Men Without Women* and a homage to Kafka's *The Metamorphosis*, presents another feminine figure with futurative significance as regards sexual relationship. The eponymous protagonist, previously an insect, has recently taken on the human form and, in his interspecies confusion, acts like a child in a grown man's body. He embodies pure innocence with a fully functioning penis that he flourishes erect with complete disregard for etiquette. His counterpart is a hunchback woman, who on account of her malformed body has learned not to accept or profit from theatricality, evoking Misaki from 'Drive My Car' who 'shoots from the hip when she talks' (2017a: 5). No wonder there is hope for this couple, where even the man need not lack the colour of desire. Indeed, Samsa, joyful with uninhibited sexuality of the infantile kind, is one of the most colourful figures in Murakami's oeuvre. His erection, evocative of the 14-year-old boy's in 'Men Without Women' – 'all it took was a warm west wind for my cock to snap to attention' (2017f: 216) – constitutes a curative answer to the feminine 'independent organ'. Recall Kizuki, Nagasawa, and Kitaru who exemplify abjection by the gap between the penis, the erection of which cannot be controlled at will, and the phallus which rules through romantic myths among others; and Toru who is a nearly mythical figure of the healer of and in sex (e.g. through Naoko's awakening and Reiko's reawakening to enjoyment). The premise of these varying cases is precisely sexuality as traumatic, that is, de/subjectivising experience. Put differently, the male biological automatism (the 'independent organ' of the penis) and discursive meaning (of sexual desire qua rights and freedom) are mutually repulsive, and their identification is possibly fatal for the subject. It is this crisis that is answered by Murakami's insistence on penile vitality as the alpha and omega of his fictional world, which Samsa nakedly brings to the fore. Murakami's fiction never doubts the value of male potency. Indeed, the innocence of the penis, stripped of its phallic significance, is valorised as the very premise of sexual, relational, even world, healing.

This is Murakami's chief contribution to the psychoanalytical theory of sexuality in the postmodern era. He neither apologies for masculine erection nor condemns feminine performance. Rather, they are the very textual logic: for each woman's 'independent organ' of lying, each man's indiscriminate penis. What we have is the asynchrony of bodily fixation and symbolic compensation between the sexes. Thus is sexual difference inscribed. Each sex has a task cut out for it. Woman, unwittingly harassed by feminine falsity (caused by the failure to be properly feminine by relating to the Other qua lack as well as to the phallus), would do well to recognise her phallic motivation to become and thus desire as man. Man, with the imposture by which he wilfully identifies the penis with the phallus and thus suffers from the superego injunction – 'Enjoy!' as Lacan says (1998b: 3) – would do well to recognise the real gap that their imaginary affinity veils.

What is central to Murakami's text then, and what the Murakamian hero finally represents, is men who have rejected, failed to fulfil, or never desired the phallic function and, as such, have no ambition for 'sexual relationship' but, precisely for that reason, harbour the capacity to explore their subjective proximity to women and thereby signal an *other* relationality, 'love' that allows both sexes to relate differently to the phallus. If colour is desire that perpetuates itself by way of phallic fantasy, the Murakamian hero ought to lack colour. This narcissistic loner, alternative to the 'sailor', offers an escape and remedy for women because his withdrawal is, minimally, a bulwark against the onslaught of the phallic logic and, maximally, a premise on which this last can be traversed. Toru of *Norwegian Wood*, to whom virtually every woman that he meets feels drawn, is the most complete embodiment of this textual logic. It is clear that the Murakamian hero's significance is inseparable from women who bear the burden of the objectification of the lack or division constitutive of the subject – as ~~Woman~~. Indeed, in the absence of women, he is immobilised.

A paradigmatic example is Kino of the eponymous story in *Men Without Women*. Cuckolded in his own bed, he goes to do what the Murakamian hero does best: settle into a simple routine. He opens a little bar in an inconspicuous neighbourhood and minds his own business, tending bar and playing music. Then begins magic: a supernatural figure by the name of Kamita – literally 'god's field' as he takes the trouble to clarify – offers advice, which is more like a riddle: 'Mr. Kino, you're not the type who would willingly do something wrong. I know that very well. But there are times in this world when *it's not enough just not to do the wrong things*. Some people use that blank space as a kind of loophole. Do you understand what I'm saying?' (Murakami 2017e: 174; my emphasis) Textually acknowledged here is the limit of inactivity as a kind of protest against the phallic logic; the anti-sailor cannot correct a world run by the sailors merely by being. Passivity is a double-edged virtue in the Murakamian world, insofar as it invariably manifests itself as affirmation. Kino does not 'understand' but decides to follow Kamita's prescription nonetheless. He leaves town in search of something, though he knows not what. Unfortunately, the text seems lost along with the character; the final pages are mostly posturing with imagery, of the snake foremost – seemingly meaningful but in fact ill-defined and confused. All that Kino can do is admit: 'Yes, I am hurt. Very, very deeply' (ibid.: 185).

This sudden deficit in narrative craftsmanship and textual integrity (for instance, we are left to wonder: Why does Kino go against Kamita's prohibition and send his aunt a postcard, and to what effect?) might nevertheless be interpreted as one instance of the larger textuality under discussion.[5] Namely, is it not the absence of women that precludes narrative direction or textual coherence – that is to say, muddles the hero's world? The most that the story manages is a vague suggestion of a relation between the 'blank space' in him – the void left by the 'heart' (ibid.: 184) – and something like feminine essence: 'Snakes are essentially ambiguous creatures. In these legends [from all over the world], the biggest, smartest snake hides its heart somewhere outside its body, so that it doesn't get killed' (ibid.: 172). This might be a moment when the author's own desire reveals itself, perhaps for a representational order not delimited by the *real* of sexual difference and, as such, *original* creation.[6]

The Murakamian hero between desire and drive

What is the upshot of Murakami's fiction? Man must own up to his lack *first*. This negative precedence demonstrates at once his proximity to femininity – the proper position of sexual difference as well as modality of subjectivity – and the persistent sexual difference whereby he resolutely remains man. This is a textual desire if there ever was one. While an obvious intertextual reference to Ernest Hemingway's earlier short story collection (1927), the title *Men Without Women*, in other words, also invites an eminently Lacanian reading: men who see that there is no such thing as (a universal, generalised) Woman (*'il n'y a pas La femme'*) because she is in the phallic order and simultaneously elsewhere; and who sustain that truth precisely by being *with* women qua instances of ~~Woman~~. In the best cases, Murakami's text is at war with itself. The obvious Oedipal thematics – evident in characters like Kafka in *Kafka on the Shore* (2005; *Umibe no Kafuka* [2002]) and Tengo – is a kind of false position, a crowd pleaser, a bait that gets lost in the larger textual structure whereby the Oedipal assumptions themselves are rendered questionable, not ideologically but ontologically. Murakami the author cannot necessarily perceive this split internal to the textuality of his own oeuvre, which is simultaneously *his* and *not his*. We might perceive authorial desire becoming as well as interfering with textual desire, but there also persists the drive of the text, which orders, limits, and pushes that desire to its truth. There, in these gaps, must lie the postmodern possibility of contemporary literary criticism.

Notes

1 In the Freudian schema of the Oedipus complex, the father intervenes in the mother–child dyad with a threat of castration aimed at the child, typically male, the consequence of which is the child's renunciation of his incestuous desire for the mother and compensatory identification with the father, the necessary step for entry into culture. Lacan, on the other hand, situates castration as the universal requisite for the subject, the primary alienation whereby the subject loses its being in order to attain its proper status. For Freud, castration is evaded in the Oedipus complex; for Lacan, castration is acceded to as the outcome of the Oedipus complex.

2 Recall his early short story collection, *The Elephant Vanishes* (1993; *Zō no shōmetsu* [2005]), which features two types of women throughout its stylistically and thematically varying narratives. The contrast ultimately comes down to that between the hero's wife and her female friend in 'Lederhosen' (1993a; 'Rēdāhōzen'), that is, between the one who facilely repeats sociocultural banalities and the other who demonstrates an understanding, if only subliminal, of the lack that defines femininity. We see more examples in *Men Without Women* analysed in the latter half of this chapter.

3 We should be careful not to impute some kind of inherent subversion to femininity; it is rather infinity that defines femininity. In Žižek's words, 'woman [qua feminine position] undermines the universality of the phallic function by the very fact that there is no exception in her, nothing that resists it' (1995). It is in this spirit that Lacan posits the possibility of feminine *jouissance* that exceeds the phallic foundation of desire and surplus *jouissance* proper to it, and goes on to theorise the *jouissance* of language, which he calls *lalangue*.

4 An exception to this thesis is the 13-year-old lesbian in *Norwegian Wood* but her case is rather obscure, related only through Reiko's recollection.

5 Perhaps a sequel or extended version will follow in the future, the same way *The Wind-Up Bird Chronicle* built on the short story 'The Wind-Up Bird Chronicle and Tuesday's Women' (1993b; 'Nejimakidori to kayōbi no onnatachi' [1986]).

6 Reading the Preface (*maegaki*) to the original Japanese edition of *Men Without Women*, I found to my amused satisfaction Murakami's admission: '["Kino"] was a very difficult story to complete. I revised it, minutely, many times over. All the other stories, on the other hand, I pretty much dashed off [*surasura to kaketa*]' (2014b: 11–12; my translation).

References

Cassegård, C. 2007. *Shock and naturalization in contemporary Japanese literature*. Folkestone: Global Oriental.

Copjec, J. 1994. *Read my desire: Lacan against the historicists*. Cambridge: MIT Press.

Freud, S. 1953. Three essays on the theory of sexuality. *In*: J. Strachey, ed. *The standard edition of the complete psychological works of Sigmund Freud*. Vol. VII. London: Hogarth, 135–243.

――― 1961. Some psychical consequences of the anatomical distinction between the sexes. *In*: J. Strachey, ed. *The standard edition of the complete psychological works of Sigmund Freud*. Vol. XIX. London: Hogarth, 248–258.

Hillenbrand, M. 2007. *Literature, modernity, and the practice of resistance: Japanese and Taiwanese fiction, 1960–1990*. Leiden: Brill.

Hirata H. 2005. *Discourses of seduction: History, evil, desire, and modern Japanese literature*. Cambridge: Harvard University Asia Center.

Iwamoto Y. 1993. A voice from postmodern Japan: Haruki Murakami. *World Literature Today* 67 (2): 295–300.

Jones, E. 1927. The early development of female sexuality. *The International Journal of Psychoanalysis* VIII: 459–472.

Kawakami C. 2002. The unfinished cartography: Murakami Haruki and the postmodern cognitive map. *Monumenta Nipponica* 57 (3): 309–337.

Lacan, J. 1998a. *The four fundamental concepts of psychoanalysis*. New York: W. W. Norton.

――― 1998b. *On feminine sexuality: The limits of love and knowledge*. New York: W. W. Norton.

――― 2006. *Écrits: The first complete edition in English*. New York: W. W. Norton.

Murakami F. 2002. Murakami Haruki's postmodern world. *Japan Forum* 14 (1): 127–141.

Murakami H. 1993a. Lederhosen. *In*: *The Elephant Vanishes*. New York: Alfred A. Knopf.

――― 1993b. The Wind-Up Bird Chronicle and Tuesday's Women. *In*: *The Elephant Vanishes*. New York: Alfred A. Knopf.

――― 1997. *The Wind-Up Bird Chronicle*. New York: Alfred A. Knopf.

――― 2000. *Norwegian Wood*. New York: Vintage International.

――― 2011. *1Q84*. New York: Alfred A. Knopf.

――― 2014a. *Colorless Tsukuru Tazaki and His Years of Pilgrimage*. New York: Alfred A. Knopf.

――― 2014b. Maegeki. *In*: *Onna no inai otokotachi*. Tokyo: Bungei Shunjū, 7–15.

――― 2017a. Drive My Car. *In*: *Men Without Women: Stories*. New York: Alfred A. Knopf, 3–40.

――― 2017b. Yesterday. *In*: *Men Without Women: Stories*. New York: Alfred A. Knopf, 41–76.

――― 2017c. An Independent Organ. *In*: *Men Without Women: Stories*. New York: Alfred A. Knopf, 77–113.

――― 2017d. Scheherazade. *In*: *Men Without Women: Stories*. New York: Alfred A. Knopf, 114–145.

――― 2017e. Kino. *In*: *Men Without Women: Stories*. New York: Alfred A. Knopf, 146–185.

———— 2017f. Samsa in Love. *In*: *Men Without Women: Stories*. New York: Alfred A. Knopf, 186–211.

———— 2017g. Men Without Women. *In*: *Men Without Women: Stories*. New York: Alfred A. Knopf, 212–228.

Nihei C. 2013. Resistance and negotiation: 'Herbivorous men' and Murakami Haruki's gender and political ambiguity. *Asian Studies Review* 37 (1): 62–79.

Salecl, R. 2002. Love anxieties. *In*: S. Barnard and B. Fink, eds. *Reading Seminar XX: Lacan's major work on love, knowledge, and feminine sexuality*. Albany: State University of New York Press, 93–97.

Seats, M. 2006. *Murakami Haruki: The simulacrum in contemporary Japanese culture*. Lanham: Lexington Books.

Strecher, M. 1998. Beyond 'pure' literature: Mimesis, formula, and the postmodern in the fiction of Murakami Haruki. *The Journal of Asian Studies* 57 (2): 354–378.

Treat, J. 2013. Murakami Haruki and the cultural materialism of multiple personality disorder. *Japan Forum* 25 (1): 87–111.

Žižek, S. 1995. Woman is one of the Names-of-the-Father, or how not to misread Lacan's formulas of sexuation [online]. *Lacanian Ink* 10. Available from: https://www.lacan.com/zizwoman.htm [Accessed 9 May 2020].

9

ESCAPE FROM STEREOTYPE?

Male–male sexuality in the fiction of Murakami Haruki

Anna Zielinska–Elliott

As every reader of Murakami Haruki knows, the male protagonist commonly found in many novels and short stories is a loner. Without a wife, children, or a 9-to-5 company job,[1] possessed of eccentric habits and an unusual way of speaking, this man in his various incarnations emerges as an archetypal outsider: an independent, thoughtful soul who does not personify the postwar Japanese hegemonic masculinity that is represented by the hard-working, patriarchal salaryman (Dasgupta 2013: 23). Yet, as a heterosexual, middle-class male, Murakami's protagonist still belongs to the mainstream, broadly defined. We may ask, then, whether in Murakami's work there are any characters who can be said to embody what R. W. Connell has termed 'subordinated masculinity', figures who have for a long time been on the margins of the social order.[2] Put simply, does Murakami write about gay men?

The answer is, yes.

Although these characters are not very numerous, their portrayals have changed over the years, and merit investigation by anyone interested in the question of gender and sexuality in Murakami. In this chapter, through close readings of selected texts and consideration of the changing social contexts, I will show how Murakami's gay characters perform their gender. Further, I will show that Murakami's attitudes toward male–male sexuality appear to have changed over the four decades of his writing, even if they remain somewhat circumscribed within older social and cultural stereotypes.

As I demonstrate, Murakami's early gay characters generally play only minor roles, but in later works go on to assume greater importance in some stories. I suggest that, at least in part, this evolution reflects changes happening within Japanese society. Murakami first writes about gays in the 1980s, when Japan saw the appearance of a small number of gay rights organisations and the beginning of the AIDS panic. With the 'gay boom' in the 1990s (McLelland 2005: 189), however, Murakami's attitude toward gay men undergoes a transformation. As I show, Murakami gradually attempts to set aside the gay man stereotypes with which he (and the majority of his generation) grew up and instead comes to portray gay men more individualistically (and, I would argue, more interestingly), according them roles of greater prominence in his stories and treating them with more sympathetic attention.

Supporting roles: Gay characters in Murakami's early works

Murakami began writing in 1979, when male–male sexuality was still to a degree a taboo topic and gay culture in Japan remained nearly entirely underground. Perhaps not surprisingly, men who desire other men therefore show up only rarely in Murakami's early work. When they do appear, we see them mainly through the male heterosexual protagonist's eyes. They are featured sporadically in brief scenes; and while the protagonist's attitude towards gay men is not necessarily negative, it is at best indifferent. One example of such a character is the young secretary to Makimura Hiraku in *Dansu dansu dansu* (1988a; trans. *Dance Dance Dance* [1994]), who gets ordered around and follows his boss's commands without a murmur, performing his many tasks impeccably and efficiently. From a conversation between the protagonist and Makimura's daughter Yuki, it becomes clear that the secretary is gay, although the protagonist had not realised it himself:

'You saw that smooth, creepy gay [*gei*] friend of Daddy's? I'm sure he takes a bath three times a day and changes his underwear twice daily'.
'He's gay?' I asked.
'You didn't know?'
'No'.
'I can't believe it. You can see it right away', said Yuki. 'I don't know if Daddy goes for that kind of thing, but the guy is definitely gay. No question. Two hundred percent gay'. [3]

(1988a: II, 58–59)

In the above passage, it is Yuki who asserts that the young man is gay. (As will become clear, Murakami uses different Japanese terms to refer to gay men, which I provide with the quotes themselves. A discussion of the issue of terms follows below.) Later, it becomes clear that the protagonist has accepted her opinion without questioning, perhaps in light of the subordinate nature of the position occupied by the secretary, whom he refers to as 'the gay houseboy, Friday' (1988a: II, 84).

The stereotype of a gay man as someone who is fastidious about cleanliness and exists in a position inferior to other men is striking here and elsewhere in Murakami's writing. For instance, we find this description in an earlier novel, *Hitsuji o meguru bōken* (1982; trans. *A Wild Sheep Chase* [1989]), where the protagonist describes the Boss's secretary, another extremely competent secretary subordinated to a powerful male boss:

He was dressed too neatly, his features were too regular, and his fingers too slender. And if it weren't for the shape of his sharply cut eyelids and the cold eyes that seemed made of glass, he would have looked like a typical homosexual [*homo sekushuaru*]. But because of those eyes, he didn't look like one. He didn't look like anybody at all.

(1982: 147)

What is it, then, according to Murakami's protagonist, that makes a man 'look like a typical homosexual'? Perhaps it is being 'too neatly dressed' and having fingers that are 'too slender'. However, the 'cold' eyes somehow defy the stereotype, as if some quality of warmth were to be expected of gay men generally. Still, his 'gay' neat attire is contrasted with the protagonist's typical 'male' casual dress, consisting of sneakers, jeans, and a T-shirt. In these descriptions, gay masculinity appears to be treated in a one-dimensional way, as fastidious and sophisticated, if not necessarily effeminate.

We find several more examples of gay males working in subordinate positions throughout Murakami's writing. One appears in a much later work, *Kokkyō no minami, taiyō no nishi* (1992; trans. *South of the Border, West of the Sun* [1999]), where we encounter a gay bartender who is meticulous about his work and produces excellent cocktails. He appears in only one scene, where, unsurprisingly, he is described as 'young and handsome'. As if to stress that he is not prejudiced against gays, Hajime, the owner of the bar and the protagonist of the novel, says,

> This young guy was homosexual [*homo sekushuaru*] and thanks to that, gay guys [*gei no renchū*] would sometimes gather by the bar. But they were a quiet bunch and I didn't mind. I liked him, and he trusted me and worked hard.
>
> (2004b: 142–143)

In his lack of prejudice, Hajime is a typical Murakami protagonist, and the bartender a typical gay man of this period in his writing – an episodic character, good looking, and prone to a certain fastidiousness. Despite Hajime's apparent lack of bias, it is nonetheless clear that he is aware of who is gay and who is not, and regards gay men as constituting an 'other' category of people.

In *Supūtoniku no koibito* (1999; trans. *Sputnik Sweetheart* [2001]) we find mention of another possibly gay secretary. Describing an Englishman who Sumire meets in France, Miu says that he was 'over fifty, did some writing, was handsome and refined. I think he was probably gay [*gei*]. It's because he had a secretary with him who seemed to be his boyfriend' (2001: 151). In the story 'Tairando' (2000; trans. 'Thailand' [2001]), we come upon one more subordinated male who used to work for a powerful boss. This time he is not a secretary, but a driver in his 60s named Nimit. Immaculately dressed and neat, he is very good at his job. He tells Satsuki, the main female character, that he worked as a driver for a Norwegian businessman for 30 years and that his former boss had taught him to appreciate music. Nimit goes on to explain: 'When you are with somebody for a long time and do what this person tells you to do, in a sense you become one in body and soul [*isshindōtai*]' (2000: 116). Upon hearing this, Satsuki wonders if 'maybe he and his boss were in a homosexual [*homo sekushuaru*] relationship' (2000: 116). She reaches this conclusion upon realising how close the two men must have been, but Nimit's neatness, hypercompetence, and subordinate position may well have something to do with her thinking.

Edging toward the spotlight

This series of rather predictable supporting actors, mainly in earlier work, is disrupted in later writing, where we see Murakami gradually becoming somewhat more adventurous, experimenting with different types of more nuanced gay characters.

The first departure from stereotypes comes in an as yet untranslated story, 'Rekishinton no yūrei' (1996; no trans. The Ghosts of Lexington). The story is written in the first person by the writer Murakami who, while living in Massachusetts, meets a certain architect, Keishī (Casey?), who owns a house in the town of Lexington, near Boston. Murakami agrees to house-sit for him. One night he hears sounds of a party from downstairs – a party, he quickly realises, that is being held by ghosts. Murakami's descriptions of Keishī are what interest us here. He lives with Jeremī (Jeremy), who is 'terribly taciturn and very pale' (2005c: 11). He himself, however, is '[a] handsome man in his fifties with graying hair. Not very tall. He liked to swim, went to the pool daily and had a muscular body' (2005c: 11). When they meet for the first time, Keishī tightly clutches the narrator's hand and lightly pats him on the shoulder with his other hand (2005c: 14), which might be seen as typically masculine behaviour. At the same time, however, the narrator draws attention to Keishī's outfit: he is dressed in a 'smart white shirt that looked Italian, buttoned up all the way, a light brown cashmere cardigan, and soft cotton pants. He also wore small Armani-style glasses. Very smart' (2005c: 14). This would appear to be intended to signal 'gay' attire, since the typical Murakami male would not be caught dead in a cashmere cardigan (or any cardigan, for that matter). Keishī is well read, knows a lot about wine and cheese, and 'gracefully tilt[s] his glass when drinking' (2005c: 15). He lives in a beautiful old house, drives a new BMW, has a large mastiff dog, and owns a fabulous record collection (2005c: 13), all of which go to let the reader know that he is particular in his tastes and financially comfortable.

This description of upper-class sophistication and domesticity is redolent of what Lisa Duggan calls 'new homonormativity', referring to a kind of politics that does not contest heteronormative 'assumptions and institutions, but upholds and sustains them', and promotes 'a privatized, depoliticized gay culture anchored in domesticity and consumption' (2003: 179). Keishī and Jeremī are shown as a perfect example of a couple living according to such norms. The narrator seems to be supportive, understanding, and tolerant precisely within that framework. However, a few months later, when the narrator meets Keishī again, things have changed dramatically:

> He looked ten years older. His hair had turned grayer and reached below his ears; dark, bag-like circles had formed under his eyes. Even his hands seemed more wrinkled. It was all unthinkable for the stylish Keishī, who was so attentive to his looks.
>
> (2005c: 33)

At first, one wonders if this change of appearance is 'unthinkable' (*kangaerarenai*) to the narrator because Keishī is gay, and therefore expected not to neglect his looks, much the way a woman might be expected to 'take care of herself'. But perhaps 'unthinkable' here is meant to express the narrator's shock upon realising that Keishī must be suffering from AIDS, the effects of which are written all over his body.

Since Murakami lived in the United States from 1991 to 1995, first at Princeton and later at Tufts University, he would certainly have known of the widespread panic engendered by the AIDS epidemic, the devastation it brought to gay communities, and the public health response it occasioned, including the development and approval of the first antiretroviral drugs in the mid-1990s. As Takeuchi Kayo has suggested, one possible reading of the story puts it in the category of 'AIDS literature' (2010: 54), wherein the ghosts who come at night to Keishī's house are the ghosts of American gay men, his friends who died from AIDS. Especially as the narrator makes clear that the events he is describing took place in the early nineties, this interpretation of the story seems quite persuasive, and would place this 1996 publication as the first real attempt by Murakami to depict gay characters as more than two-dimensional types. In this light, one interesting aspect of 'Rekishinton no yūrei' is that the word 'gay' or 'homosexual' is never used, as if the narrator wished to emphasise that he is not biased. Takeuchi suggests that Keishī may be afraid to mention his sexual orientation to the narrator, owing to the negative image of gays in the early 1990s caused by the AIDS epidemic. That does not explain, however, why the narrator would not refer to it in the story, unless we accept Takeuchi's claim that the narrator is responding to a universalised prohibition on male homosexuality and that he is not able to face the possibility that he might be gay himself (2010: 50–51).

One might argue that the fact that Keishī and Jeremī are Americans allows the author to treat the subject as one concerning the Other. But when placed in the context of Murakami's writing at this time, we can, I believe, conclude that the story is evidence not only of a greater willingness to include gay characters in leading roles, but also of a changing attitude towards gender broadly and gay masculinity more particularly.

The piano tuner in the 2005 story 'Gūzen no tabibito' (2005; trans. 'Chance Traveller'), who appears to be a composite of the figures of Jeremī and Keishī, is another example of this new attitude. He is the first, and so far the last, gay character to play a central role in a Murakami story. The structure of the story is also reminiscent of that earlier work in that there is a narrator – also here identified as the writer Murakami Haruki – who tells a story about a gay friend who is neat and polite. However, in contrast to 'Rekishinton no yūrei', in 'Gūzen no tabibito', published nine years later, not only is the protagonist Japanese, but the author immediately informs us that he is gay:

> He is a piano tuner. He lives in the western part of Tokyo, near Okutama. He is forty-one and gay [*gei*]. He does not especially hide this fact.
>
> (2005a: 16)

We learn that, like Keishī, he 'had a high-end stereo, cooked well using natural products, and went to the gym five times a week to keep the extra weight off' (2005a: 20). It is worth taking a moment to reflect on Murakami's rather unusual choice of profession for this character – a piano tuner, like Jeremī.

Writing about 'Rekishinton no yūrei', Takeuchi suggests that choices of profession may be dictated by the fact that certain professions (architect, piano tuner) allow for independence and do not require gay men to fit into rigid and conservative hierarchies such as are found in most companies (2010: 48). Reading this story carefully, however, one can see that, despite some changes, this unnamed gay character still seems to play the assigned role, displaying many of the stereotypical gay characteristics and behaviour seen in earlier writings by Murakami:

> He was well dressed, kind, polite, he had a sense of humor, and almost always had a nice smile on his face, so that many people – with the exception of those who have a physiological aversion to homosexuals [*dōseiaisha*] – felt a natural sympathy for him.
>
> (2005a: 20)

We later learn that his family does not understand him or approve, and that he has broken off relations with his sister, who had asked him to hide his sexual orientation from his prejudiced future brother-in-law. The narrator does not criticise the man or his lifestyle in any way but does not express any views about his family's homophobia, either; he simply describes it. However, our sympathies are meant to lie with him: the narrator points out that, due to his line of work, the piano tuner's partner is unable to come out as gay, which once more underscores societal discrimination and homophobia, and the reality with which many gay men in Japan (and elsewhere) have long learned to live.

That said, the similarity of the somewhat stereotypical descriptions of the main characters – in spite of the nine years separating the two stories – cautions us against assuming continuous movement towards an ever more progressive attitude on Murakami's part with respect to male–male sexuality. Kuroiwa Yūichi stresses that 'Gūzen no tabibito', like 'Rekishinton no yūrei', is also a story about AIDS. He refers to the fact that some characters speak of desire between men as if it were an 'infectious disease', a tendency that Kuroiwa connects to the AIDS panic in the 1980s and 1990s. This interpretation of Murakami's language, with its latent homophobic overtones, seems persuasive. Kuroiwa also claims that Murakami sanitises the story by removing male sexuality from it and by 'blacking out' (*anmaku*) representations of gay males. According to Kuroiwa – who is also borrowing from Duggan's 'new homonormativity' – Murakami brings in politics, but then moves away from the issue, and is still operating as before, trying to fit gays into a heteronormative world (Kuroiwa, 2016: 64–65).

Towards more fluid gender boundaries

Wherever one comes down on the question of Murakami's politics, it is beyond dispute that there is a marked expansion of complex roles for gay men in his writing beginning in the mid-1990s. At the same time, Murakami also shows greater interest in exploring the social expectations that are typically packaged with gender and sexuality. In *Nejimakidori kuronikuru* (1994–1995; trans. *The Wind-Up Bird Chronicle* [1997]), which came out just before 'Rekishinton no yūrei', we see the 16-year-old Kasahara Mei struggling to sort out her attitude toward gay male sexuality. She asks Okada Tōru, the male protagonist, '[a]re you a fag [*okama*], by any chance?' She explains that she wants to know if it is true 'that fags cannot whistle', adding later, '[y]ou may be a fag, a pervert, or something. It doesn't bother me at all' (2003: I, 114–115). Instead of referencing some more predictable stereotype, Mei comes up with something ludicrous, as if to remind the reader how absurd such assumptions about sexuality can be and to underscore the idea that gender is a contingent social construct.

While this would seem to indicate a change in Murakami's position regarding male–male sexuality, at the same time one cannot help but notice that, in spite of her claim of indifference, Mei includes 'fag' and 'pervert' in the same category, and consistently employs a derogatory term for gay men. The protagonist's response to her, though, is especially interesting. When she asks if he is 'a fag', he answers matter-of-factly, 'I don't think so. Why?' This unfazed reply suggests that he does not consider the comment to have been an insult or a challenge to his heterosexual masculinity. Indeed, it seems that he may not have ever thought about the question of his sexuality seriously before, but now that the girl has asked him, he realises that he cannot fully exclude this possibility – and does not seem terribly bothered by it.

A somewhat similar exchange underscoring the male protagonist's open-minded (or indifferent) attitude takes place in the 2004 novel *Afutādāku* (trans. *After Dark* [2007]), when Mari asks Takahashi why her sister had chosen to confide in him. Takahashi explains that perhaps he had seemed 'harmless' (*gai ga nai*) to her, and then adds: 'It's a strange thing, but sometimes I get mistaken for a gay [*gei*] guy. Strangers approach and proposition me in the street'. Mari then follows up as if to make sure: 'But you're *not* gay [*gei*]?' to which Takahashi responds, 'I think probably not …' (2004a: 172). This is another example of Murakami's tendency at this time (mid-1990s to mid-2000s) not only to refer to gay men as more sensitive – allowing that a sensitive straight male might be mistaken for a gay one on that basis – but also to allow for the existence of alternative male sexualities in society. Takahashi is the second male character in Murakami's writing who is not appalled at being mistaken for a gay man and, in fact, cannot – or does not want to – categorically deny being gay.[4] The possibility is there and he cannot exclude it. We could perhaps understand this apparent openness to alternative sexualities as an attempt on Murakami's part to stress that gender boundaries are in fact not as rigid as they might seem.

The tendency to create more 'mainstream' gay characters towards whom the narrator shows a seemingly liberal attitude is visible in other writings by Murakami in the early 2000s as well. Three years after the 1999 publication of *Supūtoniku no koibito*, with its lesbian main character, *Umibe no Kafuka* (2002; trans. *Kafka on the Shore* [2005]) appeared. Notably, this novel features the transsexual Ōshima as an important character. Clearly a positive figure in the novel, Ōshima also seems to represent Murakami's embrace of the idea that gender boundaries are less absolute than they seem to be.

As we learn, Ōshima is physically female, but with his consciousness 'completely male', or, more precisely, that of a male who is attracted to men and who, in Murakami's explicit phrasing, 'uses his anus for sex' (2002: I, 309). Describing himself as a 'gay [*gei*] man who is a woman with a gender identity disorder' (2002: I, 354),[5] Ōshima displays some of the same features of Murakami's earlier gay characters – beautiful fingers, refined taste in clothing, etc. – but being a man and a woman at the same time, he becomes an almost gender-neutral being.[6] It is no accident that it is Ōshima who talks about Plato's *Symposium* and its description of how originally there used to be three sexes: men, women, and a union of the two (all four-legged, four-armed, and two-headed) (2002: I, 65). When one of the two central characters, the teenager Kafuka, asks why Zeus cuts people in half, Ōshima explains that gods are prone to idealism, which can be understood to mean that neatly dividing people into two genders is impossible and that it is impractical to try. Later, Ōshima makes fun of two feminists who demand a separate toilet for women in the library and accuse him – physically a woman – of male chauvinism. Referring to the feminists, Ōshima later says to Kafuka:

> I don't care if somebody is gay [*gei*], lesbian, straight, a feminist, a Fascist swine, a communist or a Hare Krishna. To me it's all the same what flag people wave. What I can't stand are such *hollow people*.
>
> (2002: I, 313, emphasis in original)

As if to underscore Ōshima's open-mindedness, *Umibe no Kafuka* includes several critical remarks about anti-gay and discriminatory attitudes, as well as positive exemplars of tolerance. A good illustration of the last is found in the comments made by the truck driver, Hoshino, who has only good things to say of Ōshima: 'Very nice. […] Intelligent, neat, looks like he comes from a good family. And very kind on top of that. He might be gay [*gei*]' (2002: II, 264). The narrator notes explicitly that,

> Hoshino had no prejudices against gays [*gei*]. People had different tastes. There was nothing strange in that there were people who could converse with stones or men who wanted to sleep with other men.
>
> (2002: II, 264)

Thus in Ōshima we find a gay character who is universally liked by people from all social classes. It should be stressed that although he is genetically a woman, Ōshima suffers from haemophilia, a disease that rarely occurs in women, which underscores his male gender and raises further interesting questions about the boundary between gender and sex.

One aspect of the way in which Ōshima's life is described that seems to fall back on a stereotypical view of gay men has to do with his relationship with his partner. Ōshima says to Kafuka:

> You ask if I'm in love? [...] In other words, you dare to interfere and ask about an anti-social romance, which can give some color to my twisted private life, the life of a person who prefers the same sex [*dōseiaisha*] with a gender identity disorder? […] I have a partner. [...] Ours is not a dramatic love like those portrayed in Puccini's operas. You could say, we keep a cautious distance. We see each other extremely rarely. But I think generally we understand each other well.
>
> (2002: II, 119)

Although one could argue that Murakami characters do not tend to be wildly, passionately in love (romantic love is relatively rarely mentioned), the above descriptions seem almost too practical and non-romantic. The relationship described here appears to be mostly based on 'generally' good mutual understanding and 'rare' meetings presumably involving sex to which Ōshima referred earlier. Another somewhat similar reference appears in 'Gūzen no tabibito', where the main difference between the main gay character and the male archetype becomes visible when his sex life is discussed: 'Having previously dated a number of men, he met his current partner almost ten years ago and ever since they have been in a harmonious and satisfying sexual relationship' (2005: 20). Is the reader to assume that sex is the main thing that keeps the main characters together with their partners (*pātonā*)? Are these positively portrayed gay characters still reflecting gay stereotypes?

Not necessarily. We need to note that their relationships are more lasting than the short-lived marriages of many of Murakami's male protagonists, most of whom are divorced, estranged from their wives, or single. In several works, such as *Hitsuji o meguru bōken*, *Nejimakidori kuronikuru*, *Shikisai o motanai Tazaki Tsukuru to, kare no junrei no toshi* (2013; trans. *Colorless Tsukuru Tazaki and His Years of Pilgrimage* [2014]) or *Kishidanchō goroshi* (2017; trans. *Killing Commendatore* [2018]), the male protagonist's inability to fully understand and communicate with his female partner is the central element carrying the plots forward, in contrast to the 'generally good understanding' between the two gay men described in *Umibe no Kafuka*. This is possibly another way of showing gay characters as the Other who, contrary to heterosexual type, are able to create lasting relationships, or of commenting on the difficulty the typical male archetype usually faces in overcoming the gender gap.

The new macho gay enters the scene

In the 1990s, a new, 'macho' style brought from the West came into fashion in gay circles in Japan. Its proponents wore leather clothes and shaved their heads, a style thought by some to be a sort of a disguise (Lunsing 2003: 30–31). It took a while for this trend to find a reflection in Murakami's fiction: with one small exception, he does not include any 'tough' gay characters in his writing until 2009, when the body-guard Tamaru appears in *1Q84* (2009–2010; trans. *1Q84* [2011]). The exception in question occurs in the story 'Kanō Kureta' (1990; no trans. Kanō Kureta) about a woman who had been repeatedly raped and after years of hiding decides to begin an independent life. To protect herself, she hires a 'gay bodyguard resembling a gorilla' (*gorira mitai na gei no gādo*). Here, the fact that he is gay may serve to emphasise that he will not threaten her sexually (1993: 131), and his strength is probably a signal of his capacity to defend her.

Therefore, when Tamaru – also a bodyguard – appears in *1Q84*, he is Murakami's first fully developed macho gay character. Tamaru is constructed in a novel way: lower social class, robust physique, broad shoulders, shaved head, and a high *dan* (rank) in karate. He is able to use weapons, and can be brutal and ruthless when necessary. All these features are usually regarded as associated with macho masculinity. Interestingly, he is also said to have a friendly personality, warm eyes, and to pay great attention to clothes – characteristics which, as we have seen, had previously been ascribed to more effeminate gay characters. Tamaru is, however, much more assertive than those earlier characters and openly talks about his sexual orientation. When speaking of himself, he throws in:

> Just in case, I will tell you that I've never been investigated by the police. [...] In other words, I don't have a criminal record. The authorities might have missed a few things – I'm not denying it. But according to the record, I am a fully law-abiding citizen. Pure, without a blemish. I'm gay [*gei*], but that is not illegal.
>
> (2009: II, 28)

This amounts to a strong claim on full social membership, and a rejection of marginality. Unlike other openly gay characters, such as the piano tuner from 'Gūzen no tabibito' and Ōshima, who both spoke of social ostracism, Tamaru is even capable of joking about his sexuality, which is unprecedented in Murakami.

First descriptions of gay sex and a 'gay bad guy'

In *Shikisai o motanai Tazaki Tsukuru to, kare no junrei no toshi*, we find one key gay character, and the first-ever sex scene between men. Haida is Tsukuru's friend from college. In many respects he fits the image of most earlier gay characters: though nothing is explicitly stated about his sexual orientation, we are told that he is of small stature, is exacting about his clothes, has refined taste in music, and attaches great importance to the flavour of coffee. One day Haida spends the night on the couch in Tsukuru's living room. Tsukuru has an erotic dream in which he has sex with two women, but suddenly realises that the women have disappeared and instead he is lying next to Haida, who is giving him oral sex and swallows Tsukuru's sperm as if 'accustomed to doing this' (2013: 118). The next day, Tsukuru thinks he may have dreamt the whole thing. Therefore, we never find out whether Haida is gay and did have sex with Tsukuru, or whether Tsukuru simply had a dream that possibly made him realise that he was latently attracted to Haida. Tsukuru is disturbed by the experience, but in the morning Haida behaves as if nothing has happened. Meanwhile, Tsukuru is afraid that his friend could learn about the 'twisted elements' (*itanda yōso*) in his consciousness, a thought that overwhelms him with shame (2013: 122–123). This means that, unlike some earlier protagonists when his own sexual preferences are questioned, Tsukuru is not open-minded about it like Takahashi or Okada Tōru, able to admit the possibility that he might be gay, but a heterosexual male who is afraid that he could be gay, or be mistaken for a gay man.

Somewhat paradoxically, the reader is led to believe that Tsukuru's general attitude towards gays is liberal. We learn about this when he meets his former high-school friend, Aka, a character engaging in ethically questionable business practices. After discovering that he feels desire for men, Aka divorces his wife, but keeps his orientation a secret until he confesses it to Tsukuru when they are both nearly 40. Tsukuru is not surprised, observing matter-of-factly: 'It's not that unusual, is it?' He also suggests that Aka should be honest with himself, which will set him free. Aka responds that it is 'not so simple' in Nagoya, where everyone knows everyone else (2013: 205). This last statement may be an expression of sympathy on the part of the writer for the situation of gay men in Japan, where it is still difficult to be openly gay in many professions and communities. However, in her review of *Colorless Tsukuru Tazaki*, Tiffany Hong questions Murakami's sympathetic attitude towards gays:

> [T]he homoerotic encounter and relationship is utilized as an example of the *something* that repels those around him, and the one other (openly) gay character is depicted as an unsavory opportunist who has united military, religious, and advertising techniques – all vilified in Murakami's fiction – to spearhead a company that essentially trades in corporate brainwashing. Moreover, the male–male scene is depicted with familiar imagery – a doppelgänger, paralysis – intimately associated with the perverse and malevolent in Murakami.
>
> (Hong 2015: 449)

While one could argue whether paralysis is *always* associated with malevolence in Murakami (given the scene in *1Q84* when Fukaeri has sex with a paralysed Tengo, as a result of which Aomame inexplicably becomes pregnant with his child – a very positive outcome), Hong makes a valid criticism of depictions of gay sex and characters in this novel. In Aka we have the first negative, unsympathetic gay character and in Tsukuru a seemingly liberal heterosexual one, who is nonetheless insecure about his own heterosexuality.

A return to supporting roles, but with a twist

In the years following *Shikisai o motanai Tazaki Tsukuru to, kare no junrei no toshi*, Murakami seems to return to his somewhat stereotypical descriptions of gay men. One example of this is Gotō, the secretary of Doctor Tokai, in 'Dokuritsu kikan'

(2014; trans. 'An Independent Organ' [2017]) who is described in the following way:

> From his deep voice on the phone, I expected a man of solid build, but, in fact, he was tall and slender. As Tokai had told me, he had quite a handsome face. He wore a brown woolen suit, a snow-white button-down shirt and a dark mustard-colored tie – flawless attire. His longish hair was also nicely styled, bangs falling attractively on his forehead. He was about thirty-five. I had heard from Tokai that he was gay [*gei*], but he looked just like an ordinary well-dressed youth (he still retained the vestiges of youth). You could also tell he'd have a heavy beard.
>
> (2014a: 149)

This description includes some of the early characteristics of Murakami's gay characters – meticulous dress, handsome face – but the deep voice and what must have been a five o'clock shadow complicate the description. What is more puzzling is that the first portrayal of the secretary's competence and his impressive organisation skills ends with the following statement by the narrator about the young man's employer: 'To express his gratitude at every occasion he gave presents to this handsome secretary (he was, of course, gay) [*mochiron gei datta*]' (2014a: 129–130). Whence the 'of course'? Because the man is good looking, well dressed, competent, amiable, and of inferior social status? This appears to be a partial return to the earlier gay stereotype. These descriptions have also been criticised by Katō Norihiro, who commented on 'insensitive references (*donkan na genkyū*) to a gay young man' present in the story (Katō 2014; see also Katō's chapter in this volume).

One additional element of Gotō's behaviour that makes his character more unusual is that he cries in front of the narrator. Although women tend to cry in Murakami's works – Naoko in *Noruwei no mori* (1987; trans. *Norwegian Wood* [1989/2000]) and Kasahara Mei in *Nejimakidori kuronikuru* almost drown in tears (1987: 73; 2003: III, 486) – examples of lachrymose men are much less common. And when men do cry, they cry alone: Watanabe Tōru, for example, weeps alone on the beach after Naoko's death in *Noruwei no mori* (1987: II, 223), and Kino cries alone at the end of the story 'Kino' (2014b: 261; trans. 'Kino' [2017]). Gotō, however, starts crying during his meeting with the narrator. Does he cry because he is gay, and as such is less 'manly', or is he a new, 'sensitive man' who is not afraid to cry? When he apologises for showing weakness, the narrator assures him that 'crying because someone has died is not a sign of weakness' (2014b: 162), suggesting the injustice of the common rule that 'big boys don't cry'.

Murakami's latest novel, *Kishidanchō goroshi*, features no gay characters as such, but it does seem to apply some putatively 'gay' attributes to the heterosexual Menshiki, who has beautiful hands, is extremely neat, exceedingly particular about his clothes, and – what is perhaps even more significant – plays the piano. The town gossip also claims, '[h]e might be gay [*gei*]. But there are a few reasons to think he is probably not' (2017: I, 176). One character in the novel who might also be gay is the narrator's unmarried uncle, a scientist. He 'lived in his own world, but was very open and frank' (2017: I, 370). When the narrator goes to visit him as a child, the uncle is 30 years old and lives in a small, rented house in Kōfu with a 'friend' (*yūjin*) (2017: I, 370). The uncle might have been gay, but it was not obvious at the time to a young boy, especially given that when he visited, the uncle's friend was away.

The depiction of these men, particularly of Menshiki, would seem to suggest that Murakami continues to experiment with gender stereotypes, creating men possessing what would previously be considered effeminate characteristics, and women (such as Aomame in *1Q84*) with attributes that the early Murakami might have classified as decidedly masculine. In all the cases, he allows that such people – whose way of being defies easy categorisation according to pre-established gender norms – do exist, and not just at the margins of society.

Every word matters

Together with the changing depictions of gay men in Murakami have come changes in the words referring to them. As the attentive reader will already have observed, we find five different terms to describe gay men: *homo sekushuaru* (a loan expression from 'homosexual', written in *katakana*), *homo*, *okama* ('fag'), *dōseiaisha* ('homosexual' from '*dōseiai*' – 'same-sex love'), and *gei* (a loan word for 'gay', written in *katakana*). One interesting aspect of the term *homo sekushuaru* (which was used in the above-quoted passages from *Hitsuji o meguru bōken* and *Kokkyō no minami, taiyō no nishi*, but also in 'Gūzen no tabibito', 'Tairando', and *Sekai no owari to hādoboirudo wandārando* [1998b (1985); trans. *Hard-Boiled Wonderland and the End of the World* (1991)]) is that Murakami writes it as two words separated by an interpunct (*nakaguro*). This is different from the earlier *homo* or the newer term, *homosekushuaru* (one word) suggested by Japanese dictionaries and commonly used in written sources. Rebecca Suter, writing about the alienating effect of *katakana* in Murakami, mentions the use of such non-abbreviated forms of *katakana* words as 'instances in which this alienating effect emerges most clearly'. She continues:

> By using this form, slightly different from the common usage [...] the texts draw attention to the foreignness of the word, while at the same time 'Japanizing it' by way of transcription into *katakana*.
>
> (Suter 2008: 68)

In other words, *homo sekushuaru* written as two distinct words may appear as a more 'foreign' concept than *homosekushuaru* written as a single word, or earlier *homo*, which, according to some scholars, used to be a more common term referring to a 'masculine-identified homosexual men' until the early 1990s, when it started to be replaced by *gei* (McLelland 2005: 12, 137, 155). *Okama*, generally perceived as having a connotation of someone who is effeminate and passive (Lunsing 2003: 30), is used in *Nejimakidori kuronikuru* – as in the passage where Kasahara Mei refers to the 'whistling theory' of gayness – and, on one occasion each, in *Dansu dansu dansu* and the story 'Hanarei Bei' (2005; trans. 'Hanalei Bay' [2006]). In the former, the male protagonist refers to a famous 1980s pop singer, saying, '[e]ven an overweight fag [*okama*] without singing talent like Boy George could become a star' (1988a: I, 198). In 'Hanarei Bei', the word appears in the expression 'faggy music' (*okama ongaku*) when an American at a bar in Hawai'i says about the pianist, '[t]hat fruitcake [*frūtsūkēki*] can only play lame faggy music' (2005b: 70).[7] However, in this second example, both expressions are clearly used by a negative character in an intentional way and meet with a strong reaction from the main character.

The word *gei* appears more and more commonly in works starting from the 1988 *Dansu, dansu, dansu*, with the occasional appearance of *dōseiaisha* in 'Gūzen no tabibito', *Kokkyō no minami, taiyō no nishi, Umibe no Kafuka*, and a couple of other stories. This term began to be used with political connotations only in the late 1980s or early 1990s, although it had been introduced to Japan during the American occupation. Originally it was only seen in the expression *gei bōi*, referring to sexual partners of the members of the Occupation forces, but in the mid-1950s it began to refer mostly to transgender entertainers working in gay bars (McLelland 2005: 78, 102). Lunsing notes that Japanese gay rights organisations in the 1990s tried to promote the idea that the only difference between straight and gay men is their sexual orientation and encouraged the use of the word 'gay' (*gei*) as a politically correct term to refer to them. Nonetheless, despite their efforts, in the early 2000s the word *gei* still included some connotation of femininity (Lunsing 2003: 30).[8] It seems, however, that the increased use of the word *gei* in Murakami is accompanied by apparent further liberalisation of the attitude towards male–male sexuality. These changes may reflect the writer's changing attitude, but he may also simply be adapting the terms from general discourse, which has itself undergone dramatic shifts.

Finally, we gain a further perspective on Murakami's position with respect to terms related to homosexuality by looking at his translations of English fiction. In his 2003 translation of Salinger's *The Catcher in the Rye* (1951), for instance, Murakami generally chooses not to translate derogatory terms referring to gay characters in similarly derogatory language in Japanese. In several cases he rendered the pejorative term 'flit', common in the US in the 1950s, as *gei* (2003: 241), and 'flitty' as *geippoi* (2003: 242, 330) – although he also used *okamappoi* (2003: 146, 252, 257).[9] In a 2003 exchange with another famous translator, Murakami once mentioned that both the translation and readers' consciousness have changed, so a new translation required new wording and had to be based on new paradigms (Murakami and Shibata 2003: 129, 177). This interesting issue would likely reward further study.

Conclusion: Escape from stereotype?

Murakami's tendency over the years to describe gay men in an increasingly sympathetic and understanding manner seems clear. At the same time, gay men appear to be judged by heteronormative standards and are seen as positive if they fit that matrix. Yet, since the number of gay characters in Murakami's works is still relatively small, it is difficult to reach definite conclusions. We can only say that there is a noticeable change from gay men appearing as secondary or tertiary (and sometimes slightly ridiculous) characters in the early works, to becoming full-fledged and sympathetically described players in later works, filling ever more important roles described in a more nuanced way. How should we understand this transformation?

Attitudes towards male–male sexuality have undergone a number of shifts in modern Japan. What might be regarded as 'liberal' attitudes dominated during the Edo period, when sex between men was viewed in popular discourse as 'a "way" to be pursued and perfected', something in which any man could engage. Although the authorities created many laws to control it, they were less concerned with the practice itself (Pflugfelder 2007: 18–19). Under the modernising project pursued during the Meiji period, standards of official morality were dramatically reformulated. The government decreed that male–male sexual acts were 'a "barbarous" vice that ran contrary to "civilised" norms', and for a short time in the 1870s and 1880s male–male anal intercourse was strictly forbidden and punishable by law (Pflugfelder 2007: 20). The development of science and medicine further reshaped perceptions of male–male sexuality, which came to be seen as a sexual pathology, 'unnatural' and 'perverse'. Indeed, in the first half of the 20th century, 'same-sex-love' was a topic often taken up in medical writing, literature, and journalism (Pflugfelder 2007: 22).

After WWII, no new anti-gay laws were introduced. Male–male sexuality continued to become more visible in literature and cinema throughout the 1950s, 1960s and 1970s,[10] as transgender entertainers such as Miwa Akihiro became media celebrities and the number of gay bars increased. The latter gradually evolved from places mostly linked to prostitution to 'communication spaces' in the style of the gay bars of today (McLelland 2000: 29). In the 1970s, representations of male–male sexuality became part of mainstream culture,[11] and gay pornography began to appear in magazines addressed to the gay market (McLelland 2000: 32).

As mentioned above, by the time Murakami began writing about gay characters, Japan had witnessed the appearance of the first gay rights organisations, followed by the AIDS panic and the 'gay boom' of the nineties. As a result, as Wim Lunsing notes, general social interest in gay men and gay lifestyles increased. Whereas at first this interest was motivated by simple curiosity, and the portrayals of gays stereotypical, it also meant that gays became more visible, which strengthened their position and gave rise to new political movements (Lunsing 1997: 277–280). Romit Dasgupta agrees, observing that gay male masculinity had become a 'possible lifestyle alternative' in Japan by the beginning of the 21st century (Dasgupta 2003: 131). Yet, as in Murakami's own writing, there appear to be clear limits. Writing about gay stereotypes in the early 2000s, Lunsing argues that the dominant Japanese stereotype of a gay man is effeminacy. Analysing masculinity and gays in the Japanese media during the same period, Mark McLelland emphasises that in spite of the 'gay boom', gays continued to be portrayed in extremely stereotypical ways (McLelland 2003: 59–78).

It is only to be expected that the events and changes described above are to a degree reflected in Murakami's treatment of male–male sexuality in his writing. In addition to these influences were those that came from the United States:

as mentioned earlier, for a few years in the 1990s (and again in the early 2000s) Murakami lived in politically liberal Princeton, New Jersey, and Cambridge, Massachusetts. By this time, the American gay movement had already arrived, and Murakami may well have absorbed something of the ideologically open atmosphere of American university campuses and their surrounding communities. He would also have become quite aware of the medical, social, political, and cultural impact of the AIDS epidemic, which was a frequent topic of comment and discussion in American media at the time.

While today there may be more societal acceptance of gays and gay lifestyles, Japan remains the only one of the G7 countries where neither same-sex marriage nor civil unions are legal. It is, of course, important to remember that although Canada legalised same-sex marriage in 2005, this step was taken in France, Italy, Germany, the UK, and the United States only between 2013 and 2017 – in the case of Italy, it was civil unions, not marriages, that were made legal. Moreover, the only Asian country to have legalised same-sex marriage so far is Taiwan – a legislative move that took place in May 2019. In Japan, change is definitely occurring in that sphere, though so far mainly on a local scale, and often as a result of grassroots campaigns. The first administrative unit to recognise 'domestic partnerships' was Shibuya Ward in Tokyo in March 2015, which offered gay couples some benefits, like equal treatment in case of rental contracts or hospital visits, but no legal rights, and only within the municipality (*Nihon keizai shinbun* denshiban 2015; Shibuya ku kōshiki saito 2019). The trend seems to be gaining momentum: other municipalities have since followed, with a total surpassing 100 by 1 April 2021 (Out Japan Co., Ltd, n.d.). On 1 July 2019, the first prefecture, Ibaraki, followed suit, with the governor making the decision to recognise domestic partnerships in spite of some protests (Ibaraki ken 2019; *Asahi Shinbun* 2019). Gunma prefecture was next, in December 2020 (Out Japan Co., Ltd, n.d.). In March 2021, the Sapporo District Court ruled that the government's ban on same-sex marriage was unconstitutional (BBC News 2021).

For now, we can conclude that Murakami's treatment of gay characters to a certain degree reflects both social changes occurring in Japan as well as Murakami's own sense of responsibility as a writer to incorporate those changes into the fictional worlds he creates. He has attempted, with some success, to escape stereotypes and to create fully-formed, complex gay characters. In fashioning positive, or at least neutral, models of gay manhood, he may be seen as trying to battle homophobia and broaden his readers' horizons. Yet, such concerns have not been paramount for him: it would be hard to argue that Murakami has been at the forefront of challenging stereotypes or advancing claims for the equal and inclusive treatment of gay men in society. It remains to be seen whether Murakami will wholeheartedly embrace the cause of the gay rights movement and come round to a fully liberal, non-judgemental acceptance of male–male sexuality that is then woven fully into his writing. For now, given his popularity around the world, most readers do not demand that kind of activism or political stance from him, and are satisfied that he continues to deliver imaginative stories with compelling characters, whatever their sexuality may be, and however it may be portrayed.

Notes

1 I am referring to a typical Murakami's male protagonist here. There are a few exceptions: Hajime in *Kokkyō no minami, taiyō no nishi* is married with children, and Tazaki Tsukuru from *Shikisai o motanai Tazaki Tsukuru to, sono junrei no toshi* has a regular company job.

2 In her classification of masculinity, R. W. Connell described subordinate masculinity in this way: 'Oppression positions homosexual masculinities at the bottom of a gender hierarchy among men. Gayness in patriarchal ideology is the repository of whatever has been symbolically expelled from hegemonic masculinity, the items ranging from fastidious taste in home decoration to receptive anal pleasure. Hence, from the point of view of hegemonic masculinity, gayness is easily assimilated to femininity' (Connell 1995: 78).

3 My translation. Because the works quoted in this chapter have either been translated by three different translators, or have not previously been translated into English, for the sake of uniformity, I have decided to provide my own English translations from the Japanese.

4 When the protagonist of *Dansu dansu dansu* turns down the services of a prostitute hired for him by somebody as a surprise, to the prostitute's question of whether he is gay (*homo*), he simply says, 'I am not. I am not, but the gentleman who hired you and I have different ways of thinking' (1988a: II, 98).

5 McLelland notes that the Japanese term *seidōitsusei shōgai* is 'even more pathologizing' than the English term 'disorder' – problematic, in his view, because one cannot assume that all transgender people are traumatised by their status and want to be 'treated' (2005: 210). It is not clear whether Murakami is trying to send a political message here or simply introducing a transgender character to reflect the fact of their existence in Japanese society.

6 Murakami once noted in an interview that he needed a character in *Umibe no Kafuka* who would be 'unusual', using a word that can be read as *ikei* (atypical, of an unusual appearance) or *igyō* (fantastic, grotesque, weird-looking). He said that Ōshima's face 'would be a cross between a fish and a cat' (Yukawa and Koyama 2003: 36). Jay Rubin, writing about this statement, translates the word as 'deformity' or 'deformation' (Rubin 2005: 293), but it is rather difficult to agree with this interpretation, because the hero is more mentally than physically 'deformed'. Descriptions of Ōshima make it clear that he is quite good looking, so it seems that Murakami meant *ikei* rather than *igyō*.

7 Most Japanese readers seeing the word in *katakana* will probably not realise that, in English, 'fruitcake' can be a derogatory term for a gay person.

8 Lunsing also argues that the word *gei* is often understood as referring to *nyū hāfu* (i.e. new half). *Nyū hāfu* are men who often work in gay bars dressed as hostesses and often performing on stage. The word *nyū hāfu* is used for transvestites, transsexuals, and gays, but Lunsing suggests treating this term more as describing a profession rather than gender (2003: 26).

9 Murakami was criticised for this decision. See for example the blog of Chiyoda Natsuo, a scholar of American literature and queer studies: http://chiyodanatsuo.jugem.jp/?eid=95. I am grateful to Keith Vincent for telling me about this blog.

10 See, for example, Mishima Yukio's *Kinjiki* (1951; trans. *Forbidden Colors* [1968]) or Fukusaku Kinji's 1968 film *Kuroi Tokage* (trans. *Black Lizard*).

11 For instance, Murakami Ryū included gay themes in *Kagirinaku tōmei ni chikai burū* (1976; trans. *Almost Transparent Blue* [1977]).

References

Asahi Shinbun. 2019. *Ibaraki ken ga pātonāshippu seido jimin hantai shita ga chiji ga danketsu* [online]. Available from: https://www.asahi.com/articles/ASM6S3DFSM6SUJHB006. html [Accessed 26 July 2019].

BBC News. 2021. Japan court finds same sex marriage unconstitutional [online]. Available from: https://www.bbc.com/news/world-asia-56425002 [Accessed 22 April 2021].

Butler, J. 2007 [1990]. *Gender trouble*. New York and London: Routledge.

Connell, R. W. 1995. *Masculinities*. Berkeley: University of California Press.

Dasgupta, R. 2003. Creating corporate warriors: The 'salaryman' and masculinity in Japan. *In*: K. Louie and M. Low, eds. *Asian masculinities: The meaning and practice of manhood in China and Japan*. London: Routledge, 118–134.

———— 2013. *The salaryman in Japan: Crafting masculinities*. London: Routledge.

Duggan L. 2002. The new homonormativity: The sexual politics of neoliberalism. *In*: R. Castronovo and D. D. Nelson, eds. *Materializing democracy: Towards a revitalized cultural politics*. London and Durham: Duke University Press, 175–194.

Hong, T. 2015. Review of *Colorless Tsukuru Tazaki and His Years of Pilgrimage* by Haruki Murakami. *Room One Thousand* 3 (3): 444–449.

Ibaraki ken. 2019. *Ibaraki de pātonāshippu sensei seido o jisshi shite imasu* [online]. Available from: http://www.pref.ibaraki.jp/hokenfukushi/fukushi/jinken/ibarakipartner.html [Accessed 26 July 2019].

Katō N. 2014. *Onna no inai otokotachi: Murakami Haruki no igokochi no yoi basho kara no hōchiku* [online]. *Nikkei Shinbun*, 28 April. Available from: http://www.nikkei.com/article/DGXDZO70464510W4A420C1MZB001/ [Accessed 26 July 2019].

Kuroiwa Y. 2016. Dasseijika to iu 'sei no seiji' – Murakami Haruki no 'Gūzen no tabibito' o yomu [The depoliticization of sexual politics: Reading Murakami Haruki's 'Chance Traveler']. *Genko bunka kenkyū* (Ritsumeikan Daigaku) 28 (2): 61–69.

Lunsing, W. 1997. Gay boom in Japan: Changing views of homosexuality? *Thamyris* 4 (2): 267–293.

———— 2003. What masculinity? Trangender practices among Japanese 'men'. *In*: J. E. Robertson and Suzuki N., eds. *Men and masculinities in contemporary Japan: Dislocating the salaryman doxa*. London: Routledge, 20–36.

McLelland, M. 2000. *Male sexuality in modern Japan*. Richmond: Curzon Press.

———— 2003. Gay men, masculinity and the media in Japan. *In*: K. Louie and M. Low, eds. *Asian masculinities: The meaning and practice of manhood in China and Japan*. London: Routledge, 59–78.

———— 2005. *Queer Japan from the Pacific War to the internet age*. Lanham: Rowman and Littlefield.

Murakami Haruki. 1982. *Hitsuji o meguru bōken*. Tokyo: Kōdansha.

———— 1987. *Noruwei no mori*. Tokyo: Kōdansha.

———— 1988a. *Dansu, dansu, dansu*. Vols. I and II. Tokyo: Kōdansha.

———— 1988b. *Sekai no owari to hādoboirudo wandārando*. Vols. I and II. Tokyo: Shinchō Bunko.

———— 1993 [1990]. Kanō Kureta. *In*: *TV pīpuru*. Tokyo: Bungei Shunjū, 119–132.

———— 2000. Tairando. *In*: *Kami no kodomotachi wa mina odoru*. Tokyo: Shinchōsha, 97–125.

———— 2001 [1999]. *Supūtoniku no koibito*. Tokyo: Kōdansha Bunko.

———— 2002. *Umibe no Kafuka*. Vols. I & II. Tokyo: Shinchōsha.

———— 2003. *Nejimakidori kuronikuru*. Vols. I & III. Tokyo: Shinchōsha.

———— 2004a. *Afutādāku*. Tokyo: Kōdansha.

———— 2004b. *Kokkyō no minami, taiyō no nishi*. Tokyo: Kōdansha Bunko.

———— 2005a. Gūzen no tabibito. *In*: *Tōkyō kitanshū*. Tokyo: Shinchōsha, 7–42.

———— 2005b. Hanarei Bei. *In*: *Tōkyō kitanshū*. Tokyo: Shinchōsha, 43–79.

———— 2005c [1996]. Rekishinton no yūrei. *In*: *Rekishinton no yūrei*. Tokyo: Bungei Shunjū, 9–38.

———— 2009. *1Q84*. Vols. I and II. Tokyo: Shinchōsha.

———— 2013. *Shikisai o motanai Tazaki Tsukuru to, sono junrei no toshi*. Tokyo: Bungei Shunjū.

———— 2014a. Dokuritsu kikan. *In*: *Onna no inai otokotachi*. Tokyo: Bungei Shunjū, 117–167.

———— 2014b. Kino. *In*: *Onna no inai otokotachi*. Tokyo: Bungei Shunjū, 211–261.

———— 2017. *Kishidanchō goroshi*. Vol. I. Tokyo: Shinchōsha.

Murakami Haruki. and Shibata M. 2003. *Sarinjā senki*. Tokyo: Bungei Shunjū.

Nihon keizai shinbun. 2015. *Dōsei patonā jōrei ga seiritsu Shibuya ku gikai de sansei tasū* [online]. Available from: https://www.nikkei.com/article/DGXLAS0040010_R30C15A3000000/ [Accessed 26 July 2019].

Out Japan Co. Ltd. n.d. *Risuto: Dōsei pātonashippu shōmei seido o donyū shite iru/dōnyū yotei no jichitai* [online]. Available from: https://www.outjapan.co.jp/pride_japan/document/ [Accessed 5 June 2021].

Pflugfelder, G. M. 2007 [1999]. *Cartographies of desire: Male sexuality in Japanese discourse, 1600–1950*. Berkeley: University of California Press.

Rubin, J. 2005. *Haruki Murakami and the music of words*. London: Vintage Books.

Salinger, J. D. 1991 [1951]. *The Catcher in the Rye*. New York: Little, Brown and Company.

———— 2015 [2003]. *Kyacchā in za rai*. Translated by Murakami Haruki. Tokyo: Hakusuisha.

Shibuya ku kōshiki saito. 2019. *Shibuya ku pātonāshippu shōmeisho* [online]. Available from: https://www.city.shibuya.tokyo.jp/kusei/shisaku/lgbt/partnership.html [Accessed 26 July 2019].

Suter, R. 2008. *The Japanization of modernity: Murakami Haruki between Japan and the United States*. Cambridge and London: Harvard University Asia Center.

Takeuchi K. 2010. Murakami Haruki 'Rekishinton no yūrei' ron: kanōsei to shite eizu bungaku. *Nihon bungaku* 67 (10): 45–57.

Yukawa Y. and Koyama T. 2003. Murakami Haruki rongu intabyū: *Umibe no Kafuka* o kataru. *Bungakukai* 57 (4): 11–42.

PART III

Literary dialogues

10

ASK THE HORSE

Murakami's views on literary creation and the nature of inspiration

Giorgio Amitrano

There are writers for whom writing appears to be a means of finding themselves, of acquiring awareness, and others for whom writing seems to represent a key for forgetting the self, a way of creating an alternative reality in which they might dwell more comfortably than within their own identity. Writers such as these are not necessarily to be considered escapists. The imagination can be quite a powerful means of expression even when its goal is not self-awareness. If these categories actually exist, we may place in the first writers such as Philip Roth, J. M. Coetzee or Ōe Kenzaburō, to name but a few, and in the second authors like Roberto Bolaño and Clarice Lispector. But where would we position Murakami?

By 'forgetting the self' I mean an approach to writing in which authors, rather than masterminding their project, allow themselves to be swept away by the narration, following it wherever it may lead them. For them creative power means the ability to be receptive to any ideas and images that cross their imagination, being able to capture them and translate them into the language of literature. As Stephen King (2012: 29), another writer 'possessed' by inspiration, put it: 'Good story ideas seem to come literally from nowhere, sailing at you right out of the empty sky'.

A powerful example of the romantic vision of writing as possession, in which the author is seen as a receptacle filled with the divine inspiration poured into it by the Muse, is the short story 'The Possessed' ('Kohyō' [1942]) by Nakajima Atsushi, set in a Scythian village in ancient Greece. The protagonist, Shaku, shocked at the sight of the mutilated corpse of his brother who was killed during a barbarian invasion, starts speaking in a trance, giving voice to the dead man's spirit. But this possession does not come to an end with the close of his brother's story, and Shaku takes on the role of medium for a great variety of spirits, even animals, all of them keen to recount their experiences through him. Shaku becomes a storyteller entertaining the villagers, and his stories become increasingly complex and detailed. But one day the spirits stop visiting him and he loses his ability to tell new stories. Now that he has become useless, the villagers sentence him to death, and in the final scene he is boiled in a cauldron and devoured by the community.

This short story is a clear metaphor of a writer's uneasy relationship with inspiration. To make the metaphor more explicit, Nakajima ends the story with the following passage: 'Nobody knows that long before the blind Maeonian named Homer started to declaim his verses, a poet was devoured in this way' (Nakajima 1981: 141; my translation). Nakajima, whose works are mostly based on pre-existent sources, was particularly sensitive to the limitations of a feeble imagination, and many of his stories resound with anxiety about his own creative power, but there has hardly ever been a writer who is not concerned with the ebbs and flows of inspiration. 'Talent has a mind of its own and wells up when it wants to, and once it dries up, that's it', writes Murakami Haruki (2009: 77).

To the best of my knowledge, Nakajima does not feature among the authors cited by Murakami, but I could detect in both writers – despite their obvious differences – an attention to problems relating to the writing process and the nature of inspiration. In their own way, both of them poignantly conveyed the anxiety of being a writer in their fictional works, an anxiety Murakami did not express to the same degree when he discussed these themes directly in essays such as *What I Talk About When I Talk About Running* (2009; *Hashiru koto ni tsuite kataru toki ni boku no kataru koto* [2008]) and *Shokugyō toshite no shōsetsuka* (2015; no trans. Novelist as a Profession).

My interest in writing as awareness or forgetfulness in connection with Murakami comes from having detected in his work a sort of contradiction between two different kinds of attitudes, or more precisely between two opposite approaches to these elements. Murakami expressed his views on writing, providing insights into how he developed his personal literary style, in the works I mentioned above. In these same books he also insisted on the importance of a writer keeping fit through constant physical exercise. He seems to suggest that although talent is a prerequisite that a writer must possess to produce meaningful work, talent is also a gift which does not stand by itself. It cannot be acquired, but it could and should be controlled and wisely cultivated. In order to do so, talent must be accompanied by another important quality: 'Focus – the ability to concentrate all your limited talents on whatever's critical at the moment' (Murakami 2009: 77). And a writer also needs the energy to hold his concentration for a long time. This quality is endurance, a virtue that, like focus, should be 'acquired and sharpened through training' (ibid.: 78), in other words practising regularly as one would for physical exercise. 'This involves the same process as jogging every day to strengthen your muscles and develop a runner's physique' (ibid.: 78). In general, Murakami offered the image of a writer who has reached maturity and is in full charge of his creative power. We may say that he presented himself as an Apollonian writer, rational and self-disciplined, in contrast with a wilder, more Dionysian version he gives of himself elsewhere.

The high degree of intertextuality, as well as the use of metafiction and pastiche in Murakami's works has led some critics (notably Suter 2008 and Seats 2006) to draw attention to his connection to postmodernism. As I have explained elsewhere (Amitrano 1996: 6–7), I feel slightly uncomfortable with this view because such elements, although recurrent in his novels, lack the ironical distance and moral relativism that characterise the postmodern sensibility. His references to literary works and his use of quotations seem to me to express not so much a distance from – as a proximity to – the authors he mentions, a tribute to them rather than irony encapsulated in quotation marks. The struggle of his heroes to keep a sense of decency and loyalty is closer to Charles Dickens than to Donald Barthelme or Italo Calvino. From this perspective, a comparison with Calvino might prove revealing.

Calvino's literary style underwent an amazing transformation from his early works to his later ones. A taste for metafiction gradually spread across his pages, transforming the passionate young novelist into a sophisticated postmodern author, enamoured of mental arabesques, which somehow anticipate the conceptual photographic images of the photographer Sugimoto Hiroshi. Calvino's early works were all about *being there*; his later works were about *being somewhere else* and watching things from a distance. But Murakami's works are *all* about 'being there'. Whereas his creation of worlds becomes progressively complex, his description of human life gradually becomes de-problematised, not that it becomes shallower – it becomes more essential and humanistic: the solitude of human beings and their desperate efforts to find their place in the world is enhanced by their being portrayed as little men imprisoned in towering structures (both physical and intangible) like the tiny figures struggling in the artist Giovanni Piranesi's imaginary prisons.

Despite being an internationally acclaimed writer, Murakami seems to have remained in touch with his younger self, as if his experience as an aspiring writer needing to develop a strategy to translate an intense but uncertain desire into actual writing was still alive in his memory and played an important role in his fiction. He touched on the theme of the writers' struggle to find their way in several of his works. In his short story 'Honey Pie' (2003; 'Hachimitsu pai' [2000]), the protagonist Junpei at 36 is a writer who, after much effort, has finally managed to secure himself a position in the literary world. Determined to become a writer since his youth, Junpei has kept faith with this resolution without compromise, refusing even his editor's advice to abandon short stories in favour of novels, which would attract more attention and sell better. But despite managing to build up 'a steady readership, and a fairly stable income' (Murakami 2003: 123), he feels that his stories are not as powerful as he would like them to be. His writing is marred by the same indecisiveness that has characterised his relationship with Sayoko, the woman he has always loved but whom he allowed to be taken from him by his more persistent friend Takatsuki. It is only when he overcomes his uncertainty and makes love to the now divorced Sayoko, taking on responsibility for her and her small child Sara, that he at last feels the urge to write more effective stories.

> I want to write stories that are different from the ones I've written so far, Junpei thought: I want to write about people who dream and wait for the night to end, who long for the light so they can hold the ones they love.
>
> (Murakami 2003: 132)

This story is particularly interesting with regard to how Murakami combines the theme of a writer's search for his own truest voice with the ethical quest for right conduct towards others. Junpei's hesitation in declaring his love for Sayako, divided as he is between his shyness towards her and a sense of loyalty to his friend Takatsuki – a hesitation which, incidentally, reminds us of the attitude of Natsume Sōseki's heroes – in particular Daisuke in *Sore kara* (1909; trans. *And Then* [1978]) – is closely linked to his difficulty in fully emerging as a narrator.

It should be noted that what breaks this shell, in which both his sentimental life and creative power are imprisoned, is the earthquake and its consequences on those who Junpei cares for. Sara has been seriously affected by it; her hysterical fits and her dream of 'the Earthquake Man' who threatens to put her and the people around her in a little box is a clear symptom of post-traumatic stress disorder.

'Honey Pie' is part of a series of six short stories with the common theme of the 1995 Kobe earthquake, even if the event itself is peripheral to the main narrative in each of the stories. The Japanese versions of the first five stories were serialised in the magazine *Shinchō* under the series title 'Jishin no ato de' (2000, literally 'after the quake'), the title clearly suggesting that Murakami is more interested in the aftermath, namely the ways in which the consequences of the earthquake has altered people's daily life. The Japanese version of 'Honey Pie', called 'Hachimitsu pai', is the only one included in the short story collection *Kami no kodomotachi wa mina odoru* (2000; trans. *after the quake* [2002], lit. All God's Children Dance) as *kakioroshi* (i.e. hitherto unpublished), giving it a special relevance within the book. This collection, which in my opinion has not received the attention it deserves, marks an important stage in Murakami's literary career, because it was through it that he managed to express most effectively the sincerity of his commitment, not as a writer inclined towards social or political critique but as someone who chooses to stand with the anonymous many who suffer the injuries of the world, ignored and even ostracised. Also to this nameless multitude belong those who strive to repair the ravages of nature or, indeed, the violence of others, like Katagiri, the obscure clerk who, in 'Superfrog Saves Tokyo' ('Kaeru-kun, Tōkyō o sukuu'), also from the same collection, is approached by a giant frog to carry out the important feat of saving Tokyo. In a series of conversations with the psychoanalyst Kawai Hayao, Murakami (2016) explained how his attitude had gradually changed from one of 'detachment' to one of 'commitment', the latter increasingly becoming crucial to him over time. His 'commitment' is clearly not ideological and appears to stem from a genuine need to turn a general sympathy for people into something more effective and meaningful.

Underground (2002; *Andāguraundo* [1997]), his non-fiction book on the 1995 Aum Shinrikyō sarin gas attack on the Tokyo underground, was born of similar feelings. In its preface, Murakami writes that he was struck upon reading a letter to a magazine from a woman whose husband had lost his job as a consequence of being injured in the attack. Unable to get himself back into a work routine, he was isolated and mistreated by his boss and colleagues and forced to resign.

The letter shocked me. Here were people who still carried serious psychological scars. I felt sorry, truly sorry, although I knew that for the couple involved my sympathy was irrelevant. […] As if it weren't enough to be the victim of purely random violence, the man had suffered 'secondary victimization' (everyday corporate violence of the most pervasive kind). Why could nobody do anything about it? […] I grew curious to learn more about the woman who wrote in about her husband. Personally, I wanted to probe deeper into how Japanese society could perpetrate such a double violence.

Soon after that I decided to interview the survivors of the attack.

(Murakami 2002: 3–4)

Such personal involvement in the destiny of his contemporaries is all the more striking if we compare this attitude to that of the detached, cool narrator of *Hear the Wind Sing* (1987/2015; *Kaze no uta o kike* [1979]) and *Pinball, 1973* (1985/2015; *1973 nen no pinbōru* [1980]). Compared with the empathetic view expressed in the stories of *after the quake*, his first two novels appear to represent a solipsistic authorial vision and are more oriented towards describing his own imaginary world than to the lives of others.

Similarly, the long novel *1Q84* (2011; *1Q84* [2009–2010]) can be read both as a fictional reflection on the hardships of writing and as a meditation on humanism. There is a remarkable contrast between the extremely complex dystopian vision that Murakami creates and the simplicity of Tengo and Aomame's love story which forms the core of the novel. The two had been classmates when they were in the third and fourth years of school. One day, some time after Tengo had rescued Aomame from a bully, the two happened to be alone in the classroom. Suddenly Aomame grabbed Tengo's hand and went on holding it for a long time. Then she dropped it and dashed out of the classroom. That one moment had stayed with them throughout the years. They had gone on loving each other and hoping to fulfil that unspoken childhood promise. If Aomame represents Tengo's ultimate goal in his quest for love, Fuka-Eri, a mysterious 17-year-old girl, holds the key to fulfilling his ambition to become a writer. The characters of Tengo and Fuka-Eri symbolise two opposite approaches to literary creation: Tengo masters writing skills but lacks inspiration, whereas Fuka-Eri cannot write but is endowed with narrative power. Komatsu, the editor of the publishing house with which Tengo works, asks him to rewrite Fuka-Eri's novel, which is fascinating but badly written. In the following passage Komatsu gives an accurate description of Tengo's strengths and limitations as a writer.

This Fuka-Eri girl has something special. Anyone can see it reading *Air Chrysalis*, her imagination is far from ordinary. Unfortunately, though, her writing is hopeless. A total mess. You, on the other hand, know how to write. Your story lines are good. You have taste. You may be built like a lumberjack, but you write with intelligence and sensitivity. And real power. Unlike Fuka-Eri, though, you still haven't grasped exactly what it is you want to write about. Which is why a lot of your stories are *missing* something at the core. I know you've got something inside that you need to write about, but you can't get it to come out. It's like a frightened little animal hiding way back in a cave – you know it's in there, but there's no way to catch it until it comes out. Which is why I keep telling you, just give it time.

(Murakami 2011: 30)

Although *1Q84* may be a work that most obviously comments on this paradox on whether inspiration or skill is more important for a writer, we can already detect similar feelings in *Sputnik Sweetheart* (2001; *Supūtoniku no koibito* [1999]) through the voice of another aspiring writer – in this case a young woman – Sumire.

'My head is like some ridiculous barn packed full of stuff I want to write about', she said. 'Images, scenes, snatches of words … in my mind they're all glowing, all alive. *Write!* they shout at me. A great new story is about to be born – I can feel it. It'll transport me to some brand-new-place. Problem is, once I sit at my desk and put them all down on paper, I realize something vital is *missing*. It doesn't crystallize – no crystals, just pebbles. And I'm not transported anywhere'. […] 'Maybe I'm *lacking* something. Something you absolutely must have to be a novelist'.

(Murakami 2001: 16)

Once again, I cannot help but think of Nakajima Atsushi. He was well read both in Western literature and Chinese classics and aspired to be a professional writer, but thought he suffered from lack of creative imagination. His exquisite story, 'The Moon Over the Mountain' (2011; 'Sangetsuki' [1941]), was inspired by an ancient Chinese tale about Li Zheng, a poet whose frustration and suppressed anger for failing to realise his literary ambition turn him into a tiger. In a rare moment in which human consciousness returns, Li Zheng asks his friend Yuan Can, whom he has met in the mountains, to write down his poems to be recorded for future generations.

He recited thirty long and short poems, elegant in expression and lofty in sentiment, all demonstrating, even upon first hearing, the poet's uncommon ability. Yet Yuan Can, although deeply impressed, could not overcome a vague unease: There could be no question that the poet's talents were first-rate, but there was a subtle *lack* that kept the poems from achieving the highest quality.

(Nakajima 2011: 5)

Both Nakajima, from his position as one still striving to become a professional writer, and the world-renowned Murakami, are painfully aware of how lacking an essential element – be it inspiration, the spark of genius, imaginative power, or simply discipline – can jeopardise one's realisation as a writer.

That Murakami decided to write a novel while watching a baseball game is a well-known fact that he has mentioned on several occasions, in particular in *Shokugyō toshite no shōsetsuka* (Murakami 2015: 41–43). But of course, what leads an author to write is more complex than any single episode can convey. And even if the epiphany happened at that specific place and time, he had already felt the acute need to express himself, even though his vocation still had a very uncertain appearance. To fulfil a vocation is indeed an uneasy task, and it is especially hard if one does not know what the ultimate goal is. *Vocation* is such an impressive word. It comes from the Latin *vocare*, to call. It may be used in current speech to indicate emphatically a strong aptitude for a particular career or occupation, but it is also the word used to describe the divine calling that saints receive from above. Murakami (1984) did not express it in such mystical terms, but in a short essay he wrote as a tribute to Sasaki Maki, one of his favourite illustrators, he hinted as to what it meant to him to become a writer, and how a vocation can be strong even when it is still vague and confused.

In this essay Murakami recalls his days as a high school student, when he and his classmates discovered Sasaki Maki's drawings in the magazine *Garo*. They knew nothing about him. They knew neither his age nor where he was from, and they were not even sure whether he was a man or a woman. Murakami's idea of him was one of a mysterious being who inhabited a silent space: an old room with a high ceiling where the sun filtered through a small window. The room was empty except for a tidy writing desk, where the man sat. He had no face. Like some of the characters in his manga, he did not need one. What view this man could see from that window, Murakami did not know.

> It was just an image. But images can sometimes be stronger than the reality that produced them. Since then Sasaki Maki's drawings have been like an open window looking onto a territory that existed only within me. Of course, Sasaki Maki's drawings were not the only window. But those drawings had an effect on me that nothing else had. To put it briefly, I believe that for me they always combined originality and impact.
>
> At that time, I wasn't able to analyse it well, but for me Sasaki Maki's manga also represented a possibility.
>
> [...]
>
> 'What do these manga try to express?' I asked myself. Of course, they did not express anything in particular. But despite this, they were accomplished in themselves as works with a clear purpose and impact.
>
> I had the feeling that the crucial point was style. Sasaki Maki possessed a unique and definite style, and it was that artistic style that governed everything. In the end, that style swallowed even Sasaki Maki, and I realised confusedly, *very* confusedly indeed, that it was right there that reality – that reality essential to one's self-expression – was born.
>
> (Murakami 1984: 272–274, my translation)

What Murakami learned from Sasaki Maki was that style was more important than content. Knowing *how* to express was more important than knowing *what* to express. The content might come later. Sasaki Maki's example certainly opened the way to *Hear the Wind Sing* and *Pinball, 1973*. In them we can distinctly feel how style swallows up the plot, the narrative structure, and to a certain degree, Murakami himself. Everything seems to disappear, except style. This explains why these first two novels were at the same time exciting and unsatisfactory: they had style to burn, but they somehow lacked substance. However, what really matters is that they helped Murakami find his voice. In the 'long, long interview' he gave to Kawakami Mieko, he explained how important the voice factor was in establishing his method. This part of the conversation starts by his taking issue with the quintessentially Japanese tradition of *watakushi shōsetsu* (the I-novel).

> On the other hand, I am more interested in discovering the story I have inside of me, dragging it to the surface, and watching what comes out of it. This is why when I read Japanese *watakushi shōsetsu*-style novels I have no inkling as to what they mean.
>
> (Kawakami and Murakami 2017: 38, my translation)

> Ultimately, I think it is primarily a question of voice. If my voice resonates with that of another, or if my harmonics merge with the harmonics of another, surely that person will read me with interest. I have the feeling that people have read my first novels *Kaze no uta o kike* and *1973 nen no pinbōru* only thanks to such resonance and consonance of harmonics. I had staked everything on this. But starting from *Hitsuji o meguru bōken*, I brought that voice into the narrative world [*monogatari no sekai*], and it formed good synchronism with the backbone of the story [*monogatari no jiku*]. In broad terms I would say that this is the path I have travelled as a novelist so far. Voice first. I am quite sure that if you do not get this kind of resonance, no matter how interesting a story you write, people will not be attracted to it.
>
> (Kawakami and Murakami 2017: 38–39, my translation)

But even if in *A Wild Sheep Chase* (1989; *Hitsuji o meguru bōken* [1982]) Murakami managed to find a successful blending of style and substance or, to use his own expression, he found out how to bring his newly-found voice to the heart of the narrative world, the difficulties related to being a writer (crisis of inspiration, lack of talent, etc.) have been and still are a recurrent theme in his work. This theme even emerges in *Killing Commendatore* (2018; *Kishidanchō goroshi* [2017]) where none of the characters is a writer. The protagonist of the novel is actually a painter, so Murakami shifts the theme of creative impasse from writing to painting, but the dilemma is the same, whether writer or artist. In the following passage, the painter's creative block in front of the blank surface of the canvas is a transparent allegory of the blank page syndrome that afflicts most writers at some point. Although the protagonist is in an ideal space for an artist to focus on his work, things do not go as smoothly as he had thought.

Now that I had this environment to work in, the feeling of wanting to paint something grew stronger, like a quiet ache. And there were no limits on the amount of time I could spend for myself. […] I was utterly free to do exactly what I wanted, without worrying about anybody else.

In the end, though, I couldn't paint a thing. No matter how long I stood in front of the canvas and stared at that white, blank space, not a single idea of what to paint came to me. I had no clue where to begin, how to start. Like a novelist who has lost words, or a musician who has lost his instrument, I stood there in that bare, square studio, at a complete loss.

I'd never felt that way before, not ever. Once I faced a canvas, my mind would immediately leave the horizon of the everyday, and something would well up in my imagination. Sometimes it would be a productive image, at other times a useless illusion. But still, something would always come to me. From there, I'd latch onto it, transfer it to the canvas, and continue to develop it, letting my intuition lead the way, the work completed itself. But now I couldn't see anything that would provide the initial spark. You can have all the desire you want, but what you really need is a concrete starting point.

(Murakami 2018: 46–47)

Choosing as a protagonist a painter rather than a writer allows Murakami to analyse indirectly, which also means more freely, the theme of inspiration and also the complex relation between the creative process and the works it produces. As Rebecca Suter remarks: 'The characters and realities that come into existence through portraits and novels do not stay contained in the realm of fiction – they enter "our" reality and enact changes in it' (Suter 2020: 16). The problem of reading into the products of the creative process in order to decipher them seems to be even more troubling for Murakami than the crisis brought upon by lack of inspiration. It is as if literary creation moved on directly from the unconscious of the writer, almost out of his control. A process which 'happens "through" the writer rather than being deliberately and rationally planned by him' (Suter 2020: 5). This reading of Murakami's relation to the process of literary creation could find support in the anecdote that follows.

When my Italian translation of *Umibe no Kafuka* (2002; English trans. *Kafka on the Shore* [2005]) was published, Murakami agreed to give a rare interview with an Italian journalist, Ranieri Polese (2008) and asked me to translate for him. It was not far into the conversation before I got the impression that Murakami did not appreciate the questions much. To questions like 'Why Kafka? When did you read Kafka for the first time? What does Kafka mean to Japanese readers?' or 'Why did you choose to use names like Johnnie Walker and Colonel "KFC" Sanders that sound like commercial advertisements?', his answers were all variations of 'I haven't the slightest idea' or 'How should I know?'. To the question 'Why did you choose Shikoku as the destination for Tamura Kafuka's escape from Tokyo?', he replied: 'It wasn't me who chose it. It was Tamura Kafuka who decided to go there', then adding that:

For me, writing a long novel is like riding a runaway horse and clinging desperately to its back so as not to be thrown violently to the ground. This struggle goes on for one or two years. It is superfluous to add that clinging to the horse requires great physical strength and cold blood. There are times when I see nothing of what is around me. So when one who is clinging to a runaway horse hears someone asking: 'Why did you take this way rather than another?', he does not really know how to answer. The only thing I can say, and I am truly sorry, is: 'ask the horse'.

I think that if a writer is able to explain coherently this or that aspect of his novels, probably he does not write because he is driven to do so by real necessity. A person like this would do better writing a declaration or a statement rather than a novel. In my opinion, if a person spends one or two years writing a long novel, it is because what he has to express can be expressed only through that form. I think it is the critics you should ask for explanations, not writers.

(Polese 2008: 43, my translation)

Even if this answer was the result of insistent questioning and it may betray a certain degree of irritation on Murakami's part, it gives us a precious insight into his thoughts on the creative process of writing and its mysteries, sometimes unfathomable even to the author himself. His image of a writer desperately clinging to his horse in an attempt to avoid falling off implies a loss of control in sharp contrast with the sense of balance expressed in *Shokugyō toshite no shōsetsuka*. Which one are we to believe? As asking the horse would not prove particularly fruitful, it may be more useful to reflect on what these words may mean for Murakami.

The horse metaphor reminds me of a beautiful poem by Sylvia Plath, 'Words' (1983). It is quite short, only four five-line stanzas, and in it we find two images of horses. I quote only the relevant verses:

Axes
After whose stroke the wood rings,
And the echoes!
Echoes traveling
Off from the centre like horses.
[…]
Years later I
Encounter them on the road—
Words dry and riderless,
The indefatigable hoof-taps.

(Plath 1983: 86)

In both cases horses are evoked only obliquely: first as a simile for echoes that reverberate from a wood violently cut and gallop away from the centre, and again when the poet encounters words she once knew and finds them wandering without direction, as if their rider had deserted them or had been thrown off.

Even though Plath's poem and Murakami's sentence were produced in completely distinct contexts, I find it interesting that they, coming from different directions, converged upon a similar point. They both used the 'horse' image in relation to writing. Comparing them may help us understand a subtler nuance in Murakami's reply to the Italian journalist. In Sylvia Plath's poem the first instance of the use of 'horse' is still an image of vitality, but in the last part of the poem, in the space of a few lines, words are drained of vital energy and move on, dry and riderless, accompanied by the dull, obsessive, endless sound of hoofbeats. But Murakami's words are neither dry nor riderless. What he forgot to mention in the interview was that he is both the rider and the horse. The rider clings desperately to the horse, trying not to be thrown off, the horse finds the way for both. Now let me return to my opening question: Where would we position Murakami? Between writers for whom writing would seem to serve as a means of finding the self, of acquiring awareness? Or with those for whom writing seems to represent a key for forgetting the self, a way of creating an alternative reality?

I am tempted to say that in his case we may conclude that there is no contradiction between the two possibilities, as there is no antinomy between the Apollonian writer and the possessed one. The rider forgets himself, oblivious – or blind – to the scenes he is going through; the horse knows all and takes him to the destination. Both are saved. This could be the final answer. But of course, being a Murakami reader, I prefer to leave the ending open.

References

Amitrano, G. 1996. *The new Japanese novel: Popular culture and literary tradition in the works of Murakami Haruki and Yoshimoto Banana*. Kyoto: Italian School of East Asian Studies.

Kawakami M. and Murakami H. 2017. *Mimizuku wa tasogare ni tabidatsu*. Tokyo: Shinchōsha.

King, S. 2012. *On writing: A memoir of the craft*. London: Hodder.

Murakami H. 1984. Sasaki Maki. Shokku. 1967. *In*: Takeuchi O. and Murakami T., eds. *Manga hihyō taikei 1: Atomu. Kagemaru. Sazae-san*. Tokyo: Heibonsha, 270–275.

—— 2001. *Sputnik Sweetheart*. Translated by Philip Gabriel. London: Vintage.

—— 2002. *Underground: The Tokyo Gas Attack and the Japanese Psyche*. Translated by Alfred Birnbaum and Philip Gabriel. London: Vintage.

—— 2003. *After the Quake*. Translated by Jay Rubin. London: Vintage.

—— 2009. *What I Talk About When I Talk About Running*. Translated by Philip Gabriel. London: Vintage.

—— 2011. *1Q84*. Translated by Jay Rubin. New York: Vintage International.

—— 2015. *Shokugyō toshite no shōsetsuka*. Tokyo: Suitchi Paburisshingu.

—— 2016. *Haruki Murakami Goes to Meet Hayao Kawai*. Translated by Christopher Stephens. Einsiedeln, Switzerland: Daimon.

—— 2018. *Killing Commendatore*. Translated by Philip Gabriel and Ted Goossen. London: Harvill Secker.

Nakajima A. 1981. *Nakajima Atsushi zenshū*, vol. 1. Tokyo: Chikuma Shobō.

——— 2011. *The Moon Over the Mountain and Other Stories*. Translated by Paul McCarthy and Nobuko Ochner. Bloomington, Indiana: Autumn Hill Books.

Plath, S. 1983. *Ariel*. London: Faber and Faber.

Polese, R. 2008. Murakami: il critico letterario è l'interprete del mio romanzo. *Corriere della sera*, 5 April.

Seats, M. 2006. *Murakami Haruki: The simulacrum in contemporary Japanese culture*. New York; Plymouth, UK: Lexington Books.

Suter, R. 2008. *The Japanization of modernity: Murakami Haruki between Japan and the United States*. Cambridge: Harvard East Asia Center.

——— 2020. The artist as a medium and the artwork as metaphor in Murakami Haruki's fiction. *Japan Forum* 32 (3): 361–378. DOI: 10.1080/09555803.2019.1691630

11

MODERN JAPANESE AND EUROPEAN GENRE HISTORY IN MURAKAMI'S AND SŌSEKI'S COMING-OF-AGE NOVELS[1]

Annette Thorsen Vilslev

In his foreword to the 2009 English translation of Natsume Sōseki's *Sanshiro* (*Sanshirō* [1908]), Murakami describes both *Sanshiro* and his own novel *Norwegian Wood* (2003 [2000]; *Noruwei no mori* [1987]) as Japanese Bildungsromane, or coming-of-age novels (Murakami 2009: xxxv). In terms of genre, he writes, *Sanshiro* – with certain differences – is comparable to coming-of-age novels such as Gustave Flaubert's *Sentimental Education* (*L'éducation sentimentale*) from 1869 and Romain Rolland's *Jean-Christophe* (*Jean-Christophe*) from 1904 to 1912.

As an extraliterary source, Murakami's foreword is interesting for at least two reasons, firstly because he reflects on how the modern Japanese novel relates to its European cousins within the coming-of-age genre, and secondly because he also explicitly characterises *Norwegian Wood* as his own coming-of-age novel. He furthermore writes, '[v]irtually all novelists have such a work. In my own case it is *Norwegian Wood*', and adds, 'I don't especially want to reread it, nor do I have any desire to write another one like it' (Murakami 2009: xxxvi).

While this statement from 2009 suggests Murakami did not intend to write another coming-of-age novel, he apparently changed his mind only a few years later. As I will show, similar to *Norwegian Wood*, *Colorless Tsukuru Tazaki and His Years of Pilgrimage* (2014, hereafter *Tsukuru Tazaki*; *Shikisai o motanai Tazaki Tsukuru to, kare no junrei no toshi* [2013]) seems to insist on being read in relation to previous coming-of-age novels. In these two Murakami's works, we find archi- and intertextual references to earlier European and American Bildung classics, including Goethe (1749–1832), Flaubert (1821–1880), Robert Musil (1880–1940), Thomas Mann (1875–1955), and J. D. Salinger (1919–2010), and as I will argue, *also* to the modern Japanese writer Natsume Sōseki (1867–1916).

In the present chapter, I thus examine references and intertextualities to the coming-of-age genre in *Norwegian Wood* and *Tsukuru Tazaki*, in order to analyse how they relate to Sōseki's modern classics, *Sanshiro* and *Kokoro* (*Kokoro* [1914]) as well as

European classics.[2] The diachronic comparison will help illustrate how the Murakami novels not only recall a European genre history, but also *re*negotiate pivotal coming-of-age themes that were already circulated in earlier modern Japanese literature, for example introducing new themes such as depression, trauma, and love and sex. Thus, I suggest speaking of an interweaving of different transnational strains of the coming-of-age genre in Murakami's work.

Before we move on, I should note that I use the term *intertextuality* in accordance with the narratologist Gérard Genette's (1930–2018) definition, as a subcategory of transtextuality. The term designates the co-existence between two or more texts, eidetically, or as the actual presence of one text in the other (e.g. quotes and allusions) (Friis 2012: 146). According to Genette's narratological categories, which he summed up in the introduction to *Palimpsests: Literature in the Second Degree* (1997; *Palimpsestes: la littérature au second degré* [1982]), a *metatext* is a type of transtextuality that can be read as a direct comment on the other text without necessarily quoting it (literary criticism is of course also metatextual in this sense). A subcategory of the *paratext* is the *epitext* which, in contrast to *peritexts* (titles, epigraphs, etc.), is not in contact with the book physically. It includes other texts by the same author, letters, interviews, etc. but not the literary criticism, which is, as mentioned above, considered metatexts (Friis 2012: 147). Last but not least, *architextuality* is any generic relation to formal, transcendental text categories: types of discourse (e.g. satire) and genres.

Murakami's novels contain many explicit references and intertextualities to 'Western' literature (characters named after European novels, characters reading American novels, etc.). Here I will concentrate on describing some of the ways in which these particular novels refer to concrete works associated with the coming-of-age genre (i.e. according to Genette, their intertextuality). I will also focus on how Murakami's two novels negotiate Sōseki's modern Japanese narratives, even though – in contrast to the frequent references to the Western literature – they never explicitly refer to them. The chapter is divided into two sections: 'From *Norwegian Wood* to its "follow-up" *Tsukuru Tazaki*', and 'Thematic and narrative connections to *Sanshiro* and *Kokoro*'. My aim here is not to produce a comprehensive study of all the possible relations to the coming-of-age genre in Murakami's oeuvre, but to merely point out some of the ways in which these specific novels relate to the modern Japanese as well as the European and American coming-of-age classics. Overall, my intention is to highlight the relations between Sōseki's novels in the Meiji (1868–1912) and Taishō (1912–1926) periods, and Murakami's play with the genre in the Heisei (1989–2019) period as a creative and interpretative category. Before we take a closer look at the novels, I will briefly sum up some examples and characteristics from the long genre history of the coming-of-age novel.

A long and wide history of the Bildungsroman genre

Historically and architextually, the coming-of-age genre leads us all the way back to premodern European genres such as the Medieval and Arthurian romances.

In the 18th century, the Bildungsroman appeared in Europe and flourished with Romanticism and Goethe's *Wilhelm Meister* series, including *Wilhelm Meister's Apprenticeship* (*Wilhelm Meisters Lehrjahre* [2008, 1795/9]) and its sequel *Wilhelm Meister's Journeyman Years or the Renunciants* (hereafter *Wilhelm Mister's Journeyman Years*; *Wilhelm Meisters Wanderjahre, oder Die Entsagenden* [1982, 1821]). Since then, the German Bildungsroman (education/formation novel) has been considered a class or type of novel that deals specifically with a main character's formative years or spiritual education, and as a type of novel that, at least to some extent, explains both the moral and psychological processes by which protagonists develop from early youth to adulthood, and the reasons for these processes.[3] During the 19th century, a number of European novels in German, Irish, French, and other languages cultivated the genre through irony and parody. One very long-titled famous example of the latter is *The Life and Opinions of the Tomcat Murr Together With a Fragmentary Biography of Kapellmeister Johannes Kreisler on Random Sheets of Waste Paper* (*Lebens-Ansichten des Katers Murr nebst fragmentarischer Biographie des Kapellmeisters Johannes Kreisler in zufälligen Makulaturblättern herausgegeben* [1820–1822]) by the German Romantic writer E. T. A. Hoffmann (1776–1822). Internationally, the genre has branched off in various directions and spread to many different languages and literatures, including Japan in the modern period. The last chapters of Sōseki's *I Am a Cat* (*Wagahai wa neko de aru* [1905–1907]), in fact, comment ironically on the international competition of Hoffmann's long-titled novel in comparison with his own famous cat (Natsume 1995, vol. 1).

The genre largely continues such meta-reflexive, experimental, self-conscious parodying when it reappears in the literature of the 20th century, in modernist, neo-Romantic, and again, in German literature after the Second World War. Well known is Günther Grass's *Tin Drum* (*Blechtrommel* [1959]), whose (anti-)Bildungsheld, or (anti-)hero, Oskar, tells his story from a mental hospital (see also Enzensberger 1959). As Martin Swale, who sees Grass's novel as the end of the Bildungsroman, writes: 'even the non-fulfilment of the consistently intimated expectation can, paradoxically, represent a validation of the genre' (Swale 1978: 12). While Todd Kontje sees the term Bildungsroman as a broad superordinate umbrella term, Frederick Amrine wonders if the concept becomes useless, because 'if one takes "Bildung" in its strict and limited historical sense, then nothing is a Bildungsroman – not even *Wilhelm Meister's Apprenticeship*; but if one takes it in the loose sense, something like "development of the protagonist", then everything is a Bildungsroman' (quoted in McWilliams 2016: 10). However, a more recent focus in the theoretical discussion of the circulation of the genre has focused on how it has travelled and changed when migrating into new cultures. This tendency is seen to be mirrored in the increased use of the generic term as a literary category, for example in relation to 'women's literature' and in relation to different types of transnational currents (e.g. Summerfield 2010 and McWilliams 2016). As Ellen McWilliams writes in a recent study, the genre is now widely spread and seems 'more suited to migration than previously imagined' (McWilliams 2016: 10).

In Japanese as well as in European history, the Bildung genre relates to the modern idea of the individual's possibilities of self-realisation (from Wilhelm Dilthey's ideas of the German Enlightenment in his interpretations of Goethe) and socialisation into society. The basic characteristics include a young coming-of-age hero, Bildungsheld, leaving home in a quest for personal success. Social life is seen as a means of individual growth, but also as a chance to develop qualities, so that the hero matures and possibly returns (home) wiser. The Bildungsroman, as Dilthey later names it, presents the 18th-century humanistic ideal of self-education and the development of the individual intellect. Importantly, the early reception described it as an 'unfulfilled' rather than teleological narrative (Lukàcs 1988: 134; Ever 2013: 9). As Selin Ever writes in her study, in the later stage of modernity,

> core values of classical Bildung such as autonomy and self-formation are replaced with those of a socially pragmatic model [...] that promote capitalist-friendly subject production. Thus, the dynamism of Bildung gives way to the rigidity of institutional mode of knowledge-production that only values the end result of a given developmental process.
>
> (2013: 26).

In Japan, *Bildungsroman* has been translated as *kyōyōshōsetsu* (educational novel) but is also sometimes referred to as *seichōshōsetsu* (maturation/growing-up novel). As a genre, *kyōyōshōsetsu* differs from the much discussed autobiographical, confessional *shishōsetsu* genre (lit. 'I-novel') in being less directly focused on the author persona. The instrumentalist use of the Bildung ideal has been widely commented on, and the critic Miyoshi Masao (1974) has discussed the genre's history in Japanese literature, going so far as to suggest that there was a lack of a genuine Bildungsroman in Japan despite the influence of Western individualism. 'The problem for the Japanese novelist is that there is no general acknowledgement in his [sic] culture that noticeable personalities should be allowed to exist'. (Miyoshi 1974: 80). People are, according to Miyoshi, regarded based on their assigned slots, an oppressive hierarchical structure that 'keeps literature tied to strict role-definitions rather than tackling the problem of personality' (discussed in Mortimer 2000: 222). Dennis Washburn (1995), instead, focuses on the hybridity in relation to the translation of the genre in Japan in, among other novels, Mori Ōgai's *Youth* (*Seinen* [1910–1911]) and Sōseki's *Sanshiro*, but also raises a question about the accuracy of cross-cultural classification:

> The term ['Japanese *Bildungsroman*'] is [...] double-edged: not only does '*Bildungsroman*' call attention to the hegemony of Western standards, but even 'Japanese' signifies a conception of nation that reinforces Japan's position on the periphery of modern culture and the myth of its unique status.
>
> (Washburn 2007: 109–110, original italics)

Washburn describes the genre as the perfect vehicle for Ōgai (1862–1922) in exploring the larger issue of how to define selfhood and identity in a period of immense social upheaval, as well as an instance of the conscious and critical experiment with hybridity in literary forms.

Meiji–Taishō writers, like Sōseki, Ōgai, and Tanizaki Junichirō (1886–1965), experimented with different types of new and imported prose fiction (Washburn 2007). As I have argued elsewhere, Sōseki, among others, rejected automatically epitomising everything Western and also combined his experiments with the novel genre with previous Japanese genres and styles (Vilslev 2017).[4] In this way it can be discussed if there is indeed a lack of a serious Japanese Bildungsroman, but it is certain that we do find novels that react to the Bildung genre and related ideals in different ways in Japan. Possibly, as Ever writes in her study, it is because the Bildungsroman today 'communicates ideals that transcend any particular national situation' and 'in fact reinforces the ideology of modernity by universalizing it through aesthetics' (Ever 2013: 20). Inspired by the foreign literature, philosophy, and ideology that would arrive in Japan during the following decades, Japanese novelists and theorists eagerly discussed ideas of self-formation and individualism.[5] During a time of massive social upheaval, new ideals of selfhood, and the introduction of new possibilities of social advancement, it is not surprising that writers in Japan continue to experiment with exploring issues of personal/individual development in relation to the existing social norms in their literary works. Not surprisingly, there are also archi- and intertextualities to the Bildung genre in the Murakami novels that deal with ideas of selfhood.

From *Norwegian Wood* to its 'follow-up' *Tsukuru Tazaki*

Youthful aspirations, disillusionment, self-formation, and transition to the major cities as a sort of *rite de passage* – a string of modern Bildung-related themes are repeated in Murakami's first coming-of-age novel, *Norwegian Wood*, and what I call his follow-up coming-of-age novel, *Tsukuru Tazaki*. In *Norwegian Wood*, the 37-year-old narrator–protagonist Toru Watanabe sits on a plane when a cover version of The Beatles' 'Norwegian Wood' from the 1960s plays from the loudspeakers. As a group that characterised the youth culture of that period, The Beatles tune nostalgically brings him back to a time of complicated feelings and relations during his student days. The novel is initiated by this flashback to the late 1960s, where Toru recalls standing in a meadow with his first love, Naoko, who – during his high school days in Kobe – was the girlfriend of his best friend Kizuki. After Kizuki suddenly committed suicide, Toru moved to Tokyo to study because he 'had to get away from Kobe at any cost' (Murakami, 2003 [2000]: 29). When he runs into Naoko in Tokyo, he develops more intimate feelings for her, but Naoko is reluctant and tormented by the traumatising past. Gradually, she becomes more and more depressed, and to recover from her mental health problems she moves to a sanatorium in the countryside, where Toru goes to visit her and her roommate Reiko. Back at Waseda University in Tokyo, Toru meets another girl Midori and develops deep feelings for her too, but he cannot commit to a relationship with her because of his feelings for Naoko. When Naoko commits suicide, his world is torn apart and he embarks on a journey around Japan before he eventually returns to Tokyo.

The novel has a number of explicit references to coming-of-age works. This is first seen when Toru makes friends with the flamboyant Nagasawa in Tokyo and discovers that they both hold Fitzgerald's initiation classic *The Great Gatsby* (1925) as their favourite novel. According to Toru, they both wanted to read something else than what everybody else was reading at the time, namely Ōe, Mishima, and the modern French writers. Thus, the American Bildung classic is presented as a way in which the two young friends aim to distance themselves from the current trends of society. The concrete stories they read mirror their own development and play an important part in their self-perception during their educational years. In other words, the reading of literature has an existential, self-educational, and social function for the characters in the novel.

In addition to Nagasawa, other characters bring about explicit intertextuality to the coming-of-age genre. Halfway through the novel, when Toru meets Reiko (Naoko's roommate) at the sanatorium, it soon becomes apparent that they also share an interest in coming-of-age novels which creates a bond of understanding between them and draws them closer to each other. Early on in their friendship, Reiko remarks that Toru sounds just like the protagonist of Salinger's *The Catcher in the Rye* (1951), which is often considered the quintessential North American coming-of-age novel: "'You've got this funny way of talking [...] Don't tell me you're trying to imitate that boy in *Catcher in the Rye*?'" (Murakami 2003 [2000]: 131). While the intertextuality feels like a humorous comment on *Norwegian Wood*'s own relation to the genre, it can also be read as a meta-comment about the inspiration from the foreign language literature that is likely to have influenced how the characters express themselves in the novel. Literary research has previously discussed the degree to which Murakami's translations of American writers such as Raymond Chandler and Salinger, has influenced the language and style of his own novels (see e.g. Seats 2006: 197–201). Extradiegetically, in his essay 'To Translate and to be Translated' (2008, 'Honyaku suru koto to, honyaku sareru koto' [1996]), Murakami gives his own account of the relation between being a translator and writer (see also Akashi in this volume on translation and Murakami).

A third example of explicit intertextuality to a coming-of-age novel is seen when Toru spends the night at the sanatorium but cannot fall asleep. After a long talk with Reiko about life and about Naoko, he begins to read Thomas Mann's *The Magic Mountain* (*Der Zauberberg* [1932]), another Bildung classic. Toru immediately understands Reiko's baffled reaction to the fact that he is reading exactly this novel, a major part of which also takes place in a sanatorium in the mountains: "'How could you bring a book like that to a place like this?" she demanded. She was right of course' (Murakami 2003: 138). Reiko's comment possibly hints at how the protagonist in Mann's novel visits his tubercular cousin but contracts a bronchial infection and ends up staying for seven years at the sanatorium. The parallel is interesting not only because it shows that Reiko knows the plot of this Bildung classic well, but also because it hints at Reiko's own similarly long stay at the sanatorium. The fiction Toru is reading is, in other words, real life to her, it reminds her of their own situation of being 'stuck' at the sanatorium. With these explicit referencing to the previous coming-of-age novels, the novel again highlights actual predecessors of the genre as being important to the educational years of the protagonist Toru. During their conversations about life and love, the literary interests Reiko and Toru share ease their communication about the complex and difficult issues of mental illness, depression, and despair. Thus, the reading of the actual books and previous coming-of-age classics is presented as being important not only to the personal identity building but also to the formation of social relations between the characters.

Concrete references to classic coming-of-age novels and music-generated memories play not only an important part in *Norwegian Wood*, Murakami's first coming-of-age novel, but also in *Tsukuru Tazaki*, which I therefore will call his follow-up coming-of-age novel. When *Shikisai o motanai Tazaki Tsukuru to, kare no junrei no toshi* was first published in Japan in 2013, literary critics soon compared it to *Noruwei no mori* (see Konosu and Nakajima 2013; Konosu 2017). Structure-wise the two novels are constructed very differently, the first entering into a sudden flashback, the second embarking on a deliberate search for answers about the past with episodes of flashback. However, as in *Norwegian Wood*, the protagonist of *Tsukuru Tazaki* is a man in his late 30s looking back at the years of his early youth.

The novel opens as Tsukuru, the eponymous protagonist, has almost put his social life on hold after having been excluded by his high-school group of friends much earlier. His new prospective girlfriend, Sara, however, asks him to confront his personal trauma and repressions about the past. Through conversations, they realise that his depressions must relate to the loss of his friends who, in contrast to Tsukuru, all had colourful nicknames – Ao ('blue'), Aka ('red'), Shiro ('white') and Kuro ('black'). As he visits the past and meets his old friends from Nagoya, Tsukuru, furthermore, discovers that the break-up of the group had to do with love conflicts, jealousy, and unsolved mysteries that involved accusations of rape, mental illness, and the death of Shiro. His search for answers finally leads him all the way to Finland to meet Kuro – who now wants to be called by her real name Eri – who reveals that she previously had feelings for him but had never told him because she thought he was in love with Shiro. Murakami's first and follow-up coming-of-age novel are thus connected thematically through complicated love relations and the death of close friends. However, unlike in *Norwegian Wood*, where Toru tries to offer Naoko support before she commits suicide, in *Tsukuru Tazaki*, Tsukuru finds out only years later that Shiro accused him of rape and he is left to wonder if he actually did rape and murder her.

Furthermore, the high degree of explicit intertextual referencing to the coming-of-age genre that we saw in *Norwegian Wood* is another feature we see repeated in *Tsukuru Tazaki*, and in that way both novels very consciously intertextualise and position themselves in relation to previous coming-of-age classics. Already in the novel's long title, *Colorless Tsukuru Tazaki and His Years of Pilgrimage*, we find two intertextualities to European coming-of-age novels. The first part of the title, 'Colorless Tsukuru Tazaki' (in Japanese 'shikisai o motanai Tazaki Tsukuru' which means 'Tsukuru Tazaki without colour') recalls Austrian Robert Musil's (1880–1942) novel *The Man Without Qualities* (*Der Mann ohne Eigenschaften* 2013 [1930–1943]). Not only do we see a similar play on words here, but it soon becomes clear that the paratextual colourlessness is synonymous with the lack of particular traits or qualities throughout Murakami's novel and that the eponymous protagonist Tsukuru Tazaki quietly laments his own colourlessness – similar to Musil's anti-Bildung-hero Ulrich, a rather intelligent intellectual who, on sabbatical from life, does nothing much, apart from analysing his surroundings. The second half of Murakami's title, 'His Years of Pilgrimage' (in Japanese 'kare no junrei no toshi') suggests an intertextual link to Goethe's second Bildung classic, *Wilhelm Meister's Journeyman Years*, in which Goethe's coming-of-age hero Wilhelm moves on to the next phase of his life. Usually considered one of the most famous classic Bildungsroman, the German word '*Wanderjahre*' in Goethe's title literally means 'wandering years' or 'years of pilgrimage' as echoed in Murakami's work. Connected by the conjunction 'and', the two halves of the title *Colorless Tsukuru Tazaki and His Years of Pilgrimage*, thus strongly suggest that we read the novel with the classic European coming-of-age novels in mind.

In the meantime, apart from these explicit references, there are also a number of clear differences. For example, while Musil's Ulrich reflects deeply about the things he observes around him, he never really achieves anything, a fact that Swale refers to as an 'unrelieved discursiveness' (1978: 157). By contrast, as his name indicates, Murakami's Tsukuru (lit. 'to do/make') is always doing/making something. Designing train stations in Tokyo, he has a career that he never had doubts about because of his heartfelt interest in stations. Nevertheless, due to the abandonment by his friends, he feels lost in his private life, and in that sense Tsukuru is much more easy-going and less critically attuned to his surroundings than Musil's idiosyncratic, pre-war sabbatical Ulrich. Having encountered deep loneliness and suffered from depression, Tsukuru is self-critical, has a low opinion of himself, and feels a fundamental lack of supposedly identifiable qualities to his own person that influence his relationships with other people, in particular his friends.

As with *Norwegian Wood*, the intertextualities found in the title of this follow-up coming-of-age novel is also brought into the story itself through an extra layer of musical reference. 'Years of Pilgrimage' is actually translated from the French *Années de pèlerinage* ('years of pilgrimage'), a musical suite in which the Romantic composer Franz Listz (1811–1886) interprets Goethe's *Wilhelm Meister's Journeyman Years*. Furthermore, one of the pieces in the suite, called 'Le mal du pays', which means homesickness, is also mentioned in the novel as a piece that Shiro used to play on the piano and that Tsukuru once discussed with a friend, Haida. Musically, the piece has a recurring motif, and is supposed to evoke strong feelings for the past. Whenever the song is played or discussed, Tsukuru is reminded of a very particular feeling of homesickness or melancholia, which is described in the novel as '[t]he groundless sadness called forth in a person's heart by a pastoral landscape' (Murakami 2014: 56).

Intertextually, this metaphorical connection between melancholia and pastoral landscape might also have the reader recall the initial flashback that Toru experienced in the beginning of *Norwegian Wood* – the meadow landscape that returns him to his youth in the late 1960s. *Tsukuru Tazaki* similarly looks back to the time of youth, but this time to uncover accusations of rape, love conflicts, death, and the break-up of a group of friends during the 1980s. Compared to *Norwegian Wood*'s unfolded flashback story, the flashback in *Tsukuru Tazaki* is brief but likewise generated by a piece of music, and the descriptions of the music-generated flashbacks adds to the feeling of similarity between the two novels. In cinematic terms, we could say that the Listz piece becomes a classical soundtrack for Murakami's coming-of-age follow-up as The Beatles' 'Norwegian Wood' is for *Norwegian Wood*. In both cases, the specific piece of music theme connects the present moment with lost times that serves as an emotional gateway to the youth stories of the past.

While in this way we can point out many similarities between Murakami's two coming-of-age novels, it is again necessary to also highlight significant differences, including the fact that *Norwegian Wood* is written in the first person and *Tsukuru Tazaki* in the third person. This influences how each protagonist recollects his youth story, which in turn becomes notably different. Although Toru Watanabe and Tsukuru Tazaki are roughly the same age, Toru is on a plane when the music takes him back to a melancholic, nostalgic time of mixed feelings that makes him tell his story in order not to forget, whereas Tsukuru is haunted by past events and the break-up of his high-school group of friends. In order to move on in his adult life, he has to figure out what happened back then and he embarks on a journey to his past that physically takes him to his childhood city and as far as Finland. As he puts the pieces together, his search for answers becomes similar to that of a detective who must solve a puzzle that includes accusations of rape, and in that way Tsukuru appears more like the middle-aged hero of an American detective story than the young hero of a coming-of-age classic. The Murakami coming-of-age follow-up is thus in some ways *not* archetypal at all; it moves the plot from the early years of youth to the middle of adult life.

To sum up the comparison so far: music, flashbacks, and previous coming-of-age classics play an important part in both Murakami novels. As we have seen, both novels make multiple references – some explicit, others less so – to the European and American novels that historically speaking have been part of defining the coming-of-age genre. Compared to *Norwegian Wood*, *Tsukuru Tazaki* takes us all the way back to the beginning, namely to Goethe's *Wilhelm Meister's Journeyman Years*, the Bildungsroman generally considered the first in world literature, digging even deeper in its recapitulating of important moments of the genre history. Somewhat similar to *Journeyman Years* being the sequel to *Wilhelm Meister's Apprenticeship*, *Tsukuru Tazaki* could also be seen as a follow-up to Murakami's first coming-of-age novel *Norwegian Wood*. While Tsukuru's detective-like search for answers in the past is not very typical for the genre, architextually it does concern events that happened in his formative years. In scrutinising the psychological aspects of the youth dramas of the past, the novel is about how past events came to affect his self-perception and sense of selfhood. Suffice it to say, the inspirations from previous coming-of-age classics are obviously more associative than imitative whether they concern Goethe's style or plot, and the Murakami novels also differ in a number of ways from many of the Western coming-of-age classics that they more or less explicitly intertextualise.

In writing *Tsukuru Tazaki*, perhaps Murakami was asking himself: What could a sequel to *Wilhelm Meister's Journeyman Years* look like in a contemporary Japanese society? Can the pilgrimage be a journey back to the childhood city? Similar to Goethe or Musil, what are the challenges of living a full life, of being educated by life? Perhaps the clue is that Tsukuru cannot do it alone, and that he has to confront his past in order to be able to connect to other people. These themes, the overcoming of depression, dealing with mental illness, despair, and trauma, are far from the narratives about achieving success in modern society and more about the emotional life and psychology of the characters. The transnational intertextualities to previous coming-of-age classics are, however, not the only associations that *Norwegian Wood* and *Tsukuru Tazaki* have with the genre. Examining narrative and thematic relations to the modern *Japanese* classics, the next part of the present chapter will continue by uncovering connections to Sōseki's *Sanshiro* and *Kokoro* in the two Murakami coming-of-age-novels.

Thematic and narrative connections to *Sanshiro* and *Kokoro*

In his introduction to the English translation of *Sanshiro*, quoted earlier, Murakami describes the novel as Sōseki's only full-length coming-of-age novel, and writes that the eponymous hero's 'armsfolded, lukewarm life stance' is 'strangely comfortable for me and probably for most Japanese readers' (Murakami 2009: xxxiv). Murakami also characterises the protagonist Sanshiro as more downplayed than the classic French coming-of-age heroes: 'Compared with such novels, the course of Sanshiro's growth seems to have little straight-line continuity [...] Sanshiro merely feels surprised or moved or baffled or impressed' (Murakami 2009: xxxiii). Describing *Sanshiro* as one of his favourite Sōseki novels, Murakami writes that while he enjoyed 'the late works so widely praised for their psychology insight', he could never 'fully identify with the deep anguish of the modern intellectual depicted' in Sōseki's arguably most canonised novel, *Kokoro*, which he believes 'left something to be desired' (Murakami 2009: xxvi). This section, however, will argue that Murakami's own coming-of-age novels resemble *Kokoro* more than both *Sanshiro* and the many European and American coming-of-age classics in terms of themes and plot construction.

First, let us take a closer look at how *Sanshiro* relates to the genre. The story begins *in medias res* with the young hero making his rite of passage, an architextual coming-of-age feature. The young eponymous male hero Sanshiro is travelling by train from Kumamoto, the provinces, to the major city of Tokyo, where he will enter university. Much of the novel therefore concerns Sanshiro's immediate impressions in the new Meiji metropolis and his private reflections about the new, strange, and fascinating people he encounters during this rite of passage. Already on the train, Sanshiro imagines what the new acquaintances in Tokyo will be like:

> Sanshiro shook off these ruminations [about an unsuccessful encounter with a woman on the train the previous day] and turned to thoughts of a different

world. He was going to Tokyo. He would enter the University. He would meet famous scholars, associate with students of taste and breeding, do research in the library, write books. Society would acclaim him, his mother would be overjoyed.

(Natsume 2009: 11)

If Sanshiro is less flamboyant and more downplayed than the American coming-of-age hero, as Murakami suggests, his expectations for the future and feelings of rumination show by contrast that he is no less excited about his own potential social advancement in the new city than his London- or Paris-travelling coming-of-age cousins, such as Flaubert's Frédéric in *Sentimental Education* (*L'education sentimentale* [1869]), or Dickens's Pip in *Great Expectations* (1861). In the above quote, Sanshiro first ruminates about his encounter with a woman he meets on the train who appears to be laughing at his indecision towards her, but then he turns his attention to the potential success awaiting him in the new city, the success which he expects lies in natural prolongation of his introduction to the new modern intellectual societies. Architextually speaking, the grand expectations and disillusions are, of course, clear features that frequently appear during rites of passage in the coming-of-age genre.

While *Sanshiro* is about the young protagonist's immediate impressions, reflections, and expectations, *Kokoro* relates to the genre differently. It begins by describing the first-person narrator, a young, humble Tokyo student (the Japanese version uses the humble *watakushi*, one of the many words for 'I' in Japanese) and his accidental meeting with the older Sensei during a summer holiday in Kamakura. This first half of the novel follows the young student who wonders about Sensei's secretive character, with the first part focusing on the development of their friendship in Tokyo and the second part concerning the young student's visit to the provinces to see his father. Then, in the last part which takes up the remaining half of the novel, Sensei gives a detailed account of his own student days, revealing secrets about his own past. This part of the novel is entitled 'Sensei's Testament' and the first-person narrator here becomes Sensei, and hence can be read as Sensei's own coming-of-age story. In that sense, *Kokoro* deals with two diachronically intertwined coming-of-age stories. Sensei's account is written as a suicide farewell letter and moral testament addressed to the young student who, travelling to Tokyo after visiting his family, is eager to read the letter he has been waiting for:

When I [Sensei] read your [the young student's] letter – the last letter you wrote – I realized I had done wrong. I thought of writing to that effect, but I took up my pen, then laid it down again without writing a line. If I were to write you, it must be this letter, you see, and the time for that had not yet quite come. That is why I sent the simple telegram saying you need not come. I then began to write this letter [...] I want to write about my past, quite aside from the obligation involved. My past is my own experience – one might call it my personal property. And perhaps, being property, it could be thought a pity not to pass it on to someone else before I die.

(Natsume 2010: 122–123)

Sensei's confessional letter describes in great detail how as a young man he left the provinces to study in Tokyo and how his new university friend, K, who suffered from depression, told Sensei about his love for the daughter of their common landlady. To help, Sensei had arranged that K could also rent a room in their house. Sensei, however, was secretively in love with the daughter of the house himself, and rushed to her mother to propose. Not long after, he discovered that K, upon hearing about the engagement, had taken his own life. Horrified, Sensei believed that the platonic love triangle and his own egotism resulted in K's suicide. The letter to the young student is Sensei's confession of how it has become impossible for him to continue to live with this feeling of guilt. With the testament-cum-suicide letter, Sensei wishes to use his own example to enlighten the young student of the next generation and warn him about the direction Taishō society was taking, about the egotism and guilt that might come to prevail in modern society. Meanwhile, he insists that the young student keeps the secret to himself: 'You and I have often argued over questions of modern thought. […] You were too young to have had your own experience. [...] Now I will wrench open my heart and pour its blood over you. [...] My one request is that [my wife's] memory of my life be preserved as untarnished as possible' (Natsume 2010: 124).

In contrast to the *in media res* feeling of *Sanshiro*, Murakami's two coming-of-age stories are, like Sensei's retrospective, retold in hindsight. In order to understand their present selves or personal traumas and explain the course of events that happened in the past, the male protagonists of the two Murakami novels, both in their thirties, also either return to (for Toru) or have to search for answers in their past student days (for Tsukuru). While the works use different narrative techniques in recounting and returning to their youth stories – the letter in the train, the airplane flashback, and the detective search – in all three, the *re*collection of youth storied plays a crucial role to the mystery, suspense, and life education of the protagonists.

The narrating of a story as something that happened in the past where the older 'I' retells the story, is of course also seen in American and European coming-of-age classics like Salinger's *The Catcher in the Rye* (1951), in which the young protagonist–narrator Holden tells his own story about a significant period of his life, when he decided to travel to New York City. However, the focus on depression, mental illness, guilt, trauma, as well as suicide and death, that we see in *Kokoro* and Murakami's works are not common tropes in the American and European Bildung classics. In that sense, thematically, and in their construction of retrospective plot, the two Murakami novels seem closer to *Kokoro* than to both *Sanshiro* and the American and European Bildungsromane. *Kokoro* and Murakami's two coming-of-age novels furthermore involve romantic conflicts where two (or more) friends fall in love with the same person, and just like *Kokoro* Murakami's novels can be said to aim at overcoming heavy personal secrets and societal taboos.[6]

My comparative analysis here concentrates on examples of narrative and thematic connections between the relatively realistic coming-of-age narratives, and I will leave it to others to compare their experiments with style, language, and form. I should stress that I am not arguing that Murakami is imitating Sōseki, but that his coming-of-age novels *re*negotiate narratives and themes that were already central to and addressed in *Kokoro*. In that way, we might say that *Kokoro*'s coming-of-age narratives reverberate profoundly, albeit more implicitly than the Western classics, in the two Murakami novels. This is underscored by the open ending we see in all three works. *Kokoro* ends with the young student reading the suicide letter from Sensei on the train, but we do not get any closure about what happens next. In both Murakami novels, the final scene involves the protagonist's open-ended phone call to the woman he has come to realise he loves: Tsukuru calls Sara, while Toru in *Norwegian Wood* calls Midori, and wonders 'where am I now'. In all three, the means of communication – letters and phone calls – are used as central elements or techniques to create an open ending, elements that both connect and disconnect the characters as their coming-of-age stories come to an unresolved end, leaving it up to readers to complete the story.

Miyoshi Masao, among others, has argued that the Japanese *shōsetsu* (novel) in general tends to lack denouement, and the open ending of Sōseki's novels undoubtedly influenced this development (Miyoshi 1991). As Murakami writes, Sōseki adopted Western novel forms 'and modified them his own way' (Murakami 2009: xxxv), in continuation and discontinuation of the format of the Bildungsroman. Thus:

> As a result, in *Sanshirō*, despite its *Western framework*, cause and effect become confused here and there [...] This is the author's conscious choice of course, and Sōseki keeps the story progressing smoothly while supporting this fundamental fuzziness by bringing into play his uniquely sophisticated sense of humor, his free-ranging style, the sheer rightness of his descriptions, and above all the simple honesty of his protagonist's character.
>
> (Murakami 2009: xxxv, my italics)

In transplanting, or maybe more accurately, negotiating the 'Western framework' of the novel and the Bildung genre, Sōseki deliberately rejects linear narrative development, and intentionally, against the Western grain, confuses cause and effect.[7] Murakami's novels likewise often blur the borders or margins between different states of consciousness, and in their ways also frequently confuse ideas of cause and effect. In *Tsukuru Tazaki* for example, we read about Tsukuru's dreams and his gradually fearful realisation that he may indeed have raped Shiro in another world. The story's open end also means that the rape and death of Shiro and Tsukuru's potential involvement is never clarified beyond the protagonist's own fears, leaving it to readers to judge. In *Kokoro*, too, the open ending leaves a void that has puzzled scholars (Karatani 1989; Oshino 1994; Ishihara 1997; Sakaki 1999: esp. 33–35, 38–41). Since we never return to the young student on the train and do not know what he will do after reading Sensei's letter, the more recent reception has, maybe not surprisingly but rather polemically, speculated whether the young student's relation to Sensei's beautiful wife would turn romantic (Komori 1988 [1985]). In our comparison to Murakami, this is similar to how Toru falls in love with his deceased friend's girlfriend.

It should be noted again, however, that while it is tempting to connect Sōseki's and Murakami's works in this way, we also find significant differences, most notably concerning the *sensei* character and the position of women. While *Kokoro* and *Sanshiro* feature older male *sensei* characters who discuss the future directions of society with the young male protagonists, this type of male mentoring character is remarkably absent in Murakami's novels. Instead, it is the women – in *Norwegian Wood*, Reiko and Midori, in *Tsukuru Tazaki*, Kuro and Sara – who through conversation and intimacy help the young protagonists. It is the older Reiko who gives Toru advice about Naoko and life in general, and the slightly older Sara who suggests that Tsukuru revisit his old friends to try to heal his wounds. By contrast to Sōseki's novels, the young men and women in Murakami's contemporary coming-of-age works turn to each other, or more accurately, the young men now perceive the women as intimate conversation partners in love and life. In this sense, Murakami's novels renegotiate some of Sōseki's story worlds where women characters tended to be placed on a pedestal, uninvolved in serious decision-making, as we see in *Kokoro*. In Sōseki's first novel *I am a Cat*, we do of course see the occasional humorous interferences of the wife and the next-door she-cat, and in works like *Sanshiro*, we see young men's confusion in reading modern types of women, who do not oblige to old norms, being thematised.[8] By contrast, in the two Murakami novels, the women play a pivotal role as conversation partners and mentors for the protagonists' coming-of-age stories.

As we have seen, while Murakami's two coming-of-age novels contain explicit intertextuality to many American and European Bildung classics, they also – albeit more subtly – renegotiate Sōseki's canonised Meiji–Taishō novels. Although Murakami characterised *Sanshiro* as Sōseki's only coming-of-age novel and was less impressed by *Kokoro*, his own coming-of-age novels in fact resemble *Kokoro* more than both *Sanshiro* and the European or American genre classics in terms of theme and plot construction.

Conclusion

In 'Genre as world system', literary critic and theorist Wai Chee Dimock imagines genre as a new organising principle to literary history, in addition to existing paradigms such as temporal periods and bodies of national literatures (2009: 73–74). 'Genre' for Dimock is not a rigid taxonomy or lineage, but a family of resemblance, or a complex, interrelated, rhizomatic field. Transnationally, literatures interconnect along various paths, but the significance of their wider histories of translation and circulation is too often overlooked. To describe and see such interconnectedness, as Dimock writes, we need to look at multiple planes, also at 'far-flung kinship', 'the tangled pathways and fractional reproduction of literary forms' (Dimock 2009: 80).

This chapter followed Dimock's idea and extracted such connectedness transnationally between Murakami's *Norwegian Wood* and *Colorless Tsukuru Tazaki and His Years of Pilgrimage* with the European and American coming-of-age genre, as well as nationally with two modern Japanese Bildung classics by Sōseki who, as part of the modern Japanese novelistic tradition, was already negotiating related ideas of Bildung/formation and individualism. Murakami's works are often seen as inspired by Western, and in particular American, literature. With this chapter, however, I have wanted to stress that the two Murakami novels involve multiple traditions, not only referring to foreign classics, but also alluding – albeit more indirectly and subtly – to earlier works in modern Japanese literature, resulting in multiple layers of intertextuality.

Both *Norwegian Wood* and *Tsukuru Tazaki* have many explicit references to the Western coming-of-age classics. *Norwegian Wood* explicitly refers to European Bildungsromane as well as to American coming-of-age novels, such as Salinger's *The Catcher in the Rye*. And although Murakami did not intend to revisit the genre after *Norwegian Wood*, in 2013 he did return with an architextual follow-up that is *Tsukuru Tazaki*. The long title of this novel alone signals to a number of creative developments, beginnings, reruns, and adaptations closely related to the genre.

At the same time, both novels also renegotiate themes found in early 20th-century Japanese novels and could be said to have as much in common with Sōseki's heavy-hearted *Kokoro* as the light-spirited *Sanshiro*. Following the psychological and individual development of their male coming-of-age protagonists, all four novels architextually revolve around typical Bildung themes, such as the *rites de passage* from youth to maturity, and descriptions of transitions from the provinces to Tokyo. The Murakami novels, however, do not only recirculate the classic coming-of-age stories and themes but also bring in new themes such as psychological focuses on trauma, discussions of rape, development of close relations, and intimate conversations between men and women.

Following the magical realism of many of the novels that came after *Norwegian Wood* (see e.g. Strecher 1999), *Tsukuru Tazaki* returns to the more realist style of Murakami's first coming-of-age novel. While other novels like *Kafka on the Shore* (*Umibe no Kafuka* [2002]) can also be seen as experimenting with the coming-of-age genre, they depart significantly from the realist Bildung style due to the magical realist bend and detours into the subconscious mind.

With the comparison of these four novels, I wanted to stress that the two Murakami novels not only refer to foreign classics, but also allude to earlier works in modern Japanese literature. Intertextualising previous novels within the genre, the Murakami novels examined in this chapter, like Sōseki's before them, transplant, renegotiate, and transform the Bildung format. While *Norwegian Wood* explicitly refers to European and American coming-of-age novels, *Tsukuru Tazaki* refers us to the older European classics and to their adaptations into other art forms, resulting in a many-layered intertextuality.

Notes

1 This chapter maintains the Japanese name order with family names first, unless it is a character name from a novel's English translation. Sōseki's family name was Natsume and his given name Kinnosuke, but around 1889, he settled on the pen name Sōseki that replaces his first name. As is common practice, I refer to him as Sōseki, but list his works under Natsume in the bibliography. The same goes for Mori Ōgai, né Mori Rintarō, known by his pen name Ōgai, indexed under Mori.

2 The word *classic* here simply refers to canonised literary works, and *modern* to the period of literature of the late 19th and early 20th century.

3 For more definitions see e.g. Mayer (1992). The influential architext/genre has developed a palimpsest of signification. There are also translation variants to the term, such as the Danish *dannelsesroman*, the French *roman d'apprentissage* or *roman initiatique*, and the Japanese *kyōyōshōsetsu* or *seichōshōsetsu*, while in Spanish the German generic term *Bildungsroman* is commonly used. As this chapter can hardly do justice to its amazingly widespread literary history, suffice to say that the genre has undergone numerous developments transnationally. See e.g. Summerfield and Downward (2010).

4 In 'Questioning Western universality' (2017), I argued for relations between Sōseki's haiku-novel *Kusamakura* and his theories about the global transformations of literature.

5 The translation of foreign literature, fiction and non-fiction, undoubtedly also had a great impact on the ideals of education and selfhood formation in the development of modern society, aesthetics, and literature in Japan. Noticeably, one of the first books to be translated to Japanese after the Restoration was the so-called 'bible of mid-Victorian liberalism', *Self Help; With Illustrations of Character and Conduct* from 1859 (its second edition added *Perseverance* to the subtitle) by Scottish reformist Samuel Smiles (1812–1904), translated to Japanese in 1870 by Nakamura Keiu as *Saikoku risshi hen*, which argues for self-education as the road to individual/personal success in modern society. In 'Watakushi no kojinshugi' (1914; trans. 'My Individualism' [1979]), Sōseki notably and famously also discusses ideas of self-formation, egoism versus individualism, and the effect of the rapid modernisation of Japan.

6 Secrets and social taboos were of course also thematised by many of the earlier modern Japanese novelists in their works, such as Ōgai's 'Maihime' (1890; trans. 'The Dancing Girl' [1975]) and Tōson's *Hakai* (1906; trans. *The Broken Commandment* [1974]).

7 The early Sōseki novels often break away from genre expectations. His novel *Kōfu* (1908; trans. *The Miner*) rejects clear plot development of a beginning, a middle and an end, and is more focused on the twists and turns of the conscious mind. In *Botchan* (1906; trans. *Little Master*), the spoiled eponymous Bildung character never strives for or really achieves anything, seriously dismantling the idea of successful self-formation. These novels therefore can be seen as satires or humorous pastiches of the coming-of-age ideal of self-realisation or search for self-identity, questioning the possibility or goal of attaining a stable and coherent perception of self.

8 Indeed, some of Sōseki's other novels such as *Sanshiro* and the unfinished *Meian* (1916; trans. *Light and Darkness* [1971]) have depicted the emergence of new types of modern independent women, the *atarashii onna* (lit. new woman), which are seen as a forerunner of the *moga*-figure (short for *modan gāru*, i.e. modern girl) (see Levy 2010). He also portrayed different notions of love and marriage across his oeuvre.

References

Dimock, W. C. 2009. *Through other continents: American literature across deep time.* Princeton: Princeton University Press.

Enzensberger, H. M. 1959. Wilhelm Meister auf der *Blechtrommel*. Frankfurt am Main, *Frankfurter Hefte* 14: 833–836.
Ever, S. 2013. *The modernist Bildungsroman: End of forms most beautiful*. Dissertation. Duke University.
Flaubert, G. 2005 [1869]. *L'éducation sentimentale*. Paris: Éditions Gallimard.
Friis, E. 2012. Intertekstualitet. *In*: L. H. Kjældgaard, et al., eds. *Litteratur: Introduktion til teori og analyse*. Aarhus: Aarhus Universitetsforlag, 143–155.
Genette, G. 1982. *Palimpsestes: la littérature au second degré*. Paris: Éditions Gallimard.
Goethe, J. W. v. 1982. *Wanderjahre, oder Die Entsagenden*. Ditzingen: Reclam Verlag.
——— 2008. *Wilhelm Meisters Lehrjahre*. Ditzingen: Reclam Verlag.
Ishihara C. 1997. Manazashi toshite no tasha: *Kokoro*. *In*: *Hanten suru Sōseki*. Tokyo: Seidosha, 155–180.
Karatani K. 1989. Sōseki no tayōsei – *Kokoro* o megutte. *In*: *Kotoba to higeki*. Tokyo: Daisan Bunmeisha, 29–44.
Komori Y. 1988 [1985]. *Kokoro* o seisei suru hāto. *In*: *Buntai toshite no monogatari*. Tokyo: Chikuma Shobō, 293–317.
Konosu Y. and Nakajima K. 2013. Haruki sekai no 'kanpeki to chōwa' [online]. *Dokushojin 2389*, 17 May. Tokyo: Dokushojin. Available from: https://dokushojin.com/article.html?i=1088 [Accessed 28 February 2020].
Konosu Y. 2017. Chi o nagasu kizu to taijisuru 'mushoku no otoko' no monogatari [online]. *All Reviews*, 8 July. Available from: https://allreviews.jp/review/427 [Accessed 28 February 2020].
Levy, I. A. 2010. *Sirens of the Western shore*. New York: Columbia University Press.
Lukàcs, G. 1988. *The theory of the novel*. Translated by A. Bostock. Talgarth: The Merlin Press.
Mayer, G. 1992. *Der deutsche Bildungsroman*. Weimar, Metzler: Springer Verlag.
McWilliams, E. 2016. *Margaret Atwood and the female Bildungsroman*. London: Routledge.
Miyoshi M. 1974. *Accomplices of silence*. Oakland: University of California Press.
——— 1991. *Off center: Power and culture relations between Japan and the United States*. Boston: Harvard University Press.
Mortimer, M. 2000. *Meeting the sensei: The role of the Master in Shirakaba writers*. Leiden: Brill Publishers.
Murakami H. 1987. *Noruwei no mori*. Tokyo: Kōdansha.
——— 2002. *Kafka on the Shore*. New York: Vintage International.
——— 2003 [2000]. *Norwegian Wood*. New York: Vintage International.
——— 2008 [1996]. To Translate and to be Translated. *In*: Japan Foundation, ed. *A Wild Haruki Chase*. Berkeley: Stone Bridge Press, 8–9.
——— 2009. The (Generally) Sweet Smell of Youth. *In*: Natsume S. Sanshiro. London: Penguin Classics, xxv–xxxvi.
——— 2013. *Shikisai o motanai Tazaki Tsukuru to, kare no junrei no toshi*. Tokyo: Bungei Shunjū.
——— 2014. *Colorless Tsukuru Tazaki and His Years of Pilgrimage*. London: Harvill Secker.
Musil, R. 2013 [1930–1943]. *Der Mann ohne Eigenschaften*. Köln, Germany: Anaconda Verlag.
Natsume S. 1995 [1905–1907]. *Wagahai wa neko de aru*. *In*: *Sōseki zenshū*. Tokyo: Iwanami Shoten.
——— 2009 [1908]. *Sanshiro*. London: Penguin Classics.
——— 2010 [1914]. *Kokoro*. London: Penguin Classics.
Oshino T. 1994. Kokoro ronsō no yukue. *In*: Komori Y., et al., eds. *Sōryoku tōron: Sōseki no Kokoro*. Tokyo: Kanrin Shobō, 12–27.
Sakaki A. 1999. *Recontextualising texts*. Boston: Harvard University Asia Center.
Salinger, J. D. 2018. *The Catcher in the Rye*. New York: Penguin Classics.

Seats, M. 2006. *Murakami Haruki: The simulacrum in contemporary Japanese culture*. Lanham: Lexington Books.

Smiles, S. 1859. *Self Help; With Illustrations of Character and Conduct*. London: John Murray London.

Strecher, M. C. 1999. Magical realism and the search for identity in the fiction of Murakami Haruki. *Journal of Japanese Studies* 25 (2): 263–298.

Summerfield, G., and Downward L. 2010. *New perspectives on the European Bildungsroman*. London; New York: Continuum.

Swale, M. 1978. *The German Bildungsroman from Wieland to Hesse*. Princeton: Princeton University Press.

Vilslev, A. 2017. Questioning Western universality: Sōseki's *Theory of Literature* and his novel *Kusamakura*. *Japan Forum* 29 (2): 257–278.

Washburn, D. 1995. Manly virtue and the quest for self: The *Bildungsroman* of Mori Ōgai. *The Journal of Japanese Studies* 21 (1): 1–32.

———— 2007. *Translating Mount Fuji: Modern Japanese fiction and the ethics of identity*. New York: Columbia University Press.

12

TRUMPING *1Q84/NINETEEN EIGHTY-FOUR?*

Reading Murakami and Orwell in a dystopian era

Patricia Welch

In *1Q84* (2011; *1Q84* [2009–2010]) Murakami Haruki makes reference to George Orwell's bleak dystopic novel *Nineteen Eighty-Four* (1949) to present a tale that reveals the importance of dreams, memory, and narrative at both an individual and cultural level.[1] Despite being an immediate bestseller, the comparison between the two novels may not be instantly obvious to the reader at first read. This is reflected by the many initial book reviews on *1Q84*, which struggled to understand how the novel responded to Orwell's work, or even what the novel 'meant'. Janet Maslin (2011) of the *New York Times* begins her review of the work by saying it is a 'vague' play on Orwell and concludes: 'It used to be customary, in a book of this magnitude, to explain unanswered questions and tie up loose ends. Mr Murakami clearly rejects such petty obligations, and he leaves many of the parallels in "1Q84" cryptic and dead-ended'. Writing in *The Atlantic*, Allan Barra (2011) complained how '[e]ven the title's allusion to Orwell seems vague'. And in his positive review in *The Independent*, Boyd Tonkin (2011) states, 'allusions to George Orwell's dystopia crop up, but don't explain that much'. Indeed, apart from the direct reference of the homophonic title[2] and the fact that both novels open on chilly April days, *1Q84* only has a total of five direct references to Orwell's novel in the entire work. How can we understand *1Q84*, Murakami's seriocomic *tour de force*, in relation to *Nineteen Eighty-Four*, Orwell's iconic tragic allegory?

Following this initial confusion from the book reviews, scholars like Tiffany Kriner (2014) and Elizabeth Russell (2014) have offered ways to compare the two novels in terms of how they pay homage to Orwell's influential work. One interesting comparison, as Russell shows, is presented through the homophonic title of Murakami's novel, which swaps the number 9 (pronounced '*kyū*' in Japanese) for the letter 'Q', representing the question at the heart of the existence of the world. Russell argues that while Orwell's world is fictional politics and Murakami's is political fiction, both posit the question 'to what extent is it possible to believe in truth and where is it to be found?' (Russell 2014: 307). The two novels, however, differ in the depiction (or not) of a totalitarian dystopia and its dangers: whereas *Nineteen*

Eighty-Four uses Big Brother as an allegory of totalitarian regimes, *1Q84* highlights religious cults and ideologies as proxies of authoritarian ideologies. Published in 1949 and set in the near future, *Nineteen Eighty-Four* evokes in its earliest readers the rise of fascism in the early 20th century and then-current anxieties regarding the imminent Cold War and the threat of communism as evidenced by the ascendance of both the Soviet Union and Communist China. Orwell creates a dystopic world, positioning 'his utopia in a grim futuristic society [...] characterized by oppressive canons and the suffocation of independent thought' (Greene 2011: 2). People's allegiances were reserved solely for the state, an attitude that was maintained through constant surveillance and the threat of violence. Even family bonds of love and allegiance had been replaced with 'fear, hatred and pain, but no dignity of emotion, no deep or complex sorrows' (Orwell 1949: 31).

By contrast, published in 2009–2010 and set in the near past of 1984 when the Cold War was beginning to break down, *1Q84* presents no singular totalitarian state personified by an all-powerful Big Brother, but instead creates a religious cult group called Sakigake (meaning 'Forerunner'), whose guru has raped prepubescent girls. Sakigake clearly reminds one of the Aum religious cult (Aum Supreme Truth [*Aum shinrikyō*]) in Japan, which launched a deadly sarin gas attack in Tokyo's metro in March 1995.[3] Thus, whereas Orwell saw Stalinism as heralding the emergence of large-scale totalitarian states, Murakami sees similar and no less ominous threats in groups such as Aum, recognising them as modern successors to Big Brother. The novel makes the point that while large-scale totalitarianism of the sort seen in *Nineteen Eighty-Four* does not exist in present-day Japan, the dangers of orthodoxy and rigid thinking still do in the form of religious cults and the hard-to-define mysterious creatures called the 'Little People': these cults turn their followers into a 'brain death' and 'take the circuits out of people's brains that make it possible for them to think for themselves' (Murakami 2011: 121). Furthermore,

> If Big Brother were to appear before us now, we'd point to him and say, 'Watch out! He's Big Brother!' There's no longer any place for a Big Brother in this real world of ours. Instead these so-called Little People have come on the scene [...] The Little People are an invisible presence. We can't even tell whether they are good or evil, or whether they have any substance or not. But they seem to be steadily undermining us.
>
> (Murakami 2011: 236)

1Q84 makes clear that rigid ideological thinking and passive acceptance of the status quo is potentially dangerous, even though the world of 1Q84 is not as obviously bleak as in Orwell's dystopia. Followers of ideologies such as Sakigake submit to the fully-formed narratives handed to them, and no longer think for themselves critically.

In spite of this obvious connection via totalitarianism, however, I contend in this chapter that *1Q84* richly pays homage to Orwell in other more nuanced ways, specifically in terms of the ways that literature functions, allowing the crossing of multiple 'realities', 'histories', and 'fictions', and the ways in which an individual work's signification can vary by time and place. In particular, I offer three themes that link *Nineteen Eighty-Four* and *1Q84*: the power of writing, the power of memory, and the power of love and commitment – 'power' because through these themes, Murakami draws on Orwell's classic as a way of reasserting the transformative potential of narrative and literature. Finally, while both *Nineteen Eighty-Four* and *1Q84* were written long before Donald J. Trump became the 45th President of the United States of America, the issues concerning the dissemination of ideologies and manipulation of information and discourse that I explore in this paper are relevant to the current dystopian context, to which I will return by way of conclusion.

Orwell's narrative is tightly focused and stripped down, and contrasts significantly with *1Q84*, which is rather baroque. *Nineteen Eighty-Four* is narrated in the third person, and hews close to the focalisation of its protagonist Winston Smith, drawing readers deep into the paranoid world of Oceania. Winston Smith is a low-level functionary who rewrites documents in the Ministry of Records. Gradually becoming upset by oppressive state control, Winston Smith secretly engages in subversive activities, first by keeping a diary and then having an illicit love affair with Julia, a co-worker. Over time, he is pulled further towards overt rebellion until he is arrested and tortured into submission.

1Q84 on the other hand features alternating narratives: odd chapters feature the protagonanist Aomame, a personal trainer who moonlights as an assassin of abusive men; the protagonist of the even chapters is Tengo, a part-time maths instructor and aspiring writer who agrees to ghostwrite a novella that had been submitted for a prestigious literary award. At one point, we learn that the protagonists had been classmates in elementary school, united by their difference from their classmates. In both narrative arcs, the protagonists find themselves in an alternate reality much like the 1984 they left, and Aomame dubs the alternative '1Q84' – meaning 'world with a question' (Murakami 2011: 110) – to distinguish the two. The narrative arcs draw closer as the novel progresses, and narrative time – while moving inexorably forward – seems to fold in on itself like a Möbius strip. The conclusion is happy-*ish*, or at least carries traces of optimism, with Tengo and a pregnant Aomame hand-in-hand preparing to face another world, in great contrast to the bleak and utterly transcendent submissive love for Big Brother of Orwell's protagonist, Winston Smith.

Nevertheless, as we see how History (history in the 'real' world), history in the Q-world, and the personal histories of characters billow and merge in *1Q84*, the novel also encourages us to question our world and society in much the same way that Orwell's work does. Murakami takes the narrative position that an individual must take responsibility for his or her actions and his or her dreams, since by doing so each of us can take control over the forces that have shaped us.

The power of writing

Nineteen Eighty-Four begins with Winston Smith in despair about the current situation and unresolved emotional pain concerning his mother. At the age of 39 and old before his time, he has reached his breaking point: Oceania's culture of surveillance, his imperfect memories of a time 'before', the disconnect between messages of victory in the unceasing war and actual lived experience, but most importantly his fervent belief in the existence of objective truths have led him to the point where he is compelled to start a diary, although he knows that to do so is to commit thoughtcrime and that '[…] *thoughtcrime IS death*' (Orwell 1949: 29, italics and capitalisation in the original). One quote brings home the likely futility of his endeavour, and the absence of any ideal reader:

> For whom, it suddenly occurred to him to wonder, was he writing this diary? For the future, for the unborn. His mind hovered for a moment round the doubtful date on the page, and then fetched up with a bump against the Newspeak word *doublethink*. For the first time the magnitude of what he had undertaken came home to him. 'How could you communicate with the future? It was of its nature impossible. Either the future would resemble the present, in which case it would not listen to him: or it would be different from it and his predicament would be meaningless'.
>
> (Orwell 1949: 9)

Winston Smith wishes to write something that will allow his present to communicate with the future, but fears, under the conditions of life in his 1984, whether any possibility that he can control the discourse exists. His anxiety for posterity even against great odds motivates him to write, even though, as Tiffany Kriner suggests '[u]nder the conditions of the changeable, erasable, or ignorable word, it seems that no possible communication or relationship with the future is possible – there is no way to learn from the past' (Kriner 2014: 130).

Tengo in *1Q84* is equally compelled to write, but he has not found his story when the novel begins. Some years earlier, he had attracted the attention of Komatsu, a top literary editor, when he had submitted a story for a literary prize competition. Though he did not win the prize, Komatsu had liked his writing and offered to read any story Tengo wrote, and also began to send him a variety of small writing jobs. At the outset of *1Q84*, Komatsu asks him to do a 'fundamental top-to-down rewrite' of *Air Chrysalis*, a novella which had been submitted for a new writer's prize, because he believes that Tengo is perfect for the job. Despite his misgivings, Tengo agrees to ghostwrite the work, but only after meeting Fuka-Eri, the author. In the course of their somewhat stilted conversations, Tengo learns that Fuka-Eri hadn't actually written the novella, but had told her story to Azami, the daughter of Professor Ebisuno with whom she has lived since escaping the cult her own father led.

As a writer, Tengo begins to find his voice after reading the original draft of *Air Chrysalis*, which he describes to his editor as rough and clumsy, but having a strange power that draws in the reader. In fact, it is because he believes in the work that he chooses to engage in literary fraud: He informs Professor Ebisuno, '[i]f *Air Chrysalis* has to be rewritten, I don't want to let anyone else do it' (Murakami 2011: 118).

In the sections where Tengo ghostwrites Fuka-Eri's novella, the narrator seems to linger over Tengo's creative process. These passages are remarkably similar to the way that Winston Smith lingers over his own writing process, in his job in the Ministry of Truth, where he is employed to continuously rewrite or create documents so that they cohere with the current and constantly evolving Party line. Ironically, despite Winston's desire for objective truth, the creative process through which he alters truth is the 'greatest pleasure in [Winston's] life' (Orwell 1949: 106). For example,

> Most of it was a tedious routine, but included in it there were also jobs so difficult and intricate that you could lose yourself in them as in the depths of a mathematical problem – delicate pieces of forgery in which you had nothing to guide you except your knowledge of the principles of Ingsoc and your estimate of what the Party wanted you to say.
>
> (Orwell 1949: 44)

At one point, he must rewrite a document where a now 'non-existent person' had previously been singled out for praise. Rather than denounce this person as a traitor and a thought criminal, or invent some victory as a distraction, he creates a new hero:

> Suddenly there sprang into his mind, ready made as it were, the image of a certain Comrade Ogilvy, who had recently died in battle, in heroic circumstance […] It was true there was no such person as Comrade Ogilvy, but a few lines of print and a couple of faked photographs would soon bring him into existence.
>
> Winston thought for a moment, then pulled the speakwrite towards him and began dictating into it in Big Brother's familiar style: a style at once military and pedantic.
>
> (Orwell 1949: 47)

In this section, Orwell writes eloquently about the creative process and the retelling of stories in the same way that Murakami does in *1Q84*. Notice how Tengo describes his own creative process as he strips down and rewrites Fuka-Eri's narrative:

> I'm a skilled carpenter who's been put in charge of everything […] I don't have a blueprint, so all I can do is use my intuition and my experience to work on each separate problem as it comes up.
>
> (Murakami 2011: 66, italics in original)

Tengo engages in the creative process and mulls over Fuka-Eri's manuscript and works through it, section by section, 'improving the flow of language, and deleting superfluous or redundant passages' (Murakami 2011: 67), making the language of the tale his own. This resembles the pleasure that Winston Smith gets in his job creating new facts for the Ministry of Truth. As Tengo writes, he becomes more and more convinced that Fuka-Eri's

narrative had succeeded in the power to appeal directly to his heart and makes it possible
for him to write his own. Whereas Smith's pondering about how his work will be received
in the future suggests that he has questions whether his ideal reader even exists, Tengo
believes that he has a reader, which allows him to find his voice.

In other words, while rewriting and writing *Air Chrysalis*, Tengo comes into his
own. Readers of *1Q84* never actually *read* Tengo's new manuscript (as embedded narrative), learning instead that it borrows the setting from *Air Chrysalis*, that it is about
himself, and that in it he is rewriting the past so that the present can change. He
explains this at one point while conversing with his married girlfriend: 'If you rewrote
the past, obviously, the present would change, too. What we call the present is given
shape by an accumulation of the past' (Murakami 2011: 308). Although we do not
read Tengo's manuscript, what happens instead is even more remarkable: his written
words bring a new reality into existence – the reality of 1Q84 that will help him heal
and reconnect with Aomame.

Tengo's conversation with his girlfriend continues a conversational thread already
begun with Fuka-Eri when she had asked Tengo about Orwell's *Nineteen Eighty-Four*.
Tengo's opinion is that it is theft to rob people of their pasts by rewriting history, in
the sense that doing so robs them of their identities; that memory is both individual
and collective; and, finally, that we need both in order to be whole:

> In his novel, George Orwell depicted the future as a dark society dominated by
> totalitarianism. People are rigidly controlled by a dictator named Big Brother.
> Information is restricted, and history is constantly being rewritten. The pro-
> tagonist works in a government office, and I'm pretty sure his job is to rewrite
> words. Whenever a new history is written, the old histories all have to be thrown
> out. In the process, words are remade, and the meanings of current words are
> changed. What with history being rewritten so often, nobody knows what's
> true anymore. They lose track of who is an enemy and who is an ally. It's that
> kind of story. […] Robbing people of their actual history is the same as rob-
> bing them of part of themselves. It's a crime. […] Our memory is made up of
> our individual memories and our collective memories. The two are intimately
> linked. And history is our collective memory. If our collective memory is taken
> from us – rewritten – we lose the ability to sustain our true selves.
>
> (Murakami 2011: 257)

After this, Fuka-Eri then adroitly remarks that Tengo 'rewrites stuff', which means he
is doing exactly what he just suggested was wrong. At her comment, Tengo 'laughed
and took a sip of wine', perhaps somewhat self-reflexively (ibid.). Whereas Winston
Smith seemed to want to memorialise his memories through his diary, and use it
to fix, as in make a permanent and immutable record of, the past so that the future
might learn from their bad example, Tengo wants to fix, as in repair, the past so as to
create a better future. As writers, however, both Tengo and Winston Smith have direct
experience with the notion that truth (history, memory) is always filtered through
language.

Just as written histories can rob one of his or her 'true self', fiction has the capacity to reveal truths that are not necessarily seen in histories through the framing of events and the judgements passed on historical actors. Whereas Orwell, through his protagonist Winston Smith, appears to decry 'history' when it is written in a way that disavows any real consideration of facts, Murakami, through Tengo, recognises that fiction has transformative and emotive power that goes beyond mere historical truths as recorded in official histories and ledgers. In other words, there are ethical and emotive dimensions to fiction. Beyond that, as exemplified in these two works, fiction has a discursively constitutive function that allows writers (and their readers) to change the world. It is these dimensions that link readers and writers, and seem to bridge the gap between the fictional and the real.

The power of memory

A second critical theme found in both *1Q84* and *Nineteen Eighty-Four* is the power of memory. While we can state that someone has a good memory or a bad memory, memory is not a total recall of past events and experience but a form of selective recall and amnesia that allows one to reorder or *re-present* or *re-cognise* past experiences in terms of the present. Richard Terdiman, a pioneer in memory studies writes that the very processes of memory are what 'complicates the rationalist segmentation of chronology into "then" and "now". In memory, the time line becomes tangled and folds back on itself. Such a complication constitutes our lives and defines our experience' (Terdiman 1993: 8). Additionally, memory encompasses much more than individual, personal memories, but also those cultural memories in various forms that help groups define who they are. In varying ways, both Orwell and Murakami explore the treacherous nature of memory effects in their respective works, in that both 'investigate how to establish truth – on which the future depends – through history and memory, under conditions of the shifting text' (Kriner: 2014: 131).

Winston Smith in *Nineteen Eighty-Four* chooses to write a diary in full knowledge of the perilous nature of his task, partly because he is motivated by the desire to set the record straight, given that somehow his imperfect memories do not line up with the story that he is being told. He knows that contradictions exist 'because his memory was not satisfactorily under Party control' (Orwell 1949: 86). Put differently, he has not succeeded in forgetting that which is not to be remembered, and he chooses to record these contradictions, though his effort to record the truth is likely in vain. He knows that in all likelihood he will be found out and both he and his diary destroyed:

> The diary would be reduced to ashes and himself to vapour. Only the Thought Police would read what he had written, before they wiped it out of existence and out of memory. How could you make an appeal to the future, when not a trace of you, not even an anonymous word scribbled on a piece of paper, could physically survive?
>
> (Orwell 1949: 28)

That night he dreams of his mother and his sister, and he senses vaguely he lived because of their sacrifice. Though his memories of childhood are hazy and unclear, he knows that things (at least in terms of how people related to each other) were somehow radically different in his childhood, and he recoils in horror at the present mutability of the past in Oceania:

> If the Party could thrust its hand into the past and say of this or that event, it never happened – that surely, was more terrifying than mere torture and death.
>
> (Orwell 1949: 35)

Because of his job in the Ministry of Truth, Winston Smith knows that Oceania's history is rewritten every time the present situation changes, rendering actual memories suspect because there is no way to confirm one's memories against an objective truth. Further, because family members have been conditioned to police each other in ways that render family ties moot, he cannot be confident of verifying memories with other family members. Thus, in a world stripped of values such as love, family, and freedom of thought, he knows that he cannot even be sure of his personal memories. He plays over his incomplete and muddled childhood memories, knowing only that they were primarily of a time when 'there was still privacy, love, and friendship' (Orwell 1949: 31). And while his recent memories are more vivid, they are equally uncertain. Finally feeling stripped of any meaningful identity, he attempts to take a stand with his journal through which he plans to concretise his memories through language. Sadly, it is Winston Smith's misreading of a (false) memory that ultimately leads to his downfall and the torture chambers in the Ministry of Love later in the book.

Ironically, despite the uncertainty that constantly shifting narratives create for him personally, Winston Smith is also a writer who paradoxically takes pride in his ability to control narrative and memory through his writing. This power gives him pleasure, even though he knows he cannot trust the veracity of anything, since each document is merely 'the substitution of one piece of nonsense for another' (Orwell 1949: 41):

> Comrade Ogilvy, unimagined an hour ago, was now a fact. It struck him as curious that you could create dead men but not living ones. Comrade Ogilvy, who had never existed in the present, now existed in the past, and when once the act of forgery was forgotten, he would exist just as authentically, and upon the same evidence, as Charlemagne or Julius Caesar.
>
> (Orwell 1949: 48)

Since his words and made-up narratives have the power of the state to back them up, they have the ability to change history, rendering both objective fact and memory moot. Through his act of creation, then, real people could be erased, not just from the present but also from the past, their lives altered in ways that suit the goals of the state apparatus of Oceania. In some sense, Winston Smith's subversive act in writing a diary is to establish a coherent and stable link between his memory and fact, both of which are questionable in the totalitarian state of Oceania where everything is subject to change and no objective verifiable fact can be said to exist. To do so, Winston Smith believes, would allow him to know who he is, something he wants desperately.

In *1Q84*, as we have seen in Orwell, memory works in several ways. In the alternating narratives, both Tengo and Aomame cope with a reality that does not line up with their memories. More importantly, through memory work both Tengo and Aomame are able to independently recall why each had tried to establish themselves apart from their parent's narrow-minded mindsets, and use their insights as they work towards creating a future.

Tengo's story line begins with him in the grip of a vivid ten-second memory of himself as a toddler, with his mother, breasts bare, being suckled by a man who was not his father. Though brief, the memory wells up unbidden again and again, causing him to break out in sweat all over his body, and transporting him, somehow, 'to a new track' (Murakami 2011: 14). To Tengo, the memory was too vivid to be false, but it didn't square with what his father had told him of his mother, namely that she had died shortly after he was born. Without any evidence, and contrary to his father's story about his mother's death, he chooses to believe the memory is true, given how vivid it is and its physical effect on him. This possibly false memory seems also to be the source of Tengo's belief that his father doesn't really love him.

In rewriting Fuka-Eri's story, Tengo begins to come to terms with the formative traumas of his own unhappy childhood when his fee collector father made him be present on his Sunday rounds in the hope that people would be more likely to pay up. One day, when returning from a visit to Professor Ebisuno, the adult Tengo notices a young girl and mother on the train. The expression in her eyes triggers a vivid memory of Aomame, whom he had not seen since they were children. Her parents, members of a religious group called the Society of Witnesses, had raised her accordingly, and she had been forced to go with her mother on her proselytising missions on Sundays, in much the same way that he had been made to accompany his father. Unlike himself, Aomame had been a class outcast and later the object of bullying. Although he saw in her a kindred spirit, they never became friends. But one day, he stepped in to defend her when a peer was bullying her. Some days later, she came into a classroom where he was standing and silently took his hand instantly forging a connection between them. Now more than 20 years later, alone on the train, caught in the depths of his memory, Tengo recalls the powerful strangeness of that moment though is yet to understand its significance. The episode concludes, '[t]ime flows in strange ways on Sundays, and sights become mysteriously distorted' (Murakami 2011: 153). Although he has yet to work through his memories, they are beginning to well to the surface and will take shape in the narrative he writes.

Memory is significant for Aomame as well, both personal memories and her knowledge of historical and current events. In the opening pages of the book, Aomame is stuck in traffic in a taxi on her way to fulfil a murder for hire. Janáček's *Sinfonietta* playing on the car radio triggers multiple memories, both personal and cultural. Her recollection that the piece had been composed in 1926 brings up parallel thoughts of 1926 Czechoslovakia and 1926 Japan, as well as family history – including some musing on her unusual name. Then while climbing down the emergency stairway from the Metropolitan Expressway, she recalls with great warmth her first real friend Tamaki, who had committed suicide to escape an abusive marriage. Later, she spots a young policeman wearing a uniform she has never seen before and carrying a semi-automatic Beretta although she has no recollection of Japanese police being so heavily armed. It bothers her that she cannot recall these changes and she seeks clarification from a man that she picks up in a bar. Despite a reasonable explanation, she remains puzzled and continues to try to square events that people tell her as fact with what she knows she has experienced, and what she had learned through reading. Aomame's further research reveals that 1984 as she thought she knew it has switched into a new reality some two years earlier after a radical group with machine guns had tangled with Japanese policemen carrying 'old-fashioned six-shooters' (Murakami 2011: 86). Since she has no memory of this event and she prides herself on her command of history, she concludes that it is the world that has changed, not that she is either mistaken or crazy. Once she accepts this, she decides to adapt herself to the new world in order to survive, since as the narrative repeatedly states, there's 'only one reality' (Murakami 2011: 9, 12, 107). It is as if she has actually found herself inside the type of world that writers like Winston Smith and Tengo create. Ironically, making the cognitive step to accept the new world of 1Q84 as real is what affords Aomame the space to rediscover Tengo, whereas Winston Smith's acceptance of reality as defined by the state in *Nineteen Eighty-Four* marks his failure.

While memory effects in *Nineteen Eighty-Four* can be found mostly on the level of the plot, in *1Q84* they can be seen both in plot and form. To be specific, the jumbled nature of memory is reflected in the novel's structure, and the effect of this jumbled narrative is that the characters start in separate plotlines but gradually converge. Towards the end of Book 2, the alternating narratives begin to draw closer when Aomame is hired to kill the leader of a cult, who is suspected of having raped pre-pubescent girls, including Fuka-Eri, his own daughter. As the narrative threads draw closer, history and narrative time begin to curve and fold in on themselves. Though the basic narrative thrust moves forward chronologically, time is not presented as a measurable content, but something that moves and flows forward, backward, in the present, and the past, multi-dimensionally, a sensation shared by protagonists and reader alike. Two quotes present this nicely:

> Time became confused in her [Aomame's] memory, like a tangled string. The straight line access was lost, and forward and back, right and left, jumbled together.
>
> (Murakami 2011: 30)

> Tengo knew that time could become deformed as it moved forward. Time itself
> was uniform in composition, but once consumed, it took on a deformed shape.
> (Murakami 2011: 275)

Just as the primary characters move backwards and forwards in time through the
processes of memory, the chapters themselves do not exactly line up chronologically.
While the two primary narrative threads encompass a total of nine months (April
through December), the pacing of each differs until the narrative threads begin
to coalesce at the end of Book 2. The central episodes of each narrative, namely
Aomame's encounter with Leader, and Tengo's passive but intense sexual encounter
with Fuka-Eri, unfold over multiple chapters, leaving the impression that these events
are happening in real time despite the otherworldly aura that infuses these chapters.

In Aomame's story line, odd-numbered Chapters 7 through 15 relate how
Aomame went to the Okura Hotel to meet and kill Leader, under the guise of providing a stretching session. Chapters 13 and 15 are central to this episode, both in
terms of what she learns and within the structure of the book itself.[4] Their meeting, and her subsequent killing of Leader, is spread out over multiple chapters, with
Chapter 17 taking place the following day. While time seems to move more quickly
for most of the even-numbered Tengo chapters in this section, it slows down around
Chapters 8, 10, 12, when he visits his father in a facility for people with cognitive
disorders. At the end of Chapter 10, Fuka-Eri (now in hiding at Tengo's apartment),
tells Tengo to come home quickly. The strange sexual encounter between Tengo and
Fuka-Eri occurs in Chapter 14, presumably at exactly the same time that Aomame
kills Leader in the alternating narrative. Tengo, having fallen asleep with Fuka-Eri in
his arms – whilst trying to avoid sexual thoughts – awakens to find them both naked.
Although unable to move, his penis is fully erect. Predictably sexual intercourse follows, described in language that echoes the way Leader relates his sexual unions with
pre-teen daughters of the cult to Aomame. It is also at this moment that Tengo makes
the connection between the girl he saw on the train and Aomame. In this moment,
Leader and Fuka-Eri, father and daughter, become the means through which Tengo
and Aomame will connect. Here, Murakami's narrative functions like many layers
of an onion. As each layer is peeled back more of the story is revealed. The way that
Murakami plays with the different dimensions of the narratives in this section complicates readers' understanding of the separability of 1Q84 and 1984.

For the reader, the effect of these alternating chapters is both fragmented and
unsettling, in the sense that past and present, the fictional and the real seem jumbled
together. Significantly as well, it is – somehow – in the course of this evening that
Aomame becomes pregnant with 'Tengo's' child, despite them never actually having
physical contact since they were children. In other words, through the performative
recall of memory both Aomame and Tengo manage to breach the divide between
present and past, and the borders between bodies, through Tengo's metaphorical ejac-
ulation into what Matthew Strecher has termed a 'wormhole', or 'metaphysical zone,

freed from the constraints of time and space [...] a repository for memory, dreams, and visions' (Strecher 2014: 71).

The power of love and commitment

The third critical theme that resonates in *Nineteen Eighty-Four* and *1Q84* is the power of love and commitment, though the protagonists of each novel find themselves moving along very different experiential trajectories. Despite the fact that the Ministry of Love is central to the government of Winston Smith's Oceania, love itself is in curiously short supply. Miniluv, as dubbed in Newspeak, was responsible for maintaining law and order, and it did so by maintaining absolute control through the use of omnipresent telescreens, denunciations, and ritualised Hate – in the form of 'Two Minute Hates' and Hate Weeks, which whipped up invective and abuse towards a putative enemy, as a way of demonstrating one's unconditional love for Big Brother.

To this end all ordinary expressions of love were rendered suspect since they might weaken an individual's loyalty towards the Party. Marital unions were only allowable with permission, which was never given 'if the couple concerned gave the impression of being physically attracted to one another' (Orwell 1949: 66). Marriage was to be contracted for one purpose alone, and that was the begetting of 'children for the service of the Party' (Orwell 1949: 67). Given the State's suspicion of intimacy and sexuality even within marriage, it is no wonder that Winston Smith remembers the final days of his failed marriage to Catherine with pain. Thoroughly indoctrinated in the Party's distrust of sexuality while equally committed towards having a child, she had approached their weekly sexual encounters as a distasteful chore, so much so that he too comes to view them with dread.

The presence of children in a marriage results not in less scrutiny, but more, as the children themselves are recruited into organisations like the Youth League and the Spies, which start turning children into willing tools of the state at an early age. Early in the novel, Winston Smith unclogs the sink of his neighbour. Just as he is leaving, her children surround him, calling him traitor, thought criminal and Eurasian spy in tones 'so vicious. [...] it was not altogether a game' (Orwell 1949: 24). Back in his flat, he thinks to himself about the systematic ways that children are turned against their parents. Through the Spies and similar organisations they are socialised fully as future party members, and all tendency to rebel rooted out:

> All their ferocity was turned outwards, against the enemies of the State, against foreigners, saboteurs, thought-criminals. It was almost normal for people over thirty to be frightened of their own children. And with good reason, for hardly a week passed in which the Times did not carry a paragraph describing how some eavesdropping little sneak – 'child hero' was the phrase generally used – had overheard some compromising remark and denounced his parents to the Thought Police.
>
> (Orwell 1949: 25–26)

Yet, as indicated in my section on memory above, Winston Smith has memories, if imperfect, of a time when there were such things as love, friendship, and loyalty between people. His thoughts about his mother's sacrifice continue: 'His mother's memory tore at his heart because she had died loving him, when he was too young and selfish to love her in return, and because somehow, he did not remember how, she had sacrificed herself to a conception of loyalty that was private and unalterable' (Orwell 1949: 31).

Already committed to his private rebellion through keeping a diary, it is no wonder that when Julia, whom he had initially despised for her apparent orthodoxy, slips him a note that says 'I love you' he embarks on the most dangerous dissent of all: that of freely loving another person. Despite appearing the very model of a perfect Party woman, Julia is a kindred spirit, perhaps even more rebellious than he, and someone who likes both him and sex, which proves to him how the Party had conditioned people to political orthodoxy by strangling the powerful instincts of love and sexuality. The second section of the books reveals their growing love and commitment to each other in the face of such obstacles. It is also in this chapter, that they decide to make their dissent more public by attempting to join the Brotherhood, Big Brother's opposition. They, or more accurately, Winston Smith, sees another kindred soul in Inner Party member O'Brien, suspecting that he may actually be an insurgent. As they are interviewed for admission (of sorts) to the Brotherhood, they are asked to declare to what extent they would go to overthrow the state. The only thing they refuse to do is deny their love for each other.

As it turns out, however, O'Brien was no fellow traveller, but an utterly loyal member of the Thought Police who had allowed Winston Smith and Julia's love to flourish whilst grooming them to denounce the party. Once they had, they were arrested and taken to the Ministry of Love where, through unrelenting torture, the two lovers denounce and betray the other, sacrificing the dignity of individual emotions for their total submission to Big Brother.

By contrast, in *1Q84*, moon-crossed lovers Aomame and Tengo are able to find each other against all odds, against time and space, and a vengeful cult, once Q-world 1Q84 comes into existence. Their hearts touched the instant the child Aomame took Tengo's hand in her own, leaving an indelible mark that shaped their lives. It was that touch that allowed them to forge their own paths in the world, separate from the single-minded ways of their respective parents. But, somewhat like the characters who have only fuzzy memories of their perfect love after suffering from a terrible illness in 'On Seeing the 100% Perfect Girl One Beautiful April Morning' (1993; 'Shigatsu no aru hareta asa ni hyaku pāsento no onna no ko ni deau koto ni tsuite' [1981]), which Murakami told Sam Anderson (2011) was one of the inspirations for *1Q84*, Aomame and Tengo literally begin the novel in separate worlds. Nevertheless they manage to find each other.

As I have shown, as the story progresses, Tengo begins to recall and understand that magic moment their hearts touch more clearly, reaching clarity as his body climaxes into Fuka-Eri's at the end of Chapter 14. In the parallel narrative Aomame confesses her love for Tengo in a conversation with Leader before she kills him, a death he reveals he has already foreseen and welcomes for the crimes he committed. When Aomame hesitates (his words have touched her somehow), Leader reveals that should she not kill him, then Tengo would surely be killed for 'countering the momentum of the Little People' through the book he collaboratively wrote with Fuka-Eri (Murakami 2011: 469). Leader offers Aomame a terrible choice: if she kills him, Tengo would be saved, but Aomame would face the wrath of the Leader's group. 'They will track you down and punish you severely. That is the kind of system we have created: close-knit, violent, and irreversible' (Murakami 2011: 470). Hesitating only a moment, musing '[t]o tell the truth, though, I would have preferred to stay alive and be united with Tengo' (Murakami 2011: 472), Aomame chooses the commitment of love and sacrifice for another over her survival. Although ready for death, she does not die; instead in their respective narrative arcs (now united in focus), the protagonists acutely aware of their love, Aomame and Tengo throw themselves into the search for each other, which spans the end of Book 2 into Book 3. Significantly, this search is not mere detective work (in fact, for most of it, Aomame is holed up in a safehouse in Koenji), but primarily an inward journey of self-discovery, forgiveness, and love. While sitting in a playground near the end of Book 2, Tengo notices two moons in the sky and realises that his fictional world has come into existence. While much happens between then and the novel's conclusion, when Aomame and Tengo wake up together in a new 1984 in the final chapter, readers can take with them the notion that love and commitment really can change the world.

This brings us back to *Nineteen Eighty-Four* and its enshrinement of love as commitment to an empty idea in the name of power for power's sake. While Winston Smith knows from the outset that his mother loved him and was willing to give her life so that he might live, once he is captured and tortured by the Thought Police, he is willing to betray both her memory and his previous commitment to Julia in order to stop the pain of torture. Winston Smith ends the novel, a broken man – in our estimation – but pure and healed in the eyes of the State. By contrast, in their various ways, Tengo, Aomame, and even Fuka-Eri begin the novel broken – or at least stunted by their childhoods – but are in some important sense able to heal through love and commitment in a differently dystopic world.

Echoing the power of writing, *1Q84* draws on Orwell's *Nineteen Eighty-Four* in the way that it makes writing, or storytelling, take centre stage as a transformative act of finding love. Tengo's words literally change the world; while rewriting Fuka-Eri's novella, he also rewrites his own, which brings the world of 1Q84 into existence. In the process, he rediscovers his love for Aomame, and realises that love takes many forms. He comes to forgive his father, and understand that his father had cared for him as best he could. For her part, Aomame also moves beyond the anger and pain of her childhood. As Kriner argues about Aomame, 'love and loyalty, the sacrifice she will make for them, cleanses her hatred and in fact brings her further on in a spiritual journey that allows her to move beyond the injuries of her childhood trauma as a member of a cult' (2014: 142). Thus, love in *1Q84* is not the terrible love of transcendent submission that

Winston Smith embraces at the end of *Nineteen Eighty-Four*, or the mindless love of the cult members for Leader, which destroys the lives of many young girls, or even Tengo's father's blind acquiescence to the Japanese state. The love that Tengo and Aomame discover is one that accepts the radical alterity of the love object, and allows them to commit themselves to whatever might follow.

By way of conclusion: *Nineteen Eighty-Four*, *1Q84*, and the Trump presidency

In the early days of writing this chapter, I was exploring the deep connections and shared themes between *Nineteen Eighty-Four* and its near namesake; at that time most reviews touched on how Murakami's work differed from Orwell's rather than on what united them. Yet I believed that *1Q84* was the vehicle through which Murakami permitted readers access to a refreshing understanding of both *Nineteen Eighty-Four* and the time when *1Q84* was published. Back then, Donald J. Trump did not figure into my thoughts at all. This changed after Trump announced his candidacy for the President of the United States in June 2016. I could not help but wonder if the populist chord he struck signalled that the United States had entered a critical 'Little People' moment, with a significant minority wilfully abdicating their responsibility for critical thought.

For many, amused disbelief at the responses to Trump's candidacy in the face of his apparent disregard for truth changed to dismay when he was elected in November 2016. Between the presidential election and Trump's inauguration, Amazon saw a 10,000 per cent increase in demand for Orwell's book, along with a serious uptick in dystopian literature in general, suggesting that people thought that they could learn something from Orwell's classic and other dystopian works. Popularity remains high at the present time.

In his messaging, it seemed that Trump had taken a master course in Newspeak, the language used by the state machine of Oceania in *Nineteen Eighty-Four*, which the novel's appendix explains, 'was to provide a medium of expression for the world-view and mental habits proper to Ingsoc, […] make all other modes of thought impossible', and 'to diminish the range of thought' (Orwell 1949: 303–304). Trump, his spokesmen, and advisers wage assault on facts through language even in the face of objective evidence to the contrary, putting to the test the notion that if you repeat a claim often enough people will come to believe it regardless of corroborative evidence. Whereas *Nineteen Eighty-Four* foregrounds the process through which discursive range of thought is narrowed, *1Q84* explores how this plays out on a societal level. A figure like Trump cannot exist in a vacuum; rather, he, or others like him, are transmitters, who need receivers, receptive to their distorted narratives. Murakami explores this part of the equation. In a series of articles, sociolinguist George Lakoff (2018) has analysed the discourse strategies of Trump's Tweets, showing that he manipulates discourse through making bald assertions with authority, power, and conviction, and in constantly controlling the discourse by deflecting it from what matters by creating diversions, as well as in trying to intimidate people into buying into the narrative as he has presented it.

In a *New Yorker* article (Mayer 2016), Tony Schwartz spoke wryly about his complicity in bringing Donald Trump to greater prominence through ghostwriting Trump's *The Art of the Deal*, even creating a kind of Newspeak-like term for Trump's lax relationship with the truth: truthful hyperbole. Schwartz spoke about the ease with which Trump lies: 'Lying is second nature to him. More than anyone else I have ever met, Trump has the ability to convince himself that whatever he is saying at any given moment is true, or sort of true, or at least *ought* to be true' (Mayer 2016). Although citizens do not have to accept Trump's 'alternative facts' wholly, they just need to be brought to the point – like Winston Smith – where we begin to doubt that which can be objectively proven, or become too lazy to even care about things that cannot. We witnessed these strategies employed throughout his presidency, including the following examples: his assertions of voter fraud and his denial of any Russian meddling in the 2016 US Presidential Election. We further see this in Trump's parsing of the conclusion of the Mueller Report as a declaration of his innocence (despite the executive summary of the report having a far less conclusive evaluation) and declaring the entire investigation a witch hunt in a press conference on 30 May 2018 ('Trump unleashes', 2019).[5] Then, in the midst of the Covid-19 global pandemic, after initially denying the novel disease was of any concern, President Trump attempted to take credit for state stay-at-home orders which worked to flatten the infection curve, while simultaneously waging a counter campaign through Twitter to build momentum for quickly reopening the economy against the advice of the World Health Organization, the Centers for Disease Control, and even in contradiction to the very plan put forth by the White House Coronavirus Task Force. This contradictory messaging may have contributed to the second surge of coronavirus in the United States in the autumn of 2020.

For the first three years of the Trump presidency, Trump held few regular press conferences where reporters could ask questions following prepared remarks. Instead, he communicated primarily through Tweets and campaign-style rallies to his base using the discursive strategies identified above. Then, in spring 2020, with mass gatherings largely banned during the Covid-19 pandemic, President Trump temporarily embraced what could be called a more conventional way of getting his message across: taking centre stage at the regular press briefings of the White House Coronavirus Task Force. In this time of 'social distancing', Trump replaced his rallies with daily press briefings. Yet, in these briefings and in the Tweetstorms contradicting official messages that followed, I see a discursive equivalence between Trump's actions and the way Orwell portrays the state organised so as to direct all love towards Big Brother.

As the 2020 presidential election approached, Trump did not abandon his strategy of presenting and repeating 'alternative facts', planting seeds of voter fraud conspiracies through Tweets repeated in the echo chambers of conservative media, and he redoubled his efforts once it became clear that Joseph Biden was emerging as front runner. He then resumed campaign rallies, whilst largely eschewing any significant precautions with respect to the novel coronavirus. In particular, Trump claimed that an expansion of early voting, mail-in voting, and absentee voting in the wake of the Covid-19 pandemic would result in millions of fraudulent votes. Yet, as security officials repeatedly have pointed out, these steps may have led to an election that was both more secure and had the highest turnout in United States' history.

Even after it was clear that Joseph Biden had received enough votes to take the Electoral College and become the 46th president in January 2021, Trump stayed the course, filing suit after suit alleging voter fraud. In his opinion to one recent Pennsylvania case that was struck down, Judge Stephanos Bibas cut to the chase of the Trump strategy:

> Free, fair elections are the life blood of our democracy. Charges of unfairness are serious. But calling an election unfair does not make it so. Charges require specific allegations and then proof. We have neither here.
>
> (Donald J. Trump for President v Commonwealth of Pennsylvania,
> No. 20-3371, 27 November 2020)

Essentially what the Trump presidency reveals is confirmation of the message of Orwell's *Nineteen Eighty-Four* and Murakami's *1Q84*: namely, that the ability to write and make one's message known renders it possible to shape the present and our understanding of the past and thereby shape the future, and that without either strength or wherewithal to fashion their own narrative, people will unknowingly be led. In her essay on *Nineteen Eighty-Four*, Siobhan Chapman proposes that the real horror of the work is the way in which the Party compels the people of Oceania to hold 'both a truth-committed approach and a non truth-committed approach [to discourse] and to do so simultaneously' (Chapman 2009: 75). Doublethink of this sort only serves to strengthen the discursive control of the party. In pragmatic terms, the first approach is generally considered to be that of science or history, in that it requires empirical evidence, while the latter is generally considered to be within the realm of literary discourse. The mixed messaging emanated from the highest levels of the United States government (even in the face of medical evidence) thrust citizens into a similarly contradictory position as Winston Smith with – for many – similarly dizzying results, including the insurrection on the United States Capitol Building on 6 January 2021.

Herein is the great paradox. While human beings necessarily live their lives as though there is an objective reality or real world, in fact we only understand that world through language. Through language we create and categorise our worlds. Our identity or self exists in a continual state of creation, through the interaction of one's individual experiences with the collective. Yet, the very constitutive nature of language ensures that reality (in some essentially circular way) reflects the language of those who speak (read) the world into existence. Matthew Strecher writes:

> Indeed, having once accepted that there is no *absolute* reality to the world (the conscious world), none, at any rate, that is not filtered through the medium of

language, we recognize that language fulfills the extraordinary and necessary functions of constituting reality nonstop, creating it anew in our minds from moment to moment.

(Strecher 2014: 29, italics in the original)

Both *Nineteen Eighty-Four* and *1Q84* concern themselves on the macro-level with what Strecher calls the 'constitutive role' of language, though differently (Strecher 2014: 33). But whereas Winston Smith has the unenviable (but professionally satisfying) task of writing into existence a constantly shifting and oppressive world, Tengo – and Fuka-Eri – have the chance to write into existence a possibly better world that allows them to make sense of what came before and create a better future. To use the terms central to *1Q84* (though contra to what Fuka-Eri tells Tengo on p. 564 of the novel), both are simultaneously *Perceivers* and *Receivers* who enact and engage in meaningful interpretive acts against forces – for good or for evil – that seem to be undermining the enactment of free will against fate. Whether personified by an evil Big Brother, a band of Little People, or a politician like Trump, the human gift of categorising and making sense of their lives through stories, makes us all susceptible to the seductive lure of seemingly plausible stories.

In contrast to *Nineteen Eighty-Four*, which is a book about a dystopian future, Tengo laughs at the possibility that Big Brother could get any headway in his day and age, but he does recognise that something – the Little People – function similarly to Big Brother. Through the entrance of replicants – the *dohtas* – into the world, the world itself has become a simulacrum of itself, undermining the real. In Murakami's novel, of course, through the power of love and commitment, Tengo and Aomame set out determined to change the future, whereas Winston Smith has abandoned everything but his aweful love for and absolute commitment to Big Brother; through the power of his words, Tengo changes the past, which affects the future. Orwell's work provides a warning, while Murakami's, though signalling that we must (always/already) be living in a dystopian present, nevertheless suggests that people, with faith and love and persistence, can find a way to assert their own stories. Orwell's cautionary tale gives a means to better understand what can go wrong, while Murakami's hints that there may be a way to create a playbook to move beyond the current moment.

1Q84 ends with Tengo and Aomame hand-in-hand, having climbed their way out of 1Q84, but it is not clear that they are back in the 1984 they exited at the start of the novel. Murakami never provides an answer to this question, though one senses that it remains a different world. While we enter Aomame's world with a question thinking that answers can be found, we exit, with them, into a transformed world, knowing only that our choices create us and our world, and that we can – like Winston Smith – become enslaved by our own creation. To this end, *1Q84* is a concretisation of the way Tengo thinks about the function of stories themselves even as he creates his own: 'The role of a story was, in the broadest terms, to transpose a single problem into another form. Depending on the nature of the problem, a solution could be suggested in the narrative' (Murakami 2011: 178). Although 2020 has drawn to a close, and Joseph Biden has been inaugurated as the 46th President of the United States, we must recognise that this message continues to be important. Citizens are – or rather should be – like Fuka-Eri, Aomame, and Tengo, learning how to become active participants in their own narratives, continuing to question, and claiming the right to rewrite the ending.

Notes

1 *Nineteen Eighty-Four* was published in 1949. Murakami Haruki's *1Q84* was published as three volumes in 2009 (Books 1 and 2) and 2010 (Book 3) and the English translation in October 2011 by Jay Rubin (Books 1 and 2) and Philip Gabriel (Book 3). To avoid typographical confusion with Murakami's *1Q84*, in this chapter I refer to Orwell's novel in its full name as *Nineteen Eighty-Four*, except when characters in Murakami's novel make direct reference to Orwell's work. Quotes from *1Q84* come from the published translation.

2 In Japanese, *1Q84* is read 'ichi-kyū-hachi-yon', which is identical to how Orwell's title is read in Japanese.

3 In a 2009 *Yomiuri Shinbun* interview, Murakami revealed that Aum, together with Orwell's *Nineteen Eighty-Four*, were the inspirations that led to his writing *1Q84* (cited in Flood 2009). For further information on Aum, see Metreaux (1999) and Hardacre (2007–2008) among others. Murakami also published two volumes of interviews on Aum, respectively titled *Andāguraundo* (1997) on the sarin gas attack's victims and their families, and *Yakusokusareta basho de: Underground 2* (1998) on the cult members; the two volumes appear in English as one volume as *Underground: The Tokyo Gas Attack and the Japanese Psyche* (2000).

4 This is most readily apparent in English translation where all three volumes are published in a single volume. In Japan, Book 3 was published a year after Books 1 and 2, using a process Katō Norihiro (2020) dubbed *tatemashi* (stacking or building up), which has the cognitive effect of altering how the 'original' text is interpreted. What this technique does is replicate in a metatextual way how the meaning of texts alter through time as conditions change. For a fascinating discussion of tatemashi see Katō (2020).

5 The Mueller Report, officially titled *Report on the Investigation into Russian Interference in the 2016 Presidential Election*, refers to official findings and conclusions of former Special Counsel Robert Mueller's investigation into allegations of Russian attempts to interfere with the United States presidential election and conspiracies between the Trump campaign and Russia. In a Department of Justice press conference on 30 May 2019, Robert Mueller made the following statement: '[i]f we had confidence that the president clearly did not commit a crime, we would have said so', clearly providing no exoneration of guilt.

References

Anderson, S. 2011. The fierce imagination of Haruki Murakami [online]. *New York Times Magazine*, 11 October. Available from: https://www.nytimes.com/2011/10/23/magazine/the-fierce-imagination-of-haruki-murakami.html [Accessed 16 April 2020].

Barra, A. 2011. How Murakami's '1Q84' became 2011's biggest literary letdown [online]. *The Atlantic*, 16 December. Available from: https://www.theatlantic.com/entertainment/archive/2011/12/how-murakamis-1q84-became-2011s-biggest-literary-letdown/250119/ [Accessed 16 April 2020].

Chapman, S. 2009. 'How could you tell how much of it was lies?' The controversy of truth in George Orwell's *Nineteen Eighty-Four* [online]. *Journal of Literary Semantics* 38 (1): 71–86. Available from: https://doi.org/10.1515/jlse.2009.004 [Accessed 26 April 2020].

Donald J. Trump for President, Inc; Lawrence Roberts; David John Henry v Secretary Commonwealth of Pennsylvania; Allegheny County Board of Elections; Centre County Board of Elections; Chester County Board of Elections; Delaware County Board of Elections; Northampton County Board of Elections; Philadelphia County Board of Elections [online]. 2020. United States Court of Appeals for the Third Circuit, No. 20-3371, 27 November. Available from: https://www.govinfo.gov/app/details/USCOURTS-ca3-20-03371 [Accessed 15 December 2020].

Flood, A. 2009. Murakami reveals Orwell and Aum as twin inspirations for new novel [online]. *The Guardian*, 26 June. Available from: https://www.theguardian.com/books/2009/jun/26/murakami-orwell-aum-novel [Accessed 3 May 2020].

Greene, V. 2011. Utopia/dystopia [online]. *American Art* 25 (2): 2–7. Available from: http://www.jstor.org/stable/10.1086/6611960 [Accessed 16 April 2020].

Hardacre, H. 2007–2008. Aum Shinrikyō and the Japanese media: The Pied Piper meets the Lamb of God. *History of Religions* 47 (2–3): 171–204.

Katō N. 2020. The problem of *tatemashi* in Murakami Haruki's work: Comparing *The Wind-Up Bird Chronicle* and *1Q84* [online]. *Japan Forum* 32 (3): 318–337. Available from: https://www.tandfonline.com/doi/abs/10.1080/09555803.2019.1679225 [Accessed 28 April 2020].

Kriner, T. E. 2014. *An eschatology of reading [E-book]*. Minneapolis: Fortress Press. [Accessed 30 April 2020].

Lakoff, G. 2018. Pinned tweet: Trump uses social media as a way to control the news cycle. *Twitter*. Available from: https://twitter.com/georgelakoff/status/948424436058791937 [Accessed 27 June 2019].

Maslin, J. 2011. A Tokyo with two moons and many more puzzles [online]. *New York Times*, 11 November. Available from: https://www.nytimes.com/2011/11/10/books/1q84-by-haruki-murakami-review.html [Accessed 16 April 2020].

Mayer, J. 2016. Donald Trump's ghostwriter tells all [online]. *The New Yorker Magazine*, 25 July. Available from: https://www.newyorker.com/magazine/2016/07/25/donald-trumps-ghostwriter-tells-all [Accessed 16 April 2020].

Metreaux, D. 1999. *Aum Shinrikyō and Japanese youth*. Lanham, Maryland: University Press of America.

Murakami H. 1993. On Seeing the 100% Perfect Girl One Beautiful April Morning. *In*: *The Elephant Vanishes*. Translated by A. Birnbaum and P. Gabriel. New York: Alfred A. Knopf, 67–72.

——— 2000. *Underground: The Tokyo Gas Attack and the Japanese Psyche*. Translated by A. Birnbaum and P. Gabriel. New York: Random House, Vintage International.

——— 2011. *1Q84*. Translated by Jay Rubin and Philip Gabriel. New York: Alfred A. Knopf.

Orwell, G. 1949. *Nineteen Eighty-Four*. New York: Harcourt, Brace, and Company, Inc.

Russell, E. 2014. Haruki Murakami's *1Q84*: A homage to George Orwell's *Nineteen Eighty-Four*? *In*: P. Gallardo and E. Russell, eds. *Yesterday's tomorrows. On utopia and dystopia*. Newcastle-upon-Tyne: Cambridge Scholars Publishing, 307–322.

Strecher, M. C. 2014. *The forbidden worlds of Haruki Murakami* [Kindle edition]. Minneapolis, London: University of Minnesota Press.

Terdiman, R. 1993. *Present past: Modernity and the memory crisis*. Ithaca: Cornell University Press.

Tonkin, B. 2011. *1Q84* by Haruki Murakami [online]. *The Independent*, 21 October. Available from: https://www.independent.co.uk/arts-entertainment/books/reviews/1q84-haruki-murakami-2373438.html [Accessed 16 April 2020].

Trump unleashes fury at Mueller, 2019. *YouTube*. 30 May 2019. Available from: https://www.youtube.com/watch?v=FeSuu0trppQ [Accessed 27 June 2019].

13

MANIFESTATIONS OF CREATIVITY

Murakami Haruki as translator[1]

Akashi Motoko

Introduction

In contemporary Japan, Murakami Haruki is not only the most celebrated writer, but also one of the most admired translators, and his writing practice goes hand in hand with his translation practice. Famously, he wrote the initial part of his debut novel *Kaze no uta o kike* (1979; trans. *Hear the Wind Sing* [1987/2015]) first in English, and then translated it into Japanese. This experiment enabled him to depart from the prevailing writing style found in the *bundan*, or the Japanese literary establishment, and to create '*atarashii nihongo no buntai*' [a new style of Japanese][2] which has become his trademark (Murakami 2015: 47).

Traditionally, writers who translate tend to view translation as an exercise, a *pretext* on which their own literary works are based (Woodsworth 2017: 5–6) and, having engaged in translation from even before his own writing career began, Murakami is no exception. While he began translating the works of F. Scott Fitzgerald as a hobby, he has continued translating works by authors he admires, including Truman Capote, Fitzgerald, and J. D. Salinger (Murakami and Shibata 2000: 38, 209, 238). With no formal training in creative writing, Murakami even claims to have used translation as a means of developing his own writing skills (Murakami 2017: 156–157). As several scholars have suggested, many of the works Murakami has translated have had an observable influence on his writing. Jonathan Dil (2017) argues for example that Murakami's protagonist/antagonist relationships are typically Fitzgeraldian, and Murakami (Kawakami and Murakami 2017: 187) himself has also admitted that he has recycled structures and devices from Fitzgerald's *The Great Gatsby* (1925).

However, Murakami's translations are not merely a means of developing his own writing skills or the source of inspiration for his novels. Rather, his translations can be considered an extension of his literary works (Fujimoto 2006: 316). By taking a close look at Murakami's translation of Salinger's *The Catcher in the Rye* (2010 [1951]) in comparison to Nozaki Takashi's translation from 1964, this chapter discusses the creative aspects of Murakami's translations, departing from the traditional perception in the literary sphere which views translations as subservient to their source texts (Perteghella and Loffredo 2006: 2). Specifically, the chapter posits creativity in two senses: creativity manifested at the textual level where certain features of Murakami *buntai*[3] or Murakami-style writing influence the way the main protagonist Holden Caulfield is portrayed; and creativity during the translation process, in which Murakami's subjectivity as a writer interacts with the decisions he makes in his translations.

By evaluating the creative aspects of Murakami's translations, this chapter contributes to the discussion of creativity and translation, a relatively underexplored subject in translation studies and literary studies (Nikolaou, 2006: 19), especially in Asian language contexts. The subject of translators' artistic interventions in translations is an important area in literary study, as it concerns how world literature is read and received in the target cultures. Furthermore, this chapter will contribute to Murakami studies focusing not on his literary works nor translations of his works into other languages, but the translations he does *from* other languages. In addition, compared to some of Murakami's fellow translators who are themselves not writers, Murakami's enormous literary fame has granted him much greater creative freedom in his translations than his contemporaries would enjoy (Akashi 2018: 4). Thus, the manifestation of creativity in Murakami's translations becomes an important case study for Murakami's achievement as a translator.

'Life-writing': Tracing Murakami *buntai* in translation

Literary translation is frequently perceived as cultural and linguistic transfer, or 'writing minus the self' in which translators are expected to remain under the shadow of the source author (Nikolaou 2006: 31). Paschalis Nikolaou (2006: 21) instead views the act of literary translation as a form of writing which is comparable to 'life-writing', a vaguely defined term that refers to ways of telling a life story, such as memoirs, autobiographies, biographies, diaries, letters, and autobiographical fiction (Lee 2005: 100). Nikolaou (2006: 21) proposed that literary translations be understood as 'imaginings of "source selves" and recordings of translators as they write', which are produced through their self-expression. Thus, while translators generally aspire to avoid showing their own voice in their translations, their voice could still manifest in the target text to some degree. In cases where a translator is also a writer/poet, Nikolaou furthermore argues that their creative subjectivities tend to manifest in their translation choices which result in a personalising of the text, a phenomenon which is observable in autobiographies (ibid.).

The view of literary translation as 'life-writing' is highly relevant when examining Murakami's translations, since he is not only a translator, but also a novelist. If a novelist also publishes literary translations and incorporates his/her own writing styles or habits into those translations, readers may recognise thematic or stylistic similarities between the novelist's own creative works and the translations s/he produces; hence, the translations can be viewed as part of the writer's oeuvre (Evans 2016: 9). Indeed, Murakami is known for incorporating his idiosyncrasies as a writer into his translations, and as Fujimoto Yukiko (2006: 316) argues, Murakami's translations 'potentially give the reader the illusion that the translations are an extension of his original writings'. This perceived extension of a writer's oeuvre is available to Murakami by virtue of his dual identity as both a translator and a novelist.

While a glance at Amazon reader reviews immediately shows that Murakami's tendency to employ his own *buntai* in his translation work pleases some readers (e.g. Pigumon 2003; Keroji 2011; Kowka 2020), but some professional critics as well as readers have criticised him for disregarding the source author's voice (e.g. Mutenhakase 2019; Numano qtd in Koshikawa et al. 2003: 292–293). For example, his translation of Raymond Chandler's 1953 novel *The Long Goodbye* has been criticised for transforming classic hard-boiled fiction into '*toshigata*' [city type] contemporary literature (Ōsawa 2007). Murakami himself is aware of this criticism (Murakami and Shibata 2019: 258) and even confirms that his *buntai* may unintentionally manifest itself in his translations:

> [I guess it's similar. I often get told that. Some say the writing style in my novels is similar to the writing style of the novels I translate, while others say the writing style in my translations is too similar to the writing style in my novels.]
> (Murakami 1989: 24)

The negative reactions to the presence of Murakami's idiosyncrasies in his translations are, however, generally based on the traditional concept of literary translation which values precision and fidelity. Such perceptions may prevent readers from discovering the potential merits of Murakami's translations. Nikolaou's idea of translation as 'life-writing' allows us to move beyond a conventional evaluation of textual fidelities or merits/demerits of using Murakami *buntai* as other critics have done (e.g. Ōsawa 2007). Instead, the focus of this chapter is on examining the creativity of Murakami's translations and deepening our understanding of Japan's most famous author not as a novelist, but as a translator – not through the usual lens of his literary work, but through the synergy between his literary translations and literary creations.

As my key analysis in this chapter, I will show how Murakami *buntai* are manifest in Murakami's translation of Salinger's *The Catcher in the Rye* (Salinger 2010 [1951]) as *Kyacchā in za rai* (2003), effectively arguing that *Kyacchā in za rai* can be considered an 'extension' of Murakami's oeuvre – almost another Murakami novel. This work is one of Murakami's best-selling translations, and partly prompted an ongoing retranslation boom in Japan, where major publishers, including Kōbunsha and Kawade Shobō Shinsha, have launched imprints dedicated to retranslations of foreign classics since 2006 (Satō 2009: 1). More importantly, however, it is also one of the most controversial Murakami translations, in the sense that the characterisation of the main protagonist differs significantly from Nozaki Takashi's earlier translation entitled *Raimugi batake de tsukamaete* [lit. Catch me in the rye field] (1964). By 2002, Nozaki's translation had sold 2.5 million copies, and is regarded as a masterpiece by Japanese readers and critics alike (Satō 2009: 12–13). When Murakami's version was published the following year (and

40 years after Nozaki's first appeared) with the same publisher, it received significant attention not because it was also regarded as a masterpiece, but because of the significant amount of Murakami *buntai* present in the translation. Hence, in the following section, I will compare and contrast Murakami's translation with Nozaki's, in order to highlight how the effect of Murakami *buntai* shapes the reader's perception of the protagonist and the novel differently from Nozaki, and brings the reader closer to a 'Murakami' world. This textual creativity will then be followed by a discussion on Murakami's writerly creativity, examining the motives of his interventions, the awareness and influence of his subjectivity as a writer, and his personal views on the source text and source author.

Murakami *buntai* in *Kyacchā in za rai*

Murakami's *buntai* has several idiosyncratic features that are familiar to his readers, and in this section, I discuss three main features present in *Kyacchā in za rai*, namely *boku*, *yare-yare*, and *katakana* loanwords. What is clear across all three subsections below is that, sometimes at the expense of losing fidelity with the source text, Murakami has provided a rendition of Salinger's novel and protagonist that reminds readers strongly of Murakami's own characters and stories.

Boku

One of the best-known features of Murakami *buntai* is the use of the first-person pronoun *boku*, and in *Kyacchā in za rai* this is clearly detectable as Murakami almost always renders the novel's male protagonist Holden with *boku*. The Japanese language has a variety of first-person pronouns, depending on the speaker's gender, position in the social hierarchy, and the nature of the relationship between the speaker and listener (Hadley and Akashi 2015: 467). While the English first-person pronoun 'I' is most commonly rendered as *watashi* used by both men and women (ibid.), *boku* is used as an informal term reserved for males. Contrasted with *ore*, another male first-person pronoun which represents vulgarity and is often perceived as displaying masculinity (Lee and Yonezawa 2008: 754), *boku* evokes a passive character (Nihei 2013: 69). Murakami's consistent use of *boku* however greatly contrasts Nozaki's Holden who, in addition to *boku*, also uses *ore* whenever Holden is attempting to play the bad boy. For example, when a pimp approaches Holden and offers sexual service, he is dumbstruck and answers: 'Me?' (Salinger 2010 [1951]: 99). Murakami renders this as '*boku ga kai?*' (僕がかい?) (2003: 155), while in Nozaki's text, Holden switches tone and answers '*ore ga?*' (おれが?) (1984: 142). Because *ore* is a Japanese pronoun that is generally associated with dominance, manliness, and machoism, Nozaki's choice of translating 'I' as *ore* rather than *boku* shows how he sees Holden trying to act tough here, an implication that is absent in Murakami's rendition of *boku*.

Similarly, in the following passage where Holden rants about having his gloves stolen by someone and imagines how he would confront the suspect, Murakami and Nozaki differ again on pronoun use:

Salinger's original:
'All I know is my goddam gloves were in your goddam galoshes.' Right away then, the guy would know for sure that I wasn't going to take a sock at him, and he probably would've said, 'Listen. Let's get this straight. Are you calling me a thief?' Then I probably would've said, 'Nobody's calling anybody a thief. All I know is my gloves were in your goddam galoshes'.

(Salinger 2010 [1951]: 97)

Nozaki's translation:
「**おれ**が言ってるのはただ、**おれ**の手袋がおまえのオーバーシューズに入ってたって、それだけのことさ」ってね。するととたんに相手は、僕が奴を殴りはしないことを見てとって「おい。このかたをつけようじゃねえか?おまえ、**おれ**を泥棒だと言うのか」っていうだろう。すると僕はたぶん「誰も泥棒なんて言ってやしない。**おれ**はただ、**おれ**の手袋がおまえのオーバーシューズに入ってたって、そう言ってるだけだ」と言う。(Nozaki 1984: 139–140)

'**Ore** ga itteru no wa tada, **ore** no tebukuro ga omae no ōbāshūzu ni haitteta tte, soredake no koto sa' tte ne. Suruto, totan ni aite wa, <u>boku</u> ga yatsu o naguri wa shinai koto o mite totte 'Oi. Kono kata o tsukeyō janeeka? Omae, **ore** o dorobō dato iu no ka' tte iu darō. Suruto, <u>boku</u> wa tabun 'Daremo dorobō nante itteya shinai. **Ore** wa tada, ore no tebukuro ga omae no ōbāshūzu ni haitteta tte, sō itteru dake da' to iu.

Murakami's translation:
「はっきりしてるのは、<u>僕</u>の手袋がお前のろくでもないオーバーシューズの中にあったってことさ」ってね。そこで相手の男は、一発くらわせるつもりが<u>僕</u>にはないんだってことを即座に見抜いてしまう。そこでやつはかさにかかって言う。「おい、話をはっきりさせようぜ。お前は**俺**がそれを盗んだって言うのか?」で、たぶん<u>僕</u>はこう言うだろう。「別に誰が盗んだとか、そういうことを言ってるわけじゃないんだ。言いたいのは、<u>僕</u>の手袋がお前のろくでもないオーバーシューズの中からみつかったってことだけだ。

(Murakami 2003: 152–153)

'Hakkiri shiteiru no wa, <u>boku</u> no tebukuro ga omae no roku demo nai ōbāshūzu no naka ni atta tte koto sa' tte ne. Soko de aite no otoko wa, ippatsu kurawaseru tsumori ga <u>boku</u> ni wa nain da tte koto o sokuza ni minuite shimau. Soko de aite no yatsu wa kasani kakatte iu. 'Oi, hanashi o hakkiri saseyōze. Omae wa **ore** ga sore o nusunda tte iu no ka?' De, tabun <u>boku</u> wa kō iu darō. 'Betsuni dare ga nusunda toka, sō iu koto o itteru wake ja nain da. Iitai no wa, <u>boku</u> no tebukuro ga omae no roku demo nai ōbāshūzu no naka kara mitsukatta tte koto dake da'.

Both Murakami and Nozaki use *ore* (in bold above) for the imaginary stealer that Holden is confronting; for Murakami's passage, this is the only time that *ore* is used. What is different between the two translations, however, is the pronoun Holden uses to refer to himself. Murakami uses *boku* (underlined above) consistently, but Nozaki uses a mixture of *boku* and *ore*, with *ore* being used when Holden is confronting the suspect, giving the impression that he wants to assume a toughened personality. The *ore* in bold in Nozaki's text then, can either refer to the suspect or to Holden himself, while in Murakami's, under no circumstance will Holden switch to using *ore*. By doing so, Nozaki's Holden sounds as if he deliberately attempts to hide his weakness and sound tough, while Murakami's Holden gives off a heavier sense of passiveness.

This contrast between toughness and passiveness also demonstrates a difference in personality; in other words, the two translations shape Holden's personality differently for the reader. In addition to the pronouns *boku* and *ore*, there are other linguistic features that demonstrate this divide in personality. In the following passage, Holden imagines himself doing things that would annoy his elder brother D. B., who despises war:

> Salinger's original:
> If there's ever another war, I'm going to sit right the hell on top of it. I'll volunteer for it, I swear to God I will.
>
> (Salinger 2010 [1951]: 152)

> Nozaki's translation:
> 今度戦争があったら、僕は原子爆弾の<u>てっぺん</u>に乗っかって<u>やるよ</u>。自分から志願してやってやる。誓ってもいいや。
>
> (Nozaki 1984: 219)

> Kondo sensō ga attara, boku wa genshibakudan no <u>teppen</u> ni nokkatte <u>yaru yo</u>. Jibun kara shigan shite yatte yaru. Chikatte mo ii ya.

> Murakami's translation:
> もし次の戦争が始まったら、爆弾の<u>上</u>に進んでまたがってやろう<u>と思う</u>。僕はそういう役に志願しよう。ほんとに、真面目なはなし。
>
> (Murakami 2003: 238)

> Moshi tsugi no sensō ga hajimattara, bakudan no <u>ue</u> ni susunde matagatte yarō <u>to omou</u>. Boku wa sō iu yaku ni shigan shiyō. Honto ni, majime na hanashi.

In Nozaki's text, Holden's voice appears to have a tone of assertiveness that seems to correspond to the voice of the source text: in the underlined parts, Nozaki uses the slang *teppen* (meaning 'top'), the construction *te yaru* (which expresses a rough tone for harsh actions), and the emphatic end particle *yo* to convey the emotion of the phrase 'sit right the hell on top of it'. In contrast, Holden's tone in Murakami's text seems softened by the standard word *ue* and the verb *to omou* ('to think'), which is often used in Japanese to soften a statement by giving it an amount of subjective judgement. Holden here speaks in a rather neutral tone, sounding as if he were merely referring to a future plan of his rather than an outburst of determination.

As can be seen, the characteristics of Holden in the two texts are rather different. Whereas Nozaki's Holden seems to be a closer rendition to Salinger's original with his rough tone and bad-boy pretension, Murakami's Holden is more soft-spoken. Murakami himself is very aware of this and even says that some critics have questioned his use of *boku* in his translation work, because they believe that the pronoun is more suitable for a middle-class male character than a character who is unemployed, working class, or of a passionate personality (Murakami and Shibata 2019: 249–250). Examples of *boku* characters in question include the unemployed protagonist in his translation of Carver's 'Collectors' (1975) and the narrator who is struggling to overcome his alcohol problem in 'Where I'm Calling From' (1982). However, rather than being a question of translation fidelity, I focus here instead on the affinity between Murakami's Holden and the protagonists in Murakami's own novels. In this light, the consistent use of the first-person *boku* is the first feature of Murakami *buntai* that connects *Kyacchā in za rai* with other Murakami novels.

Boku is one of the trademark features found in Murakami novels, with the majority of Murakami's male protagonists adopting this pronoun (Koshikawa et al. 2003: 292). His American translator, Jay Rubin (2002: 37), claims that Murakami's employment of *boku* is what distinguishes his works from those of his contemporaries, who prefer the term *watashi/watakushi*, which is 'the long-established fixture of serious Japanese fiction'. Nihei Chikako (2013: 69) even comments that *boku* is 'one of the essential elements' in the popularity of Murakami's fiction. Indeed, the characteristics of *boku* have not gone amiss on Murakami's readers and critics, which can be seen from how frequently *boku* is discussed in Murakami-related magazines and websites. For example, the popular magazine *Bessatsu Takarajima* (Hasegawa et al. 2003: 108–112) has dedicated a special issue to Murakami and featured a roundtable discussion on why Murakami's protagonist is almost always *boku*. Similarly, *Murakami Haruki Shinbun* [Murakami Haruki Times], a digital newspaper run by Murakami's fan base, has synthesised the characteristics of *boku* characters in four novels and a short story from Murakami's early works into a profile of *boku* with biographical details and habits, such as listening to The Beach Boys' *California Girls* while drinking beer ('*Kaze*', n.d.).

Some critics even hold the view that Murakami's *boku* is akin to Murakami himself. After all, he also refers to himself as *boku* in his non-fiction writing including his numerous essays. Rubin has also suggested that the fictional *boku* in fact resembles Murakami's own personality:

> Murakami was by no means the first Japanese novelist to adopt *boku* as the 'I' of a nameless male narrator, but the personality with which Murakami invested his Boku [sic] was unique. First of all, it resembled his own, with a generous

fund of curiosity and a cool, detached, bemused acceptance of the inherent strangeness of life.

(2002: 37)

Murakami (2000: 115) himself admits that although he and the fictional *boku* should be treated separately, there may be some resemblance between them. Either way, Murakami's *boku* is widely regarded to have a defined and recognisable personality as a pacifist who likes to play it safe, bottling his lust and emotions (Kazamaru 2006: 30), and when Murakami uses *boku* also in his translations, this pronoun choice gives the protagonists a similar air to those in his fiction, irrespective of the characteristics of the protagonists in the source texts (Hadley and Akashi 2015: 467). In *Kyacchā in za rai*, we see a clear overlap with how Murakami's Holden sounds more passive and subdued than Nozaki's, but similar to Murakami's own *boku* stories.

Yare-yare

I have established so far that Murakami's *boku* is more than simply a narrative pronoun – in fact, it suggests a different personality to a character. This different personality is also reflected in the way the character speaks, particularly in the verbal tics that Murakami tends to use both for his translations and his novels. A hallmark example commonly seen in his novels is '*yare-yare*' (Katō 2006: 141), an interjection employed often 'when the protagonists are confronted by confounding situations' (Rubin 2002: 37).

In *Kyacchā in za rai*, the presence of the term is particularly important because Murakami renders the majority of Holden's habitual use of 'boy' as *yare-yare*, which appears some 41 times (based on a one-time manual count I conducted), hence an important marker that shapes Holden's personality. In Chapter 2, for example, Holden tells his teacher that his parents are yet to be informed that he has been expelled from school:

Salinger's original:
'And how do you think they'll take the news?'
    'Well… they'll be pretty irritated about it,' I said. 'They really will. This is about the fourth school I've gone to.' I shook my head. I shake my head quite a lot. '<u>Boy</u>!' I said. I also say '<u>Boy</u>!' quite a lot.

(Salinger 2010 [1951]: 9)

Nozaki's translation:
「それにしても、ご両親は、おしりになってどうお思いになるかな?」「さあ・・・・・・相当怒るでしょうね。きっと怒りますよ。僕の入った今度がだいたい四つ目の学校ですからね」そう言って僕は首を振った。僕はよく首を振るくせがあるんだ。そして「<u>チェッ!</u>」って言った。「<u>チェッ!</u>」って言うくせもあるんだ。

(Nozaki 1984: 17)

'Sore ni shite mo, goryōshin wa, oshiri ni natte dō oomoi ni naru kana?' 'Sā …
sōtō okoru deshō ne. Kitto okorimasu yo. Boku no haitta kondo ga daitai yottsume no gakkō desu kara ne' sō itte boku wa kubi o futta. Boku wa yoku kubi
o furu kuse ga arun da. Soshite '*che!*' tte itta. '*Che!*' tte iu kuse mo arun da.

Murakami's translation
「ご両親はそれを聞いてどう思われるかな?」「あの‥‥‥かなりかり
かりするだろうと思います」と僕は言った。「まじめな話。なにしろこの学
校は四つめくらいですから」、僕は首を振った。僕はまたよく首を振るん
だ。「やれやれ!」と僕は言った。ついでに言うと、この「やれやれ!」っての
も**口癖**なんだ。

(Murakami 2003: 18)

'Goryōshin wa sore o kiite dō omowareru kana?' 'Ano … kanari karikari suru
darō to omoimasu' to *boku* wa itta. 'Majime na hanashi. Nanishiro kono gakkō
wa yottsume kurai desu kara', *boku* wa kubi o futta. *Boku* wa mata yoku kubi
o furun da. '*Yare-yare!*' to *boku* wa itta. Tsuide ni iu to, kono '*yare-yare!*' tte no
mo **kuchiguse** nan da.

While Murakami renders the interjection 'Boy!' as *yare-yare*, Nozaki translates it as
che' (チェッ), which is a tutting sound one expresses when disappointed but which also
has a different implied tone to *yare-yare*. For example, the Japanese–English online
dictionary *Weblio* translates *yare-yare* as 'thank God', 'dear me', and 'good grief' (*Yare-
yare*, n.d.), while *che* is rendered as 'shoot', 'shit' and 'dammit', clearly expressions of
irritation and annoyance (*Che'*, n.d.). As with the *boku* pronoun, Holden's personality in Murakami's *Kyacchā in za rai* is again significantly different from Nozaki's
translation, with Murakami's *yare-yare*-musing Holden much calmer than Nozaki's
che'-spewing one.

Like *boku*, *yare-yare* has its share of criticism as well. Numano Mitsuyoshi for
example said that '[it is certainly a phrase that Murakami's readers are familiar with,
but for a high school student to be saying "*yare-yare*" certainly sounds anachronistic to
me]' (qtd in Koshikawa et al. 2003: 292–293), while Koshikawa Yoshiaki comments
on the use of *yare-yare* in Murakami's translation of Raymond Carver's works:

> [In Carver's case, many of the protagonists are working class, so they use swear
> words and slang such as 'goddamn', or even stronger words. In Murakami's
> case, expressions that sound quite fierce to the listener in English become '*yare-
> yare*' or '*iyahaya*'.[4] For better or worse, these are standard expressions found in
> 'the world of Murakami'.]

(ibid.: 293)

These critiques focus on Murakami's deviation from the source text, and are thus
based on the traditional view of translation as precision and fidelity.

By taking a different approach to translation, however, Murakami's use of *yare-yare* strengthens the association readers may make between Holden and other Murakami protagonists. The term *yare-yare* first appeared in *1973 nen no pinbōru* (1980; trans. *Pinball, 1973* [1985/2015]), and is used habitually by the protagonist of *Hitsuji o meguru bōken* (1982; trans. *A Wild Sheep Chase* [1989]) (Nakamura and Dōzen 2018: 172). Nakamura and Dōzen (ibid.) further observe that Murakami himself uses the term regularly in his essays, creating an interlinkage between his own personality and his protagonists. As in the case of *boku*, *yare-yare* receives significant attention from readers. This is for instance evident in the special feature in the *Murakami Haruki Shinbun* titled '*Murakami Haruki yare-yare chōsadan* [The Murakami Haruki 'Yare-yare' Investigation Committee]' ('Murakami Haruki "*yare-yare*"', n.d.). As of June 2020, this ongoing investigation lists the uses of *yare-yare* from 33 Murakami works including novels and short stories.

Given that '*yare-yare*' is a representative expression in Murakami's literature and his own habitual language, its usage in his translations demonstrates the thorough influence of his *buntai*. What is important about the above example of *yare-yare* from *Kyacchā in za rai* is that it echoes a passage almost verbatim from Murakami's 1982 novel *Hitsuji o meguru bōken*, where the nameless protagonist *boku* says after having had an unproductive day:

「やれやれ」と僕は言った。やれやれという言葉はだんだん僕の口ぐ せのようになりつつある。

(Murakami 1982: 238)

'Yare-yare' to boku wa itta. Yare-yare to iu kotoba wa dandan boku no **kuchiguse** no yōni naritsutsu aru.
['"*Yare-yare*", I said. The word *yare-yare* is gradually becoming my **pet phrase**'.]

In addition to the use of *boku* and *yare-yare*, the two lines are joined intertextually by the hinge word *kuchiguse* (in bold, meaning 'pet phrase'). The unmistakable similarity invites readers to create resonance between Holden in *Kyacchā in za rai* and the *boku*s in Murakami own novels, therefore effectively reading *Kyacchā in za rai* as an extension of Murakami's oeuvre.

Katakana loanwords

The final feature of Murakami *buntai* examined here is his frequent use of *katakana* loanwords.[5] Table 13.1 shows examples of transliterated foreign terms that I have found in Murakami's *Kyacchā in za rai* in comparison with Nozaki's translation.

As is evident from Table 13.1, Nozaki consistently renders words into their Japanese equivalents (except for 'gorgeous' which is omitted), while Murakami often transliterates English words and phrases into *katakana*. For example, 'nervous' becomes *nāvasu*, 'sex life' *sekkusu raifu*, 'friendly' *furendorī*, and 'old sport' *ōrudo supōto*, all of which Nozaki translates into Japanese vocabularies, respectively *fuan*, *seiseikatsu*, *aiso ga ii*,

TABLE 13.1 Comparison of *katakana* loanwords in Murakami with Nozaki. Page numbers (not exhaustive) are in brackets.

	Source Text	Murakami	Nozaki
1	The Catcher in the Rye	キャッチャー・イン・ザ・ライ (*Kyacchā in za rai*)	ライ麦畑で捕まえて (*Raimugi batake de tsukamaete*) [catch me in the rye field]
2	Old sport	オールド・スポート (*ōrudo supōto*) (238)	親友 (*shin'yū*) [best friend] (218)
3	Good luck!	グッド・ラック (*guddo rakku*) (342)	幸運を祈る (*kōun o inoru*) (314)
4	Vocabulary	ボキャブラリー (*bokyaburarī*) (18)	語彙 (*goi*) (17)
5	Nervous	ナーバス (*nābasu*) (165)	不安 (*fuan*) [uneasy] (151)
6	Necking	ネッキング (*nekkingu*) (134)	抱擁 (*hōyō*) [to hug, cuddle] (124)
7	Sex life	セックス・ライフ (*sekkusu raifu*) (243)	性生活 (*seiseikatsu*) (223)
8	Fuck you	ファック・ユー (*fakku yū*) (342)	オマンコシヨウ (*omanko shiyō*) [Let's have sex] (314)
9	Complex	コンプレックス (*conpurekkusu*) (229)	劣等意識 (*rettō ishiki*) [a sense of inferiority] (210)
10	Friendly	フレンドリー (*furendorī*) (48)	愛想がいい (*aiso ga ii*) (43)
11	Gorgeous	ゴージャス (*gōjasu*) (333)	—
12	Roommate	ルームメイト (*rūmumeito*) (113)	同じ部屋にいる友達 (*onaji heya ni iru tomodachi*) [A friend in the same room] (104)
13	Crazy	クレイジー (*kureizī*) (193)	いかれた (*ikareta*) (177)
14	Jesus Christ	ジーザス・クライスト (*Jīzasu Kuraisuto*) (193)	これはねえ (*korewa nē*) [Well, this is …] (178)
15	Yes, sir	イエス・サー (*yesu sā*) (318)	ええ、分かります (*ee, wakarimasu*) [yes, I understand] (296)

and *shin'yū*. When Nozaki does use *katakana* words, they are either proper names or nouns that are by now commonly used in Japanese, such as *shawā rūmu* [shower room] and *dauntaun* [downtown] (Nozaki 1984: 33, 95). Murakami's heavy use of transliteration, however, is not necessarily comprehensible in the target language – 'old sport' for instance is an English slang term of endearment, and when transliterated into Japanese, *ōrudo supōto* does not convey the same connotation of friendship to a Japanese speaker, both because *supōto* has no meaning in Japanese for 'sport' is transliterated as *supōtsu*, not *supōto*, and because even if it had been *ōrudo supōtsu*, it would have meant simply 'a sport with an old history'. Yet, instead of evaluating such transliteration in a negative light, it is more constructive to identify the potential for interpretation *katakana* loanwords have given rise to, which can already be detected from the title of the work itself.

Unlike Nozaki who translates *The Catcher in the Rye* into *Raimugi batake de tsu-kamaete*, a phrase that can be immediately understood by Japanese readers to mean 'catch me in the rye field', Murakami's title, *Kyacchā in za rai*, is not immediately comprehensible and is the first instance where readers become aware of his idiosyncratic usage of *katakana*. Nozaki supplements the reader with additional information when he expands the word 'rye' in the English title into *raimugi batake* (ライ麦畑), a rye 'field'. In Murakami's title, the word *rai* (ライ) stands alone without any suggestion of a field, but because of this, it may also be understood as a proper noun, or the term 'lie' used in golf, causing ambiguity. Similarly, the term *kyacchā* (キャッチャー) could also be understood as 'a catcher' in baseball, whereas Nozaki's *tsukamaete* (つかまえて) simply means 'catch (me)'. Here we see Murakami's deliberate emphasis on the ambiguity offered by the *katakana* title: defending his choice, he notes that Salinger's novel has now become a household name and therefore the title does not have to be semantically comprehensible (Murakami and Shibata 2003: 60). In fact, he predicts that the peculiarity of his *katakana* title will help make it recognisable to readers, and also allow them to have their own interpretation, which was previously less possible to do because Nozaki's semantically comprehensible title limits interpretive possibilities: the phrase 'The Catcher in the Rye' in fact comes from Holden's misinterpretation of a poem by Robert Burns called 'Comin' Thro' the Rye' (1782), and this information becomes clear to the reader only in Chapter 22 of the novel. Hence, for Murakami, a semantically comprehensible title such as *Raimugi batake de tsukamaete* does not reflect the mis-rendition and the opacity of the source title (Murakami and Shibata 2003: 60–61).

Like *boku* and *yare-yare*, Murakami's tendency to employ transliteration is also observable in his other translations and novels. A conspicuous example is perhaps the phrase *ōrudo supōto* (old sport), which appears in *Kyacchā in za rai* (see Item 2 in Table 13.1) but also in Murakami's translation of Fitzgerald's *The Great Gatsby* for instance – there, 'old sport' is habitually uttered by the character Jay Gatsby and appears on some 42 occasions, which Murakami consistently renders as *ōrudo supōto*. As discussed, *ōrudo supōto* is not immediately comprehensible to a Japanese reader, and in contrast to Murakami, other translators have opted for readability in their translation, like Ogawa Takayoshi who completely avoids translating the term, or Nozaki who, like in *Raimugi batake de tsukamaete*, again translates it into the Japanese word *shin'yū* (Akashi and Hadley 2014: 193; Hadley and Akashi 2015: 469). More broadly in his fiction, Murakami frequently uses *katakana* words for a variety of purposes and effects, ranging from (1) transliterating foreign brand names and Western foods – such as *Jonī Wōkā* for Johnnie Walker in *Umibe no Kafuka*, or *rōsuto bīfu sandoicchi* for roast beef sandwich in *Dansu dansu dansu*; (2) keeping the full word in the source language rather than using a more common abbreviated form spoken by Japanese people – such as *sūpāmāketto* for supermarket instead of just *sūpā*, or *conpūtā* for computer instead of *pasokon*; and (3) introducing transliteration of foreign words usually unfamiliar to Japanese readers – such as *burasshu appu* for 'brush up', *aidentitī* for 'identity', *rēzon dēturu* for 'raison d'être'. Furthermore, similar to *Kyacchā in za rai*, titles in *katakana* are seen from time to time in Murakami's own stories, including 'Famirī afea' (1985; trans. 'Family Affair' [1993]), 'Tairando'[6] (1999; trans. 'Thailand' [2001]), *Afutādāku* (2004; trans. *After Dark* [2007]), 'TV pīpuru' (1989; trans. 'TV People' [1990]), and so on, some of which are even rather ambiguous at first sight, such as 'Doraibu mai kā' (2013; trans. 'Drive My Car' [2015]), where both 'doraibu' and 'mai kā' are common used in Japanese separately, but the combination of these two works produces a layer of ambiguous meaning.

Katakana loanwords appearing in Murakami's translations have previously drawn the attention of scholars and literary critics (e.g. Kawahara 2016: 42; Numano qtd in Koshikawa et al. 2003: 294–295; Fujimoto 2006: 314); however, they tend to centre on the 'modernising' and 'foreignising' effects of loanwords in his texts and their contributions to the Japanese language, rather than approaching it from his overall oeuvre. Traditionally, heavy use of foreign vocabulary was not considered appropriate for serious Japanese literature but, as Suter (2008: 67–69) argues, the popularity of Murakami's novels and the extensive usage of loanwords in them have together improved acceptability of loanwords among mainstream writers of serious literature. Specifically in the context of *The Catcher in the Rye*, Nozaki's translation was already considered to contain a high number of *katakana* words when it was first published in 1964 (Hokujō 2004: 153), but as we have seen in Table 13.1 and Murakami's comment on the ambiguous title, *Kyacchā in za rai* further drifts the reader closer to contemporary times, to the extent that critics have credited Murakami for creating 'new Japanese terminology' with his idiosyncratic *katakana* words (Koshikawa et al. 2003: 294). Furthermore, Suter (2008: 68–72) suggests that Murakami's avoidance of the commonly used abbreviated *katakana* forms (e.g. *conpūtā* not *pasokon*) and introduction of hitherto unpopular *katakana* terms (e.g. *rēzon dēturu*) help highlight the foreignness of these words, creating a sense of 'estrangement'. What needs to be pointed out too, however, is that Murakami's use of *katakana* in *Kyacchā in za rai* – and right from the title at that – builds rapport with the abundance of *katakana* loanwords in his own novels and, as the pervasiveness of *ōrudo supōto* has shown, the foreignising effect is also achieved in Murakami's translations as much as in his novels. Simply put, the presence of *katakana* transliterations induces in the reader a familiar connection with his novels.

Writerly creativity: Negotiating Murakami's subjectivity as a writer/translator

Having analysed the textual creativities Murakami makes in introducing his *buntai* in *Kyacchā in za rai*, almost effectively turning it into another Murakami novel, this section will extrapolate to discuss how Murakami's subjectivity as a writer is manifest in the translation project and process on the whole, in order to further contextualise Murakami's textual interventions in his dual writer/translator identities. Across all three aspects of Murakami *buntai* explored in the last section, namely *boku*, *yare-yare*, and *katakana* loanwords, it can be concluded that Murakami's interventions at the textual level resonates strongly with similar features in his own novels and stories. However, these similarities are far from habitual; to the contrary, Murakami has expressed clear awareness of the effect of his translation style and conscious reflection on the reasons behind his creative interventions. On several occasions Murakami is seen discussing his subjectivity as a writer openly and sharing his thinking process with the reader. As far as *Kyacchā in za rai* is concerned, several important considerations governed Murakami's translation style.

The first factor has to do with the fact that Murakami wrote *Umibe no Kafuka* (2002; trans. *Kafka on the Shore* [2005]) just before he began translating Salinger's novel. Murakami admits that the characterisation of Holden may have been influenced by his own protagonist Kafuka, a 15-year-old boy who is of similar age to Holden and who also uses the *boku* pronoun to refer to himself (Murakami and Shibata 2003: 27). In other words, Holden in *Kyacchā in za rai* is not simply a Japanese reiteration of Holden in Salinger's original novel, but a hybrid character whose personality is also constituted by Murakami's own protagonist Kafuka. This is, for example, telling in how for both characters their inner voice materialises as second-person narratives. In *Umibe no Kafuka*, the boy named Karasu [Crow], who is an imagining of the protagonist himself, keeps Kafuka company and guides him throughout his journey. Karasu narrates in the second-person pronoun '*kimi*', mirroring Kafuka's inner voice. In the passage below, Karasu's voice can be interpreted as how Kafuka is coming to term with himself (the pronoun '*kimi*' is underlined):

Umibe no Kafuka
[...] なぜかといえば、その嵐はどこか遠くからやってきた無関係ななにかじゃないからだ。そいつはつまり、<u>君</u>自身のことなんだ。<u>君</u>の中にあるなにかなんだ。

(Murakami 2002: 10)

[...] Nazeka to ieba, sono arashi wa doko ka tōku kara yatte kita mukankei na nani ka ja nai kara da. Sore wa tsumari, <u>kimi</u> jishin no koto nan da. <u>Kimi</u> no naka ni aru nani ka nan da.
[[...] Because this storm isn't something that came from faraway and has nothing to do with you. It's <u>you</u>. It's something that exists inside <u>you</u>.]

The resemblance between Murakami's Holden and Kafuka/Karasu becomes clear in the following episode from *The Catcher in the Rye*, in which Holden, who is revisiting the museum he went to as a child, comes to realise that he is not the person he once was. In Nozaki's translation, the protagonist appears to be talking to himself with the use of the pronoun *kotchi* – which usually means 'here' as a place, rather than as a person – while in Murakami's text, Holden appears to be coming to terms with himself or communicating with his inner self, but addresses this inner self with – like in Kafuka – the second-person pronoun *kimi* (corresponding personal pronouns are underlined):

Salinger's original:
The only thing that would be different would be you. Not that you'd be so much older or anything. It wouldn't be that, exactly. You'd just be different, that's all.

(Salinger 2010 [1951]: 131)

Nozaki's translation:
変わるのはただこっちのほうさ。といっても、こっちが年をとるとかなんとか、そんなことを　言ってるんじゃない。厳密にいうと、それとはちょっと違うんだ。こっちがいつも同じではないという、それだけのことなんだ。

(Nozaki 1984: 188)

Kawaru no wa tada kotchi no hō sa. To itte mo, kotchi ga toshi o toru toka nan toka, sonna koto o itterun ja nai. Genmitsu ni iuto, sore to wa chotto chigaun da. Kotchi ga itsumo onaji de wa nai to iu, sore dake no koto nan da.

[What changes is me. I'm not saying that I am getting old or anything like that. Strictly speaking it's a bit different. It's that I'm not always the same – that's all.]

Murakami's translation:
ただひとつ違っているのは君だ。いや、君がそのぶん歳をとってしまったとか、そういうことじゃないよ。それとはちょっと違うんだ。ただ君は違っている、それだけのこと。

(Murakami 2003: 205)

Tada hitotsu chigatte iru no wa kimi da. Iya, kimi ga sono bun toshi o totte shimatta toka, sō iu koto ja nai yo. Sore wa chotto chigaun da. Tada kimi wa chigatte iru, sore dake no koto.
[The only thing that would change is you. No, it's not that you'd aged or anything like that – that's not it. It's a bit different from that. It's just that you'd be different – that's all.]

The influence of writing *Umibe no Kafuka* on *Kyacchā in za rai* can also be observed in Murakami's interpretation of Phoebe, Holden's younger sister. Murakami has said that he understood her not as a physical character but as an illusion, or a mirror image of Holden's other self (Murakami and Shibata 2003: 49), which reminds us of the Kafuka–Karasu relationship. In Murakami's *Kyacchā in za rai*, Phoebe addresses Holden as '*anata*' [you], while Nozaki's Phoebe calls Holden '*nīsan*' [brother] (Hadley and Akashi 2015: 468). In Japanese it is standard to call an older male sibling '*nīsan*' and not 'anata', and it therefore becomes clear that in Nozaki's text the two are physical siblings, whereas in Murakami's, Phoebe should not be understood as Holden's physical sister, but as an inner self. As a writer by profession, Murakami's works, no matter their genres, form an oeuvre and speak to each other. The two examples here – the use of second-person pronouns and the interpretation on Phoebe – exemplify what Evans (2016: 15–17) calls a 'dialogue' between the translation and the author: 'When an author undertakes translation because "it appeals to the author", or "as an extension of their artistic project", there will be interactions with other writing by the author both before and after the translation', in this case, between the translation *Kyacchā in za rai* and the novel *Umibe no Kafuka* written before it.

More important than the influence from Kafuka, however, is that Murakami had carefully studied Salinger's biographical information prior to translating the novel, and he concluded that *The Catcher in the Rye* could be interpreted autobiographically: the life story of Holden could be taken as the lost-in-life Salinger searching for an answer to '[what I might do with my life?]' (Murakami and Shibata 2003: 30, 66). With this interpretation, he also set out his own aim for the translation project:

> [I started feeling like I wanted to try translating *The Catcher in the Rye*, which had become a modern classic, with my own hand. My interest was mainly in its *buntai*. I wondered what I could do with this modern classic, *The Catcher*, in terms of its *buntai*. I suppose it was a bit like a kind of challenge.]
>
> (Murakami 2003: 22)

This challenge of *buntai* eventually became a writerly experiment as we have seen where Murakami incorporates features of his *buntai* into the translation. Here lies the key contrast between Murakami's approach to translation and conventional literary translators such as Nozaki: where Murakami's *Kyacchā in za rai* has always been a subjective interpretation of the source text, Nozaki operates in 'the shadow of the source text' – that is, without showing his own voice and rather focusing mostly on linguistic/textual manoeuvring between the languages (Nikolaou 2006: 20). As Murakami claims, he takes *The Catcher in the Rye* in 'his own hand' and produces *his* version, not *the* version, of the text. This is also why it is less productive to employ traditional understandings of translation (focusing on fidelity) to evaluate Murakami's *Kyacchā in za rai*, because Murakami never meant it to be a 'reproduction' of the source text.

This difference in approach can further be seen in what Nozaki and Murakami aimed to achieve with their work respectively, and here the modernising effect of Murakami's prose discussed in the previous section becomes relevant. Nozaki uses his translator afterword to mainly describe the author Salinger's background information without mentioning any issues concerning the translation processes. The only exception is that he mentions the difficulty of rendering the colloquial language of American teenagers of the 1950s (Nozaki 1984: 338), but even here, his aim is to recreate what he believed to be a '1950s American' flavour in Salinger's novel.[7] Murakami, as can be seen from his thoughts about the novel being autobiographical, is more forthcoming with the vision he has for the translation. He has also said that he deliberately attempted to move the source text away from the 1950s, the time period the novel is actually set, to the 21st century, in the belief that the content of the novel, which portrays the personal struggles of a youth, could apply to the present era (Murakami and Shibata 2003: 63).

Ultimately, it is these visions of Murakami's on the translation project that have informed the textual creativities I have discussed. His intention to transport the target text into the present era explains the frequent occurrence of *katakana* loanwords: unlike the mid-1960s when Nozaki's translation was published, Murakami believed that by 2003 when his translation was released, Japanese readers have become familiar with the American lifestyle, and hence felt it unnecessary to replace terms such as 'fuck you' with Japanese equivalents as Nozaki did (Murakami and Shibata 2003: 64–65). And as he takes on the challenge of the *buntai* in *The Catcher in the Rye*, he mixes his own *buntai* into the target text and creates, through phrases like *yare-yare* or the pronoun *boku*, what Evans calls a 'dialogue' between his writing and his translation. This in turn forms an experimental version of Holden based on Murakami's interpretation. Responding to Shibata Motoyuki's observation that Murakami's Holden uses old-fashioned Japanese idioms such as *seiten no hekireki* (青天の霹靂, a bolt from the blue), Murakami explains that although this is not the kind of language used by regular 16-year-olds, incorporating such language into Holden's speech has helped create a unique personality for the protagonist in Japanese (Murakami and Shibata 2003: 133). Furthermore, speaking of Nozaki's Holden who rebels against the hypocrisy and social values set by adults, Murakami comments that he wanted to show instead a boy who struggles not with society primarily but with himself (ibid.: 25–26). For this reason, Murakami deliberately avoided signs of aggression in the protagonist's voice even though he is aware that *boku* may seem too good to readers, deviating from the familiar image of Holden in Nozaki's existing translation (ibid.: 69).

In short, then, the deviations one may find in *Kyacchā in za rai* from Salinger's original, or indeed from Nozaki's version, are deliberate on Murakami's part. Echoing Nikolaou's 'life-writing' argument, Murakami interprets *The Catcher in the Rye* as a kind of 'life-writing' for Salinger, and accordingly produces a translation that also creatively demonstrates features of his own *buntai*, as another 'life-writing' extension of his oeuvre. As a project of artistic exploration, Murakami re-engineered Holden's personality and created a textual surface reminiscent of his own novels, shifting the target text away from the source context and transporting the reader closer to the world of Murakami, all of which, he is highly aware, is at the expense of translation accuracy and fidelity.

Conclusion

Through comparing Murakami's translation of Salinger's *The Catcher in the Rye* with Nozaki's earlier translation, this chapter has demonstrated how two interconnected senses of creativity, namely textual creativity and writerly creativity, are deeply integrated into Murakami's translation process. Features of Murakami's *buntai*, including *boku*, *yare-yare*, and *katakana* loanwords, are present in *Kyacchā in za rai* not as a matter of habit, but as a result of a combination of factors that demonstrate his subjectivity as a writer: the influence of writing *Umibe no Kafuka* prior to translating *The Catcher in the Rye*, his desire to experiment with the *buntai* of Salinger's novel, as well as his knowledge about Salinger's life. *Kyacchā in za rai* can be considered a biography of Holden, or an autobiography of Salinger imagined and narrated by Murakami. By doing so, Murakami also consciously challenges the novel's established reception in Japan due to Nozaki's earlier translation. Last but not least, Murakami's willingness to share insights to his writerly stance with readers also reminds us that his translation projects are part of his artistic endeavour, and therefore should not be evaluated in the same light as translations made by other translators who are not writers themselves.

A sizeable portion of Murakami's literary production is his translations (for a full list see Murakami 2017), and these therefore deserve to be evaluated as part of his oeuvre as well. Examining Murakami's translations based on the traditional perception of translation as seen in critics' reviews would, however, limit us from appreciating the creativity demonstrated in his translations beyond semantic and stylistic resemblance. A more fruitful evaluation, as this chapter has shown, is to consider Murakami's translations as 'a bidirectional relationship between two texts [source and target texts], two writers', to use Nikolaou's wording (2006: 23), rather than between a translator and a source author.

The idea of translation as 'life-writing' (Nikolaou, 2006: 21) and my sample analysis with *Kyacchā in za rai* here open new opportunities for future research on Murakami's translations of other writers, especially F. Scott Fitzgerald, since Murakami also interprets Fitzgerald's works as autobiographical (2006: 344). Just as Murakami's study of Salinger's life has influenced his translation of *The Catcher in the Rye*, it would be interesting to examine how Murakami's personal understanding of Fitzgerald's life story might have influenced the way his *buntai* and subjectivity as a writer might have interacted with the author's works.

Notes

1 I would like to thank Dr Jonathan Dil for his kind advice and expert opinion on Murakami's works, and Dr Christopher Hayes for reading and commenting on an earlier version of the manuscript.
2 Per conventions in translation studies, the square brackets indicate the author's translations from Japanese originals, unless otherwise indicated.
3 *Buntai* [writing style], a vaguely defined term, can be understood as an author's personal style of writing which consists of particular words and expressions that are repeatedly selected by the author (Makino 2013: 1).
4 The term *iyahaya* is rendered as 'dear me' in the online dictionary Weblio: https://ejje. weblio.jp/content/%E3%81%84%E3%82%84%E3%81%AF%E3%82%84 [Accessed 13 February 2019].
5 *Katakana* is one of the three Japanese syllabaries, typically used for the transcription of foreign words such as loanwords and proper nouns. See Rebuck (2002).
6 The usual Japanese word for Thailand is *Tai* (タイ), and the official Japanese name is *Taiōkoku* (タイ王国), so *Tairando* is idiosyncratic to the Japanese ear.

7 In reality, of course, *The Catcher in the Rye* was serialised in 1945 and released in one volume in 1951, so perhaps 'a 1940s American flavour' would have been more accurate. However, Nozaki might have known the work in its 1951 novel form, hence 1950s.

References

Akashi M. 2018. Translator celebrity: Investigating Haruki Murakami's visibility as a translator [online]. *Celebrity Studies* 9 (2): 271–278. Available from: https://doi.org/10.1080/193923 97.2018.1458531 [Accessed 12 June 2019].

Akashi M. and Hadley, J. 2014. Chomei-hon'yakuka/tekusuto-bunseki/kashisei-gainen: Murakami Haruki ni miru dōka/ika-ron no shinten [Celebrity translators, textual analysis, and the visibility paradigm: How Haruki Murakami can advance domestication–foreignisation thinking]. *Tsūyaku hon'yaku kenkyū* [Interpreting and Translation Studies] 14: 183–201. Available from: http://jaits.jpn.org/home/kaishi2014/14_011-akashi-hadley.pdf [Accessed 9 June 2019].

Dil, J. 2017. *Murakami Haruki and the great Fitzgerald. 23rd Annual Japan Studies Association Conference*, 5–7 January, Honolulu.

Evans, J. P. 2016. *The many voices of Lydia Davis: Translation, rewriting, intertextuality*. Edinburgh: Edinburgh University Press.

Chandler, R. 1953. *The Long Goodbye*. London: Hamish Hamilton.

Che' [online]. n.d. *Weblio*. Available from: https://ejje.weblio.jp/content/%E3%81%A1%E3% 81%87%E3%81%A3 [Accessed 9 June 2019].

Fitzgerald, F. S. 2012/1925. *The Great Gatsby*. London: Harper Collins.

Fujimoto Y. 2006. Bungei hon'yaku no shinjidai: Hon'anshōsetsu kara Murakami Haruki made [From *The Black Cat* to *The Catcher in the Rye*: The evolution of literary translation in Japan] [online]. *The Waseda Journal of Social Sciences* 8: 305–318. Available from: http:// hdl.handle.net/2065/32046 [Accessed 12 June 2019].

Hadley, J. and Akashi, M. 2015. Translation and celebrity: The translation strategies of Haruki Murakami and their implications for the visibility paradigm [online]. *Perspectives: Studies in Translatology* 23 (3): 458–474. Available from: http://www.tandfonline.com/doi/full/10.10 80/0907676X.2014.998688 [Accessed 9 June 2019].

Hasegawa E., et al. 2003. Shujinkō ga itsumo 'boku' na wake: 'Boku' to iu yobitkata no himitsu o saguru [Why the main protagonists are always called *boku*: Discover the secret of the term of address 'boku']. *Bessatsu Takarajima* 743: 107–112.

Hokujō F. 2004. *Hon'yaku to ibunka: Hon'yaku to 'zure' ga katarumono* [Translation and foreign culture: What 'deviation' in translation describes]. Tokyo: Misuzu Shobō.

Katō N. 2006. *Murakami Haruki ronshū (1)* [Murakami Haruki study books 1]. Tokyo: Wakakusa Shobō.

Kawahara K. 2016. Preliminary analysis of translation shifts and translators' conscious and unconscious thinking [online]. *Kinjō Gakuin University Repository* 13 (1): 33–46. Available from: http://id.nii.ac.jp/1096/00000783/ [Accessed 9 June 2019].

Kawakami M. and Murakami H. 2017. *Mimizuku wa tasogare ni tobitatsu: Kawakami Mieko kiku; Murakami Haruki kataru* [The horned owl takes off into twilight: Kawakami Mieko asks/Murakami Haruki speaks]. Tokyo: Shinchōsha.

Kazamaru Y. 2006. *Kikyō suru 'boku': Murakami Haruki, hon'yaku buntai to katarite* [Transgressing borders: Murakami Haruki, translation stylistics and the narrator]. Tokyo: Shironsha.

'*Kaze no uta o kike*' '*1973 nen no pin bōru*' '*Hitsuji o meguru bōken*' '*Dansu dansu dansu*' no shujinkō no 'boku' [The protagonists 'boku' in *Hear the Wind Sing, Pinball, 1973, A Wild*

Sheep Chase, and *Dance Dance Dance*] [online]. n.d. Murakami Haruki Times. Available from: https://murakami-haruki-times.com/boku/index.html [Accessed 9 June 2019]

Keroji. 2011. Hon'yaku shōsetsu no ii tokoro [Good things about translated literature] [online]. Customer review, *Amazon.co.jp*, 14 September. Available from: https://www.amazon.co.jp/product-reviews/4560090009/ref=cm_cr_arp_d_viewopt_srt?ie=UTF8&showViewpoints=1&sortBy=recent&pageNumber=8 [Accessed 8 June 2020].

Koshikawa Y., et al. 2003. Sarinjā futatabi: Murakami Haruki o yomu [Salinger revisited: Reading Murakami Haruki's translation]. *Bungakukai* 57 (6): 284–304.

Kowka. 2020. Jitsu o iu to geri gimi datta [I felt like diarrhoea, to say the truth] [online]. Customer review, *Amazon.co.jp*, 26 February. Available from: https://www.amazon.co.jp/product-reviews/4560090009/ref=cm_cr_arp_d_viewopt_srt?ie=UTF8&showViewpoints=1&sortBy=recent&pageNumber=1 [Accessed 8 June 2020].

Lee D.-Y. and Yonezawa Y. 2008. The role of the overt expression of first and second person subject in Japanese. *Journal of Pragmatics* 40 (4): 733–767.

Lee, H. 2005. *Body parts: Essays on life-writing*. London: Chatto & Windus.

Makino S. 2013. *Murakami Haruki no nihongo wa naze omoshiroinoka: Buntai o chūshin ni* [The reason why the language Murakami Haruki uses is interesting: A focus on his writing style] [online]. *In*: Kubota S., ed. *24th Annual Conference of the Central Association of Teachers of Japanese (CATJ24) Proceedings*, 5–6 October 2013. Ypsilanti: Department of World Languages, Eastern Michigan University, 1–19. Available from: https://commons.emich.edu/catj/1/ [Accessed 9 June 2019].

Murakami H. 1982. *Hitsuji o meguru bōken*. Tokyo: Kōdansha.

——— 1989. Boku ga hon'yaku o hajimeru basho [Where I Start Translation]. *Hon'yaku no sekai* [The World of Translation] 3: 22–29.

——— 2000. *'Sōda, Murakami-san ni kiitemiyō' to seken no hitobito ga Murakami Haruki ni toriaezu buttsukeru 282 no daigimon ni hatashite Murakami-san wa chanto kotaerareru no ka?* ['Oh yeah, let's ask Mr Murakami' Can Mr Murakami Properly Answer 282 Questions that the General Public Throw at Him]. Tokyo: Asahi Shinbunsha.

——— 2002. *Umibe no kafuka*. Tokyo: Shinchōsha.

——— 2003. *Kyacchā in za rai*. Translation of *The Catcher in the Rye* by J. D. Salinger. Tokyo: Hakusuisha.

——— 2006. *Gurēto Gatsubī*. Translation of *The Great Gatsby* by F. S. Fitzgerald. Tokyo: Chūōkōron Shinsha.

——— 2015. *Shokugyō toshite no shōsetsuka* [Novelist as a Vocation]. Tokyo: Switch Publishing.

——— 2017. *Murakami Haruki hon'yaku (hotondo) zenshigoto* [(Nearly All) Translation Works of Murakami Haruki]. Tokyo: Chūōkōron Shinsha.

Murakami H. and Shibata M. 2000. *Hon'yaku yawa* [A Casual Talk on Translation]. Tokyo: Bungei Shunjū.

Murakami H. 2003. *Hon'yaku yawa 2: Sarinjā senki* [A Casual Talk on Translation 2: A Record of the Salinger War]. Tokyo: Bungei Shunjū.

——— 2019. *Honto no hon'yaku no hanashi o shiyo* [Let's Talk About Real Translation]. Tokyo: Switch Publishing.

Murakami Haruki 'yare-yare' chōsadan [Murakami Haruki 'yare-yare' investigation committee] [online]. n.d. *Murakami Haruki Shinbun* [Murakami Haruki Times]. Available from: http://murakami-haruki-times.com/yareyare/ [Accessed 9 June 2019].

Mutenhakase. 2019. Rikai suru no dewa naku kanjiru shōsetsu [A novel that you should feel rather than trying to understand] [online]. Customer review, *Amazon.co.jp*, 20 March. Available from: https://www.amazon.co.jp/product-reviews/4560090009/ref=cm_cr_arp_d_viewopt_srt?ie=UTF8&showViewpoints=1&sortBy=recent&pageNumber=2 [Accessed 8 June 2020].

Nakamura K. and Dōzen H. 2018. 'Yare-yare' ni tsuite kataru toki ni wareware no katarukoto [What we talk about when we talk about '*yare-yare*']. *In:* Dōzen H., ed. *Murakami Haruki go jiten* [Dictionary of Murakami Haruki words]. Tokyo: Seibundō Shinkōsha, 172–173.

solaou, P. 2006. Notes on translating self. *In:* M. Perteghella and E. Loffredo, eds. *Translation and creativity: Perspectives on creative writing and translation studies*. London/New York: Continuum, 19–32.

Nihei C. 2013. Resistance and negotiation: 'Herbivorous men' and Murakami Haruki's gender and political ambiguity [online]. *Asian Studies Review* 37 (1): 62–79. Available from: http://www.tandfonline.com/doi/abs/10.1080/10357823.2012.760528 [Accessed 9 June 2019].

Nozaki T. 1984. *Raimugibatake de tsukamaete*. Translation of *The Catcher in the Rye* by J. D. Salinger. 2nd ed. Tokyo: Hakusuisha.

Ōsawa A. 2007. Murakami Haruki ban '*Rongu guddobai*' Shimizu yaku kara hanseiki [Murakami Haruki's version of *The Long Goodbye*: Half a century since translated by Shimizu]. *Asahi Shinbun*, 14 March.

Perteghella, M. and Loffredo, E., eds. 2006. *Translation and creativity: Perspectives on creative writing and translation studies*. London/New York: Bloomsbury.

Pigumon. 2003. Haruki san gomennasai watashi yappari raimugi ga suki [I'm sorry Haruki, I like *Raimugi* after all] [online]. Customer review, *Amazon.co.jp*, 23 April. Available from: https://www.amazon.co.jp/product-reviews/4560090009/ref=cm_cr_arp_d_viewopt_srt?ie=UTF8&showViewpoints=1&sortBy=recent&pageNumber=14 [Accessed 8 June 2020].

Rebuck, M. 2002. The function of English loanwords in Japanese. *Nagoya University of Commerce and Business Administration Journal of Language, Culture and Communication* 4 (1): 53–64.

Rubin, J. 2002. *Haruki Murakami and the music of words*. London: Harvill Press.

Salinger, J. D. 2010 [1951]. *The Catcher in the Rye*. London: Penguin Books.

Satō M. 2009. Shin'yaku o meguru hon'yaku hihyōhikaku [An analysis of the current reviews of literary retranslations in Japan] [online]. *Media and Communication Studies* 57: 1–20. Available from: http://hdl.handle.net/2115/40054 [Accessed 12 June 2019].

Suter, R. 2008. *The Japanization of modernity: Murakami Haruki between Japan and the United States*. Cambridge/London: Harvard University Press.

Woodsworth, J. 2017. Introduction: 'One more possession of beauty'. *In: Telling the story of translation: Writers who translate*. London: Bloomsbury, 1–10.

Yare-yare (やれやれ) [online] n.d. *Weblio*. Available from: https://ejje.weblio.jp/content/%E3%82%84%E3%82%8C%E3%82%84%E3%82%8C [Accessed 13 February 2019].

PART IV

Personal stories
from the industry

14

CHASING WILD SHEEP

The breakthrough of Murakami Haruki in the West[1]

Elmer Luke

The Shōwa era (1926–1989) was in its final year when I landed in Tokyo, and the Heisei era (1989–2019) soon to launch. I don't know how aware I was of the big picture at the time, but without a doubt it was a moment larger than the passing of an emperorship after 62 years – a moment, given history, of no insignificance itself. It was a moment that coincided with Japan's spectacular emergence onto the global stage.

Japan had been undergoing enormous changes within and without. The economy was thriving, companies were expanding, people had cash they weren't used to having, technology was exploding, fashion designers were recognised internationally, and writers were writing (as they always have). Suddenly, it seemed, Japan was in the world's eye. Suddenly, this unfamiliar, non-Western, non-European, non-white nation, with a funny non-Romance language based on Chinese ideographs, was the newest, flashiest kid on the block. Japan, long associated with Zen, had broken through with yen, even as few countries seemed to have more than a cursory familiarity with anything culturally Japanese. Soon, from around the world, newspapers, magazines, press agencies – the media of those days – had flooded into Tokyo, setting up bureaus, eager for intelligence, curiosities, exposés, and inside stories of corporate life, MITI [the then-Ministry of International Trade and Industry], technology, and the stock market, but also about sushi, the bullet train, trains that ran on time, kabuki, common courtesy, and, it turned out, literature.

For most people reading this, the reprise of those times may seem obvious, unnecessary background, but now that we have entered Reiwa – after Heisei lasting a mere half as many years as Shōwa – and time seems to pass at hyper-speed, it may be easy to forget the context that brought us to a volume such as this – and, by extrapolation, to the state of Japanese literature today.

In any case, this was my entry onto the scene where I was to become the first English editor of Murakami Haruki as he made his way in the anglophone world.

Modern Japanese literature as the Big Three

At the time, as regards Japanese literature as I knew it, and probably as most Western readers knew it, modern Japanese literature was comprised primarily of Japan's Big Three (which is not to conflate them with car manufacturers, even as vital as they were): Tanizaki Jun'ichirō, Mishima Yukio, and Kawabata Yasunari. There were others on the radar screen – Abe Kōbō and Ōe Kenzaburō were an important two, following a long literary tradition before them. But for the most part, and for good or bad, the Big Three controlled the Western popular awareness as far as Japanese literature was concerned.

Of course, the indisputable reason why the Big Three were known to Western readers and seemed to define the entire field of Japanese literature – was quite simple or, some might say, simplistic. It was because they got translated. And they happen to have been translated very well. In fact, they got translated so well that some scholars have claimed that the Big Three skewed Western perception of Japanese literature because of the particular literary or sexual tastes of the translators and publishers and writers themselves. Interesting notion, but I'll leave that bit of territory for others to wade into.

The thing about writers, whether Japanese or Chinese or Korean, or French or Russian or Portuguese, or Arabic or Pakistani, is that they *need* to be translated if they are to have an international audience, and it helps tremendously if they are translated by people who do them justice. Moreover, the terrible fact of life is that English is, for the foreseeable future, the closest there is to a lingua franca of the world, and English translations thus are key to an international readership. It also accounts for why I am here, writing this, in English. English is the language anyone who works at the United Nations needs to know; it's the language of medicine and science (which once used to be German); it's the language taxi drivers in Tokyo and Bangkok and Shanghai and Milan and Mexico City understand. I can even attest to the fact that new Chinese immigrants in New York, if they do not speak the same dialect, will speak to each other in English! Anyway, the point here is that in order to be known beyond Japanese borders, Japanese writers needed to be translated; they needed to be translated well; they needed the translations to attract interest and admiration and, even, passion.

Which is how these Big Three Japanese authors got to be known in the West and why they have endured. How these three authors got to be the Big Three has a history of its own – and it's not a history about money; it's about love.

From what I can piece together, in 1946, during the US Occupation of Japan, an army officer by the name of Harold Strauss was stationed in Kyoto. Because of his recently acquired ability with the Japanese language, he was given the task of monitoring publications – reviewing the contents and trends of magazines and books. Strauss, who was then in his late 30s, was dazzled by what he discovered, developed a genuine appreciation and respect for Japanese culture, and had, one might be led to imagine, an affair with a Japanese woman. In the short story 'Ayamé' that Strauss published in 1954 in *The New Yorker* magazine, the main character, a white American by the name of Harry, located in Tokyo during the Occupation, embarks upon a love affair with a Japanese woman. The woman is very accomplished in the arts, but she is a geisha, which means she is 'owned' by a house, which ordinarily looks after a geisha's daily necessities. The woman dares to break this arrangement and move in with Harry. In time, Harry's orders take him out of Tokyo, on to a ship, and eventually back to the US. It's a not-unfamiliar theme that evokes strains from Puccini's *Madama Butterfly* (1904) as well as James Michener's novel *Sayonara* (1953) that was captured on screen with Marlon Brando in the main role.

In Strauss's story, the lovers keep in touch by letter, with Harry sending her gifts and food and money. But the woman, alone now, is tainted by having lived openly with a *gaijin* [foreigner],[2] and when anti-American sentiment grows nasty, she is subjected to taunts of *rashamen, rashamen*, the rude word for women who sleep with foreigners. She tries to make a living as a seamstress of Western clothing, but no one gives her work. To survive, she is forced to find a patron. … Six years later, the US Occupation has ended, and Harry returns to Japan eager to pick up where he left off. Yet, however much his lover wishes to see him, she now must not: she is committed to her patron. The story ends heavy with heartache.

But the story wasn't over. Harold Strauss, the author of the story, had been working at a publishing house in New York before he was sent to Japan during the Occupation. Japan, actually, was a surprise destination for him; he'd thought it'd be Europe, which he had some familiarity with. Instead, it was Japan, which proved to be so different, so culturally rich and mannered, and – it might not be too much to say – thrilling. When he returned to New York, he returned to his job as editor-in-chief of Alfred A. Knopf, bringing back with him a passion for contemporary Japanese literature. Now, with care and deliberation, he proceeded to create a programme of Japanese literature in translation; it would be a publishing breakthrough. His reading ability in Japanese was good but limited, so he consulted with scholars and writers in the US and Japan, and he cultivated young translators. One translator was Edward Seidensticker, who two years earlier had published 'The Izu Dancer' – a translation of Kawabata's short story 'Izu no odoriko' (1926) – in *The Atlantic* magazine. (Seidensticker, incidentally, had also served in the military, also as a language specialist.)

For his first title in the series, Strauss settled on a novel by Tanizaki about the psychological complexities of a disintegrating marriage, a novel that bore the unwieldy title *Tade kuu mushi*. The novel opens with an epigram, which Seidensticker translated as: 'Every worm to his taste; some prefer to eat nettles'. This, for an apt breed of readers of English, is the kind of line that makes traffic stop. (Indeed, the title translates into something on the order of 'insects that eat an unappetising weed with spikes'.) Seidensticker was good from the beginning, and Strauss was his impresario. The novel was published in 1955 with the title *Some Prefer Nettles*. It was a brilliant title, a brilliant translation, and the first time the Western world had been given the chance to hear a Japanese voice in a modern context. It also lent a stunning view into a culture that had existed only remotely in the imagination, touching emotions shared even as their expression differed, and fuelling at the same time visions of an inscrutable kimono-clad Japan.

I have no numbers at my disposal, but I doubt that this novel was anywhere near a bestseller when it was published. I do know that the novel made a strong enough impact to be significant for opening the door, through literature, to this culture in the East. The book has never gone out of print, turning out to be a very wise publishing investment.

Harold Strauss's love affair with Japanese literature did not fade. *Some Preferred Nettles* was followed by *The Sound of the Waves*, by Mishima Yukio (1956, trans. by Meredith Weatherby; *Shiosai* [1954]); *Snow Country*, by Kawabata (1956, trans. by Seidensticker; *Yukiguni* [1935–1937]); *The Makioka Sisters*, by Tanizaki (1957, trans. by Seidensticker; *Sasameyuki* [1943–1948]); *Thousand Cranes*, by Kawabata (1958, trans. by Seidensticker; *Senbazuru* [1949–1952]); *The Temple of the Golden Pavilion*, by Mishima (1959, trans. by Ivan Morris; *Kinkakuji* [1956]); *After the Banquet*, by Mishima (1963, trans. by Donald Keene; *Utage no ato* [1960]); *The Sailor Who Fell from Grace with the Sea*, by Mishima (1965, trans. by John Nathan; *Gogo no eikō* [1963]) … One begins to see how the Big Three came to be.

Who were these first translators of Japanese literature? For several of them, it was the military that first brought them to Japan. That was the case with Seidensticker, as it was with Donald Keene, who has achieved Japanese sainthood; it was the case with Howard Hibbett, Ivan Morris, and Dale Saunders. The subsequent group of translators included John Nathan, an academic who was the first Westerner to attend the University of Tokyo; Alfred Marks, who began his career teaching early American literature; and Michael Gallagher, who was a Jesuit scholar and had been a paratrooper in Korea. Corny to say, but if I may repeat, these guys weren't doing it for the money (because one does not get rich from translation); they did it for love.

In 1968, as Strauss was cutting back his duties at Knopf, the publisher brought in Robert Gottlieb to be editor-in-chief. Strauss continued to work as consulting editor, however, and continued to publish his true love, Japanese literature. That year he published *Forbidden Colors*, by Mishima (trans. by Marks; *Kinjiki* [1951–1953]), which was shocking for its homosexual content; and the next year he published *Thirst for Love*, also by Mishima (1969, trans. by Marks; *Ai no kawaki* [1950]); this was followed by Mishima's final tetralogy: *Spring Snow* (1972, trans. by Gallagher; *Haru no yuki* [1965–1967]), *Runaway Horses* (1973, trans. by Gallagher; *Honba* [1967–1968]), *The Temple of Dawn* (1973, trans. by Saunders; *Akatsuki no tera* [1968–1970]), and *The Decay of the Angel* (1974, trans. by Seidensticker; *Tennin gosui* [1970–1971]). And then Strauss really retired. He was a very hands-on editor. He might not have known the Japanese language well enough to discern the literary nuances of a novel in its original, but he knew whom to seek advice from – people whose taste and intelligence he trusted – and from this bit of research decided which books to publish; he worked closely with the translators on language and wording and even the titles of the books; and he corresponded directly with the Big Three themselves – the letters can be found in the Knopf archives.

I might add as an extended footnote that Strauss also published five novels by Abe Kōbō, starting with *Woman in the Dunes* (trans. by Saunders; *Suna no onna* [1962]) in

1964, which sold very well following upon the remarkable 1964 film by Teshigahara Hiroshi that won the Special Jury Prize at Cannes. Abe's other novels, some of which had a kind of science-fictional bent, were less accessible, and less successful. Even after Strauss retired, Knopf continued to publish Abe, but Abe never achieved the elevated status of the Big Three.

Knopf never published Ōe, who went on to win the Nobel in 1994.

It was Robert Gottlieb, who as editor-in-chief of *The New Yorker* published 'TV People' (1990; 'TV pīpuru' [1989]), the first story of Murakami Haruki's to appear in the magazine.

And Knopf has for 30 years been Murakami's US publisher.

Japan and Murakami at the cusp

Which brings me back to the question: What did I know about Japanese literature when I moved to Tokyo at the turn of the eras from Shōwa to Heisei? As I said, it was primarily the Big Three, the legacy of Harold Strauss, which had been a monopoly for an entire generation.

But Japan, like its literature, had been changing in those years. Its economics had changed, its culture had changed, manners had changed, priorities, tastes, human needs, and desires had changed; hair colour, however, had *not* changed yet. (If a high school student had a natural *chapatsu* – brown or reddish 'tea-coloured hair' – the poor kid would have had to dye his or her hair black. *That* surely has changed!) Japanese literature was beginning to reflect these changes – in detail as in style as in creativity.

I first met Katō Norihiro in the early 1980s in Montreal. I was visiting Tada Michitarō, a Kyoto University professor whom I had worked with earlier and who was on sabbatical there, and Katō-sensei happened to come by. A few years later, when I was a junior editor visiting Tokyo from New York, I had the opportunity to meet Katō-sensei again, and over dinner I remember asking him which writers young Japanese were reading and whether he had any recommendations about what should be translated into English. His answer was quick and enthusiastic: a writer by the name of Murakami Haruki, and the novel he recommended was *Sekai no owari to hādoboirudo wandārando* (1985; trans. *Hard-Boiled Wonderland and the End of the World* [1991]), which had just been published to great acclaim. There were a few other authors and titles that he suggested, writing them down on a torn-off piece of paper. I kept the little piece of paper for years (although I no longer can find it) and remember at one point checking off the titles and authors from the list. *Sekai no owari to hādoboirudo wandārando*, yes, of course – it was his magnum opus then. (Murakami Ryū and Takahashi Gen'ichirō were on the list too, and I was pleased to eventually have had occasion to edit translations of short stories of theirs.)

So that was how the great Haruki experience began for me. I didn't know much. I was in many ways a beginner. And like Harold Strauss, although our shared deficiencies in language are the limit to any comparison, I had some help along the way:

from Katō-sensei, from academic acquaintances, from colleagues, from friends both Japanese and not.

In the late 1980s, with the many changes Japan was undergoing, the moment seemed ripe for introducing this new writer to the West (at least it is in retrospect; at the time it was a lot of wishful thinking). In a way similar to Japan's opening up to the West – in finance, in baseball, even in publishing houses – the West was opening up to what Japan could offer. There was, more than ever before, this predisposition to mutual discovery.

And this was what I walked into when I arrived in 1988 at Kodansha International. I had by then been a book editor for several years in New York. This was the time of the 'bubble', Japan was on everyone's mind, and books on Japan were in vogue. Most were nonfiction – about finance, business, the automobile industry, and the threat of Japan. Chalmers Johnson's *MITI and the Japanese Miracle* (1982) and Ezra Vogel's *Japan as Number One* (1979) were important texts. I had got into the act myself when I published *Japanese Business Etiquette*, which was a simple handbook for *gaijin* who knew little about simple Japanese etiquette, like bowing and presenting *meishi* (business cards) and pouring drinks for your host. The book was far from a bestseller, but it did find its market and it sold and sold and sold and sold, for a dozen years it sold. As regards fiction, there'd been a constant trickle of translations from the Japanese, but no title, or author, had ever risen to anywhere near Big Three status. Fiction, translated fiction, however worthwhile, was not an easy sell. (*Rising Sun*, the thriller by Michael Crichton, was of course not Japanese but capitalised on fears of Japan; it was published in 1992, was set in Los Angeles, and was a huge commercial success.)

Tokyo, even in modern 1988, was a shock. The commute was shocking (in New York it had been a ten-minute subway ride to work), the company was shocking (I had to punch a time clock – which I'd only ever done at a pineapple cannery during a summer job); I had to photocopy manuscripts by myself (no such thing as an assistant); and everything was so expensive it was like haemorrhaging cash.

The other New York editor who arrived with me was a fellow by the name of Leslie Pockell. He was to be co-editorial director at the publishing house with Asakawa Minato, who was Japanese, had attended Stanford University, was well experienced in Japanese publishing, and has since written several books. They were very smart, very good men. The organisation at Kodansha International was such that there were six *gaijin* editors and six Japanese editors. A *gaijin* editor would be partnered with a Japanese editor on specific books, and each editor seemed to have a specialty carved out: crafts, language study, art, architecture, popular culture, travel, cookbooks, and literature in translation that leaned toward the traditional, that is to say, deep Shōwa. It was what the West had become used to.

In 1988 Murakami Haruki was not an unknown writer in Japan. Far from it. In 1987 he had written, and Kōdansha had published, *Noruwei no mori* (trans. *Norwegian Wood* [1989]), which turned out to be a serious blockbuster. At the time, the book had already sold, in two volumes, around three million copies. Murakami fled to Rome – Italy – where he and his wife Yōko could find peace and quiet, far from the madding Japanese media crowd, and where Murakami could work. This guy didn't know how to relax! When he wasn't writing novels, he was translating – and at the time, I believe he was translating a collection of stories by Raymond Carver.

Kodansha International had previously published translations of Murakami's first two novels – *Hear the Wind Sing* (1987; *Kaze no uta o kike* [1979]), and *Pinball 1973* (1985; *1973 nen no pinbōru* [1980]) – in *eigo bunko* format, which were pocket-sized editions aimed at the high school and university market in Japan. Essentially they were English language lessons – utterly literal, nearly word-for-word translations that included footnotes to explain tricky terms. The translator was Alfred Birnbaum.

Hitsuji o meguru bōken (1982; trans. *A Wild Sheep Chase* [1989]), Murakami's third novel, however, was, in Murakami's own words, 'the first book where I could feel a kind of sensation, the joy of telling a story. When you read a good story, you just keep reading. When I write a good story, I just keep writing' (Devereaux 1991). And Murakami was absolutely right. *Hitsuji o meguru bōken* was a good story, a very good story, and it made you want to just keep on reading. It was also, according to Katō-sensei, the last novel Murakami had written by hand, as opposed to tapping it out on a keyboard. Anyway, the novel represented a huge leap for Murakami. The directors at Kodansha International understood this and, perhaps seeking an editorial sense different from what had been the standard, or perhaps just wanting to try this New York editor out, asked me to take it on and edit it. The decision was made to treat this title as a *real book*, not as a language lesson, and to publish it in hardcover, as a big, debut novel – which may have been a first such publishing decision for Kodansha International. This was explained to the translator Birnbaum, who, it seems, was suddenly set free – because what he produced was nothing like what he'd done before.

Birnbaum's translation of the title alone was an indication of things to come. *Hitsuji o meguru bōken* literally means 'Adventures with a Sheep'. The excitement dulls. Birnbaum suggested instead *A Wild Sheep Chase*; I don't know how he came up with it, because it's not readily obvious, but it captured the tone of the novel perfectly. In fact, today, everyone, including Murakami himself, refers to *A Wild Sheep Chase* as if it were a literal translation of the original – in the way that other English language titles of his novels really are literal translations of the original. So, with the title alone, things were looking promising.

Ditto with Birnbaum's translation of the novel. I had never read a translation like it before. It had style, wit, humour; it had irony, self-deprecation, and a moral centre. It had, in other words, captured the essence of what Murakami intended – which Katō-sensei suggested as well. In what may not be the most appetising of comparisons, Birnbaum had ingested both Murakami's words and the meaning of the words, and coughed them back up for the reader, rather like what a mother bird does to feed her young, in words and tone and sense that could be appreciated in another culture. The sound of his words – the *sound*, to my mind, is the test of all language – was spot on.

Perhaps Japanese readers came to understand a little of this when they read Murakami's translations of Raymond Carver. (That I cannot judge myself, but it is notable that Murakami has translated several writers besides Carver – including J.

D. Salinger – for whom sound was also critical.)[3] Some have said that Carver's sensibilities even infuse Murakami's own writing – but that's another matter. As regards Murakami's translations of Carver's work, circumstantial evidence suggests Murakami sells more copies of Carver in Japanese than Carver has done in English!

I went to work editing Birnbaum's translation, and Kodansha International gave me the enormous support of affording me the time to do it. When you get something good, you want to spend time on it to make it *really* good. I sounded out every word, every sentence, knew the novel inside and out. I knew no moderation. And I had the support of the company behind me while I was at it.

I suspect that in the beginning we – Birnbaum and Murakami and I – were a little wary of one another – I was this excitable Asian American from New York whose *nihongo* [Japanese] was broken at best – but in time we learnt to trust each other and became friends.

What did we do in preparation for this debut novel of Murakami Haruki? In close coordination with Kodansha's marketing office in New York, we worked out a strategy. The novel would be positioned not only as postmodern, but post–Big Three. No kimono, no inscrutability; instead there was jazz and Scotch whisky and regular old alienation with a nice guy of a narrator who has otherworldly experiences. And in this case, it is an encounter with a Sheep Man who spoke, in the brilliant language of Birnbaum, in sentences that had no spaces between the words. We situated Murakami as the vanguard, the voice of a new Japan, an author whose characters were current, accessible, and knowable – in a break from the old Japan, where the flowers of an *obi* or a flick of the wrist could convey sentiment and social standing. We reminded people that not since the spectacular suicide in 1970 of Mishima Yukio – a dazzling writer with issues – had there been a writer to capture the Western imagination.

We printed Advance Reading Copies, known as ARCs, which were bound galleys with the four-colour art of the actual jacket art of the book to come. These ARCs were sent to bookstore buyers, reviewers, film producers, writers, publishers, editors, friends, relatives – anyone who could talk about the book and generate interest. And I was convinced there would be. (A buyer for the Elliott Bay Book Company, a landmark in Seattle, remembers to this day receiving his ARC of *A Wild Sheep Chase*.)

I was right. Before the publication date, Kodansha International was able to secure a very respectable floor price for the paperback rights to the book; book club rights were auctioned off; and we were on our way.

I laboured on the promotional copy and I dreamed about the flap copy. Flap copy is a critical thing. Its purpose is to place the book into context for a potential reader, to give them a sense of the plot and theme and background of the book – and, most importantly, to persuade them to buy the book. In other words, you tell the reader what and how and why to think about this novel, and by doing so, you also give reviewers and critics a handle with which to understand the book. Sometimes, I discovered, reviewers will even use flap copies in their reviews as if the words were theirs. Here is how the flap copy read:

With the publication of *A Wild Sheep Chase*, readers in the West will be introduced to the prodigious talents of Haruki Murakami, the leading novelist of modern Japan. Murakami has been lauded by Japanese critics and readers alike, hailed as the distinctive voice of a new generation. It is a voice that readers, literally in the millions, have given themselves over to, a voice the likes of which no Western reader of Japanese literature will have encountered before.

The time is now, the setting is Japan – minus the kimono and the impenetrable mystique of an exotic, distant culture. The narrator, identified only by a pronoun, is on principle an ordinary fellow. Thirty years old, he has more intelligence than an overachieving businessman, but no ambition and little purpose. Enter into this lacklustre life a young woman, apparently ordinary as well but with ears so gorgeous that all conversation stops in the presence of their unveiling; a right-wing boss with a golfball-sized blood cyst on his brain who's unaccountably been spared standing trial as a Class A war criminal; a sinister, all-efficient lieutenant with beautiful hands and a degree from Stanford; and a brilliant professor permanently sidetracked by an animal experience that in forty-two years has not dimmed in significance.

Inexorably all are impelled into the bizarre pursuit of a dream-induced sheep. But this is no ordinary sheep. With a star on its back, eyes as clear as spring water, and a near-irresistible spiritual allure, the sheep embodies a perverse Nietzschean will to absolute power. The pursuit of this fantastic *super*sheep begins in the urban haunts of Tokyo, continues at a garish suburban estate, and culminates in the lonely mountainous snow country of Hokkaido.

Here, in Haruki Murakami's dazzling debut in the West, is a feat of the imagination, a tale – not easily forgotten – of enchantment, suspense, and human mystery.

A Wild Sheep Chase was published in the US in October 1989. Much of the groundwork for publicity and promotion had been laid, and it paid off with a *New York Times* review on the date of publication. It was like a seed planted, and soon reviews popped up everywhere.

And the critical reception was tremendous.

The *New Yorker* wrote: 'It is difficult not to regard *A Wild Sheep Chase* as an event larger even than its considerable virtues merit. Many years have elapsed, after all, since any Japanese novelist was enthusiastically taken up by the American reading public – and this may soon be Murakami's destiny'.

The Los Angeles Times: 'In a staccato, hard-boiled American style, Murakami tattoos out short, snappy sentences of world-weary deadpan. [...] Alfred Birnbaum's excellent translation has gotten his sentences down exactly right'.

The Observer of London: 'A cross between Woody Allen and Franz Kafka'.

The Michigan Daily: 'Unreal, extraordinary, exceptional. [...] It's weird. It's not particularly traditional. It's damn fun to read'.

The Toronto Globe and Mail: 'A metaphysical mystery tour'.

The Wall Street Journal: 'It's refreshing to read a Japanese author who clearly does not belong to the self-aggrandizing "we-Japanese" school of writers who perpetuate the notion of the unique Japanese, unfathomable to others'.

My memory of dates may be off here, but I recall arranging for Murakami and his wife to go to New York for publication of the novel. I met them there, accompanying them to various events and places. We had a small publication party for the then-unknown Haruki Murakami – rather as a way to introduce him to editors, publishers, agents, writers, translators, select magazines, and media, to get him into the flow of things. Murakami of course did not know any of these people, though he now may – certainly they all now know who he is – and I imagine it was nervous-making for him, a shy guy, to be suddenly the centre of attention at a cocktail party in a foreign city, with people speaking to him in English with New York accents at New York speed. To be honest, I suspect people then were more curious than anything else, they'd only just heard of this guy: who was he, what was the deal? But New Yorkers love a cocktail party, and I do remember that Andrew Wylie, one of the smartest – and most aggressive – literary agents in the world (people call him 'The Jackal'), suggested that we all go off for a *nijikai* (afterparty), and he paid for the drinks!

During the day, I accompanied Murakami and Yōko to bookstores, if only to show them what New York bookstores were like and how his book was displayed. At Three Lives & Company, a terrific, charming independent bookstore in Greenwich Village that was a favourite of mine, I introduced him to the manager. She was gracious, but ignorant. I don't mean anything ill by that: Murakami was a new author – and in New York new authors were, and still are, a dime a dozen. And he was foreign. But fast forward 25 years, and like many other bookstores around the world, Three Lives is holding midnight – yes, midnight – book launch parties to commemorate the publication days of Murakami's books. At the stroke of midnight, stacks of books go on sale. In the meantime, the store is packed, spirits are high, and people are playing games: the Murakami Bingo Board, Name That Novel (which work a memorable sentence is from), Murakami Trivial Pursuits.

It's quite laughable now. Because I remember walking along then, fantasising at how amazing it would be if readers connected with Murakami and this book made it to the bestseller list. Well, that *would* have been amazing, and it didn't happen. But now it does, with regularity. It's safe to say that readers the world over have connected with Murakami, and he with them, and his books are now on bestseller lists everywhere.

Post-publication, back in Tokyo, I talked up Murakami every chance I could. The city was full of journalists from the West, there to provide a record of the 'bubble', and I ate and drank with bureau chiefs and hungry correspondents every chance I got. This being the time of great interest in Japan, I didn't have to beg, although I had to persuade. People wanted the story, saw the news value, asked for interviews. This wasn't so easily arranged, since Murakami was living in Rome and had an allergy to the media. In any case, in these times and under these circumstances, the word about

Murakami got out, almost in reverse *gai-atsu* [foreign pressure ordinarily exerted on Japan from abroad]. That is, articles were filed from Tokyo and published in the West.

Translations, translators, and …

There was also the matter of foreign rights. Perhaps every author wants not only to be read but also translated, whether from Japanese to English – or vice versa – or to any other language. It is the elation of being heard, and listened to, extending one's voice, one's reach, far beyond one's own national borders. With the publicity surrounding *A Wild Sheep Chase*, suddenly there was interest from publishers in Europe wanting to purchase translation rights. My memory is hazy on this too, even though I actually was the person to sell the rights: I believe rights were sold to France, Germany, Italy, and maybe Sweden too. I remember holding an auction in the middle of the night with two Dutch publishers. And in the UK there was the sale to Hamish Hamilton, then a part of Penguin.

When the British edition of *A Wild Sheep Chase* was published a year later, Murakami and his wife were invited to London to promote the book and I accompanied them there. All this was but a prelude, it has turned out, to the reception that Murakami now always gets around the world.

I wrote earlier of how, no matter how good an author is in his or her own language, it is necessarily the translator that is the deliverer of the author's words to another language. I said this in reference to Edward Seidensticker, who was first asked by Harold Strauss at Knopf to translate Tanizaki's *Some Prefer Nettles*. Seidensticker – as fine a translator of Japanese literature as there's ever been – then went on to translate Kawabata: *Snow Country*, *Thousand Cranes*, *The Master of Go* (1972; *Meijin* [1951–1954]), *The House of the Sleeping Beauties* (1969; *Nemureru bijo* [1961]). There was, obviously, a simpatico in literary sensibility that Kawabata and Seidensticker shared, but there is also no doubt that Seidensticker's translations were significant in the Swedish Academy's decision to award Kawabata the Nobel Prize for literature in 1968.

Kawabata was the first Japanese author to receive the Nobel prize, and Kawabata, in full acknowledgement of Seidensticker's efforts, not only invited him to the Nobel award ceremony in Stockholm but also offered Seidensticker half the prize money (the full prize of which is today worth USD 1.15 million; then it was around $350,000). Seidensticker was happy to go to Stockholm, but he declined Kawabata's generosity.

Similarly, it was Alfred Birnbaum's words – in *A Wild Sheep Chase*, in *Hard-Boiled Wonderland and the End of the World*, and in *Dance Dance Dance* (1994; *Dansu dansu dansu* [1988]) – that first brought the novels of Murakami Haruki to readers in the West. (As it was John Nathan's words – in *A Personal Matter* (1968; *Kojinteki na taiken* [1964]) – that first brought the writing of Ōe to English readers.)

So in the sense of being the first translator to introduce a Japanese writer to a Western readership, what Seidensticker did for Kawabata, Alfred Birnbaum did for Murakami. Many readers, and even judges of translation prizes, have said to me, with a drink in hand, that *A Wild Sheep Chase* may still be the best of Murakami's works in

English. (Jay Rubin, another translator of Murakami, contends Birnbaum went too far in some instances; Rubin surely has a style of his own, but nothing of Birnbaum's out-of-the-box imagination.) Whether one agrees or not is one thing; what cannot be argued is that Birnbaum's translation of *A Wild Sheep Chase* introduced Murakami to his Western readership and jumpstarted the interest in him. Without this translation it is not certain that Murakami Haruki would be the international phenomenon we know today.

Finally, a coda, coming round to my perhaps facile comparison of eras in Japan to eras of Japanese literature. Since Harold Strauss's launch of the Big Three in Shōwa, followed by the flourish of Murakami in Heisei, the publishing environment has broadened significantly. For all sorts of reasons, the world has grown more expansive, and less provincial, but as far as Japanese literature is concerned, I dare say it has been lifted by an ever-developing excellence in writing and in translations and translators. While eras are arbitrary and overlap, Reiwa, just a few years in, has already been witness to this abundance: Ogawa Yōko's *Memory Police* (2019; *Hisoyaka na kesshō* [1994]), translated by Stephen Snyder, published by Pantheon, an imprint of Knopf, named one of the Notable Books of 2019 by *The New York Times*; Murata Sayaka's *Convenience Store Woman* (2018; *Konbini ningen* [2016]), translated by Ginny Tapley Takemori, published by Grove, named a Best Book of 2019 by *The New Yorker*; Yu Miri's *Tokyo Ueno Station* (2019; *JR Ueno Eki Kōenguchi* [2014]), translated by Morgan Giles, published by Riverhead, declared the winner of the 2020 US National Book Awards' Translated Literature Prize; and Kawakami Mieko's *Breasts and Eggs* (2020; *Natsu-monogatari* [2019]), translated by Sam Bett and David Boyd, published by Europa Editions, enjoying as wide critical acclaim as an author can attract in this pandemic year. (The listing is not conclusive, let me hasten to add, with several very well-received authors and titles that precede and follow the limited time period I speak of here.) In no small way, this breakthrough has been spurred by the success Murakami Haruki has commanded.

Notes

1 This chapter was adapted from a 2009 lecture given at a class on Japanese literature taught by Katō Norihiro at Waseda University. It was edited for this volume in October 2020.
2 Usage of the term *gaijin*, meaning literally 'outside person', can be controversial. Objectively it distinguishes between insider (a person of Japanese heritage) and outsider (a person of non-Japanese heritage, whether a resident of Japan or not, a foreigner), but it also carries the connotation of exclusion: if you are not in, you are out. I have used the term in this chapter to suggest both its objective distinction and the connotation of exclusion.
3 See Akashi in this volume for a discussion of Murakami's translations of J. D. Salinger.

Reference

Devereaux, E. 1991. PW interviews: Haruki Murakami. *Publishers Weekly*, 228 (42), 113–114.

15

TWO OLD TRANSLATORS RECALL THE MURAKAMI PHENOMENON

Jay Rubin and Ted Goossen

When Gitte Marianne Hansen and Michael Tsang, the editors of this volume, suggested that friends Jay Rubin and Ted Goossen co-author an article on their respective experiences translating the works of Murakami Haruki, the two ageing translators decided to adopt the conversational *taidan* (dialogue) form commonly used in Japanese literary publications. The following is a transcription of the discussion they had on 16 May 2019, in Jay's home in Bellevue, Washington, USA.

JAY RUBIN (JR):	We first met in April 1992 when we participated in a panel on Murakami at the annual meeting of the Association for Asian Studies (AAS) in Washington, DC. Somehow we got the AAS to accept the idea of academics getting up and talking about a current popular writer, and it worked out well. My only regret was that we didn't play the tape I brought with me of 'The Girl from Ipanema', the song that inspired one of my favorite Murakami stories, '1963/1982 nen no Ipanema musume' (1983; trans. 'The 1963/1982 Girl from Ipanema' [2002/2018]). I was sort of planning to plug it into the sound system at some point if possible. It crossed my mind that it might be even more outrageous if the four of us on the panel (which included Charles Inouye of Tufts and Hosea Hirata of Princeton [later Tufts]) sang 'The Girl from Ipanema' in front of this staid academic audience.
TED GOOSSEN (TG):	But it wasn't really a staid academic audience. That was what I found so interesting. Usually those attending a panel sit around looking at their laps and taking notes, but that was a totally different room. There were no empty seats – it was standing room only. People were lined up around the edge of the room. There was a look of expectancy on their faces, quite unlike what I had ever seen before in an academic meeting. The atmosphere was completely different.

JR: And did they get what they were paying for? (laughter)

TG: I don't think they were disappointed. I don't know if what we said was as important to them as the topic, because Murakami had not been respected by some of the 'greats' of Japanese literature, like Ōe Kenzaburō (though he later changed his mind).

JR: Don't forget to mention Donald Keene. He had doubts about Murakami's validity as a writer.

TG: Yes, we were dealing with a writer considered to be 'outside the bounds' of proper academic inquiry. So singing 'The Girl from Ipanema' would have fit right in with what we were doing. Too bad it didn't work out.

JR: Yeah, I've been kicking myself ever since. Twenty-seven years is a lot of years to kick yourself!

TG: How did you start reading Murakami?

JR: That was a totally passive thing on my part. In 1989 I got a letter from an editor at Vintage Press saying that they had been sent the translation of a Japanese novel for potential publication, and they wanted the opinion of someone who could read the original. They didn't want an opinion of the translation, but of the Japanese book itself to see if it was worth publishing in translation. They tracked me down at the University of Washington where I was still teaching and asked me to write a report. You know, we get these requests once in a while. I took the job on because I was curious about current writers. I had always worked on Meiji or Taishō literature – Natsume Sōseki, Kunikida Doppo etc., and I had a very definite prejudice against working on living writers thanks to Edwin McClellan, my mentor at the University of Chicago. He believed in working on the classics, period. If you're going to get involved in translating a book, it should be one that has already proved its staying power. So I tended to be rather snobbish as far as current literature was concerned. I think I had at least become vaguely aware of Murakami, mainly from occasional trips to Tokyo where I would see his books piled up in bookstores – stacks of them lying on their sides. I would think, 'here's another popular writer' – 'popular' in the bad sense, pandering to a young audience, with characters hopping in and out of bed, that kind of thing. I was curious to see what kind of junk was being read then. So they sent me the book – a two-volume Japanese *bunkobon* paperback with the long, crazy title *Sekai no owari to hādoboirudo wandārando* (1985), which later came out as *Hard-Boiled Wonderland and the End of the World* (1991). I read the thing and was absolutely amazed by it. I was not expecting to be *so* impressed by a Japanese writer. To me, Japanese writing all tended to be rather low-key, realistic black-and-white depictions of the real world, but here's this guy whose hero puts his fingers on a unicorn skull and all these colours go floating out of the skull into space, and these turn out to be the dreams of the people who lived there in the town. It was so colourful and amazing and imaginative, I could hardly believe that a Japanese writer could do stuff like that. So I wrote to them and said, boy, this is an amazing book, you should definitely publish a translation, and if by any chance you don't like the translation that's been sent to you, let *me* do it, I'd love to translate this book. Well, it didn't take them long to completely ignore my advice. They didn't want to publish the book at all, let alone in my translation. They weren't ready to take chances on an unknown writer like Murakami. As big as he was becoming in Japan, he was still an unknown quantity here. This was in 1989, a few months before Birnbaum's translation of *Hitsuji o meguru bōken* (1982; trans. *A Wild Sheep Chase*) got so many people – especially publishers – excited about Murakami. I got that translation and was impressed by it, though I didn't like *Hitsuji* as much as *Sekai no owari*. Still, I was soon reading nobody but Murakami. I stopped reading Sōseki and other classic writers and concentrated on Murakami for the next 15 years or so, especially his short stories, very few of which had been translated into English. You were already well into Murakami's world, though.

TG: Yes, I started reading him in 1986, when my family and I were living in Tokyo. I had got a postdoctoral fellowship, but it was in Canadian dollars, which didn't go very far in those days. So I took various part-time jobs and, in my free time, read all kinds of stuff. I had no particular plan in mind. I sure didn't want to go any further with my thesis research. I was just happy to have got through that.

JR: What was your thesis about?

TG: It was on Shiga Naoya (1883–1971), who certainly would have counted as one of your 'classics'. Anyway, I had a good friend who said, 'You've got to read this guy Murakami', so I read *Hitsuji o meguru bōken*, and loved it. As it happened – though I wasn't aware of this at the time – Murakami and I had arrived on the campus of Waseda University in 1968 within a month or two of each other. We were both 19. I was an exchange student from Oberlin College, while he was a first-year student who had been a *rōnin* for one year. We never met then, of course, but there were references to his experience, really concrete things, that clicked with me. It had been my first time in Japan, so my memories – the clatter and whistles of the radical students' on-campus drills, the cheap student dives, the filthy university buildings, the clumsy hookups, the heightened fears and expectations we all felt – were very distinct. I had read and enjoyed a lot of different writers, but I had never related to a Japanese writer in such a direct and personal way before.

Then I read *Sekai no owari to hādoboirudo wandārando*, and I was won over. It had just come out, and it blew me away. It was intensely pleasurable. In the years leading up to that time, most of my reading was connected to my thesis, or to something I was writing. I enjoyed it, but at the same time it was work, if you know what I mean.

JR: Welcome to the club. Actually, Dazai Osamu was the first writer I read for pleasure.

TG: It leaves an imprint, doesn't it? I think a lot of factors were involved in why I reacted so strongly to *Hitsuji* and especially *Sekai no owari*. The accessibility of Murakami's style was one. The fact we're so close in age was another. Japanese and American 'baby boomers' went through a lot of similar stuff. Whether we attended a US school like Oberlin or a Japanese school like Waseda, we all were affected by the student movement. I don't know if it mattered that much if we were deeply involved or not. And when it collapsed, many of us faced the same problem: how to find a way to live without 'selling out' to the establishment. Those early novels seemed to grapple with that issue in a way I could relate to. The fact that at the time I was pushing 40 with no job prospects probably made it more relevant too!

But *Sekai no owari* was special. I liked it so much I became a bit depressed when I finished reading it. I didn't want it to end.

JR: Wow, that was my reaction exactly. I wanted to stay in Murakami's world.

TG: I still have that pink hardcover. Murakami wasn't that big in Japan in 1986 when it came out. But his popularity skyrocketed in 1987, with the success of *Noruwei no mori* (trans. *Norwegian Wood* [1989/2000]).

JR: So the timing of our AAS panel in 1992 was good. People were aware of Murakami and wanted to hear more about him.

TG: Yes, the timing was excellent. The audience was younger than is usual at the AAS, too. Lots of grad students, I guess. I think people had a feeling that something was changing. I mean, a lot of people had assumed that you couldn't really study living writers, especially young ones.

I don't think we disappointed our audience. I think the three of us – Hosea Hirata, Charles Inouye, and me – were excited to be part of it. And you were the guy who set it up. You talked about how Murakami handled the song 'The Girl from Ipanema' in one of his stories, I remember.

JR: Which is why I brought the tape with me to begin with.

TG: That tune is an unforgettable piece. It can easily become a kind of ear worm. You can hear it in the back of your mind as you read the story. I think a lot of his works are like that. Which means, too, you can also hear it as you translate.

JR: Yeah, at times, I've put on the piece of music in question to listen to while I translate.

TG: Right from the start, you seem to have made that connection between Murakami's style and music, and a few years later you gave your study the title *Haruki Murakami and the music of words*.

JR: Yeah, that book came out in 2002. In it, I used my translation of 'The 1963/1982 Girl from Ipanema' as a kind of introduction so the reader can get a taste of a whole Murakami work right at the beginning – it's only about five pages long. They made me take that out, you know. It's not in the book anymore. You can find it in the original 2002 edition and the 2005 rewrite, but that story never appeared in English again until my *Penguin Book of Japanese Short Stories* came out in 2018. It was supposed to be in the 2006 Murakami collection, *Blind Willow, Sleeping Woman* that I did with Philip Gabriel. Just before that book was due to come out, the publishers became aware that the [Antônio Carlos] Jobim estate hadn't given permission to quote the lyrics in English. When Murakami published the story in Japanese, it had carried a notice to say the lyrics quoted in the story were there with permission. So when I translated it – I didn't know anything about copyrights and stuff – I assumed that was it, the permission was all taken care of. I got permission from Murakami's agent to print the story in my book, but when it came to a new anthology of Murakami stories, [Alfred A.] Knopf and Harvill [Press] were more careful about permission for the lyrics quoted in the story. Knopf did a better job than Harvill in removing the story from *Blind Willow, Sleeping Woman*. The British and American editions are almost identical, but in the British version, Murakami mentions the Ipanema story in his introduction, while there is no such mention in the American version of his introduction. A British reader could look for the story in the Table of Contents without finding it and might notice that the book contains only 24 stories though the dust jacket claims there are 25. Knopf left behind no such evidence that 'The 1963/1982 Girl from Ipanema' had been suppressed. Once Harvill became aware of the problem, they made me take my complete translation out of my *Haruki Murakami and the music of words* beginning with the 2008 rewrite (which is dated 2005 just to confuse people) and substitute a summary. We did such a rush job in 2008 that there's a big blank space on one page as if the story had been physically ripped out of the book. We did a much smoother job in the 2012 edition. I liked that story so much, I was sorry to think that only readers of my 2002 and 2005 editions would have access to it in English, so I started pestering Penguin to arrange for the missing permission, which they successfully did, and now English readers can find 'The 1963/1982 Girl from Ipanema' in *The Penguin Book of Japanese Short Stories*, page 516 of which carries a permission notice that seems almost as long as the story itself.

TG: Murakami has used music from the very beginning, yet the type of music varies, and it's constantly changing. You're just 30 pages into his first novel *Kaze no uta o kike* (1979; trans. *Hear the Wind Sing* [1987/2015]), for example, when he gets started. And it's 'The Mickey Mouse Club Song'! He even gives the reader a line or two. Then in the next few pages we get Brook Benton's 'A Rainy Night in Georgia', Creedence Clearwater Revival's 'Who'll Stop the Rain?', and the Beach Boys' 'California Girls', complete with the lyrics! The next page has references to Miles Davis's 'A Gal in Calico' and Glenn Gould's performance of Beethoven's third piano concerto. From 'The Mickey Mouse Club Song' to Beethoven and Glenn Gould – that's some range for a writer just getting started.

I read *Sekai no owari* before *Kaze* so I didn't know where Murakami was coming from. But I could tell that there was a musical subtext to the novel. I remember when I hit the scene with the couple in the white convertible playing Duran Duran on their car radio I broke out laughing. Their superficiality matched the superficiality of the music just so perfectly!

The closeness in age means that, to a large degree, Murakami and I were listening to the same songs on the radio growing up. It was easy to access popular American music in Japan during the 1960s and 1970s – all you had to do was turn on FEN [Far East Network], the US armed forces network, or one of the Japanese radio hosts who were playing those tunes. Of course, our tastes in music change as we get older. Different kinds of music become associated with different times in our lives. I think that, unconsciously, I was propelled by the songs of the 1960s when I was translating *Kaze* and *1973 nen no pinbōru* (1980; trans. *Pinball, 1973* [2015]). They were playing in the back of my mind and were connected to the way I thought and felt back in my late teens and 20s. I could also pilfer them for words and rhythms when that seemed appropriate.

Murakami went on to classical music and now opera, something I don't enjoy quite as much as he does. So I didn't have the same experience when I was translating the second book of *Kishidanchō goroshi* (2017; trans. *Killing Commendatore* [2018]). I think my musical interests and yours are different, though I'm not sure that influences our translating all that much.

JR: Yeah, I do like opera, especially in recent years. I remember when I translated *Nejimakidori kuronikuru* (1994–1995; trans. *The Wind-Up Bird Chronicle* [1997]) I had to familiarise myself with *The Thieving Magpie*, which appears prominently in the novel. One thing I had to decide was whether to call it by its original Italian title, *La gazza ladra*, which is the usual practice with opera, or by the English translated title. I ended up using the English because there's a passage where the reader needs to know the meaning. The protagonist is wondering to himself, 'was *The Thieving Magpie* really the story of a magpie that engaged in thieving? If things ever settled down, I would have to go to the library and look it up in a dictionary of music. I might even buy a complete recording of the opera if it was available' (Murakami 1997: 558). The funny thing is that Murakami himself didn't know the opera very well. He and I were in [UC] Berkeley, where he was giving a talk, in November 1992. We went downtown together just to kind of poke around, and we stumbled into the San Francisco Opera House, where the gift shop had all sorts of opera recordings available, one of which was *The Thieving Magpie*. He immediately bought a VHS video of it because, he said, he wanted to find out how the story turned out. Of course, this was long after he had used the title, *The Thieving Magpie*, in the 1986 story 'Nejimakidori to kayōbi no onnatachi' (trans. 'The Wind-Up Bird and Tuesday's Women' [1990]), and also long after he had given the first of the novel's three volumes the title *The Thieving Magpie* and mentioned 'the overture to Rossini's *The Thieving Magpie*' in the opening paragraph, where that overture is described as 'the perfect music for cooking pasta'. In other words, he had committed to using the overture – just the overture – as a formative element in both the story and the novel, without knowing much about the opera itself.

TG: I guess we tend to assume that a writer only refers to works they know well. Back in graduate school at the University of Toronto, I attended Northrop Frye's seminar on T. S. Eliot and James Joyce, and I remember he talked for three or four hours about the opening of Joyce's *Finnegans Wake*. I couldn't believe the range of references Joyce had packed into those few pages, and the digging that was required to unearth them. The implication was that only a scholar of the magnitude of Frye could understand what the author was doing.

This, though, is the opposite, isn't it? The critic might plunge into the opera *The Thieving Magpie* expecting all sorts of connections to the novel when, in fact, the connection was limited to the overture and the title itself.

JR; I'm sure when he has his protagonist think, in Volume 3, 'I might even buy a complete recording of the opera if it was available' (Murakami 1997: 558), he was thinking of his own purchase of the recording in November 1992. Volume 3 didn't appear in Japanese until 1995. I'm convinced he cited Rossini's overture at the beginning *precisely* because it's a piece of music that everybody knows without being able to name or analyse it. It's commonly used in TV commercials, and [Stanley] Kubrick used it in *A Clockwork Orange*. I think Murakami's drawing a parallel between the half-known music and the existence for most Japanese (particularly those of his generation and younger) of World War II as something that hovers on the edge of consciousness.

TG: I guess a lot of what we do when we try to uncover the 'subtext' of a work of art is more for our own benefit, or that of our readers, than to figure out the artist's creative process, and what he or she 'intended'. For example, *Sekai no owari* ends with Bob Dylan's 'A Hard Rain's a-Gonna Fall' playing on the car radio. It's a song I know pretty well. It has a lot of verses, some of which can be connected in fairly concrete ways to the themes of the novel in one way or another. I guess I always assumed Murakami was referencing the whole song, but it may have been the title alone that he had in mind. The 'hard-boiled/ hard rain' link could have been the whole story. I may enjoy imagining how the song and the novel fit together, but a reader unfamiliar with Dylan – a younger reader, perhaps, or someone from another country – might get just as much if not more out of the novel.

JR: Yes, speaking of readers from other countries, Murakami's popularity around the world is a real riddle isn't it? I mean, how often have you been asked about that by journalists?

TG: Yeah, and I don't have an answer.

JR: That's too bad – I was hoping you could answer that question once and for all today.

TG: You know, I teach at York University in Toronto. Over half a million Chinese Canadians live in or around Toronto, so some of my students read Murakami in Chinese translation. Several have written papers comparing translations from various places – Taiwan, mainland China, and Malaysia, primarily. All the translations are apparently quite different, reflecting the backgrounds of the readers. Yet, that difference doesn't seem to affect Murakami's popularity one way or the other.

JR: So you're not going to explain why he catches on so well?

TG: I'm not sure. I'm not even sure why *Noruwei no mori* in particular should be so popular in Asia. There it tends to be everyone's favourite, here not so much.

JR: Some readers here like it too. I sent a copy to a historian of Japan who was tremendously moved by it. In his case, he strongly identified with the generation of the student movement. I was kind of surprised to have this gruff old guy so moved by the love story, but he really was. But I don't know, I make up something different every time I'm asked why Murakami is so popular in so many different places. I usually talk about how plain his language is, how simple the images are, how accessible it makes his fiction beyond cultural boundaries. But that doesn't really answer the question.

TG: I still think there's an 'Asian difference' when it comes to the popularity of various novels. If I ask Murakami fans here [in Canada] which is their favourite, they usually say *Hard-Boiled Wonderland*, *Wind-Up Bird*, or sometimes, *Kafka on the Shore* (2005; *Umibe no Kafuka* [2002]). If I ask Chinese or Korean readers the same question, most name *Noruwei no mori*. Maybe part of the reason is that the novel is an introduction to a wide variety of possible sexual and romantic relationships – the mistakes that you can make, the abuses that can occur, but also the pleasures. I think young people here work through those issues by talking to each other, and maybe sometimes even with their parents. I don't know if that happens to the same extent in most Asian communities. I remember listening to my daughters at the age of 14 or 15 talking on the phone with their friends. They could go on and on about what was and wasn't appropriate between boys and girls, what was going on with their classmates, and so forth. They were constantly checking: Is that okay? No. How about that? Possibly. It's like they were setting up a whole protocol to govern how young adults should act in romantic relationships.

   Perhaps *Noruwei no Mori* is less of an eye-opener for readers who have grown up engaged in those kinds of conversations.

JR: So you think readers from more sexually conservative societies are more responsive to the novel?

TG: Yes. Or at least societies where love and sex aren't discussed so openly.

   When *zenjo kōsai* [compensated dating] was being so hotly discussed, one of the points that kept coming up was that Japanese girls of 15 or 16 were susceptible to the idea of exchanging sex with older men for money precisely because they were so innocent. They hadn't been involved in conversations with their peers or their families about sex, and what the issues are, so they were operating in a moral vacuum. In a sense, *Noruwei no mori* filled that vacuum for some young readers by providing that kind of discourse in novelistic form.

   Then again, your historian friend is a big fan of the novel, too, so obviously there's more going on here.

JR: He liked the presentation of the student movement primarily.

TG: I think that's another draw in Asia. Koreans experienced the violent repression of student protests in Gwangju in 1980, and China had the same sort of thing in 1989 with the Tiananmen Square massacre. So there are parallels that are a lot more recent than Kent State in the US or the ANPO protests in Japan.

JR: That's one book. Conversely, I've got very little sense that our favourite, *Sekai no owari*, is the favourite of many people. To me, it's his great accomplishment, more so than *Nejimakidori*. *Nejimakidori* has tremendous impact for its historical content, but I just love the sense of interiority of the central character in *Sekai no owari*, and how he's bifurcated and how the two parts of his brain interact, but not that many people are that crazy about the book.

TG: Yeah. When I read the dialogues between Murakami and the Jungian psychologist and author Kawai Hayao, I got a sense for why that shift may have happened. Kawai was such a charismatic man, and he was convinced that Murakami should use his fiction to 'heal' the hearts and minds of his readers.

JR: Yes, I think that kind of Jungian analysis may have compromised Murakami's spontaneity. It made him too conscious of what he was doing. I think others have said the same thing.

TG: The 'Murakami effect' can be powerful in a number of ways. Have I told you what happened last October at the literary festival in Cheltenham, England?

JR: A bit, but I'd like to hear more.

TG: It's a pretty big festival in one of the picturesque towns that circle London. Over 300 people attended the panel on Murakami, which included the novelists David Mitchell and David Peace – they've spent years in Japan and know a lot about Murakami's work – and myself. Each of us was asked to choose a passage from Murakami's writing, which would be read to the audience by the very talented actor, Julian Rhind–Tott. Maybe a bit too talented, actually, given what took place. I chose Chapter 40 from *Killing Commendatore*, 'I Could Not Mistake the Face', since it was the shortest, and Philip Gabriel's and my translation had just come out. One of the other panelists (neither of the Davids, by the way), however, chose that excruciating scene in *The Wind-Up Bird Chronicle* where a Japanese spy, Yamamoto, is skinned alive.

The reading of that scene was partway through when we became aware of a small commotion in the audience. The stage lights were too bright, though, to let us see what the cause was, so we just continued on our merry way. Later, we found out that a woman had fainted dead away at that point – she just toppled out of her seat and into the aisle. When I emailed Murakami to let him know what had happened, his response was, 'why the heck would anyone choose that passage to read?'

JR: When you first told me about this, I felt great, as if my writing had had some impact. It reminds me of a story Murakami himself told a long time ago. There was a young woman who got so turned on by one of the more erotic passages in his work that she went to her boyfriend's place, sneaked into his room and forced him to make love to her. Murakami was just so delighted to hear that his words were able to influence someone in the real world in this way. To make them do something. So when you told me about this, I felt the same sense of satisfaction. Like, wow, my translation made this woman faint. It's very satisfying to me as a translator. Of course, Murakami wrote the scene, but she never would have heard this and fainted away if I hadn't put it into English.

TG: Yes, it's one of the unspoken pleasures of being a translator. The knowledge that all over the world people are reading our words and feeling fear or lust or beauty.

JR: That's what I always hope for. People talk about whether translations should be accurate or not, but I think the thing that they have to be accurate in doing is conveying these qualities of the original – the fear, the lust, the, you know, humour. Humour especially. I want my readers to laugh when Japanese readers would laugh, and be scared when something is scary in Japanese. That's the most important thing to try to be faithful to – that emotional baggage of the text. Certainly not grammar – that's the least important element. Just because the writer used a noun for a certain concept, you're not bound to use a noun. You might be able to convey it better with a verb in English.

TG: Then is it necessary for a translator to feel fear when handling a scary scene, or be sexually aroused when the scene is erotic?

JR: I think the translator *has* to become sexually aroused. I mean you have to have those feelings that are created by the text. Whatever it is. If it's sexual arousal, fine. I once wrote a story about this. It was about prostatitis – a prostatitis comedy. It was about a writer whose agent insists that he give his readers more sex scenes. So he sits down and tries to write sex scenes, which arouses him, but he has no way to release that feeling, so that in the end he develops prostatitis. I thought it was pretty funny, so I sent it to a couple of magazines – *Esquire* was one – but they didn't print it. In my case, I think it's absolutely crucial for me to feel what the writer wants me to feel so that I can get across these things in my own language.

I can imagine, though, that not everyone works in the same way. Someone like the late Howard Hibbett, who died in March 2019 at the age of 98, did a lot of research on women writers in English, looking for the proper style to convey the Osaka-dialect feeling of *Manji* (1928–1930, by Tanizaki Jun'ichirō; trans. *Quicksand* [1994]), since most of the original uses that idiom. He was very methodical in how he went about this, and I have never been that analytical and thoughtful about things. I suspect a translator who is so intellectual wouldn't necessarily have to go through that process of 'feeling' the text – he or she could do it all verbally. This is guesswork, though.

For me, Howard Hibbett is one of the great touchstones of translators, partly because I'll never forget how analytical he was in translating *Manji*, and also for his collection of Tanizaki stories, *Seven Japanese Tales*. That was a tremendous accomplishment. Each of the stories is translated in a very different style – some sound more like medieval Japanese, while some are clearly modern. Seven very different tales that come out in seven different styles in English. I don't know anybody else who could do that.

TG: Some have said that a translator must 'love' the work being translated. Murakami has said this, I know, and I feel the same.

JR: Yes, I'd agree with that.

TG: So then can we see the world of translation as a kind of dating site, where texts and translators find one another?

JR: Oh come on, Ted, there's too much involvement of publishers and contracts and things for it to be that simple – that sexy!

TG: It's true, though. I'm finally stepping out with one of my old dates after 35 years. It's the novella *Wakai* (1917; trans. *Reconciliation* [2020]) by Shiga Naoya, which he wrote a century ago and which I translated for my PhD thesis. There's a scene, the most powerful in the entire work, that describes the death of a baby. The baby begins crying in the middle of the night, the mother's frantic and the father says, don't worry, it'll be okay, and then it's clear it's not going to be okay, so the father runs through the mud to get the doctor, the baby rallies, then fades and in the end the baby dies. It's a long scene, the longest in the novella.

   I remember, when I launched that translation my own kids were about four and two, and I just found it excruciating. It took me days to complete. And all that time I was having trouble eating and sleeping – the scene was coming into my dreams. I was all screwed up! I looked at my children differently, I was so fearful of losing them. Anyway, a few years later it was going to be published by a Canadian press, so I went through that scene again. And exactly the same thing happened. I *knew* the outcome, yet that didn't make any difference. I was back in the scene, feeling all those emotions. Unfortunately, the publisher went under, so the translation never came out.

   Now *Reconciliation* looks like it's coming out from Canongate Press so I'm going over it again. And that scene still gets to me! I think it's a testament to how Shiga wrote it. And the fact I'm spending a lot of time with my year-old grandson probably has something to do with it too.

JR: Yeah, I'm familiar with how intense feelings about grandchildren can be. It's like, here we go all over again. It doesn't answer the question whether translators *need* to feel those things. I can imagine an argument for just the opposite – that translators should distance themselves from the feelings they get from the text and deal with them more objectively.

TG: I think both happen. There's a range of how close or how far we allow ourselves to get to the text, even within the same work. It's not as though you're emotionally engaged to the same degree from beginning to end.

   One thing we have in common now is that both of us have translated scenes from Murakami's novels that describe wartime atrocities – *Nejimakidori* has several, while *Kishidanchō goroshi* includes a gut-wrenching beheading scene set during the massacre in Nanjing. Obviously you have to distance yourself from something like that. You can't be there in every gory detail.

JR: Really? I'm not sure. You have to be disgusted by it…

TG: You have to be there, but at the same time you have to maintain some sort of distance from it.

JR: True, you have to have enough distance to be able to write coherent sentences. Your logical brain has to function to write decent text.

TG: How about the skinning scene, the one that made the lady faint? Did that bother you at the time?

JR: It bothered not only me but the author himself. I tried to talk about it once with him, and he turned the conversation off immediately. It was just too awful, he said. He wouldn't talk about it. I like to say that he had it easy – he just had to write it, but I had to translate it, a much slower process (at least the way I do it). Of course, I'm just kidding, it must have been an excruciating act of imagination to create the scene, but afterwards he could forget about it. I, though, had to live with it in my imagination for several days so that I could make it work in my own language. You can't be passive when you translate: you can't skim or shut your eyes the way you can when you're reading a book or watching a horror movie. I wrote an article about this in *The Guardian* back in 2005, but it's still online with the title 'Close My Eyes'. It quotes from the beginning of the scene *before* things get really gory: 'His men held Yamamoto down with their hands and knees while he began skinning Yamamoto with the utmost care. It truly was like skinning a peach. I couldn't bear to watch. I closed my eyes. When I did this, one of the soldiers hit me with his rifle butt. He went on hitting me until I opened my eyes. But it hardly mattered: eyes open or closed, I could still hear Yamamoto's voice. He bore the pain without a whimper – at first. But soon he began to scream' (Murakami 1997: 159). If you close your eyes when you translate, though, that soldier starts hitting you with his rifle butt.

TG: I recall I imagined the beheading scene as much as was necessary to translate it, but I think I shut my imagination down immediately after I finished. I severed my emotions in a way I couldn't with the death of the baby. To protect myself, I guess.

JR: Before we finish, I'd like to hear more from you about the AAS panel, the one we did in 1992.

TG: I think the reason the room was filled with expectancy and a certain happiness was that a writer like Murakami could be discussed in a very formal, academic setting. It was new, not so much because we were talking about a contemporary writer – Nakagami Kenji and writers of that sort were academically kosher by that point – but because there had been a dismissive attitude toward writers who were 'entertaining', popular with a young audience. Until then, the division between 'serious' and 'popular' literature had been observed in universities, even though it was eroding in Japan. I mean, the popular and the so-called serious were merging. That meant the literary establishment – the *bundan* – was losing its influence. This had been going on for a while in Japan, but I think our panel signalled a recognition of that fact in the academy. I've heard many younger writers talk about how Murakami liberated them, freed them from the rules and strictures of the *bundan*.

I think the audience at the AAS reflected that somehow. I think they were happy that a writer like Murakami could be discussed without worrying about whether he should be placed on the 'serious' or 'popular' side of the ledger. So maybe our panel did something to liberate Japanese literary studies, allowing younger scholars in the field – our audience was younger than the AAS norm – to work on writers for whom they felt a special affinity.

JR: Of course, it's not as if the dismissive attitude toward Murakami just disappeared at that point. There's still a strong prejudice against treating him seriously. For some, anyway. Come to think of it, I was there at an event that signalled a shift in the establishment's attitude toward Murakami. Ōe Kenzaburō, one of Murakami's most vocal critics, gave the keynote address at the ceremony awarding the prestigious Yomiuri Literary Prize to Murakami on the evening of 23 February 1996, and spoke in praise of *Nejimakidori*. The two men nervously bowed to each other and chatted about jazz for ten minutes during the reception afterwards, and things have never been quite the same. (There's a more detailed account of this in my *Haruki Murakami and the music of words*. See Rubin 2002: 234–236.)

TG: So when Murakami and Ōe bowed to each other it was cementing a shift that was taking place around the time of our panel, a shift that still wasn't widely accepted in our field at that point.

JR: Aren't you glad you got old and wrinkly enough so you could say something like that?

References

Murakami H. 1997. *The Wind-Up Bird Chronicle*. London: Vintage.
Rubin, J. 2002. *Haruki Murakami and the music of words*. London: Harvill Press.
Rubin, J., ed. 2018. *The Penguin Book of Japanese Short Stories*. London: Penguin.

16

TO BUILD A PILE OF SLEEPING KITTENS, TRYING NOT TO WAKE THEM

Rebecca Suter interviews Murakami Haruki

Rebecca Suter with Murakami Haruki

I began researching the literature of Murakami Haruki during my doctoral degree at the beginning of the new millennium. A few years later, while I was a postdoctoral fellow at the Reischauer Institute of Japanese Studies at Harvard University, serendipitously Murakami happened to be a writer in residence at the Institute, and I had the good fortune of meeting him in person. During those months I had the opportunity to engage with the author in thought-provoking conversations on a variety of topics, but seldom about his literature; I had the impression that Haruki was not keen to discuss his writing process, and I respected that. On my part, as someone trained in literary theory and cultural studies, I also felt that it was my job, as a scholar, to offer my own analysis of texts, and that asking the author what his intentions were when writing them, or what his own interpretation was, would be somewhat pointless if not downright misleading. I still do, to an extent, think this. Another author whose works I have studied in depth and written about, Kazuo Ishiguro, often complained about how much time he has had to spend on book tours and similar events over the course of his career, and how he found himself resenting having to devote his energies to talking about his writing, rather than just doing it. While there are of course numerous writers who see engaging in public debate as an integral part of their work, and they do that excellently, personally I have always felt much sympathy for Murakami and Ishiguro's view that a writer's primary task is to tell stories, not to analyse and theorise.

As a result, when several years later I was commissioned by an Italian publisher to interview Murakami, I found myself in a bit of a quandary.[1] I wanted to balance between asking about things I was curious to know, particularly surrounding his work as a translator, and letting the conversation become, as much as possible, another form of storytelling, that would complement rather than explain Haruki's writing. It would appear that I succeeded at least in part, since Murakami noted that he was glad I had not asked him what kind of novels he wrote. I believe the conversation went smoothly, and I learned much from it. The interview took place at the Ebisu Westin Hotel in Tokyo. It was a very Murakamiesque moment. Jazz music was playing in the background the whole time; I wish I could say we drank whisky, but I am afraid it was just coffee. We talked about travel, translation, global literature, the smell of books, and the importance of grocery shopping as a sociological exercise.

Since I had never translated the interview into English, I thought it was time to make it available to a broader audience. It was very interesting to revisit our conversation almost a decade later. It was uncanny to notice that many of our reflections on broader social, economic, and political issues, from the sense of crisis of Southern European countries like Italy and Greece to the rise of economic inequality in the United States, still rang true ten years later. It was inspiring to see that some of Haruki's considerations on the power of literature to connect us globally also remain valid and valuable. Most interesting to me was probably to look back at Haruki's comments about the translations he was doing at the time and the ones he intended to do, as well as his musings on what he was going to write after finishing one of his longest and most complex works, *1Q84* (2009–2010; trans. *1Q84* [2011]). Spookiest of all was to realise that Murakami's final remark in the interview was that, when looking at literary texts, 'it's best to let time do its work'. I hope readers will appreciate time's work on Haruki's words on this occasion as much as I did when re-reading and translating them.

25 October 2011
Ebisu Westin Hotel, Tokyo

MURAKAMI HARUKI (MH): Oh, are you going to record with that? Nowadays you can do all sorts of things with mobile phones!

REBECCA SUTER (RS): Actually, it's not a mobile phone, it's an iPod.

MH: Oh, it's not a phone! You can record also on an iPod! I only have the small version … I use it when I run.

RS: Do you listen to music while running?

MH: Of course.

RS: What kind of music?

MH: Usually rock.

RS: Really? Not jazz?

MH: No, I cannot run to the sound of jazz. Rock music has a regular rhythm, tum-tum-tum … Jazz is different, it changes all the time, it's not ideal for running. I like to create playlists, to choose different pieces and combine them. I have three different ones at the moment, and I keep changing them, adding songs, deleting others. It's a real pleasure.

RS: What kind of music do you choose for your playlists?

MH: All sorts. Recent stuff, 1960s rock, even rap sometimes.

RS: Rap!

MH: Yeah, why not? It actually suits the rhythm of running quite well. By the way, on 11 December [2011] I will run in the Honolulu marathon.

RS: But that's very soon! Do you train every day?

MH: At the moment I am travelling, but in Honolulu I have signed up for a marathon training group. It's been interesting. I am the only Japanese in the group. A marathon training session is about three or four hours, it can get pretty boring to run alone for such a long time. Running in a group is more interesting.

RS: Do people talk while running?

MH: Yes, they often do. My group is quite chatty. I ended up in a group mostly composed of girls in their 20s. I don't really know what to talk about with them!

RS: Do you ever use these situations as material for your stories?

MH: I try not to. I know there are writers who use their real lives as story material, but I can't do that. In general, I prefer to avoid using real events in my work. But they do act as a trigger. They set something in motion, and that something becomes a story. For example, during the 2000 Olympics I stayed in Sydney for a month. Many curious things happened during that time, but no specific episode became part of a novel. It's more as though I put the events in a drawer and forget about them. Then, inside the drawer, they turn into something else, and after a while, that something else is ready to become a story.

RS: Speaking of living overseas, I know that lately you have been dividing your time between Tokyo and Hawai'i. What's it like to live in Honolulu?

MH: It's great for exercise. When it comes to culture, well, compared to Boston or New York, there isn't all that much happening. For example, there are no second-hand bookstores or vintage record stores. In that sense it's a bit disappointing.

RS: Speaking of this, I always wondered, when you left Japan for the first time, why did you choose to go to Rome, rather than, say, Boston or New York?

MH: In the 1980s I had a friend who was married to an Italian, and they lived in Rome. They had invited me to visit them several times. At the time I was tired of living in Japan, so I thought, let's try Italy. I had been to Greece before and I had loved it, so I also wanted to go back there. Moving back and forth between Italy and Greece, which are so close to each other, seemed like an ideal arrangement.

RS: And yet I think that many of your readers, including me, find it puzzling that a big fan of American literature and music like you would not choose to move to the US.

MH: Europe seemed more appealing as a destination. America was easy to imagine, whereas I knew very little about Europe. In hindsight, I think it was the right choice. Later in life, I didn't get that many opportunities to travel to Europe, so I am glad I went when I had the chance.

RS: Well, recently Italy has also gone through tough times …

MH: Indeed! Your Prime Minister is quite something! But you know, even when I was living there, 30 years ago, everyone was talking about the economic crisis, and worrying about the future of the country … In the end it all worked out. In fact, people seemed to be doing well, they looked happy, they were eating out …

RS: (laughs) You're right, I have the same impression whenever I go back to Italy.

MH: Same for Greece. Of course, nowadays young people have a hard time, and unemployment is very high, but when you travel there, you don't get a sense of crisis. The nation may be struggling, but people maintain a positive spirit. In this sense it's very similar to Italy: the country may be doing poorly, but people are happy. I remember thinking at the time that it was the exact opposite of Japan: the country was getting rich, and people were not. Now the situation has changed in Japan too; the country is struggling more.

RS: And what about the US, how would you place them in this picture?

MH: What always struck me in America is the huge gap between the rich and the poor. Nowadays you hear a lot about the 'occupy' movement, about the 'one per cent' … It's true that the economic inequality is striking. I find it shocking that it has reached such proportions.

RS: Is it noticeable in Honolulu?

MH: In Hawai'i there are many foreigners and Americans from the mainland who purchase real estate, and they drive the prices up to the point that locals cannot afford to buy. This phenomenon is probably specific to Hawai'i, and it may be less pronounced in other parts of the US. But that's another example of inequality I guess: you see people from outside building these huge villas and local residents who cannot even afford an apartment.

RS: On a different note, I wanted to ask you about your work as a translator. For many years now you have alternately published your own fiction and translations of American literature. After *1Q84*, you translated *Winter Dreams* by Francis Scott Fitzgerald and *But Beautiful* by Geoff Dyer, a collection of life stories of famous jazz musicians. I was wondering: Why did you choose these two works?

MH: I have been translating short stories by Fitzgerald for a very long time now; there were some I had not translated yet, so I decided to do them. There wasn't a particular reason for choosing those ones, it was more like continuing an ongoing work.

RS: And what about Dyer?

MH: I read the book by chance, and I found it extraordinary. I thought: I must translate this! It's great to translate a book about jazz. All along, I worked while listening to jazz. When I was doing the chapter on Charles Mingus, I listened to Charles Mingus, and so on. It was fantastic. When I work on a novel, the pace of the story is so important to me that I cannot listen to music. It would interfere with my inner tempo. But translating to the sound of music works really well.

RS: So when you run you listen to rock, and when you translate you listen to jazz?

MH: Actually, when I translate, I listen mostly to classical music, like, say, Mahler's. Normally it's hard to find the time to listen to a whole symphony, that lasts over an hour, right? But if I listen to it while I work, it's easier to make time for it. So I try to choose that kind of long piece. Sometimes I also listen to opera.

RS: Really? Don't you get distracted by the lyrics?

MH: Oh, since I don't understand Italian, that's not a problem! (laughs)

RS: Myself, I tend to listen to music without words when I work, but it's true that if it is a language I don't know, and I don't understand the meaning …

MH: If you don't understand the meaning, words do not interfere with your own thoughts, right?

RS: And what else are you working on now?

MH: It took me three years to write *1Q84*, so I needed a break! For a while I divided my time between translation and nonfiction. Over the past year I did a series of interviews with Ozawa Seiji, the music conductor, and I collected them in a volume that will come out next month.[2]

RS: Is it a long book?

MH: Yes, pretty long. It was very interesting work. We talked only about music, for hours. I really needed to do something like this, different from literature.

RS: Any plans for the near future?

MH: Now that I have finished the book with Ozawa, I am writing some short stories. I'm not sure what they will be like. *1Q84* is a strong text, almost aggressive; I think my next book will be something calmer, more subdued. A quiet book, without too much movement. *1Q84* was so intense! I think a long novel must be like that, it has to keep the readers a bit on edge, otherwise they get bored and stop reading halfway through (laughs). But now I want to write something less intense.

RS: What about translation?

MH: At the moment I am translating a novel by Marcel Theroux, the son of Paul Theroux. The title is *Far North*.[3] It's an exceptional book. I know the father's work well, and when I heard on the radio program *National Hour* that the son had also written a novel I got very curious. When I read it, I thought, I have to translate this. I love it when this happens: when you discover an author you have never heard of, and you like their work so much that you want to translate it. After that I would like to translate *The Big Sleep* by Raymond Chandler. There are already translations in Japanese, but I would like to try my hand at it. It's a book I loved when I first read it, and it's always been a pet project of mine to translate it. I like the idea of treading the same path other translators have walked before me. Of course, in the process of translation, the original text is important, but translators also add something significant, so in the end it becomes a new text. And yet, at the same time it also needs to be accurate, faithful to the original. It's like playing a game. I never play board games or videogames, but I guess this is my way of playing.

RS: Do you ever get asked to translate something by a publisher?

MH: Usually not. Typically I translate something that I like, and then see if a publisher would be interested. Translating is a long-term endeavour; you spend many months with a book. If you don't like it, it can get really stressful! If it's a shorter work, for example an illustrated book, I may take someone else's suggestion, because it's something I can finish relatively quickly. But with a longer work, I have to like it, or I cannot finish it.

RS: Speaking of translation, there is something you said many years ago that really struck me. I don't know if you remember it, but there is an essay of yours from the 1980s entitled 'America as sign'. It's an essay on translation, and it talks about the expression 'cooking with Crisco'.

MH: Ah, yes, 'cooking with Crisco', I remember that! I had to ask Roger Pulvers what it meant.

RS: In the essay, you said that you had come across the expression 'you're cooking with Crisco' and you struggled to translate it because you could not find it in any dictionary. But when you finally learned that it is similar to the expression 'you're cooking with gas', meaning 'you're doing great', you were disappointed, because the words had lost the charm that they had when they were unintelligible, a pure sign.

MH: Yes, that kind of realisation is always a bit sad!

RS: I completely agree! But I was wondering if living in the US for many years made a difference in this respect. Can you still feel the magic of an unintelligible word?

MH: To this day, when I translate from English, I often encounter expressions that I don't fully understand. Sometimes it dawns on me if I let it sit for a few days, sometimes I end up asking an American friend. Even they don't always have an answer! There are many nuances that even a native speaker does not fully grasp. It's the same for me, there are plenty of Japanese expressions I don't really understand. But the fun is precisely in trying to understand. It's like those chess problems where you have to guess in how many moves the white will win. I am hopeless at chess, but I love translation problems. Some people find them very frustrating, but I treasure those moments when I encounter a phrase that seems impossible to translate, and I have to think about it for days. Most people would think I'm crazy!

RS: What about the translators of your works, do they ever ask you questions?

MH: Oh yes, all the time! Jay Rubin, one of my English translators, for example often contacts me. I cannot think of any concrete example off the top of my head, but he might point out that a sentence could be interpreted in two ways, and he would ask me which one was the right one. Other times he would ask for clarifications on details, names of places, things like that.

RS: Does that make you self-conscious when you write, for example do you find yourself thinking about how a sentence would sound in a different language?

MH: To be honest, not so much. When I write I don't really think whether it would sound good in English. Generally speaking, I think my Japanese is easier to read than that of other writers, say someone like Kawabata Yasunari.

RS: I agree, friends and students often tell me they find your work very approachable as readers! But to translate it can be quite hard.

MH: Really? Well now that I think about it, I have been translating Raymond Carver for many years, and his style is also a bit like that: very easy to read, but very difficult to translate. I read a review of one of my novels in a

British magazine that described it as 'enormously readable but outrageously incomprehensible' (laughs). I think it captures well my ideal in literature. I've always wanted to write novels that are extremely readable but highly incomprehensible.

RS: Do you have a favourite writer among the ones you translate?

MH: Maybe Raymond Chandler? I love the style of Scott Fitzgerald: it's irrational, exuberant; it goes in all sorts of directions, you lose track of where sentences begin and end. Raymond Carver is the opposite: logical, straightforward, and powerful precisely because of that. I love both. And Truman Capote of course. Capote's images are – how should I put it – dense, brimming with meaning. It's a style I love to read and translate, although when I write myself, I don't try to come up with such complex sentences. I prefer a simpler, more straightforward language.

RS: When you translate works that have already been translated, do you consult existing translations, or do you prefer to avoid them?

MH: Usually I try to avoid them. After I have rewritten and edited everything, in the final revision phase, I may use older translations as reference. But if I read those first, they would influence me too much, so I try to avoid that. As an author, too, I have not really looked at other writers for inspiration … one day, I simply tried to write. But even then, I did not look for a model, I did not start reading Mishima or Kawabata in order to find my voice.

RS: Is this still the case, in your own creative writing?

MH: Now I feel that I have found a format that suits me, so writing has become much easier. But even now, I don't think I have really been inspired by other authors. When they ask me to name the Japanese authors that have influenced me, I am a bit at a loss. I am an anomaly! In fact, originality is probably the one thing I am confident about.

RS: In many of your works from the 1980s, the narrator describes the difficulty of writing. There is a metaphor that I particularly like, where the narrator compares the act of writing to piling up kittens …

MH: Wow, that is such an old story! Yes, I do remember it. To build a pile of sleeping kittens, trying not to wake them.

RS: And like the pile of sleeping kittens, writing is something soft, unstable.

MH: That's right.

RS: How does it feel now? Are you still trying not to wake the kittens?

MH: Not anymore, no. My relationship with writing has changed. It comes more naturally to me; I don't have to think so much about it. I can put my thoughts on paper with less effort. I wrote that story when I was 30 years old, and now, 30 years later, I feel that I have learned to write more smoothly. At the time I was trying to write things that had not yet completely formed in my head; now I put on paper what I think, as it is. It's convenient. Maybe I shouldn't say that, but to be honest it really is convenient (laughs).

Back then, when I thought of a story, I was not sure I could tell it the way I wanted, so I ended up changing a lot of details. That doesn't happen anymore. For example, let's say I want to write the story of two girls in their 20s, and let's say they are lesbians. When I was young, I would not have been able to write a story like this, because I knew nothing about these things, these people. I felt I could not write it. But now, with some effort, I can imagine them, I can put myself in their shoes. I think that if an author of fiction genuinely tries, they can understand many things about the human heart. Although real-life 20-year-old lesbians may be completely foreign to me.

RS: Would you say that your imaginative power has changed?

MH: Yes. And my literary technique too, the ability to write seamlessly.

RS: So the kittens have become more stable?

MH: I'm not sure that the kittens have really become stable … but I stopped worrying about them.

RS: Changing topic slightly, in your novels there are often characters who cook, and elaborate descriptions of the dishes they prepare. It made me wonder whether you also cook in daily life.

MH: Yes, I cook quite often. When I work for many hours in a row, it makes me want to cook, to do something different. When I was in Italy, I cooked a lot of different dishes. Vegetables are so good over there. I made some great tomato sauces … Italian tomatoes are something else!

RS: I know, right? As an Italian, I find it hard to live in Japan in this respect.

MH: I can imagine!

RS: Veggies in Japan are few and expensive … What about you, do you usually do your own grocery shopping?

MH: Yes, always. It's such an interesting activity. I like to look at the price of groceries as a sociological and socioeconomic exercise. Social changes are very obvious in the fluctuation of prices. If a cabbage head costs 250 yen, we know immediately if that is cheap or expensive. Personally, I think it's very important.

RS: How about when you are in the States?

MH: In the US I shop at farmers' markets rather than supermarkets. In Paris, and in Rome, too, there are these large open-air markets. I like them. In the US supermarkets are too rigid and controlled. In Hawai'i there are many farmers' markets, and a lot of small local producers. That's a great thing about Hawai'i.

RS: Changing topic, when you read for fun, not for work, what kind of books do you like?

MH: Mostly detective fiction. Recently I read the Dragon Tattoo series, it was pretty good. I love Henning Mankell. Who else? Ian Rankin, Elmore Leonard. The kind of novels one buys at the airport.

RS: Do you always read on paper, or do you use electronic devices like Kindle?

MH: Ah, no, I only read real books, printed on paper. I have nothing against Kindle, but I don't see the need for it. Paper books are more than enough.

This may show my age, but I like the smell of books, the texture. It's the same reason I prefer vinyl records to mp3 and even CDs. I like their physicality. When I run, I put my music on an iPod, so it's not as though I am opposed to technological innovation, but personally when I want to listen to music properly, I choose vinyl records. With the Kindle it's the same thing, I am not critical of it, but personally I prefer not to have one. I like things that I can touch.

RS: Like used books?

MH: Exactly, I love used books, I love looking for them in second-hand stores. Although in the US, too, eBooks are becoming very popular.

RS: In some cases, though, these devices add to the physical experience too. For example with manga, it becomes possible to zoom into the image, view more detail …

MH: Ah, manga! I used to read them, but now I don't have the time. When you're young you have time for so many things, but as I get older I feel that time becomes more precious. For example, like I said, I never play videogames, and I don't watch TV. Well, apart from baseball of course (laughs). I almost never read newspapers.

RS: Really?

MH: Yes, I find them boring. I don't read literary magazines either. When I lived in Boston, I often went to used records stores, though. That's something I never get bored of. Every time I go, I think I won't find anything interesting, and bam! I end up buying something.

RS: Do you buy used records in Honolulu too?

MH: They don't have dedicated used records stores, but Goodwill and Salvation Army have 99-cent records, and if you look you can find really good ones. I don't really need them, but it seems a crime to sell them so cheap, I feel the urge to save them from this embarrassing situation. My own kind of salvation army! Seriously, sometimes there are classical music LP in mint condition, sold at 99 cents apiece, it's a shame! So I buy them, take them home, dust them, look after them. Nowadays collectors buy LP in good conditions for 500 dollars or more, on eBay you see that all the time. Me, I prefer to buy a 99-cent record and treat it with great respect. It's not like I don't have the money (laughs). If I wanted to buy a 500-dollar record, in theory I could do that, but I can't, it feels wrong. Whereas for a 99-cent record, maybe even a bit mouldy, you take it home, you polish it carefully, put it on the plate, and it plays just fine. It's a priceless feeling.

RS: Do you have a favourite record?

MH: Ah, no, if I play favourites they get upset! (laughs) I try to love them all in the same way. Of course, secretly I do have favourites, but I don't tell them (laughs).

RS: How many records do you have?

MH: I am afraid of counting them! I think there must be around ten thousand, but I don't know the exact number.

RS: What do you do when you travel? Where do you keep them?

MH: Most of them are in my house in Kanagawa, but I ran out of space, so I had to start storing some in Tokyo, and there are some more in Honolulu. It's not easy!

RS: It's not indeed!

MH: What about Italy, when I was there, they didn't have many used records stores. Is that still the case?

RS: I'm not sure, but LPs are back into fashion. I have a much younger brother, he is 23 years old, and I see that he and his friends are all buying vinyl records.

MH: You mean as deejays?

RS: No, they listen to them at home. To be honest I don't have any statistics on how popular they are, but compared to my generation, it seems that there is more interest in vinyl records today.

MH: It's a good generation! (laughs)

RS: But going back to what you were saying, it's true that as we become more mobile, owning things becomes complicated. For me it is books …

MH: Books, usually I don't keep them. After I've read them, I give them away. Otherwise they pile up!

　　You know, I'm glad you did not ask me what kind of novels I write. That question always makes me uncomfortable. Is it detective fiction, romance, science fiction? I don't know! I never know what to answer. So I say that I write 'sushi noir' (laughs). At that point it's the other person that gets uncomfortable. Those who understand that I'm joking laugh, but others have no idea what I'm talking about! But to be honest writing novels that are not easily categorised has always been my dream, so I can't complain. In the Japanese publishing industry, there is a tendency to always try to fit literature into categories, like '*watakushi-shōsetsu*' or 'avant-garde novel'. When they find a book that does not fit any of these labels, critics struggle. Sometimes they get really upset! (laughs) This is why I have never been at ease in Japan. Overseas it's easier.

RS: Would you say that the American publishing world is different in this respect?

MH: My impression is that European and American publishers care more about the quality of a text than about labels. They look for originality. In Japan, originality often makes critics uncomfortable, sometimes even hostile. So rather than writing what they want, emerging authors often try to fit the existing categories, and I think that limits their creativity. Japan has a population of a hundred and thirty million. And let's say something like a hundred million readers. It's a huge market! A Japanese author can write exclusively for the domestic market and is able to make a living. In South Korea, for example, it's not like that at all. The Korean audience alone would not be enough to support many writers. So they need to think more broadly, try to address an international audience. But in Japan, a novelist can write just for the domestic audience, all their life. I think that's a problem. It always seemed limiting to me. I couldn't feel I could grow much: I needed a breath of fresh air. That's why I wanted to be published overseas. I looked for a publisher, an agent, a translator … at first I was not selling at all! It was hard. Americans don't like foreign literature. Even in movie theatres, subtitled movies are not very popular. To make Americans read a foreign book is not an easy task. But over time my books began to sell a bit better. *Kafka on the Shore* (2005; *Umibe no Kafuka* [2002]) was the first of my books to make it to *The New York Times* Best Sellers list, in 16th position. And now *1Q84* is in second position on that list. In a way, I am glad that the process was slow and difficult; now the satisfaction is so much greater than if it had been an instant success.

Although sometimes I wonder if a society that appreciates my books is desirable! (laughs) In a happy, stable society few people would read novels like mine. But in a confused society, where values are distorted, a chaotic literature like mine has an appeal for the audience. In the Reagan years I would not have sold a single copy!

RS: Probably not!

MH: Probably not. They say my novels are non-realistic, but I feel I am describing society in a realistic way. The more I think about the world in a realist way, the more non-realist my stories become. A society that appreciates this kind of literature is one where the boundary between reality and fiction has become thin, confused. It's like *Alice in Wonderland*. Everywhere in the world people read that book, even though it's such a crazy story! I think it's because the confusion it describes corresponds to the confusion readers have inside them. No one wants to read simple absurdities. Alice's absurdity speaks to us because it touches upon something deep: it accurately describes a confusion that we recognise inside our soul, and this generates a feeling of connection, of empathy. This is my ideal literature, works that connect the confusion that lies deep inside the hearts of readers all over the world. If a book like that is read all over the world, somehow it creates a connection between people. And this is what I aim for with my own books.

RS: It's probably also responding to a need that comes from readers. When a society reaches that level of confusion, naturally this kind of literature emerges.

MH: Exactly. Readers are looking for a connection. And this is what narrative fiction has to offer. It's the same with music. Everyone is talking about globalization as this new thing, but in the world of literature globalization is a given. *Alice in Wonderland* is a global text that connects readers all over the world. Mahler's music is the same: it creates a connection between its listeners, a global connection. We have reached an era where we can listen to Mahler, a society where we feel more empathy for the chaotic world of Mahler than the one of Beethoven or Brahms.

You know, recently a friend pointed out that compared to Kawabata or Mishima my style is sort of 'neutral'. It doesn't sound very Japanese; if anything, it sounds like a foreignised Japanese language. To an extent this is a deliberate stylistic choice, but another reason for this, I think, is that for me, the more neutral the language is, the more the content can be Japanese, or even Asian. For example, in Europe and in the US religion is mostly monotheistic, right? There is only one God. But in Japan, and in other parts of Asia for that matter, there is a plethora of deities. In the cupboard there is the cupboard god, in the toilet the toilet god. So it's not so strange to think that in Kentucky Fried Chicken there would be the spirit of Colonel Sanders. *Kafka on the Shore* has as one of the characters the spirit of Colonel Sanders; American readers found it odd, whereas Japanese readers may have found it funny, but were not particularly surprised. Because the idea that there is a spirit for everything, even trivial, daily things, is a familiar concept. What I'm trying to say is that no matter how neutral my linguistic style is, geocultural elements would still be present.

RS: You mean that these elements emerge more clearly because the language is neutral?

MH: Exactly, they stand out, by contrast. So even though foreign readers say that my novels don't sound Japanese, one reason they like them is this Japaneseness that emerges in the stories. They probably don't notice it, but I think that's there.

RS: And are there things you would like readers to notice?

MH: No, I don't think so. Readers can interpret my texts however they prefer; I don't have a message that I want to convey. In fact, if I wanted to impose on readers a specific interpretation, then I would run the risk that they misunderstood me. But I have no such intention. For me, a text, once it is published, belongs to the readers, and they can do what they want with it. This has always been my position. If they interpret it in a completely different way from my own, I cannot complain. I cannot say, no, you're wrong. The text belongs to everyone; it doesn't belong to me.

RS: Don't you ever think, 'this person has misunderstood my story'?

MH: No. No matter how much you misread a text, I am convinced that the power of a story continues to work in the consciousness of the reader. Many readers send me emails, and sometimes they do misunderstand what I wrote. But if you put together thousands of misunderstandings, the final result is a perfect comprehension. What emerges is a collective interpretation, and that is inevitably correct. It's such an interesting phenomenon! So I am not bothered by individual misunderstandings. True, sometimes when critics come up with particularly bizarre interpretations I am tempted to say, what are you talking about?! But I keep quiet. In my experience, sooner or later critical interpretations change, or they fall out of fashion. The power of a story lasts much longer. So it's pointless to complain. It's better to let time do its work.

Notes

1 The interview was published in Italian as: Suter, R. 2013. Come costruire una pila di gattini addormentati … cercando di non svegliarli: Rebecca Suter intervista Murakami Haruki. *In:* G. Coci, ed. *Japan Pop: Parole, immagini, suoni dal Giappone contemporaneo*. Rome: Aracne, 43–60. My thanks to Aracne Editrice for the permission to publish an English translation.
2 This refers to: Ozawa S. and Murakami H. 2011. *Ozawa Seiji-san to, ongaku ni tsuite hanashi o suru*. Tokyo: Shinchōsha; now translated into English as: Murakami H. and Ozawa S. 2017. *Absolutely on Music: Conversations*. Translated by Jay Rubin. New York: Vintage International.
3 This refers to: Theroux, M. 2009. *Far North*. New York: Farrar, Straus and Giroux, now translated into Japanese as *Kyokuhoku*. Tokyo: Chūōkōronsha (2012).

ACKNOWLEDGEMENTS

First and foremost, we would like to thank each and every author who tirelessly considered our edits and suggestions for this volume. Our discussions with all of you were enlightening, and we learnt more than we could give from the privilege of working with you. At Routledge we thank everyone for their belief and support with this book from the start, especially Stephanie Rogers, Emily Pickthall, and the copyediting team.

The generous funding by the Arts and Humanities Research Council (AHRC) for the project *Gendering Murakami Haruki: Characters, Transmedial Productions and Contemporary Japan*, enabled us to host the 'Eyes on Murakami' event series in March 2018 where many of the chapters included in this volume were first presented. In addition to the main funder, we are also thankful to a number of other funding bodies and institutions for their financial and administrative support towards the project and events. These include: The Great Britain Sasakawa Foundation, Japan Foundation, Japan Foundation Sakura Network, Newcastle University Humanities Research Institute, Newcastle University Institute for Creative Arts Practice, and the School of Modern Languages at Newcastle University.

Besides financial and institutional support, there are many people we would like to thank for their invaluable help and support during our work on this project. We thank all contributors and speakers at the event days in Newcastle, including the keynote speakers at the conference, (in no particular order) Katō Norihiro, Rebecca Suter, Matthew Strecher, and Shibata Motoyuki; the speakers at the translation symposium and workshop, Jay Rubin, David Karashima, Anna Zielinska–Elliott, Michael Emmerich, and Elmer Luke; the filmmakers Lucas Akoskin, Carlos Cuarón, and Yamakawa Naoto as well as film specialists Kate Taylor–Jones, Sabrina Qiong Yu, Guy Austin and Philippa Page; and the artists Christopher Jones, Yuasa Katsutoshi, Anna MacRae, Fujimoto Akiko, and James Quin. We especially thank Christopher Jones who kindly supplied the cover image of this volume. We are grateful to Carolyn

Taylor for her administrative support throughout the project; Nigel Harkness for his guidance; and Mitsumori Tomohide, Angel Leigh Anderson, Marcus Forrester, and Nihei Chikako for logistic assistance at the events. Last but not least, thanks are due to all the conference presenters and event participants – you all helped shape our thoughts and ideas that have now come into form with this volume.

CONTRIBUTORS

Akashi Motoko is Postdoctoral Research Assistant for the European Network for the Education and Training of Literary Translators (PETRA-E). She completed her PhD in Literary Translation at the University of East Anglia in 2019. Her thesis explores translator visibility through investigating celebrity translators in contemporary Japan. Her key publications include 'Translator celebrity: Investigating Haruki Murakami's visibility as a translator' (*Celebrity Studies*, 2018).

Giorgio Amitrano is Professor of Japanese Literature at L'Orientale University of Naples. From 2013 to 2017 he has been Director of Italian Cultural Institute in Tokyo. He has translated works by Murakami Haruki, Yoshimoto Banana, Kawabata Yasunari, Miyazawa Kenji, Nakajima Atsushi into Italian. In 2001 he was awarded the 12th Noma Award for the Translation of Japanese Literature. In 2020 he received the Order of the Rising Sun, Gold Rays with Neck Ribbon. Among his publications are *The New Japanese Novel: Popular Culture and Literary Tradition in the Work of Murakami Haruki and Yoshimoto Banana* (ISEAS, 1996) and *Yama no oto: kowareyuku kazoku* (Misuzu Shobō, 2007).

Ted Goossen is Professor of Japanese literature at York University, Canada. He was an exchange student at Waseda University in 1969 when Murakami Haruki arrived on campus, and has translated a number of Murakami's works including his first two novels, *Hear the Wind Sing* and *Pinball, 1973* as well as *Killing Commendatore* (the last with Philip Gabriel). His most recent translations are of Shiga Naoya's *Reconciliation* (Canongate) and Kawakami Hiromi's *People from My Neighbourhood* (Granta). With Motoyuki Shibata and Meg Taylor he edits the new literary journal, *Monkey: New Writing from Japan*, successor to *Monkey Business*.

Gitte Marianne Hansen is Senior Lecturer in Japanese studies at Newcastle University, UK. She is an AHRC Leadership Fellow and PI for the Gendering Murakami Haruki project on Murakami Haruki – an interest she first developed while working as a teaching and research assistant to Katō Norihiro at Waseda University (2004–2009). More generally, her work focuses on Japanese culture since the 1980s, especially issues related to gender and character construction. She is the author of *Femininity, Self-harm and Eating Disorders in Japan: Navigating Contradiction in Narrative and Visual Culture* (2016).

Katō Norihiro (1948–2019) was Emeritus Professor at Waseda University. He has published more than 50 books, including eight on Murakami, and is one of the first critics to widely recognise Murakami's contribution to Japanese literature. He has also written extensively on other topics related to Japanese literature, history, and contemporary affairs. His article, 'The problem of *tatemashi* in Murakami Haruki's work: Comparing *The Wind-Up Bird Chronicle* and *1Q84*' was translated into English and published in *Japan Forum* (2020, trans. by Michael Tsang).

Astrid Lac is Assistant Professor of Comparative Literature at Underwood International College, Yonsei University, in South Korea, where she teaches literature, film, and critical theory. Her recent publications include 'Losing melancholia: Between object, fidelity, and theory', Cultural Critique (Minnesota UP) and 'Difference, trauma, and affect: Accounting for literary desire in psychoanalysis', in *Knots: Post-Lacanian Psychoanalysis, Literature and Film* (ed. Jean-Michel Rabaté, Routledge).

Elmer Luke has edited translations of many Japanese authors – including early works of Murakami Haruki and most recently Mizumura Minae, Ono Masatsugu, Kawakami Mieko, and Murata Sayaka – working with translators Juliet Winters Carpenter, David Boyd, Ginny Tapley Takemori, and Michael Emmerich among others. He co-edited with David Karashima *March Was Made of Yarn*, the anthology of reflections on the Tōhoku tsunami and nuclear meltdown, and was consulting editor of the *Granta* Japan issue. He lives in upstate New York.

Nihei Chikako is Assistant Professor at Yamaguchi University in Japan. She recently published *Haruki Murakami: Storytelling and Productive Distance* (Routledge, 2020), and with Andrew Houwen co-translated poems of Naka Tarō, an award-winning Japanese post-war poet, into English in *Music: Selected Poems* (Isobar, 2018). She is currently researching works of Japanese American writers and 'repatriate literature' written by Japanese immigrants who returned home after August 1945.

Jay Rubin, Professor Emeritus of Japanese Literature, Harvard University. Translator of Murakami Haruki, Natsume Sōseki, Akutagawa Ryūnosuke, among others. Author of *Injurious to Public Morals*, *Making Sense of Japanese*, *Haruki Murakami and the Music of Words*, *The Sun Gods*, and *Murakami Haruki to watashi*. Editor of *The Penguin Book of Japanese Short Stories*.

Matthew C. Strecher is Professor of Japanese Literature at Sophia University in Tokyo. He is the author of *Dances With Sheep: The Question for Identity in the Fiction of Murakami Haruki* (2002/2020), *The Forbidden Worlds of Haruki Murakami* (2014), and numerous articles on Murakami Haruki. He has also published on Japanese literary history, 'poison women', and literary journalism in Japan. When he's not busy professing things, he enjoys kayaking and composing music.

Rebecca Suter is Associate Professor of Japanese Studies at the University of Sydney. She specialises in modern Japanese and comparative literature. She is author of *The Japanization of Modernity: Murakami Haruki between Japan and the United States* (2008), *Holy Ghosts: The Christian Century in Modern Japanese Fiction* (2015), and *Two-World Literature: Kazuo Ishiguro's Early Novels* (2020).

Barbara E. Thornbury is Professor of Japanese in the Department of Asian and Middle Eastern Languages and Studies at Temple University. She is the author of four books, including *Mapping Tokyo in Fiction and Film* (2020) and *America's Japan and Japan's Performing Arts: Cultural Mobility and Exchange in New York, 1952–2011* (2013). She also co-edited and contributed to *Tokyo: Memory, Imagination, and the City* (2018).

Michael Tsang is Leverhulme Early Career Fellow based at the School of Modern Languages, Newcastle University. Prior to this he was Research Associate on the AHRC-funded Gendering Murakami Haruki project. He researches in postcolonial and world literatures with an East Asian focus. He has published in *Inter-Asia Cultural Studies*, *Japan Forum*, *Wasafiri*, *Sanglap*, and other journals and edited volumes. He is the founding editor of the world's first bilingual academic journal on Hong Kong, *Hong Kong Studies*. He is due to take up lectureship in Japanese Studies at Birkbeck, University of London.

Annette Thorsen Vilslev, PhD in Comparative Literature, University of Copenhagen, Denmark, has published book chapters, translations, and academic essays on Japanese literature and world literature, including 'Questioning Western universality: Sōseki's *Theory of Literature* and his novel *Kusamakura*' (*Japan Forum*, 2017). She was a Monbukagakusho student and a JSPS Postdoctoral Fellow at Waseda University and has taught at universities in Denmark.

Patricia Welch is Professor of Japanese and Comparative Literature at Hofstra University. Research interests include Murakami Haruki, *rakugo*, and Japanese mysteries. Publications include 'Responsible dreaming: Dreamscapes and trauma response in Murakami Haruki's *Kafka on the Shore*', 'Excess, alienation and ambivalence: Edogawa Rampo's tales of mystery and imagination', and 'A consideration of *Kokoro*: Hints and echoes of Japanese inner life'. With Mari Fujimoto, she authored *NipponGO! An Introduction to Elementary Modern Japanese Language*.

Anna Zielinska–Elliott is the director of the MFA in Literary Translation at Boston University. She is a translator of modern Japanese literature into Polish. Best known for her translations of Murakami Haruki, she has also translated Mishima Yukio, Yoshimoto Banana, and Tanizaki Jun'ichirō. She is the author of a Polish-language monograph on gender in Murakami's writing, a literary guidebook to Murakami's Tokyo, and several articles on Murakami and European translation practices relating to contemporary Japanese fiction.

INDEX OF KEYWORDS

INDEX OF WORKS BY MURAKAMI HARUKI

Editors' Note: The Harvard system of referencing dictates that book and article titles be in sentence case (capitalisation only in the first letter of the first word and proper nouns). In this volume, all non-literary (e.g. academic or journalistic) titles in English and all titles in Japanese will observe sentence case. However, it is our preference that all literary titles in English (novels, short stories etc.) be expressed in title case instead (capitalisation in all content words).

In the following index, if a work has an official English translation (as of July 2021), the English title will be provided in the second column.

Japanese title	English title	Page
Novels		
1973 nen no pinbōru	*Pinball, 1973*	23, 26, 44, 53, 56, 84–85, 97, 173, 176, 228, 249, 260
1Q84	*1Q84*	6, 8, 13–14, 17–18, 20, 26, 40, 61–62, 111, 124, 129, 140–141, 156–157, 159, 173–174, 199–217, 269, 271–272, 278
Afutādāku	*After Dark*	7, 67, 82, 109–124, 153, 231
Dansu dansu dansu	*Dance Dance Dance*	67–69, 76–77, 83, 86, 88, 96, 100–101, 148, 159–160, 163, 230, 253
Hitsuji o meguru bōken	*A Wild Sheep Chase*	23–24, 26, 30–33, 44, 56, 67, 97, 148, 155, 159, 176, 228, 249–254, 257
Kaze no uta o kike	*Hear the Wind Sing*	7, 44, 51, 83–84, 87, 97, 102, 173, 176, 219, 249, 259–260, 283

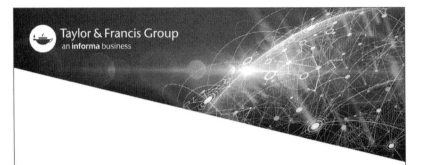

Printed in Great Britain
by Amazon

67595709R00176